Statistical Modeling and Inference for Social Science

This book provides an introduction to probability theory, statistical inference, and statistical modeling for social science researchers and Ph.D. students. Focusing on the connection between statistical procedures and social science theory, Sean Gailmard develops core statistical theory as a set of tools to model and assess relationships between variables – the primary aim of social scientists. Gailmard explains how social scientists express and test substantive theoretical arguments in various models. Chapter exercises require application of concepts to actual data and extend students' grasp of core theoretical concepts. Students will complete the book with the ability to read and critique statistical applications in their fields of interest.

Sean Gailmard is Associate Professor of Political Science at the University of California, Berkeley. Formerly an assistant professor at Northwestern University and at the University of Chicago, Gailmard earned his Ph.D. in social science (economics and political science) from the California Institute of Technology. He is the coauthor of *Learning While Governing: Institutions and Accountability in the Executive Branch* (2013), winner of the 2013 American Political Science Association's William H. Riker Prize for best book on political economy. His articles have been published in a variety of journals, including *American Political Science Review*, *American Journal of Political Science*, and *Journal of Politics*. He currently serves as an associate editor for the *Journal of Experimental Political Science* and on the editorial boards for *Political Science Research and Methods* and *Journal of Public Policy*.

Analytical Methods for Social Research

Analytical Methods for Social Research presents texts on empirical and formal methods for the social sciences. Volumes in the series address both the theoretical underpinnings of analytical techniques as well as their application in social research. Some series volumes are broad in scope, cutting across a number of disciplines. Others focus mainly on methodological applications within specific fields such as political science, sociology, demography, and public health. The series serves a mix of students and researchers in the social sciences and statistics.

Series Editors:

R. Michael Alvarez, California Institute of Technology
Nathaniel L. Beck, New York University
Lawrence L. Wu, New York University

Other Titles in the Series:

Event History Modeling: A Guide for Social Scientists,
    by Janet M. Box-Steffensmeier and Bradford S. Jones
Formal Models of Domestic Politics, by Scott Gehlbach
Data Analysis Using Regression and Multilevel/Hierarchical Models,
    by Andrew Gelman and Jennifer Hill
Essential Mathematics for Political and Social Research, by Jeff Gill
Ecological Inference: New Methodological Strategies, edited by Gary King,
    Ori Rosen, and Martin A. Tanner
Political Game Theory: An Introduction, by Nolan McCarty and
    Adam Meirowitz
*Counterfactuals and Causal Inference: Methods and Principles for Social
    Research,* by Stephen L. Morgan and Christopher Winship
Spatial Models of Parliamentary Voting, by Keith T. Poole

$\forall$ for all
$\exists$ there exists
$\nexists$ there doesn't exist
$\exists!$ there exists but unique

p-value $\uparrow$ cannot reject the null

To Gina, for continuing to roll the dice with me

Statistical Modeling and Inference for Social Science

SEAN GAILMARD

University of California, Berkeley

CAMBRIDGE
UNIVERSITY PRESS

CAMBRIDGE
UNIVERSITY PRESS

32 Avenue of the Americas, New York, NY 10013-2473, USA

Cambridge University Press is part of the University of Cambridge.

It furthers the University's mission by disseminating knowledge in the pursuit of education, learning, and research at the highest international levels of excellence.

www.cambridge.org
Information on this title: www.cambridge.org/9781107003149

© Sean Gailmard 2014

First published 2014

Printed in the United States of America

A catalog record for this publication is available from the British Library.

Library of Congress Cataloging in Publication Data
Gailmard, Sean.
Statistical modeling and inference for social science / Sean Gailmard, University of California, Berkeley.
    pages   cm. – (Analytical methods for social research)
Includes bibliographical references and index.
ISBN 978-1-107-00314-9 (hardback)
1. Social sciences – Statistical methods.   I. Title.
HA29.G136   2014
519.5–dc23   2013050034

ISBN 978-1-107-00314-9 Hardback

Contents

List of Figures

List of Tables

Acknowledgments

Various drafts of what became this book have been inflicted on various people. That I still count many of them as friends is a testament to their willingness to forgive and forget. I wish to thank them without implicating them for the results that follow. I have been fortunate to receive feedback, remarks, and critiques from Fred Boehmke, Henry Brady, Wendy Tam Cho, Doug Dion, Jamie Druckman, Chris Elmendorf, Andrew Gelman, Jeff Gill, Sandy Gordon, Shigeo Hirano, Jeff Jenkins, Joel Middleton, Benjamin I. Page, John Patty, Kevin Quinn, Jas Sekhon, Laura Stoker, Dustin Tingley, and Jonathan Wand. Miranda Yaves, Fred and Doug field-tested an early version of this manuscript with their graduate students at Iowa and produced critically important feedback as a result.

Numerous Ph.D. students at Berkeley and Northwestern used this manuscript, mostly with good cheer, as a proto-text in their introductory statistics course. I received useful feedback (and typo corrections) from many. I am especially grateful to Rachel Bernhard, Toby Bolsen, Caroline Brandt, David Broockman, Richard Hay, Chris Chambers Ju, Sebastian Karcher, Elsa Massoc, Gustav Nedergaard, Hong Min Park, David Steinberg, and Jan Vogler. My teaching assistants in various iterations at Berkeley – Sara Chatfield, Shinhye Choi, Stephen Goggin, and Adrienne Hosek – were extremely helpful as I tried to figure out how to explain the concepts in this book to graduate students unfamiliar with them.

Jamie Druckman and Jeff Gill provided essential encouragement in my decision to translate the mish-mash of notes I wrote as supplements to existing texts into this book. Mike Alvarez and Neal Beck, as co-editors of the Analytical Methods for Social Research series at Cambridge, provided extensive, much needed critique, feedback, and support that substantially improved the content and exposition. I am extremely grateful to them for their efforts, and to Mike for shepherding the manuscript and my responses to (very constructive and helpful) anonymous reviewers through the various stages of the publication process.

I have been fortunate to work with two editors at Cambridge – Ed Parsons on the initial proposal and, for most of the review and publication process, Lew Bateman – who were judicious and supportive in considering the unique features of this manuscript and tolerant of my seemingly interminable delays in revising it.

Most tolerant and helpful of all was my family: my children, William, Aidan, and Collin, and my wife Gina. It was always a delight to try to explain to my small children what I was writing about, even more so to see my efforts partially inspire their proposed manuscripts on the finer points of Minecraft, spiders, and zombies. Our continuing collective struggle with type 1 diabetes is an object lesson in randomness. Whenever I thought I faced daunting demands, the resilience of very small people confronting the vicissitudes of this disease brought me back to earth. It is only because of Gina's graceful management of our real life that I could dedicate time to writing this book, and thus, this book is dedicated to her.

1

Introduction

This text is written for a first course on statistics and quantitative methods for Ph.D. students in social science and allied fields. Anyone undertaking to write such a book must sooner or later confront the question of whether the world really needs another introductory statistics textbook. In my surveys of the market for my own classes on this subject in two social science Ph.D. programs, I clearly decided that it does.

Students in social science Ph.D. programs outside of economics have widely divergent levels of previous exposure to statistical methods, as well as comfort with mathematical expression of concepts. The typical Ph.D. program does not have the luxury of multiple "tracks" to suit different backgrounds, so one course must accommodate all of them. That course must be accessible to students with divergent levels of preparation but must also prepare them technically for future quantitative methods coursework ahead of them.

More important, I have found that students of whatever background will plunge relatively enthusiastically into methods training once they understand why it is essential for the purely substantive elements of their research. Simply put, many students, particularly those without much prior exposure to statistics, do not understand what it is or how it can help them as social scientists. Without this understanding they lack the buy-in necessary to make the technical rigors of the course seem worthwhile.

I never found a textbook that was pitched at the right technical level for introductory students and also focused on what social scientists in particular can do with statistics. Textbooks on mathematical statistics, although useful for the technically ambitious students (and entirely suitable for use in conjunction with this text), leave most students behind at a formal level. They also tend to focus, at least in their core, on univariate inference. This framework allows for

1

clarity of statistical theory – but it obscures what social scientists can do with statistics and leaves many students wondering why they should bother when they have social science research to do. Statistics textbooks at an intermediate level may be technically suitable for most Ph.D. students in social science but are not much better at explicating the integrative link between social science theory and statistics. These problems with the textbook market are widely enough recognized that instructors often assemble reading lists culled from various textbooks and research papers published in home-discipline journals, but this approach is inherently piecemeal and obscures the overall integration of the material from the students.

This text is my attempt to redress these limitations of current offerings. Mathematically, I assume students have had exposure to and a solid grasp of algebra for scalars. Prior exposure to calculus is helpful (especially for some proofs) but not strictly necessary; when I use calculus notation and concepts in the main text, I explain them on the fly. I essentially do not use matrix algebra in this text except for occasional use of vector notation as a shorthand. Other than this, the text is mostly self-contained, conceptually and mathematically. That is not to say it will be technically easy for most students; it is not for most of mine. But prior formal training in higher-level mathematics is not the limiting factor. What students really need to be able to do is integrate formal definitions and notations into their thinking right away when they are introduced.

This in itself is not a substitute for deep training of future methodologists or theoreticians of statistical modeling but should suffice for students who need solid intuition about the tools they are using more than anything else. The text does not skimp on formal proofs and derivations of core results, for example, of the law of iterated expectations, the expected value of ordinary least squares regression coefficients, canonical formulas for standard errors, and the like. My conviction is that any intelligent user of statistical methods should understand the connection between assumptions they make about their data and inference problem and the properties of the resulting statistical output; formal proofs are simply the arguments that we use to establish those connections. To keep the length and formal demands manageable, I also often present an important theorem or approach verbally (e.g., the Cramér-Rao theorem, derivation of the F distribution, properties of parametric bootstrapped standard errors) to alert students to the key issue and indicate important topics for work in more advanced quantitative methods courses.

This approach implies that mathematical demands of the presentation are not uniform across chapters and topics. For example, the formal presentation of the sampling distribution for least squares regression coefficients (Chapter 7) is much more intense than my presentation of the concept of maximum likelihood estimation (Chapter 9), which is rather more intuitive. Because the purpose of the book is to develop solid understanding of core ideas in statistical inference and modeling rather than to present a formally complete and precise treatment of every topic for its own sake, this seems to be a useful compromise. In any case, like many instructors, I have always found that many students in more advanced courses are not clear enough on the *ideas* – irrespective of the mathematical technicalities – that are to be covered in a course such as this. So my treatment is an attempt to stress those ideas. I hope thereby to reduce the incidence of students proceeding to later courses or self-study without a clear idea of the meaning of a regression, sampling distribution, p value, estimator, likelihood function, statistical model, and the like.

As far as my treatment of what statistics does for social science, I focus early and throughout on theoretical arguments about relationships between variables and statistics as a set of tools to assess those relationships in data. Early and sustained focus on this is one of the principal distinguishing features of this book. In our published research that uses quantitative methods, this is almost always what we social scientists are doing with statistics and statistical models. Understanding how theories are couched in terms of relationships and that statistical models are good ways to measure relationships, makes for a good motivation to learn statistical modeling. I have sought to write a book that introduces students to this way of thinking as soon as possible. I have found this to be unusual in a textbook, but it is probably the most important thread running through this one. I understand "theory" in social science as an argument that two or more concepts are related and the reason why; it is therefore not an accident that the substantive core of social science is intimately linked to statistics.

This focus on relationships in both social science theory and statistical modeling is reflected at several points that are unusual in first treatments but are formally no more difficult than what is usually covered. First, canonical families of probability distributions are introduced not as abstract and mysterious entities that students must suffer through today for some unknown future good but rather as convenient models for various types of social processes. I introduce them immediately with common functional forms linking the parameters of these distributions to covariates of theoretical interest to a social scientist as such and with derivation of marginal effects of these covariates. The student therefore encounters formal probability models as a way to structure and express their theorizing about some dependent variable. This is, by design, entirely separate from statistical issues involved in estimating the parameters of these models. When a student wonders what a logit model or a negative binomial model is all about, the first thing he or she needs to understand is how it expresses dependencies of what is explained on what does the explaining, not on how the magnitude of that dependency is estimated or on its numerical stability.

Second, the core statistical concepts of sampling, estimation, and hypothesis testing are all covered with an early and sustained focus on inference for parameters in regression models, not just univariate inference. The idea of a sample regression coefficient as random in repeated sampling is no more difficult than the idea of a sample mean as a random variable (which is not to say either concept is simple or intuitive for newcomers to the field; they are not), so there is no reason not to introduce these concepts at the same time. Yet doing so saves endless heartache as students learn regression in earnest, both through their own research and in further coursework. To be sure, in preference for a "clean" analytical approach, I typically focus on plain-vanilla regression and simple extensions in these discussions but also attempt to explicate how the concepts translate to parameter estimates from more intricate estimators.

Upon finishing this book, students will know how to use and critique the application of several workhorse techniques for establishing and interpreting relationships in social science research and will have developed a framework for evaluating and understanding the contribution made by more advanced techniques (the details of which they may grasp only loosely). Concretely, through the theory and applications discussed subsequently, students should finish the book with the ability to understand and critique journal articles and books in their field that make use of linear models, generalized linear models, maximum likelihood estimation, and classical hypothesis testing, among other techniques. (In my experience, this is not the case after completing most introductory treatments.) In addition, upon finishing, students will have built a solid foundation in the theory of statistics for future quantitative methods course work – and more importantly, for teaching themselves new methods as necessary for their own research. The last result is one of the most important for any scholar doing quantitative empirical work; the field of quantitative methods in social science is huge and expanding much more rapidly than any person has the ability to grasp. Therefore, the need to master a technique for a research project that one has not learned in formal coursework is a normal state of affairs.

SCOPE

In basic and abstract terms, a *positive theory* in social science asserts that two or more concepts or events are related to each other and specifies the reason why.[1] To maintain abstraction and for lack of better names, we might as well call these concepts x and y. Often a theory is useful and important because it postulates a process or channel or "mechanism" through which x causes y. So when x changes, it will cause y to change in a fashion that is explicated by the theory. It is possible that the theory says that x and y are only related conditional on some third concept z. That does not pose any conceptual problems for what follows.

For example, in political science, a theory of the "democratic peace" asserts that two nation-states are less likely to go to war with each other if both are

---

[1] By "positive" theories I mean ones that attempt to specify how social or political processes actually work, as distinct from "normative" theories. Positive theory in my usage does not imply derivation from any particular type of reasoning, such as formal or mathematical modeling. Nor does my usage imply that one developing or exploring positive theories must adhere to positivism as a philosophy of science.

democracies than if both are not. So here y indicates the concept that two states are "at war" with each other, and x indicates that both are democracies. The theory asserts that these concepts are related to each other in a specific way: the chance that a dyad of nation-states go to war is greater when they are not both democracies than when they are.

To show that a theory deserves a place in the conversation and debate of some field of research, a researcher advancing it should show that it organizes and renders intelligible actual events in the world. This requires confronting the theory with data to see if the former explains the latter. To wit, as a matter of fact, does x cause changes in y as the theory asserts? If it is, then at the very least, x and y should be associated with each other or should "move together" in some specific way spelled out by the theory. A major reason social scientists pursue formal statistical analysis is to answer that question of how things play out in fact and whether they comport with the theory in question. This empirical analysis of theory constitutes the stock-in-trade of a great many social scientists and comprises a large portion of the research published in disciplinary journals.

The main ingredient of that analysis, of course, is data. Needless to say, in social science there are often no uncontested, cut-and-dried measures of the concepts to which a theory pertains. With respect to the democratic peace, a political scientist interested in empirical analysis would first have to consider an operational definition of "war" as well as "democratic nation-state." Careful and sensible measurement are obviously crucially important for meaningful quantitative analysis, but these issues are mostly beyond the scope of the coverage in this book, save for some cursory discussion in Chapter 2 and sprinkled in a few other places. For the most part, I take as given a set of observations of variables that are tied to theoretically important concepts in a substantively meaningful way but do not offer much advice about how to obtain them.

With data in hand, an analyst can explore whether x and y are related as the theory asserts. That is what this book is about. Statistics provides a set of tools for assessing relationships in data. That is the main reason social scientists use it. Statistics provides a battery of formulas and techniques, simple in their basics, for assessing relationships among variables. Social scientists also often (and increasingly so) want to know if a relationship is causal and, if so, what is causing what (i.e., x causes y, vice versa, both, or neither). Statistics provides a useful conceptual framework for assessing what causal inference means and what it requires, although it provides no simple formulas that ensure valid causal inferences are possible in a given context.

A significant complication in assessing relationships is introduced because social scientists often deal with data that has some uncertainty behind it. You only get to see one dataset, but the data in it might be generated by some type of random or *stochastic* process. It might be that the observable data represents only a part of a larger, unknown universe of possible observations; it might be that the social processes and behind the data involve behavior that can only be described as (at least partly) random. Assessing relationships in the presence of data with randomness behind it, and expressing the degree of uncertainty about those assessments, is difficult. That assessment is what a lot of the theory of statistics, especially statistical inference and modeling, is about. The difficulty explains why we have to spend so much time on it.

This text explains (*i*) tools for summarizing data and assessing relationships in data, (*ii*) sources of uncertainty in the data social scientists can see, (*iii*) tools for formalizing and analyzing uncertainty and randomness, and (*iv*) tools for assessing relationships in the face of randomness. It also briefly discusses (*v*) concepts for assessing the extent to which an observed relationship is a *causal* relationship.

This book's coverage of these topics is almost entirely based on "classical" or "frequentist" statistics. It almost entirely excludes nonparametric approaches in the frequentist tradition. It also pays little attention to Bayesian statistics, which is achieving a status approaching standard fare for some types of estimation and in some fields. For a variety of reasons, some good and some less good, most quantitative research in social science still builds on the classical, parametric approach. There will be more than enough balls in the air with the restriction to that topic, even for students who have some solid statistics training, so that introducing whole new schools of thought as well seems ill advised.

OUTLINE

More specifically, the plan of the book is as follows. Chapter 2 introduces descriptive statistics. One of the most important sources of insight about political and social processes, and in practice a necessary precursor to formal statistical analysis, is simply "playing around with the data." This exercise gives researchers a feel for the behavior of variables, which can serve as a guide to specific modeling choices, and can suggest relationships for further analysis. Students and scholars that dive into modeling exercises without understanding their data are not uncommonly exposed to embarrassingly simple questions about specific observations that they cannot answer. This chapter develops several important benchmark techniques to structure such investigations. It introduces the concept of a distribution and variable, and presents tools for creating information from mere data. These tools are designed to distill a mass of numbers into a few useful summaries that are readily interpretable and comparable across distributions. In the case of distributions of several variables, these tools include summary measures of *association* among variables – that is, relationships –which are the bread and butter of most efforts to test theories in empirical social research.

Chapter 3 discusses the need for inference about unobservable quantities based on observable ones – not just when using statistics but when performing almost any kind of theoretically guided research based on observed data. It makes the distinction between observable data, from which summary measures and descriptions can be computed, and the crucial concept of a "data-generating process," which is itself unobservable but which gives rise to the observable data. It is this data-generating process that, in virtually all conceivable cases (even when it doesn't seem like it at first), is the ultimate object of theoretical interest to a social scientist. Furthermore, most data-generating processes that might interest anyone involve uncertainty and randomness (or at least what looks like randomness to an analyst or researcher): that is, they give rise to particular sets of observations not with certainty but only with some probability.

Chapter 3 discusses reasons for randomness in social and political data and some important implications of that randomness for the observable data from which descriptive statistics are derived. The most important such implication for the practice of empirical research is that any summary of observed data – quantitative or otherwise – itself has some randomness bound up in it. This chapter is somewhat "metaphysical," but it covers important (although often unstated) philosophical commitments and disagreements behind different approaches to empirical research.

Given the importance of uncertainty and randomness in the data social scientists can observe, a language for discussing and analyzing randomness precisely is necessary. Such a language allows for analysis and evaluation of the information provided in observable data about its underlying data generating process. That language is provided by the theory of probability, which is introduced in Chapter 4. The discussion starts from the primitive idea of an experiment and the set-theoretic ideas of a sample space and event. Probability measures are defined in terms of these foundations, and some important properties of probabilities of events are presented. The discussion then turns to the crucial concept of a random variable and the cumulative distribution function and mass or density functions associated with random variables. These functions are the central tools for modeling data-generating processes in statistical research. This chapter also introduces multiple random variables and multivariate probability distributions.

Probability distributions convey much information about the behavior of random variables that can be compressed into more compact summaries of their behavior. These summaries are addressed in Chapter 5. In particular, this material focuses on expectation and variance for univariate distributions, and conditional expectation and covariance for multivariate distributions, as important characteristics and summaries of data-generating processes. In many ways, these summaries of probability distributions are analogous to the ones that descriptive statistics offers for data distributions, as covered in Chapter 2.

Theories in social science often suggest or imply certain features of a data-generating process, such as the behavior of its summary characteristics as some variable changes. For example, many theories that assert that one variable is associated with another imply something about the behavior of a conditional mean. Chapter 6 develops the link between positive theory in political and social science and the form and characteristics of a data-generating process. This chapter introduces several important families of probability distributions that are useful as models of specific kinds of social and political processes. It explores the relationship between theoretical assertions that variables are related and the statistical comparison of expectations, variances, or other features of distributions. It also notes that many theoretical assertions of association imply that the conditional mean of one variable is a function of another, thereby introducing regression modeling as a central tool of theory evaluation. This chapter also explores the expression of additive as well as multiplicative effects of one variable on another. The main point of this chapter is that many positive theories in social science are essentially assertions about specific aspects of data-generating processes. Therefore, it establishes a crucial link between statistical modeling and the theory development and assessment that are the ultimate purpose of most empirical research in social science.

The chapters up to this point explore (i) the description of information in observable data, (ii) the distinction between observable data and the data-generating process, (iii) the data-generating process as a probability model and properties of these models, and (iv) the link between theory and data-generating process. But any empirical conclusion about theory can (by definition) only be based on observable data. Therefore, the use of observable data as a basis for theory assessment in social science requires an understanding of the connection between this observable data and the data-generating process. That connection was hinted at in Chapter 3. The rest of the book from Chapter 7 to the end focus on formally analyzing it. Collectively these chapters comprise the discussion in this text of inferential statistics, as opposed to the descriptive statistics and probability theory that occupied attention before Chapter 7.

The first step is to explore how the process of sampling or essentially taking "draws" of observable data from a data-generating process affect the connection between the data and the generating process. This is discussed in Chapter 7. The discussion draws heavily on the canonical concept of a "random sample." With such a sample, the summary statistics introduced in Chapter 2 have particularly appealing connections to the underlying data-generating process. This chapter formally defines a statistic and discusses the foundational statistical concepts of a sampling distribution and the central limit theorem. The chapter then explores how the linkages between summaries of observed data and characteristics of the data-generating process are modified by various violations of the random sampling assumption. Because these violations are commonplace in actual data in social science, these modifications cannot be treated as mere footnotes to the main point. Instead, whenever possible and necessary, they must occupy a central place in empirical investigation because they strongly affect the link between observable data and data-generating process, and therefore between observable data and theoretical question.

Chapter 6 argues that positive theories in social science often imply a comparison of conditional means or other features of data-generating processes.

The use of observable data to compare data-generating processes is the subject of hypothesis testing, covered in Chapter 8. Hypothesis tests assess the degree of support in observed data for specific conjectures pertaining to underlying data-generating processes. They are inherently linked to the sampling distributions of statistics used to estimate the features of the data-generating process that are of ultimate theoretical interest. The chapter discusses the conceptual aspects of hypothesis testing and develops methods for several important and commonly used tests (e.g., for difference in means, proportions, and variances; for the sign of regression coefficients; for categorical and tabular data).

The linkage reviewed in Chapter 7 between summaries of observable data and the data-generating process can be used another way: if we don't know some important characteristics of the data-generating process, we can use summary measures from observable data to estimate them. Estimating characteristics of the underlying data-generating process in this way is "point estimation" and is the subject of Chapter 9. This chapter presents several criteria for evaluating point estimators and uses them to evaluate the summary measures familiar from previous discussions. In so doing, it presents a version of the law of large numbers, an important theoretical result, and extends the discussion of sampling distributions for several important estimators. The chapter then discusses important techniques for developing estimators, specifically the methods of maximum likelihood, least squares, and (briefly) Bayesian estimation.

The book then briefly considers causation. Social science needs statistics because our theories typically concern relationships among variables, and statistics has a variety of tools to estimate relationships among observable quantities. But most of these statistical tools used in social science focus on *association* among variables, whereas most of our positive theories assert *causal* relationships among variables. "Correlation does not imply causation" is a mantra in empirical research and deservedly so. Chapter 10 discusses the distinction between association and causation and how and when one can bridge that gap in empirical research. This chapter covers the meaning of causation, in terms of the potential outcomes causal model and what causation looks like at an empirical level. It discusses specific conditions under which one can interpret a demonstration of mere association as an assertion of causation, and how the source of the data (e.g., experimental data vs. observational data) affects how strong a case can be made that these conditions hold. The chapter demonstrates implicit assumptions in important empirical techniques that are necessary for assertions of causation based on observable data. This material is essential and rapidly growing in importance for many social scientists, given what we hope to get out of empirical analysis. Although the treatment here is terse, I believe it is useful to present the themes and simple technicalities in a style of notation and exposition to which students are already accustomed. I hope this will make for a smoother transition to further coursework covering these issues in depth.

Finally, a brief afterword puts what is covered in this book in the larger context of empirical social science research, research that in many or most cases attempts to find what events or variables in social and political processes are related to each other, how strongly, and why.

I have taught the sequence of topics around which this book is written numerous times in the political science departments at U.C. Berkeley and Northwestern University. In each department, the course was the first in a sequence on quantitative methods. In a semester-length class at Berkeley, I typically make it through most of the text, with time for at least an overview on Chapter 10. In a quarter-length class, a few more choices must be made. The content to de-emphasize depends somewhat on the course that comes after the one for which this book is used.

This book includes a relatively large amount of material on regression for a course on foundations of probability and inference. I have found this essential to motivate the technical details for the many students for whom an interest in methods follows an interest in social science. That said, if this course is followed by a full course dedicated to regression or statistical modeling, a few (lengthy) sections of this book can be covered briefly or skipped to save time: Sections 6.7, 6.9, 7.5, 8.5, and 9.5 all deal with modeling and inference for regression. Most of Chapter 6 is written around the concept of a statistical model, but most of this is interwoven with canonical families of probability distributions. It is inadvisable to skip that material for introductory students, although it can be downplayed. In addition, Chapter 10 is self-contained, and the core theory of probability and inference is completed before this chapter. So that chapter can also be skipped or left for self-study if the course runs short on time.

It is tempting to skip Chapters 2 and 3 because they provide background material but not the core theory of probability or inference, but I have always found it important to cover these chapters. It is simply not that unusual for introductory Ph.D. students to have a hazy idea or less about the basic toolkit of descriptive statistics or the sorts of questions one can ask (and maybe answer) with these tools, so Chapter 2 is important for making the core theoretical ideas concrete. As for Chapter 3, most social science disciplines continue to have ongoing, alive-and-well research traditions drawing on methods one might call "qualitative," or at any rate far outside the ambit of statistics. This chapter is important because it provides a framework for thinking about what kinds of assumptions one must make so that a statistical approach is coherent and that is an essential part of helping Ph.D. students understand what they are doing with research methods and why. Discussions of the sort engaged in this chapter might even have the ancillary benefit of reducing the amount of incoherent quantitative research done.

I have taught from this text to students with widely divergent levels of math preparation, including some without a "math camp" or "prefresher" before this course begins. I have found that once students buy in to the material, they can grasp enough of what is here to move forward, even without such preparation. Obviously, more mathematics preparation is better, but for students less comfortable with this background, I've found it useful to schedule an optional course session or two to review some key ideas and notation of calculus, a few important functions and properties, and simple algebra for sums and exponents. Because the text is written essentially entirely in scalar notation, no formal exposure to linear algebra is necessary.

The text allows for a self-contained course, but the course website has some useful supplemental material: additional exercises, datasets, and extensions of Chapters 6 and 10. The extensions of Chapter 6 cover families of probability distributions (such as the negative binomial, beta, and gamma distributions) that are important but slightly more technical or less widely applied than the distributions in the text. The extensions of Chapter 10 cover the potential outcomes theory in somewhat more depth, as well as additional methods for addressing causal inference in observational research.

While I write this passage convinced that this text is pristinely free of mistakes, experience says otherwise. The course website also contains the inevitable errata. It is probably best to check it before a course term starts and before students begin the ritual banging of heads into walls to understand the incomprehensible. The URL is www.ocf.berkeley.edu/~gailmard/smiss.html.

Finally, an instructor's solutions manual is available on request by e-mailing the author.

2

Descriptive Statistics: Data and Information

Moving from a mass of data to an informative description of patterns within that data is a basic point of quantitative techniques social science, an area of quantitative analysis called *descriptive statistics*. It is not the fanciest math, nor does it comprise the most subtle concepts, but it requires serious attention in any quantitative work. Descriptive statistics is an important part of constructing an argument using data and includes making apparent the tendencies, patterns, and relationships in that data. Equally important is that descriptive statistics helps a researcher get a feel for the behavior of the variables in a dataset and for conjectures about relationships that are worth further analysis, both statistically and theoretically.

Before meaningful analysis can proceed, it is necessary to understand how we observe and measure the concepts of interest in any research. Thus this chapter begins with a brief overview of empirical measurement of variables. It then discusses common graphical and statistical summaries and descriptions of aggregate data, first for one variable at a time (*univariate distributions*) and then for relationships (*bivariate* or *multivariate distributions*). It also covers some important theoretical properties of these descriptive tools.

Some basic concepts are important. To fix ideas, imagine a dataset with a set of observations of one or more characteristics of some collection of units. For instance, on the "democratic peace" (see Chapter 1), the units might be pairs of nation-states. The characteristics observed for each unit would be (at least) whether they are (or have ever been) at war with each other and whether they are both democracies. Another example is a public health researcher who might have a dataset on the birth weight of newborns, along with various behaviors or traits of the baby's parents or attributes of the mother's environment while pregnant (e.g., whether the mother used tobacco, the mother's household income). Throughout, I generally suppose that the

TABLE 2.1. *Social Capital Index, Urbanization, and Bachelor of Arts (B.A.)
Attainment by State, 1998*

State Name	Social Capital Index	Urbanization	B.A. Attainment
Alabama	−1.07	87.3	10.1%
Arizona	0.06	67.5	13.3%
Arkansas	−0.50	45.1	8.9%

observations are arrayed in rows and columns as in a spreadsheet. The rows
(horizontal) consist of observations for a single unit.

The columns (vertical) contain observations of a single characteristic across
all units. Table 2.1 shows a sketch of this. The units are U.S. states, and the
characteristics are levels of "social capital" (discussed further subsequently),
percent of residents living in metropolitan areas, and percent of residents with
a bachelor's degree or higher in 1998. This table shows entries for the first
three units alphabetically.[1]

The characteristics measured in the columns are *variables*. A *distribution* of
a variable is a list of its observed values, one for each unit. The units in the
rows are also referred to as the *unit of analysis* or unit of observation. So in
the democratic peace example, the unit of analysis is nation-state dyads. The
variables are whether the members of a dyad have or have not ever been at war
with each other and whether they are or are not both democracies. Usually I
refer to a dataset as having N observations on each variable and k or $k + 1$
variables.

The data may consist of observations of multiple units at a given point in
time, a single unit at multiple points in time, or a combination of the two. If the
data consists of N different units each observed at a single point in time, the
data is *cross sectional*. For instance, the list of gross domestic products (GDPs)
of all members of the United Nations from 2012 is cross-sectional data. If the
data consists of N observations from a single unit at successive points in time,
it is *time series*. For instance, the list of annual GDPs for the United States from
1945 to the present is time series data. Data that mixes both time series and
cross-sectional elements is *longitudinal, panel,* or simply *time series–cross-
sectional* data. Different scholars have slightly different uses of these three
terms, and they are not always used interchangeably, but the differences are
not essential here. As an example, a list of the annual GDPs from each current
UN member state from 1945 (or the date of the state's creation) to the present
is time series–cross sectional data. The unit of analysis is a country-year.

[1] Alaska is not in the dataset because of small sample size and unreliable survey responses. Social
capital index data come from Robert Putnam, www.bowlingalone.com; urbanization and educational attainment data are from the *Statistical Abstract of the United States.*

2.1 MEASUREMENT

Any reasonably inquisitive or critical person should wonder about where the observations in such a dataset come from. In empirical analysis, social scientists face issues of choosing the context in which observation of data will take place and of defining the concepts to observe or measure in the first place. I have more to say about the context later, but as for this chapter, we take it as given and instead turn to issues of summarizing data regardless of context. In brief, social science research makes use of data from experiments, surveys, and observational studies.

The difference in these contexts stems largely from the degree to which the researcher's presence or involvement is obvious to the units being observed. In *experiments*, researchers purposely manipulate the context in which individuals make choices or express beliefs. In *surveys*, researchers make it known to units of analysis that they are recording the characteristics, beliefs, and choices of the units before those aspects are expressed. In *observational studies*, researchers record choices or attributes of the units of observation as they take place in their "natural" context with relatively little disturbance by the researcher. These categories are not mutually exclusive, nor is it useful at this point to be fastidious about the defining the features of each. They are noted here simply to point out the range of contexts in which data is observed. There are costs and benefits to each that we are not prepared to consider yet but touch on later.

How are the variables in the dataset defined so that these characteristics of each unit can be quantified or categorized? The democratic peace example is a good illustration of this because neither "war" nor "democratic nation-state" are self-evident conditions in all possible cases. Social scientists face these kinds of thorny measurement problems as a matter of course in empirical research. It is tempting, especially at first, to despair over the difficulties involved in good measurement, but because that is tantamount to ignoring empirical analysis in social science, it is not acceptable. Whether empirical analysis is statistical in nature or of some other form, it always requires measurement, so we might as well confront it explicitly.

A basic precondition for application of statistics to summarize data in social or policy research is the measurement of social activity or behavior. A *metric* is a set of rules or scales by which the value of a variable for a particular unit is ascertained.

2.1.1 Measurement Scales

In some happy cases, a variable has a "natural" metric, in the sense that it would be considered relatively unexceptional even by a critic of some research making use of it. Infants' birth weight is a good example. Durations also come with a natural metric, for example, the duration of wars, the persistence of a governing coalition in a parliamentary system, or the length of a marriage.

In cases like these, in which a social activity or event has a natural numerical metric attached to it, we are in decent shape for the application of quantitative methods to summarize data and compress it into information. The natural metric furnishes quantities, which can be analyzed with quantitative methods.

Lengths (in time or space), weights, incomes, population or group sizes, and proportions or percentages are all measurable on the *cardinal* scale. Cardinal numbers are numbers that can be added and multiplied meaningfully. These are cases in which it is informative to say that one number is, for instance, half as big as another; the smaller one indicates that half as much of a characteristic is present.

Other measures still use numbers to denote different values, and the numbers order the observations, but it does not make sense to add or multiply them and interpret the result on the same scale. These measures are *ordinal* scale measures. For example, social psychologists studying the affect that a person has for something might use a point scale or "feeling thermometer." In studying party identification and partisanship in the United States, an analyst might ask an individual to place him- or herself on a 7-point scale, where the points range from strong Democratic affiliation to neutral or independent to strong Republican affiliation. The scale assigns numbers 1 to 7 to possible answers. If someone self-identifies as 7 and someone else self identifies as 1 (and the respondents have similar understandings of the terms), we know that the 1 is more Democratic than the 7, but it is not sensible to say the 7 is seven times as Republican as the 1. For another example, the extent to which a country is ruled by a democratic government can be measured ordinally, with absolute autocracies scored 0, complete democracies scored 10, and gradations along this spectrum occupying integers in between. A country scoring 10 is more democratic than a country scoring 5, but is it twice as democratic? The ordinal scale of this measure does not purport to say so, and it is probably wise not to try. The ordinal scale is based on the more modest idea that we can tell when one country is more democratic than another (although perhaps even that is arguable).

Much of social science deals with behaviors or events that have identifiable categories but cannot be meaningfully ordered or quantified. So an important type of metric is a *categorical* measurement scale. Here again, numbers are used to name the values of the variables. But the numbers are literally just placeholders. They have no numerical meaning at all, they do not order the values of the variable in any meaningful way, and they certainly cannot be added or multiplied sensibly. An eligible voter in an election can either turn out or not turn out to vote. A nation-state can have a system of government that is democratic, autocratic, or something else. A state either recognizes marriage between same-sex couples or does not. With few exceptions since World War II, members of the U.S. House and Senate are either Republicans or Democrats.

Each category in a categorical scale is assigned a numerical label, for example, Democrat = 0 and Republican = 1; turnout = 1 and abstention = 0. The numbers have no intrinsic meaning. Of course, they can be combined with other observations assigned the same number to arrive at something that *does* have numerical meaning, for example, the proportion of Democrats in the U.S. Congress at a given time: in the categorization above this is $\frac{\text{Number of 0's}}{\text{Number of 0's+Number of 1's}}$. When the categorization has just two possible elements (e.g., Republican and Democrat), the variable constructed from it is *dichotomous, binary,* or *binomial.* When it has three or more possible elements, it is *polychotomous, multichotomous,* or *multinomial.* Again, there is no meaningful ordering of the elements in these cases, and the category labels are arbitrary.

All of this labeling obscures what makes good measurement hard and sometimes controversial in social science. For many concepts we want to study, there is no single, objective measurement strategy, or *operationalization,* of a concept. Earlier it was mentioned that governments can be "scored" along an autocracy–democracy continuum. What makes a country democratic? Competitive elections and broad suffrage would seem to be two important ingredients, but there may well be others, for example, can the will of the people expressed in an election be stymied by entrenched institutional actors insulated from elections, such as courts? The issue is the concept of democracy, and its components are not entirely clear. Moreover, measurement may be problematic for any one component. For example, what makes elections competitive? Is a two-party system enough? What is "widespread" suffrage? If universal adult suffrage is the standard, we must conclude that no nation-states were democratic much before the twentieth century, yet that standard judges early-nineteenth-century states (e.g., the United States, Great Britain) by standards that are ahistorical. This merely scratches the surface of the measurement of democracy, and the point here is not to flesh out that concept. Rather, it is that specifying a concept carefully and measuring its components accurately is (*i*) important and (*ii*) hard. (Several organizations have attempted this measurement for democracy and autocracy specifically, such as the Polity IV dataset housed at the University of Maryland, and Freedom House.)

The contestability of a metric is not necessarily related to whether it is cardinal, ordinal, or categorical. Consider a dataset on family structure and children's scholastic achievement. It would be useful in such a dataset to establish the number of parents in a child's household – a cardinal measure. But what does "in the household" mean: only at the time the achievement measure is recorded, for some period of time before the measure is recorded, or for most of the child's life even if one parent exited the household some years before the achievement measure is recorded?

For another example, consider the duration of civil wars in states around the world over a particular time period, say, post–World War II. Durations have a natural cardinal measure, as noted earlier. But what is a civil war? How is it different from a garden-variety insurgency? When the Bureau of Alcohol, Tobacco, and Firearms raided the Branch Davidian property in Waco, Texas, in 1993, nobody considered it a civil war. Is the Basque separatist movement in

Spain fighting a civil war? Was the Irish Republican Army? When does a civil war start, and when does it end? There may be natural units for a duration, but deciding the beginning and end of a conflict does not have natural or objective guideposts.

In short, measurement does not become more "objective" or "subjective" simply because the measurement scale is cardinal or categorical.

A helpful strategy for dealing with concepts that have no objective metric is to obtain several measures of them and look for patterns and conclusions that are robust across multiple measures. The rationale for this is that alternative measurement strategies will each have their own unique and idiosyncratic flaws that decouple the measurement obtained from the underlying concept of interest. By relying on multiple measures, researchers can mitigate the effect of these idiosyncrasies on the conclusions drawn.

For example, some measures of democracy may be ordinal-multichotomous, and some categorical-dichotomous. A subset of ordinal measures may include measures of legal rights and the right to due process; another subset may be based only on extent of suffrage and competitiveness of elections and access to the ballot for candidates. If a conclusion holds up across all these measures, one gets a much greater sense of robustness of the conclusion – it actually does occur in any meaningful conception of the concept and is not simply an artifact or quirk of a certain measurement. For example, the conclusion that democracies are wealthier than autocracies would be expected to hold in datasets that measure democracy in a wide variety of ways.

Of course, such a strategy is often infeasible. This is especially true given the logic of progress in research for individual scholars. The need for original findings often pushes scholars to analyze previously unstudied or understudied phenomena, which means there is a dearth of good measures to use as robustness checks.

2.1.2 Index Construction

Defining a concept carefully, breaking it into components, and measuring those components rigorously are among the most important contributions social scientists can make with quantitative methods. The value of this work can last far beyond any particular argument that a researcher makes with the measurements she or he constructs. When scholars attempt to advance the discussion and debate in the literature on a particular topic, they often do so by introducing new concepts into it or reformulating existing ones. It is common for scholars attempting this to break a concept down into several components, each of which is separately measurable, and then aggregate these measurements into one index that is supposed to tap into the concept as a whole.

Consider Robert Putnam's [2000] seminal analysis of social capital in *Bowling Alone*. Putnam writes in a literature that spends a great deal of effort defining what social capital is and discussing how to measure it. To Putnam

(p. 19), "social capital refers to connections among individuals – social networks and the norms of reciprocity and trustworthiness that arise from them . . . [s]ocial contacts affect the productivity of individuals and groups." Putnam has constructed a metric of social capital at the state level based on 14 dimensions taken from state-level survey data (see http://www.bowlingalone .com/data.htm). Some dimensions measure beliefs (e.g., percent of state survey respondents who believe most people are honest); others measure behaviors (e.g., state turnout in presidential elections, percent of survey respondents who serve as an officer in a club or charitable organization, average number of times survey respondents volunteered in the past year).[2] To be sure, Putnam and others have found interesting relationships between social capital scores and other variables, but a definition and measure of state-level social capital is an achievement of this research that will stand no matter what types of relationships researchers find. The measurement itself provides a focal point for debate about both the effects and determinants of the concept that is measured.

When constructing such an index, it is usually worth pausing to ask whether the individual components in it should really be combined into one grand variable. That combination necessarily obscures the variation in individual components of it across units. Moreover, when the index is used either as an explanatory device for something else (e.g., does social capital affect crime?) or as an object of explanation itself (e.g., does urbanization foster or inhibit social capital?), combining submeasures into one index constrains the types of explanations a scholar can give.

Take the case in which the index is used as a variable to explain something else. Using the index as a whole implies that every component of it has to affect the "something else" variable in the same way.[3] Breaking the index apart and using each subvariable on its own allows more flexibility because each subvariable has its own effect on the outcome of interest that can be ascertained.

A similar issue arises if the index variable is used as an object of explanation itself. Doing so requires that every variable that does the explaining has the same effect on every subvariable in the overall index. Breaking the index apart and analyzing the determinants of its subvariables one by one is more flexible: it allows explanatory variables to affect different components of the index differently.

Combining the subvariables into one index makes sense if all the subvariables in the index tap into the same basic concept because the theory underlying

---

[2] All 14 dimensions are cardinal measures, but this does not mean the resulting social capital scores are cardinal measures. The dimensions, although cardinal, do not share a single common metric. Thus the state-level social capital scores are ordinal, not cardinal.

[3] This will be more apparent, and will be noted again, in the subsequent treatment of descriptive statistics for relationships.

the construction of such an index necessitates this. And the flexibility noted earlier from breaking the index apart does not come without a cost (generally, in statistical modeling, flexibility always has a cost): more information in the data is "used up" to ascertain all the effects and dependencies related to each subvariable, and so less information is "left over" to ascertain the precision of each effect.

Whether the subvariables do in fact tap into a single underlying concept is at least worth exploring. This can be done with the help of a statistical technique called *factor analysis*, which is closely related to some of the techniques presented later in the chapter but is the subject of a large literature in its own right (e.g., Harman [1976]).

A good example from the political science literature is found in Fortin's analysis of executive power in governmental regimes around the world (Fortin [2012]). Previous literature (Shugart and Carey [1992], Frye et al. [2000]) had identified several aspects of executive power – to veto legislation, issue decrees, determine government budgets, initiate legislation, form a cabinet, dissolve a legislature, and the like – then measured the presence and extent of each of these powers in various countries and aggregated them into a single index of executive power. Fortin analyzed whether each of these measures appear to tap into a single underlying "dimension" or concept of executive power and found important evidence to believe that they do not. She also identified combinations of executive powers that do seem to stem from a single underlying concept.

At this point, and based on material later in this chapter, students should at least be aware that combining variables into one index is not necessarily the ideal approach. Even when theory suggests that a concept is coherent and measured by combining various submeasures, empirical analysis may not bear this out. This is not particularly surprising; a concept definition and measurement strategy is itself a theoretical commitment of sorts, and like all theoretical commitments, it may or may not hold up to empirical scrutiny in specific cases. At the very least, rather than digging into a fruitless conviction that one index is necessary or ideal, researchers can analyze the support for an argument depending on whether the components of an index are aggregated.

2.1.3 Measurement Validity

The *validity* of an operationalization is the extent to which it adequately measures the concept it is intended to measure. Validity is itself the subject of a large literature on measurement theory (see, e.g., Nunnally and Bernstein [2007], de Gruijter and van der Kamp [2007]). Although there are formal definitions of different types of validity, and in some cases it is possible to quantify them, these labels are often used qualitatively to help researchers trace out the qualms they have about a specific operationalization. Three such labels are widely encountered in social and political research. *Face validity* is a colloquial label for subjective judgments about whether an operationalization "seems relevant" to the concept of interest. If an operationalization (absurdly) attempted to measure a prison inmate's likelihood of recidivism by his or her favorite color, it would not have a great deal of face validity.

Content validity refers to whether an operationalization captures all important facets of a concept. For instance, one could measure whether the United States is at war at any given time by whether Congress has formally declared war according to the constitutionally prescribed process. This operationalization has low content validity because it does not reflect the active engagement in hostilities that characterizes war in practical terms. It would, for instance, miss all American "wars" since 1945. As another example, in David Mayhew's seminal study of whether divided government in the United States (which occurs when different political parties control Congress and the White House) affects the passage of important legislation, the definition of the concept of "important legislation" was obviously crucial. Mayhew recognized that one could measure a law's "importance" according to whether it was considered important at the time of passage or according to whether it was considered important in retrospect or in a historical judgment. These are two facets of the concept of "important legislation." Mayhew combined these submeasures into one measure – a law was considered "important" in his dataset if it was important both contemporaneously and retrospectively – that was superior to either of its component parts alone.

Construct validity is the extent to which an operationalization is related to other measures of the same concept specified by theory or in previous research. For example, in 2003, a researcher at the Congressional Research Service published a book listing the laws of each Congress since 1789 that were, in his opinion, "landmark laws." This is one person's retrospective judgment, and it lacks the contemporaneous component of Mayhew's definition of important laws. Thus it is not surprising that the two measures of the same concept do not completely comport with one another.[4] Which of these measures is "better" in the sense of construct validity depends on the definition of the concept of important legislation, but this example also illustrates that differences in content validity can give rise to problems of construct validity: one principal reason for the differences in these measures is that they tap into different facets of the underlying concept.

In the end, when operationalizing a concept, an analyst can little more than inform himself or herself of the substantive literature on the topic, apply good judgment, and explain the steps used to construct a variable. In all cases, the measurement has to be informed by an idea about how the social process in question works and the meaning of the concept in question. The concept

---

[4] See Clinton and Lapinski [2006] for a comprehensive analysis and aggregation of various measures of legislative "productivity" in Congress.

definition and measurement thus becomes a part of the research design and subject to criticism just as much as choice of statistical models or procedures and interpretation of results. Indeed, concept definition and operationalization are arguably the most important foundations of empirical research because carelessness at this stage renders even the fanciest modeling and analysis of the resulting variables moot. Researchers steeped in quantitative methods are often inclined to cut too much slack to themselves or others on this point or gloss over concept definition because they are used to dealing with partial measures of a concept to make some headway – when the term paper or conference submission has to be finished next week, it is tempting to conclude that "some results are better than no results." That is a good way to reach faulty conclusions that time will not bear out. Careful attention to this part of the research process will always be repaid, and may well generate higher returns on the marginal hour spent than mastering the latest modeling technique.[5]

It is crucially important for the concepts behind measurement to be sound and well specified for statistical analysis of those measurements to be meaningful or insightful. In this respect, statistics is basically parasitic on the disciplines in which it is used. Beyond techniques to analyze whether components of an index tap into a single underlying concept, statistics offers no substantive guidance on the right way to measure a concept: that is inherently the province of the substantive experts who deal with that concept for a living. Thus, the rest of this text does not focus on measurement. It focuses on how to learn things from measurements and variables that, presumably, are meaningful measures of some social science concept. The question of that meaning must always be present, however, when statistical analysis is performed or consumed.

2.2 UNIVARIATE DISTRIBUTIONS

A distribution containing observations on a single variable is a *univariate distribution*. For example, a list of the number of people in each of a collection of households is a univariate distribution: it contains a numerical entry for every household indicating the number of people living in it. The number of people is the variable, and the households are the units. Another example is a distribution of the length of time since a country's most recent civil war (however defined), for each of a collection of countries. State-level social capital measured for each state in a given year also forms a univariate distribution: there is one observation per state. The unit of observation in this example is a

---

[5] Of course, innovation in technique can and has been addressed to this very problem; for instance, there is a large literature on statistical inference in regression models estimated with data subject to measurement error. Such techniques will obviously never rescue findings based on invalid operationalizations of a concept. Validity or lack thereof does not just mean a concept is measured noisily; it means that even in a noiseless world the measurements obtained from an operationalization would not adequately reflect the concept in question.

state, and the value of social capital for each state is a variable. For generality, we can refer to the variable as simply x; its value for North Dakota is x_{ND}, its value for Vermont is x_{VT}, and so on. Also for generality, a unit of observation in general is denoted simply i, so that the value of the variable for unit i is x_i.

Univariate distributions are not a common end point in social research because we usually want to know how several variables relate to each other. However, the univariate distribution is a useful place to begin a discussion of data exploration.

2.2.1 Sample Central Tendency

One of the most important questions about a distribution of data is what the "typical" value in it is. There is, of course, no single meaning of this term in natural language, and there are several versions of it as numerical summaries of a distribution. By any of these definitions, every distribution of observed values does have a typical value (or possibly a set of them).

Mean
By far the most common definition of "typical value" is the *sample mean*. This is the arithmetic average of the values in the distribution, obtained by summing each observation and dividing by the number of observations, which is typically denoted by N. It is denoted by $\overline{x}$ for a variable x. If the observations are numbered $1, \ldots, N$, the mean is defined as

$$\overline{x} = \frac{x_1 + x_2 + \cdots + x_N}{N} = \frac{1}{N} \sum_{i=1}^{N} x_i. \tag{2.1}$$

The capital sigma $\sum_{i=1}^{N}$ is a notational device that makes the formula easier to write. It is called "sigma notation." All it ever does is shorten an expression. An arithmetic operation can be validly performed on a sigma-notation expression if and only if it can be validly performed on a sum (e.g., factoring out a constant from every term in the sum). The parts $i = 1$ and N below and above the sigma are the "limits of summation." The letter i is the index, and so the notation says that we sum x_i, starting at the index value $i = 1$ and continuing up to index value $i = N$ (the largest index value, not necessarily the largest value of x). Often, the limits of summation i and N are obvious because all observations are summed, so the limits are left implicit in the expression and not written down, as in $\sum x_i$. To reduce clutter but keep the index explicit, this can also be written as $\sum_i x_i$. But the limits are still there in the concept.

A few useful arithmetic properties: first, obviously, a mean is always at least as large as the smallest observation in the distribution, and never larger than the largest. If there are at least two values of x, "at least as large" is replaced with "strictly larger" and "no larger" is replaced with "strictly smaller." Second, the mean need not equal an observation that actually exists in dataset, and it may be an infeasible value of the variable. Third, if every observation is transformed so that $y_i = k \times x_i$ for any constant k, so every observation is multiplied by the same constant (say, dollars are converted to euros in a distribution of prices), the mean of the transformed data is $\bar{y} = k \times \bar{x}$. This property holds because a mean is a sum; if every component of the sum is multiplied by the same number, that number can be factored out of each component and instead simply multiplied by their sum. Finally, if every observation is transformed such that $y_i = x_i + k$ for some constant k, so the same number is added to every observation, the mean of the transformed data is $\bar{y} = \bar{x} + k$. Adding k to all N components of the sum increases the sum by $k \times N$, and when the mean is computed, N in the denominator cancels the one in the numerator, leaving only k. Fourth, the mean value for a distribution is always unique.

The sample mean is a useful summary of the "typical value" in a distribution because it has a nice property: if all the observations of a variable are written on a slip of paper and placed in a box, the box is shaken, and one slip is drawn out, then $\bar{x}$ is, in a specific sense, the single best guess about the value that will be drawn.

That "specific sense" is this: $\bar{x}$ is the one and only number that minimizes the mean squared difference between a variable's values and any guess about its value. A number with that property is necessarily the mean. Simple algebra allows us to show this formally: suppose we get to see the distribution of x and make one guess about the value of an observation that will be drawn blindly out of a box. That guess is a number; call it g for short. Because there are multiple values of x in the distribution, the guess will not be exactly right for a lot of possible draws. Instead, for any draw x_i, there will an *error* in the guess, defined as[6] $e_i \equiv x_i - g$.

The *mean squared error* or MSE of the guess g is

$$MSE(g) = \frac{\sum_{i=1}^{N}(x_i - g)^2}{N}. \tag{2.2}$$

Ignoring the specifics of the numerator for a moment, note that this is a sum of N items divided by N – it is, by definition, a mean of something. Now back to the numerator: it is the squared difference between the guess g and an actual value x_i, summed over all possible values of x_i – more compactly, it is the sum of all the possible squared errors e_i. The name MSE is handy because it literally describes the components. Note that in the numerator, x_i is indexed by i, but g is not: we only get to make one guess about x, not to make a specific guess for each x_i.

A simple trick helps us make headway in proving that $\bar{x}$ minimizes MSE: add and substract $\bar{x}$ from the squared error: $(x_i - g)^2 = (x_i - \bar{x} + \bar{x} - g)^2$. Obviously this does not change the value of MSE but lets us group terms

[6] An equal sign with three bars, $\equiv$, means the equation is true by definition, i.e., it holds for all possible i.

and expand the square: $(x_i - g)^2 = (x_i - \bar{x})^2 + 2(x_i - \bar{x})(\bar{x} - g) + (\bar{x} - g)^2$. The mean squared error is therefore the mean of this expression:

$$MSE = \frac{\sum(x_i - \bar{x})^2}{N} + \frac{\sum 2(x_i - \bar{x})(\bar{x} - g)}{N} + \frac{\sum(\bar{x} - g)^2}{N}. \tag{2.3}$$

The first term is not affected by the guess g. The second term is necessarily 0: $2(\bar{x} - g)$ can be factored out because it is not indexed by i, and $\frac{\sum(x_i - \bar{x})}{N} = \frac{\sum x_i}{N} - \bar{x} = 0$. Finally, the last term is 0 if and only if $g = \bar{x}$ but is positive for any other guess because the difference is squared and hence never negative.

In short, MSE for any guess g is a sum of three terms: one not a function of g, one always zero, and one that attains its minimum value only when g is the mean. Therefore, $\bar{x}$ uniquely minimizes MSE of g. If we take MSE as a characterization of what a "good guess" is, then $\bar{x}$ is the best possible guess.

Weighted Mean

The sample mean gives every observation in a distribution equal weight – $\frac{1}{N}$ – and it can be important to be careful in light of this when interpreting means. For example, California is widely regarded as one of the most reliably Democratic states in the United States in presidential elections. But in 2004, the mean vote share for George W. Bush by California counties was 52.4%. This figure was obtained by summing each county's 2004 vote share for George Bush and dividing by the number of counties (58). Thus this mean gives equal weight to populous, liberal counties (Alameda, Los Angeles, Santa Clara, San Francisco) as it does to sparsely populated, conservative counties (Del Norte, Inyo, Kings). Of course large counties contribute many more ballots to California's total than small ones, and if each county's Bush vote share is weighted to reflect its size – here, the county's ballots cast divided by all ballots cast in the state – then the *weighted average* exactly equals the overall state 2004 George Bush vote share (which was 44%). That is, each county receives a weight $w_i = \frac{\text{county ballots}}{\text{total state ballots}}$, and the weighted mean is $\bar{x}^W \equiv \sum_i w_i \times x_i$. The (simple or unweighted) sample mean results as the special case with $w_i = \frac{1}{N}$. This does not mean that the by-county average of 52.4% is necessarily "misleading"; this depends on the question asked. The unweighted average is the right answer to some questions and the wrong answer to others. If one wants to know, for instance, whether all California counties had essentially the same vote share, the by-county average is a useful quantity to compare to any given county's vote share. But if one wants to know about the state in general, obviously unweighted averaging over all counties is misleading. The remedy to this is not to mistrust any particular type of average; it is to be sure that you know the quantity you are interested in before you set out computing anything.

Somewhat relatedly, it can be hazardous to make inferences about groups of units based on the average over a larger collection of units. For example, suppose that average SAT scores among all test takers decline from one year to the next (and that the test scores are not renormed or changed in any way). Does this imply that average scores have declined among any individual demographic group (e.g. African American, White, or Latino)? It does not: average scores can in fact rise among *every* subgroup, and the overall average can still decline. The reason is that the subgroups have different averages, and the proportion of test takers from each subgroup may change from one year to the next. For instance, it is well documented that non-Latino White students score higher on the SAT, on average, than Latino students. Even if both groups' averages increase from one year to the next – and even if the "achievement gap" between the groups narrows – the overall average can decline if the share of Latino test takers increases. This is sometimes called *Simpson's paradox* in statistics and is an example of the fallacy of composition. This example is also an illustration of the *ecological fallacy*, that is, we cannot necessarily infer individual characteristics from group characteristics. Simply put, even though a group of observations as a whole behaves a certain way, every single member of the group *may* behave in a completely different way. They don't always behave differently, but they might; there are no guarantees. In the SAT example, this logic can have important policy implications; to wit, having observed a decline in average SAT scores, we cannot automatically conclude that any particular problem of student achievement has grown, either in general or in any particular group. Further investigation into the constituent parts of the group is required.

Median

Because there is no single meaning of "typical," the mean is not the only statistical summary with a good claim to capture it. Another common and useful summary measure of central tendency is the *sample median*, denoted sometimes as $\tilde{x}$, x_M, just M, or something else as specified (that is, it does not have a universally accepted symbol as the sample mean does). This is the "middle observation" in the distribution if all x values are ordered from lowest to highest. The median is the observation such that (at least) half the observations have values at least as great, and (at least) half the observations have values no greater. Thus, it is identified by ordering all the variable's values from lowest to highest.

Formally, if a whole dataset is denoted X, individual members are x, and the sample size is N,

$$x_M = \{x \in X : |y \geq x_M| \geq \frac{N}{2} \quad \text{and} \quad |z \leq x_M| \geq \frac{N}{2}, \forall y \in X, \forall z \in X\}. \quad (2.4)$$

Because the concept of a median is so simple, this formal expression is mainly just a good way to learn how to parse formal expressions, and this book is full of them. First, x_M is defined to equal an expression in curly brackets, {, }. These brackets denote a set of things. So "the" median is really a collection of numbers, not necessarily just a single number as the mean is. The part in the curly brackets before the colon denotes what kind of objects x_M is defined to be: here, members x of a dataset X. The part after the colon indicates what conditions the members x have to satisfy to get into the set x_M. In this part, the notation $|X|$ denotes the size of a group X. So $|y \geq x_M|$ refers to the number of points y satisfying $y \geq x_M$. Now, of course, we have taken more words to explain the formal definition than we saved by writing it instead of the English meaning of the median. But we will use these notational conventions many times, and it will come to be much simpler to keep track of many ideas at once if we can master and quickly parse this kind of notation.

For an odd number N of observations, the median is in position $\frac{N+1}{2}$ in an ordered list of sample members, so that it is unique (even if a given value of x occurs more than once). For an even number N of observations, *every number* between the values in positions $\frac{N-1}{2}$ and $\frac{N+1}{2}$ is a median, so that the median is not unique.[7]

While the sample mean minimizes the MSE, the sample median minimizes the mean absolute error, $MAE(g) \equiv \frac{\sum_i |x_i - g|}{N}$. So in the sense of MAE, the median can also be considered the "single best guess" about the value in a distribution.

The median is a type of *order statistic*. That means it is defined in terms of where it falls in an ordered or ranked list of the variable's values. That also gives the median an appealing property of being insensitive to extreme observations, which are sometimes loosely referred to as "outliers."[8] That is, once you know the median of a distribution, you can increase the largest values in it by any amount without changing the value of the median. This is clearly not true of the sample mean. As a result, many analysts believe that the median is a more realistic or informative picture of central tendency when a distribution has a small number of extremely large observations. For example, central tendency in a distribution of income or house prices is often reported as the median.

Order statistics don't have to refer to central tendency only. *Percentiles* are order statistics. The pth percentile in a distribution is the observation such that at least $p\%$ of the observations are below it, and at most $(1 - p)\%$ are above it. *Quartiles* are important summaries of location: the 1st quartile is the 25th percentile; the 2nd quartile is the median, and the 3rd quartile is the 75th percentile in a distribution. *Quintiles* are also important, particularly when summarizing income inequality (e.g., the average income in the top quintile may be divided by the average income in the bottom quintile). Quintiles divide a distribution into 5 parts, as quartiles do into 4 and percentiles do into 100. A general name for an order statistic defined at an arbitrarily fine-grained level

---

[7] Often when N is even, an analyst reports the midpoint of the values in positions $\frac{N-1}{2}$ and $\frac{N+1}{2}$ as "the" median. There is no reason to do this except an insistence on a misplaced degree of precision.

[8] The term "outlier" does have an actual, rigorous (if arbitrary) definition in descriptive statistics, which cannot be offered yet because it depends on other concepts. Usually people use the term loosely.

(e.g., dividing a distribution into 1,000 parts) is a *quantile*. At the qth quantile, a fraction q of the observations are smaller.

Mode

On occasion, a measure of a "typical" value is the most common observation, the one that occurs most frequently in a dataset. This is the *mode* of the distribution, or the *modal value*. With 328 unique values in a dataset and a single value that occurs twice, that single value is the mode, even if it is 10 times as large as any other. As with the median, the mode is always an observed value in the distribution, and it is not necessarily unique.

As with the mean and median, the mode can also, in one sense, be considered the single "best guess" about the value of a variable in a distribution. If you win $1 for correctly guessing the number drawn from a distribution and $0 for an incorrect guess, the mode is the one guess that maximizes the expected winnings. Because it is the most common observation, it has the greatest probability of being the correct guess, and the probability of a correct guess is the expected amount won. So what all three of these common measures of central tendency have in common is that, if one wants to make a "single best guess" about the value of a variable, the mean, median, or mode may be the right guess, depending on how correct and incorrect guesses are "rewarded."

2.2.2 Sample Dispersion

Although every distribution has a "typical" value by any of these definitions of central tendency, "typical" values in a distribution may be, in another sense, atypical. A measure of central tendency may be the "single best guess" in some sense, but that is different from whether it adequately describes very much or any of the actual observations. The question of "how typical is typical?" is reflected in how widely dispersed the data is over its possible values.

Standard Deviation and Variance

By far the most common measure of sample dispersion is the *standard deviation*, denoted simply by s. In a sense, this is a measure of the typical departure from the mean of a dataset. It is actually based on the *variance* in the sample, denoted by s^2. The variance is obtained by finding the sample mean, computing the difference between each observation and the mean, squaring all of those individual differences, and then dividing by N, the number of observations.

The main problem with variance as a summary of dispersion is that it is not in the same units as the observations themselves: it is in units-squared because deviations from the mean were squared to compute it. So to return to the natural units of the data, and therefore meaningfully interpret spread in this way, we take the square root of the variance. This number is the standard deviation. For example, in a distribution of scores on an exam, if the average is measured in percent of questions answers correctly, the standard deviation is measured in percent answered correctly as well, but the variance is measured in terms of percent-squared, which is not useful.

The definition is cumbersome at first but becomes natural with 700 repetitions or so and is useful to internalize well:

$$s = \sqrt{\frac{\sum_{i=1}^{N}(x_i - \bar{x})^2}{N - 1}}. \tag{2.5}$$

The formula for standard deviation itself is instructive for understanding the quantity it returns. Inside the radical, the formula looks similar to the definition of the mean: it is a sum of things, divided by almost the number of things in the sum. So the standard deviation is an attempt to figure out the "typical" value of something, in roughly the same sense as a mean.

The "things" are the squares of each observation's difference with the mean. Because the "things" are squares, the portion inside the radical – the variance of x – is "almost" a mean of these squares. We want an "almost-mean" of the original units, not of squares, so we take the square root of the variance to get it. The reason for the squaring-and-square-rooting is that the ostensibly more appealing measure of the mean departure from the mean is necessarily and identically zero. On average, a variable does not depart from its average.

Altogether, the standard deviation can be loosely interpreted as the "typical" departure of a variable from its mean. So if a variable is less than $\bar{x} - s$, it is an unusually low value; if it is below $\bar{x}$ by less than s, it is below average but not by more than a typical amount.

A simple example with some intuition about standard deviation comes from a binary distribution. Suppose $N = 100$ and 50 of the observations are 1s while 50 are 0s. Then the sample mean is .5 (the mean for a binary variable is always the proportion of 1s in the distribution). Now each observation differs from the mean by .5, so the typical departure of the variable from its average is also .5. The standard deviation is .503 – about the typical departure of the variable from its average.[9]

A few useful properties of standard deviation: First, if there is only one value of x in the distribution, the standard deviation is 0. No observations depart from the average, so the typical departure from average is 0. Second, adding the same constant k to every observation does not change the standard deviation. This simply shifts every observation up or down the number line by the distance k; it does not change how far apart they are. Constant addition changes the mean but does not change the spread around, or typical departure from, the mean. Third, if every observation is multiplied by the same constant k, the standard deviation is also multiplied by k. Multiplication does change

---

[9] If N is used in the denominator of standard deviation rather than $N - 1$, the standard deviation of this variable is exactly .5.

how spread out the values of x are; bigger numbers change by a larger quantity than smaller ones. So this increases the spread in the distribution.

Why bother with an "almost-mean" (denominator $N - 1$) rather than an actual mean (denominator N) in defining variance? There are two justifications, theoretical and practical. The theoretical justification will wait until much later.[10] The practical reason is that $N - 1$ in the denominator makes the whole expression a little larger than when N is in the denominator. So this makes the typical departure from average look a little larger. This in turn makes it a little harder to argue that an observation is atypical. As will become clear in later chapters, this amounts to a conservative move in statistical analysis: it is harder to argue that a maintained guess about the mean is wrong. Of course, for even modest sample sizes, the difference from using $N - 1$ versus N is very small.[11]

An equivalent but sometimes computationally simpler formula for the variance is $s^2 = \frac{\sum_i x_i^2}{N-1} - \frac{(N)(\bar{x}^2)}{N-1}$. This is obtained from the definition of variance by expanding the square $(x_i - \bar{x})^2$, breaking the sum into pieces, and applying the definition of $\bar{x}$. Given the ubiquity of computers for carrying out such calculations, this is actually not of tremendous significance in computational terms. But it is useful sometimes in theoretical derivations involving the variance, as we will see with regression coefficients in the appendix to this chapter.

Interquartile Range

Just as the sample mean is affected by extreme observations, so is the standard deviation. A measure of dispersion not so affected is based on order statistics. Specifically, the *interquartile range* or IQR is simply the difference between the third and first quartiles of a distribution. This provides bounds on the location of the "middle 50%" of the observations in a distribution.

The IQR is also useful in identifying outliers formally, if somewhat arbitrarily. Specifically, an *outlier* is any observation that is at least 1.5 times the IQR above the third quartile, or that is at least 1.5 times the IQR below the first quartile. So you identify the quartiles and look for anything more than 1.5 times the IQR away from them, on the opposite side of the median. That's pretty far away. Few observations are really outliers. What to do about them can be controversial, but you should never just discard them because they are inconvenient. You should at least try to figure out what is going on; they should make you suspect that something went awry in the measurement of the variable. If we were chemists measuring grams of salt (or something else that chemists

---

[10] If you read the last page of a novel first, it turns out that using N in the denominator leads to a biased estimate of DGP variance, whereas $N - 1$ is unbiased. However, using N in the denominator gives an estimator of DGP variance with lower mean squared error than using $N - 1$. The concepts of "biased estimation" and "DGP" are formally introduced in later chapters.

[11] Note that with N in the denominator rather than $N - 1$, the variance is exactly the MSE of $\bar{x}$; see Equations 2.2 and 2.3.

do), these are the observations where we would suspect we accidentally put a thumb on the scale.

Generally, an adequate summary of data requires at minimum a measure of sample central tendency in conjunction with a measure of sample dispersion. By far the most common approach is simply to report the sample mean and standard deviation for every variable in the dataset. Another approach, especially useful when distributions have a few extreme observations, is to report the median and IQR.

Measures of dispersion are frequently used as a way of conveying how much one understands about the behavior of a variable by understanding the behavior of its central tendency. This is a reality check of sorts: we may understand the behavior of the mean well, but to what extent does that pin down the behavior of the variable in general? Not much, if the variance is large. (In techniques designed to study the behavior of means, like regression, the variance is repackaged as "percent of variance explained," so there is a meaningful notion of "large.")

Measures of dispersion may of course also be the focus of inquiry in their own right. For example, in the United States, many interest groups score the voting records of Senators and Representatives according to how much they agree with the group's causes. Americans for Democratic Action (ADA), affiliated with the AFL-CIO, reports scores based on support for liberal public policy in general. These scores are frequently used by political scientists to gauge how liberal or conservative the voting behavior of a congressperson is.[12] It would also be possible to use the standard deviation of ADA scores in each session of Congress, as a measure of the breadth of the political spectrum represented in each session.

2.2.3 Graphical Summaries: Histograms

The purpose of descriptive statistics is to convey information about the distribution to the reader (and the researcher) in a compact, simple, accessible format. Often the best way to do that is with graphical summaries.

There is an endless variety of devices for graphically summarizing information in a distribution.[13] One of the most important graphical devices for depicting a distribution is a *histogram*.

A histogram is a frequency distribution in the form of a bar chart. It shows how often different values of the variable occur. The range of the variable is partitioned into a relatively small number of "bins" or subintervals of values.

[12] Poole and Rosenthal [2007] have developed a technique called NOMINATE or DW-NOMINATE to scale roll call votes into several basic dimensions, which has largely overtaken ADA scores and the like in political science. But NOMINATE-like techniques are harder to explain so I went with ADA scores.

[13] For good illustrations of the importance and variety of statistical graphics see Tufte [2001] or Gelman and Hill [2006].

State-Level Social Capital: Relative Frequency

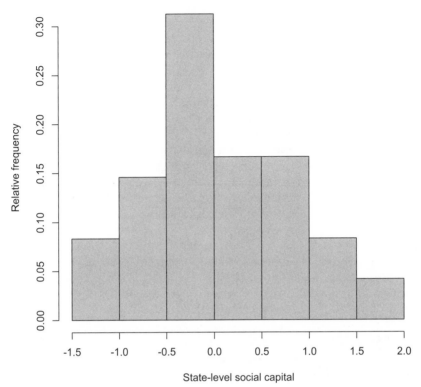

FIGURE 2.1. A histogram.

Then the frequency or number of occurrences of each subinterval in the distribution is recorded. The bins are arrayed on a horizontal line, from lowest to highest if there is any sensible ordering. The frequency of each bin is plotted in the height of a vertical bar emanating from it.

Histograms show an entire distribution in one picture. They show at a glance whether the distribution of the variable tends to have a lot of "moderate" values, or whether it has a number of very small ones and a few large ones, and so forth. In addition, to compare two distributions of a particular variable – say, household income distributions in a city versus a suburb of that city – then histograms for each distribution can be plotted on the same graph. This will give a quick visual impression of whether one distribution tends to above the other, whether one is more spread out, whether one is more skewed or has a "longer tail," and so on.

For example, Figure 2.1 shows a histogram of state-level social capital scores due to Putnam. These scores are based on the 14 dimensions described previously and are scaled to have an average of about 0. The scores range from −1.4 to 1.7. As in all histograms, the horizontal axis shows ordered bins of the variable (here, bins of width .5) and the vertical axis shows some measure of frequency (here, relative frequency or percent of all states[14] in the respective bins). The histogram shows that a plurality of states have moderately low levels of social capital, the distribution has one peak and relative frequencies trail off for relatively extreme values, and there is a slightly longer right tail than left tail (the distribution is slightly skewed to the right).

If all the bins in a histogram have the same width on the horizontal axis, it is natural to use frequency (a tally of the number of observations in each bin) or relative frequency (the proportion of all observations in each bin) as the scale on the vertical axis. However, if the bins have markedly different widths, frequency or relative frequency can give a strange and difficult to interpret shape for the histogram. The reason is that the relatively wide bins may have high frequency or relative frequency not because any one of the observations in that bin are especially common but rather because there are so many possible observations in it.

For instance, suppose a survey of personal income asks individuals to place their household income in ranges of $10,000 starting at $0, all the way up to $100,000, but lumps all household incomes above $100,000 in the same bin. Because almost 20% of U.S. households have income above $100,000, a histogram of this distribution will show the relative frequency of the largest category to be about 0.2, about as large or larger than any other single bin with a width of $10,000. Overall, the histogram will appear vaguely bell-shaped – except for a large spike in the largest income category. The problem is that these relatively high incomes are not especially common, but there are so many individual values in this bin that the relative frequency is high.

The solution to this issue is to use *density* as the scale for the vertical axis. Density is relative frequency per unit on the horizontal (x) axis. So the density of each bin is obtained by dividing its relative frequency by its width in terms of units of the x variable. In the household income example, the relative frequency of each of the first 10 bins is divided by $10,000, whereas the relative frequency of the largest ($100,000 and over) bin is divided by the width of that interval – the largest reasonable household income minus $100,000. Clearly, when all bins have the same width, the shape of a histogram on the density scale is the same as its shape on the relative frequency scale, although the units on the vertical axis are different.

Fewer people are familiar with density than with relative frequency, so presenting data in this way requires a little more explication so that it is understood. But this is not difficult and is a small price to pay for a histogram that provides a reasonable depiction of a distribution.

---

[14] The state-level social capital index is defined only for the 48 contiguous states in this distribution.

2.3 BIVARIATE DISTRIBUTIONS

A *bivariate distribution* consists of an observation of two variables for each unit in a collection of N units. For example, for a collection of households, we might observe the number of people living in each one and its total income. The units are the households themselves, and the variables are number of residents and income. The bivariate distribution is two univariate distributions for the same collection of units. The "units" comprise the *unit of observation* – here, a household. Recording a distribution of household size for N_1 households and appending it to a distribution of income for N_2 *different* households does not make a bivariate distribution, it simply makes two univariate distributions. The analytic tools defined below cannot be sensibly applied because the variables do not come from the same units.[15] A *multivariate distribution* consists of an observation of $M \geq 2$ variables for each unit in a collection of N units.

A simple case of bivariate distribution has one continuous variable (or at least one with many possible values) and one binary variable. For example, a dataset might consist of the number of "major" laws enacted by the U.S. Congress in each year, as well as a binary indicator for whether the branches of government are held by the same party ("unified government") or different parties ("divided government"). If we want to know the relationship between lawmaking activity and divided government, it is often more convenient to treat this as two univariate distributions of a single variable – a distribution of the number of landmark laws under unified government and a distribution under divided government – rather than as one bivariate distribution. Nevertheless, it certainly is a bivariate distribution by our definition, and the unit of observation is the year.

Of course, for each variable in a bivariate distribution, the summary measures of the previous section can also be computed. That is, a multivariate distribution can be taken as a collection of univariate distributions, with observations on the same group of units, joined together. Each such univariate distribution can be explored with the tools described earlier.

However, the reason bivariate distributions are important is that they are a necessary foundation for exploring relationships between two variables. Analyzing relationships is the stock-in-trade for theoretically motivated social science and for most of public policy research. In terms of theory, we may want

---

[15] Sometimes, of course, two distributions with different units can and may be aggregated into a bivariate distribution in the sense defined earlier. For instance, suppose we observe mean household size for each city in a state, and we observe mean household income for each county in a state. These univariate distributions have different units of observation – city and county, respectively. Then we can aggregate household sizes from different cities in a county (using a weighted average) to arrive at a bivariate distribution of mean household size and income, by county. Here the aggregation is natural because each city is in exactly one county (or some unit that can be taken as identical to a county, in unusual cases such as St. Louis, Missouri).

to know, for example, whether people with some characteristic (intelligence, attractiveness, etc.) are more likely than other people to have mates with those characteristics (associative mating); whether voters are more likely to vote for candidates they perceive as "closer" to themselves ideologically than "more distant" candidates (spatial voting); or whether "democratic" nation-states are less likely to go to war with each other than pairs involving a "nondemocracy" (the democratic peace). In terms of policy, given some variable of public interest – for example, poverty rates, student achievement, environmental quality – we want to know if some policy instrument helps us affect it (and there is some at least implicit theory of behavior or social interaction that makes the question reasonable): for example, do job training programs alleviate poverty? Do smaller class sizes raise students' standardized test scores? Do "spare the air" announcements in the Bay Area improve air quality? All of these questions are about relationships; we want to know if one variable (measuring the outcome of interest) changes as another variable (measuring the policy intervention) changes. The ability to answer such questions is arguably the single most important reason why social, political, and policy researchers use statistical methods.

Each one of these questions can be phrased in terms of a common structure: does one variable tend to get bigger as another variable gets big? If so, they are *positively related*; the variables grow together. Does one variable tend to get smaller as another variable gets big? If so they are *negatively* or *inversely related*. Or does one variable tend not to change in any systematic way as another variable gets big? If so they are unrelated.[16] By using specific measures of the central tendency of each variable and interpretations of what "big" or "small" mean, we arrive at alternative tools to measure relationships and express them as quantities.

2.3.1 Graphical Summaries: Scatterplots

A visual representation of association is often invaluable in assessing relationships among variables. *Scatterplots* are a useful tool for displaying this. Before launching into quantitative measures of relationships described later, it is useful simply to look at a few scatterplots to get a visual sense of the relationship. Although quantitative measures of relationships are precise and easy to report and (sometimes) to compare, a picture is worth a thousand numbers.

A scatterplot is a two-dimensional graph of the value of each variable for each unit in a bivariate distribution. The first, horizontal dimension represents the x value for any unit (x_i, y_i). The second, vertical dimension represents the y value. So a scatterplot is simply a cloud of dots, one for each ordered pair in the dataset. It is a good way to display a relationship. If the cloud generally slopes up, it is because the relationship is positive. If it is formless or

---

[16] At least through their means.

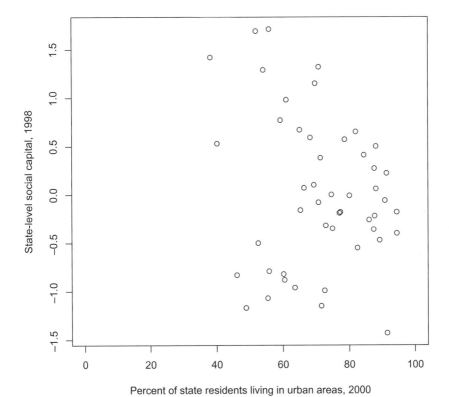

FIGURE 2.2. A scatterplot.

generally flat, there is roughly no relationship. And obviously if the cloud of dots slopes down, the relationship is negative. The scatterplot can have a definite but nonlinear shape, meaning that the relationship between x and y is more complicated than a straight line can fully capture. This does not require any modification of a scatterplot; it simply shows the data as it is.

For example, Figure 2.2 shows a scatterplot of Putnam's 1998 state-level social capital scores and the 2000 share of the state's population in urban areas (from the *Statistical Abstract of the United States*). Each point in the scatterplot represents a state or district (Washington, DC, is included but Alaska and Hawaii are not). Dropping down from any dot to the x-axis shows the share of the state's population in urban areas; moving left from any dot to the y-axis shows its social capital score. The scatterplot shows a general downward drift in the points: the average social capital score for states between 40 and 60 on the x-axis is positive (0.16), whereas it is negative (−0.12) for states above 80 on the x-axis. The scatterplot also shows that the dispersion of state-level social capital changes as the population becomes more urbanized: the points are more widely dispersed for relatively low values on the x-axis than for relatively high values. Apparently, social capital is negatively associated with urbanization. The social science question is, why? Does the anonymity of urban life undermine social capital? Putnam has also shows that demographic and ethnic diversity are negatively associated with social capital; because urban areas tend to be more diverse than rural ones, might the scatterplot reflect the effect of diversity? Or does it go the other way – do people in states with low social capital choose to live in cities because the social ties that make rural life appealing are absent? The scatterplot can suggest a relationship but cannot by itself answer the social science question. These questions also illustrate the interplay of theory and data in social science: armed with a theory predicting a particular relationship, we can use quantitative and graphical tools to explore whether the relationship holds. At the same time, after some descriptive exploration of the data, we can discover a relationship that needs further theorizing to help us interpret it.

2.3.2 Numerical Summaries: Crosstabs

We have seen that histograms are valuable tools to present an entire univariate distribution in graphical form. The clarity achieved in this way is just as useful for bivariate distributions, and in principle it is simple to present a multidimensional histogram. Whereas a histogram is a two-dimensional figure, a multidimensional histogram has three axes: one for bins or categories of the x variable, one for bins or categories of the y variable, and a third for the frequency, relative frequency, or density of each bin created by the intersection of x and y values. In practice, multidimensional histograms plotted on a graph are often hard to read because it is difficult to interpret intricate relationships in a three-dimensional graph on two-dimensional paper.

A more common way to display this information is in a table, with numbers or percentages to represent (relative) frequencies rather than bars in a graph. When a multidimensional histogram is displayed in this tabular form, it is called a *crosstab* or *contingency table*.

For instance, Table 2.2 contains a crosstab drawn from the General Social Survey (GSS), an important representative survey of American adults administered for many years by the National Opinion Research Center at the University of Chicago.[17] The rows show frequency of respondent's church attendance, and the columns show the frequency of the respondent's attempts to influence the votes of others in elections. For example, 15 of the 1,134 respondents answering both questions report that they never go to church and often attempt to influence the votes of others.

---

[17] The GSS website contains a huge treasure trove of downloadable data, as well as online tools for analysis of that data. It is a good idea for any social scientist to have a passing familiarity with it, and poking around in it is also a fun way to kill time.

TABLE 2.2. *Attempts to Influence Others' Votes, by Frequency of Church Attendance*

| Church Attendance | Attempts to Influence Others' Votes: | | | | |
	Often	Sometimes	Rarely	Never	N
Never	15	31	23	127	196
Several times/year	20	61	48	141	270
Once/month	22	37	16	78	153
Once/week	35	93	46	195	369
> Once/week	16	33	15	82	146
N	108	255	148	623	1,134

The table indicates that regardless of church attendance, most respondents report that they never try to influence the political behavior of others in the sense of voting in elections. For each row of the table (indicating self-reported church attendance), over half of the respondents say they never try to influence the votes of others (again, these are self-reports; whether others see their behavior differently is another matter). The bottom row of the table shows the distribution of self-reported attempts to influence others, aggregated over all church attendance behavior; again, 623 of the 1,134 respondents indicate that they never do so. The data also indicates that, regardless of attempts to influence others, a little less than half the respondents report that they attend church at least once a week. The overall behavior of each variable by itself, reflected in the bottom row and right-most column, respectively, makes up the *marginal distribution* of each variable. The marginals are obtained simply by adding up the cell totals for each row or column, as applicable.

In addition to these marginals, the crosstab also reflects information about the relationship between the two variables. In particular, although the majority of respondents for each church attendance category indicate that they never attempt to influence the votes of others, the proportion of individuals who report attempting to influence others grows as church attendance grows. The effect is not constant across cells; there are plenty of twists and turns in this pattern. That is a good thing about crosstabs; they remind us that even when relationships are present, it is best not to be procrustean about assuming they are inexorable or the same in every cell.

Crosstabs show relationships between the variables in a distribution, as well as the overall behavior of each of the variables separately. They are sometimes considered "low-tech" devices compared with some of the statistical approaches for summarizing relationships described later, but it is not clear that this makes them undesirable. In particular, they impose low "barriers to entry" on the reader, and more important, they make no (possibly questionable) assumptions about a specific mathematical function relating the variables (e.g., that it follows a straight line). For this reason, crosstabs at the very least offer a useful reality check for any conclusions that are obtained from regression methods described later.

2.3.3 Conditional Sample Mean

A simple way to see relationships is with the sample mean of variable y, assuming the other variable x takes a specific value. This is the mean of y *conditional on* x, or just *conditional mean* for short. We will denote it $\bar{y}(x)$. This suggests that $\bar{y}$ is a function of x. As we consider different specific values x, we might get different values of the conditional mean $\bar{y}(x)$.

In view of that, this conditional mean can be compared to the conditional mean of y for other values of x to get some idea of how y tends to change as the value of x changes. With multiple observations of y and k different values of x, this gives us k different values of the conditional mean of y, one for each of the k values of x. This conditional mean function is one specific way to measure the relationship between x and y. Plainly, it measures one facet of what we previously said a relationship is: whether and how one variable tends to change as another variable changes.

To compute a conditional sample mean, simply pick out the subset of observations for which the condition $x = x_1$ holds. Then, for this subset, compute the mean of y. Repeating this for each value of x of interest gives the conditional sample mean of y as a function of x. Resulting patterns or relationships between x and y will be a lot easier to spot if the data is ordered by x before conditional means are computed.

Conditional means computed in this way are actually not often used to measure relationships, but they are important building blocks of more widely used techniques, in particular regression (discussed later in this section). An exception to this – a case in which conditional means computed in this way are widely used – is when one variable x is multichotomous (whether ordinal or categorical) and has a small number of categories; in this situation a conditional mean function is a useful tool. If we want to understand how x and y are related, then the conditional mean of y as a function of x is a simple way to find out. For example, in Mayhew's data from 1947 to 1990, on average 11.7 major laws are passed in Congresses under divided government, whereas on average 12.8 major laws are passed in Congresses under unified government. This is the conditional mean of the number of major laws (measured on a cardinal scale) as a function of divided government (measured as a binary categorical variable). The change in the conditional mean (about 1.1) alone does not tell us whether the change is "large" or "important" because a deviation from a mean does not specify whether the deviation is larger than typical. The standard deviation does tell us that, and in Mayhew's data on 22 Congresses, the standard deviation in the number of major laws passed is about 5. So the average difference between unified and divided government is much smaller than the typical deviation from average in a Congress. This is one way to see, with simple tools, that divided government does not have a stunning impact on Congress's ability to pass landmark laws.

Even if x has a large range, that is a large set of possible values, a conditional sample mean function can still be a useful way to visualize relationships: we can simply group x values into a small number of categories. For example, consider the bivariate relationship between income inequality and per capita income in a nation-state. Although income inequality may be damaging to some conceptions of political equality, some social theorists have argued that it provides powerful incentives for economic performance (Aghion and Williamson [1999]). A simple version of the logic is as follows: if everyone winds up with about the same income, so that income inequality is low, there is not much point in working hard to accumulate income. But if income inequality can be high, there may be a big payoff to intense effort and high performance in the labor market. This theory implies something about the relationship between income inequality and per capita income, to wit, it should be positive.

The degree of inequality in any distribution (including income) is a subtle concept, and there are a variety of ways to measure it, one of which is the Gini coefficient. The Gini coefficient measures the degree of difference between a perfectly equal income distribution (i.e., in which all units have the same income) and any particular income distribution. It ranges from 0 (perfectly equal income distribution) to 1 (a single person has all income); it is a cardinal variable on an interval scale. Per capita income is more straightforward to measure;[18] for instance, per capita gross domestic product adjusted for purchasing power parity.

The Gini coefficient takes many different values across nation-states in any given year; in 2004 data from the *Penn World Tables*, it ranged from a low of about 20 to a high of about 65, with scores of different values and few values repeated exactly. So a conditional mean of per capita GDP as a function of the Gini coefficient would be impractical to deal with. But the Gini coefficient can be grouped into "bins" of similar values, analogous to the procedure of constructing a histogram; for instance, we can group together ginis of 20 to 25, 25 to 30, 30 to 35, and so forth. Then we can construct the mean value of per capita GDP for all nations in each bin – the conditional mean of y, given that x is in a particular bin.

Constructing this conditional mean and plotting the results reveals an interesting, uncluttered, readily interpretable relationship between income inequality and average income (Figure 2.3). A graph of conditional means will have the same general pattern as a scatterplot but is a bit "cleaner" because many individual observations are compressed into a single average. As Figure 2.3 shows, apparently (at least for 2004) there was a rather steep *decline* in per capita GDP as the Gini coefficient increased. However, although these results

---

[18] But still not entirely unambiguous because we can either convert currencies at market exchange rates or attempt to hold constant the purchasing power of a currency in its local context.

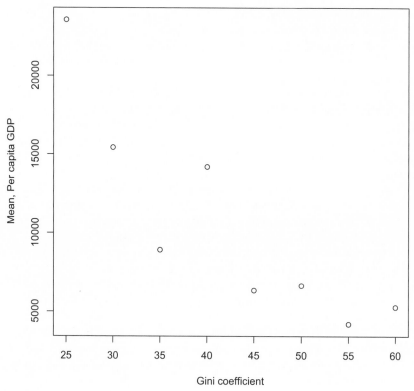

FIGURE 2.3. Mean of per capita GDP by range Gini coefficient.

do provide a clear counterpoint to some versions of the theory that greater income inequality improves economic performance, they must be interpreted with caution. They do not report what *would have happened* to a country's GDP if its Gini coefficient changed. The results only tell us what did in fact happen to per capita GDP as we move from low-inequality countries to high-inequality countries. The answers to the "what would have happened" and "what actually did happen" questions do not have to be the same.[19]

2.3.4 Association between Variables: Covariance and Correlation

When both variables in a bivariate distribution can take a large number of different values, there are less cumbersome ways to measure the general contours of their relationship. Additionally, these techniques compress relationships into a single number or a small set of numbers – and thus can be clearer than a

---

[19] The issue is that the countries with high Ginis do not represent *counterfactual outcomes* for the countries with low Ginis. This issue is taken up in greater depth in Chapter 10.

conditional sample mean function, albeit it at a cost of some extra assumptions. They take advantage of the following idea, which is further explicated later: when two variables are positively related, they tend to be "big" at the same time (and "small" at the same time), but when two variables are negatively related, one tends to be "big" when the other tends to be "small."

A straightforward way to capture this idea formally is through a summary measure called their *covariance*. Covariance expresses a relationship in a single number. When two variables are each "big" or "small" at the same time, covariance returns a positive number. But if one variable is "big" and the other is "small," covariance returns a negative number.

Formally, the covariance of x and y is defined as

$$Cov(x, y) = \frac{\sum (x - \bar{x})(y - \bar{y})}{N - 1}. \qquad (2.6)$$

As for standard deviation, this looks a lot like an average. Consider the numerator first: for each observation i, each variable's mean is subtracted from that observation's value of each variable, and the differences are multiplied. When the variables are positively related, they tend to both be above their means at the same time and below them at the same time (i.e., they tend to be "big" and "small" simultaneously), so the product $(x - \bar{x})(y - \bar{y})$ is either a positive times a positive or a negative times a negative – either way, a positive number. But when the variables are negatively related, one tends to be above its mean and the other is below its mean, so the product is a positive times a negative – a negative number. The covariance is something like the average of all of these products for each observation. If there are a lot of positive products in the numerator, the covariance is positive, whereas if there are a lot of negative products, the covariance is negative. So the covariance between two variables is a single number, and its sign reports the direction of the overall relationship between two variables.

The covariance can be alternatively written as $Cov(x, y) = \frac{\sum_i x_i y_i}{N-1} - \frac{N(\bar{x})(\bar{y})}{N-1}$. This has some use as a computational simplification but is mainly useful as an alternative way to write the covariance in theoretical derivations, as we use it in the appendix to this chapter.

The covariance of two variables is affected by scale changes of either one of them (i.e., increases in spread or variance). Often this scale-dependence is confusing or misleading, and it implies that covariance is not readily comparable for different bivariate distributions. For example, the covariance of incumbent campaign spending and incumbent vote shares in U.S. Senate elections is not necessarily comparable to that same covariance in U.S. House elections because the variance of incumbent vote shares is much higher in Senate elections. More strikingly, the covariance of a distribution changes whenever the units of measurement of a variable change. The covariance between per capita GDP and income inequality across countries changes if GDP is measured in dollars or euros.

This scale effect is not difficult to overcome. A scale-independent measure of association that is comparable across any bivariate distributions is the correlation between x and y. It is obtained by scaling the covariance between x and y by their respective standard deviations.

This rescaled covariance is the sample *correlation coefficient* or correlation, sometimes denoted r_{xy} or just r. It is defined formally as

$$r_{xy} = \frac{Cov(x, y)}{s_x s_y}. \qquad (2.7)$$

The correlation coefficient, like the covariance, is always positive when the covariance is positive and negative when the covariance is negative. This is because it is simply the covariance divided by the product of two positive numbers, so it inherits the sign of the covariance. Furthermore, unlike covariance, the correlation coefficient is always between -1 and 1. Suppose for example that $y = x$, so x and y are obviously perfectly correlated. Then the covariance is simply the variance of x; the covariance formula collapses to the variance formula. To get the correlation, this variance is divided by the squared standard deviation – otherwise known as the variance. So the same number is in the numerator and denominator.

Correlation is unaffected by changes in scale in a variable, because they affect both the covariance and the standard deviation of the rescaled variable in the same way. So their effects cancel each other out, leaving the correlation unchanged. For example, if we compute the correlation between average income in U.S. states in 2004 dollars and Republican share of the state's presidential vote in a given year, we'd get the same answer had we used 1994 dollars instead.

Correlation and covariance return one single number as a measure of an overall relationship, no matter how many peaks and valleys exist in the conditional sample mean function. For example, the correlation between state-level social capital and state urban population share is $-.19$. This is because covariance and correlation measure *linear* relationships between two variables. There may be lots of ways two variables are related, for example, various curves or sharp peaks, but the correlation captures a special kind of relationship – one that can be described by a straight line. That is not necessarily the entirety of the relationship, but it does make reporting the strength and direction of a relationship, at least as an overall tendency, simple. In addition, linearity is somewhat less restrictive than it might sound. If the relationship is actually quadratic rather than linear (i.e., y is related to x^2 rather than x, so the graph of means is a parabola rather than a straight line), then there is a linear relationship between y and $z \equiv x^2$. The upshot is that if you already know or suspect there is nonlinear association, this is easy to pick up with correlation-based tools (including regression, on which see more later). But if you are simply exploring relationships between x and y, the correlation between these variables won't alert you to nonlinear relationships.

The strength and direction of a linear relationship captured in correlation corresponds to the shape of the cloud of points in a scatterplot. When the cloud of points in a scatterplot tends to "drift upward," the correlation between the two variables displayed in it is positive. Imagine a vertical line in the scatterplot at the overall mean of x, and a horizontal line at the overall mean of y, then focus on the (single) point where they intersect. "Upward drift" means exactly that the points tend to fall in the quadrants above and right of the intersection, and below and left of the intersection. Above the intersection means y is above average; right of the intersection means x is above average. Similarly, when the cloud of points tends to "drift downward," the correlation is negative. In this case, the points in the scatterplot tend to fall in the quadrants above and left of the intersection, and below and right. Above and left occurs when x is below its average and y is above its average; below and right occurs when x is above its average and y is below its average. Whether the drift in the scatterplot is up or down, when the points are tightly clustered around a straight line, the correlation is close to 1 in absolute value. When the points are widely dispersed, the correlation is closer to 0 in absolute value.

2.3.5 Regression

We have already seen that a scatterplot displays all available information about the patterns by which two variables are related. Although the information in a scatterplot is rich, it is inevitably irregular: interesting data in social science rarely conforms to a perfectly tidy relationship that is self-evident from a cloud of data points. A graph of conditional means is useful for precisely this reason; it throws the basic patterns of a relationship between two variables into stark relief by eliminating irregularities from the graph and focusing only on general tendencies. Again, a conditional mean is by definition a regression, so the graph of conditional means is simply the graph of the regression function relating one variable to another. Because there are two variables involved, y and x, this is a *bivariate* regression.

An even more pronounced simplification of the relationship between two variables is revealed by a linear approximation to this regression or conditional mean function. A straight line is about the simplest possible description of an overall relationship or pattern between two variables, and although it obscures nuance, it shows general tendency clearly. When a straight line is used to approximate a regression function in this way, it is called a *linear regression*. The linear regression of y on x expresses the conditional mean of y as a linear function of x. A linear regression smooths out the jagged edges and peaks of the scatterplot and the conditional mean function. Neither the scatterplot as a whole nor a linear regression simplifying its patterns should be understood as the one true depiction of a relationship; these descriptive devices are more useful in conjunction with each other than as substitutes.

The basic idea in linear regression is that the slope of the regression line says something about the strength and direction of the relationship between the variables. If two variables are uncorrelated, the regression line is flat. Uncorrelatedness means exactly that one variable does not change on average as another variable changes, and when a regression line is flat, it means that the conditional mean of y is the same for all values of x. If two variables are positively correlated, the regression line slopes up; if they are negatively correlated, it slopes down. Thus the regression slope presents a compact and easily interpreted numerical summary of an overall relationship. Because it compresses the drift of a whole scatterplot into one number, it necessarily loses some information relative to the scatterplot, but it also clarifies the information that is available and makes it possible to compare across situations.

When we take the conditional mean of y to be a function of x in a regression, x is called a *covariate, explanatory variable, independent variable, conditioning variable,* or *regressor*. The variable y is called the *dependent variable, outcome variable, response variable,* or *regressand*.

The language of "dependent" and "independent" can be misleading. At this point we are simply describing a linear relationship between two variables, and no theoretical claim about the dependence of y in x in any social process is implied by exploring their relationship through regression. It is always possible to reverse the roles and take x as a function of y, for instance. This results in another (generally different) regression line that describes the exact same relationship in the data in a different way. Later we shall see that claims about the dependence of y on x, or even the causal effect of x on y, play a crucial role in theorizing and and theoretically guided empirical work in social science, but for now, regression is simply a tool for describing relationships between variables.

Any straight line can be defined by two numbers, the *slope* (how much y changes as x changes by one unit) and the (vertical) *intercept* (the value of y when $x = 0$). The slope and intercept are also called the *coefficients* of the regression line. So to capture a straight-line approximation of the regression of y on x, we need to identify these two coefficients.

The slope is typically denoted b, which represents a single number that means "a one-unit change in x is associated with an b-unit change in the average value of y." Because the relationship is a straight line, b captures the response of y to a one-unit change in x no matter what value of x we start with. The intercept is typically denoted a, which represents a single number that means "when $x = 0$, the average value of y is a." The intercept may not be substantively meaningful in a regression; if 0 is an absurd value of x (think about a regression of a nation's degree of democratization on its gross domestic product; GDP, the x variable, is never 0), the intercept may not make a lot of sense. But it is still necessary to pin down a line that approximates the regression.

To summarize, if $\bar{y}(x)$ denotes the mean of y conditional on x, a linear regression can be written

$$\bar{y}(x) = a + bx. \tag{2.8}$$

Given a specific value of x, we can then use $a + bx$ as a guess about the value of y, just as we used $\bar{x}$ as a guess about the value of a variable x drawn out of a box. And also as in that case, we do not generally expect these guesses always to be exactly right; instead they will typically involve some error for particular values of y.

The *error* or *residual* in the guess is simply $e = y - \bar{y}(x)$, the difference between the actual value and the guess. This is equivalent to $e = y - (a + bx)$. Put differently,

$$y = a + bx + e. \tag{2.9}$$

A specific value can always be expressed as a guess of its value plus the error in that guess.

To describe a linear relationship between x and y, there are lots of choices of a and b, just as there are many guesses to make about the value of y for a given value of x. How do we know which values of a and b return a line that is a "good" approximation of the conditional mean of y on x?

Recall that we found the sample mean $\bar{x}$ to be the "best" guess about x in the sense that $\bar{x}$ gives a smaller value of the average squared error than any other possible guess. We can use the same criterion to establish a and b values that give the "best" possible approximation of the conditional mean in exactly the same sense.

This is fleshed out formally in the appendix to this chapter, but to get the idea, consider the error $e_i = y_i - (a + bx_i)$ for every possible observation of x and y in a dataset, where i indexes the unit of observation. There is just one regression line, but there is an error specific to each observed value y_i. Now suppose we take all those errors, square each one, add them up, and take their mean value: that's the same mean squared error we saw for $\bar{x}$, only this time it's for the regression line. Because the errors depend on the values of a and b (apparent from the fact that a and b both appear in the definition of the error), we can use mathematics to identify the intercept a and slope b that lead to the smallest possible value of the mean squared error of the regression. If this made sense in the context of $\bar{x}$, it should still make sense now, because it's essentially the same problem.

The a and b values obtained in this way produce the smallest possible mean squared error of the linear approximation to the regression. For this reason they are said to define the *least squares regression line*. In the sense of MSE, the least squares regression line is the best possible approximation to the conditional mean of y as a function of x. The appendix goes through the math to show that the least squares regression coefficients are defined as follows:

$$b = \frac{r s_y}{s_x} \tag{2.10}$$

$$a = \overline{y} - b\overline{x}. \tag{2.11}$$

Here r is the correlation coefficient and s_x and s_y are the standard deviations. In terms of measuring relationships, primary attention goes to the slope b. This formula for b is equivalent to $b = \frac{Cov(x,y)}{Var(x)}$, that is, the covariance of x and y over the variance of x. The slope formula says that when x increases by one standard deviation, y changes by r times the standard deviation of y on average. Equivalently, when x changes by 1 unit, y changes by b units on average.

Note that b inherits its sign from r but b is not confined to the $[-1,1]$ interval. Any value of b can be meaningful. The slope term b is sometimes called the *marginal effect* of x on y. It is important insofar as it specifies the strength and direction of the relationship between x and y, and assessing this is the reason social scientists usually use correlational techniques.

When reporting and discussing regression coefficients, a researcher should always remember that she or he is communicating with an audience that usually knows the data far less well than the researcher. From this standpoint, the one-standard-deviation-change interpretation of b is often helpful to the reader because a one standard deviation change in x is a typical deviation of x from its mean. Any reader versed in statistics will know how to interpret a standard deviation, so this interpretation is substantively meaningful. This interpretation of b can be more useful than the (typically more common) b-unit-change-in-y-per-unit-change-in-x interpretation, because readers often do not know or recall whether a 1 unit change in x is particularly large or small. For instance, if x is a percentage measured as a decimal (say, the percent of a population with a college degree), a 1-unit change in x is unreasonable.

As for the intercept, note that the intercept a is defined so that the best fit line passes through the joint mean of the data, the ordered pair $(\overline{x}, \overline{y})$. So when x is equal to its mean, the least squares line says that y is equal to its mean. One way to interpret this is that you have no particular information about the value of x, so what value of y should you predict given that fact? To minimize the squared distance between the prediction and the actual result, which the least squares regression line attempts to do, $\overline{y}$ is the best guess, as we already discussed under central tendency for univariate distributions.

Obtaining a and b by minimizing the MSE of the regression also implies some important properties of the error term e. First, the mean value of e_i is always 0 for any least squares regression line with both a slope and intercept. This is analogous to an observation we made about the "prediction" error for the sample mean: on average, a variable does not depart from its average. The same holds true for its conditional average as expressed through least squares regression. Second, with a least squares regression line, the errors

e_i are always uncorrelated with the covariate x_i. Intuitively, this is because least squares regression extracts all systematic information about the linear relationship between x and y and places it in the slope b. If x and e were correlated, it would mean that some available sample information about the relationship between y and x were still left in the error. These two properties of least squares errors are discussed further in the appendix.

As an example of regression, the least squares regression equation for state-level social capital y as a function of state urban population share x is $0.72 - 0.01x$. This is a cross-sectional relationship, and the unit of analysis is U.S. states; social capital data is from in 1998 and urbanization data is from 2000. Here x is measured from 0 to 100. So when a state's urban population share increases by one percentage point, the social capital score of that state drops by about .01 points on average. Because the scales and standard deviations of both of these measures are not readily known to most readers, it is difficult to get a sense for the magnitude at stake here. Is a one percentage point change in urbanization large? Is a .01 unit change in the composite social capital index large? To get a feel for this, consider that the standard deviation across states of the share of residents living in urban areas is about 15, and the standard deviation of states' social capital indices is about .78. So, when state-level urbanization (x) increases by a standard deviation – a typical increase in this variable from its mean – state-level social capital falls by about $\frac{1}{7}$ of a standard deviation (i.e., .15). This regression describes a pattern by which these two variables are related in this sample, and nothing about this relationship or the language used to describe it should be understood to imply a cause–effect relationship. The intercept in this regression is not substantively meaningful because it does not make sense to consider a state with no residents living in urban areas (the minimum level of urbanization for a state in 2000 was about 38%, for Vermont).

To take another example, consider the cross-sectional relationship between per capita GDP (y) and the Gini coefficient (x). The unit of analysis is a country. The regression line is $31,900 - 498x$. The standard deviation across countries of the Gini coefficient is about nine and the standard deviation across countries of per capita GDP is about $16,500. So when the Gini coefficient changes from its mean by a typical amount, per capita GDP falls by about $4,500 – a little more than a quarter of a typical change from its average. This regression simply describes an overall negative relationship between income inequality as measured by Gini and economic development as measured by per capita GDP. Again, this is not a demonstration that increasing income inequality causes a decline in GDP; it simply describes a pattern in observed data and provides information for which a theoretical explanation might be developed to account.

As noted at the start of this section, a regression is simply a smoothed-out, straight-line version of a graph of means of y conditional on the value of x. As such it is at the polar extreme of simple ways to report a relationship. It

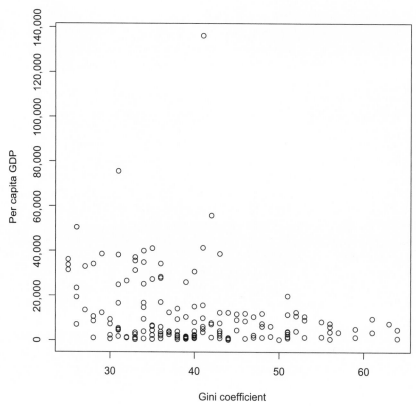

FIGURE 2.4. Scatterplot: Per capita GDP and Gini coefficient.

is concise, precise, and readily interpretable, although the linearity assumption can obscure a great deal of dispersion and peaks in the scatterplot. At the other pole, reporting a relationship in maximum complexity, we might put the scatterplot itself. It leaves nothing about the relationship to the imagination, although the complexity may sometimes obscure the forest for the trees. The graph of means is somewhere in between these poles. Graphs of these three representations of the bivariate relationship between per capita GDP and the Gini coefficient (2004 data, GDP in purchasing power panty terms) are presented in Figures 2.4 through 2.6.[20]

---

[20] To capture the relative advantage of each pole in one figure, it is common to present a scatterplot with the bivariate least squares regression line superimposed. This approach shows all the nuances, curves, and dispersion in the raw data (which readers typically want to see) and also the simplicity of a regression line. They are shown in separate figures here to illustrate the increasing simplicity and abstraction of moving from scatterplot to plot of means to regression line.

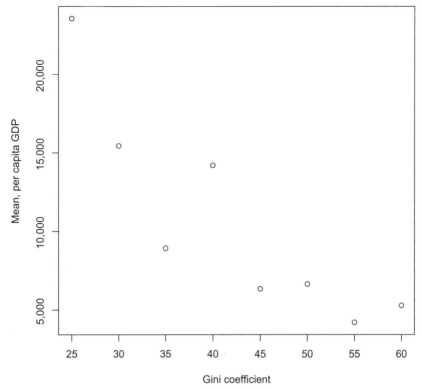

FIGURE 2.5. Graph of means: Per capita GDP and Gini coefficient.

R^2 *and Regression Diagnostics*

Earlier we defined the regression error e_i such that $y_i = a + bx_i + e_i$. It turns out that whenever two variables are uncorrelated, the variance of their sum is the sum of their variances. As was noted earlier, in least squares regression, it is always true that x and e are uncorrelated. So the variance of y_i can also be decomposed in terms of regression and error term:

$$Var(y) = Var(a + bx) + Var(e). \tag{2.12}$$

This says that the total variance of y (left-hand side) can be expressed as the variance of $a + bx$ plus the variance of e. Put differently, it says that *total variance* is the sum of *regression variance* and *error variance*. The regression variance may also be referred to as "explained variance," and error variance may be referred to as "residual variance." Note that it is impossible for either the regression variance or the error variance to exceed the total variance; generally speaking each variance on the right-hand side is strictly smaller than the total variance on the left.

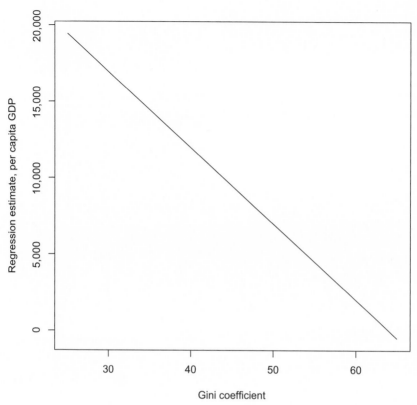

FIGURE 2.6. Regression line: Per capita GDP and Gini coefficient.

Now if the least squares regression does a good job of explaining the behavior of y – that is, how it varies from one observation to the next – then the errors e will tend to be close to 0 for all observations i. If they are all close to 0, they do not vary much from one observation to the next, so their variance $Var(e)$ is small. If this is the case, $\frac{Var(e)}{Var(y)}$ will be close to 0, and so $1 - \frac{Var(e)}{Var(y)}$ will be close to 1.

If the least squares regression does a poor job of explaining the behavior of y, then the errors will be nearly as variable as y itself. The covariate x and the regression provide little information about y's behavior from one observation to the next in this case; most of y's behavior is unexplained by x, so most of its behavior, and therefore variation, is left for e. In this case, $\frac{Var(e)}{Var(y)}$ will be close to 1, so $1 - \frac{Var(e)}{Var(y)}$ will be close to 0.

This logic leads to one of the most widely reported diagnostics of a linear regression, called R^2 or the *coefficient of determination*.[21] R^2 reports the

---

[21] The name "coefficient of determination" is uncommonly encountered in applied work.

percent of the variation in y that is explained by variation in x, and as such it is said to measure the *goodness of fit* of the regression, that is, the extent to which the observed values of y "fit" onto the least squares regression line.

In a bivariate regression, another way to think about R^2 is that it is simply the square of the correlation coefficient r. In fact this falls mechanically out of Equation 2.12. One of the properties of variance noted earlier is that for constants a and b, $Var(a + bx) = b^2 Var(x)$. Furthermore, from the definition of b in least squares regression, $b^2 = \frac{r^2 Var(y)}{Var(x)}$, so $b^2 Var(x) = r^2 Var(y)$. Plugging this back into Equation 2.12 gives $(1 - r^2)Var(y) = Var(e)$, or $r^2 = 1 - \frac{Var(e)}{Var(y)}$.

Because $Var(y)$ can be decomposed such that $Var(e)$ is one of its components, it follows that $Var(e) \leq Var(y)$ in all cases. Because $Var(e)$ is a variance, $Var(e) \geq 0$. Therefore, $0 \leq R^2 \leq 1$ in all cases.

Also note that because least squares regression gives a smaller mean squared error of the regression than any other procedure for identifying the coefficients a and b, it necessarily also produces a smaller value of $Var(e)$ than any other linear regression. Therefore, no straight-line approximation to the conditional mean function of y on x gives a higher R^2 than the least squares regression line.

Component parts of R^2 may also be reported as regression diagnostics: the total, residual, and explained sum of squares (or error and regression sum of squares). These are simply the numerators of the respective variances, and because the denominators all have the same number $(N - 1)$, the denominators do not affect the ratio of one of these quantities to another. Computer programs also commonly report the "root mean squared error" of the regression or RMS error (or RMSE). This is the standard deviation of the residuals. It is the "typical" departure of y from the regression line, unconditional on any value of x.

For an example, in the bivariate regression of state social capital on state urban population share, $R^2 = 0.036$. So urban population share by itself explains only about 3.5% of the variation in state social capital. This is a pretty small number. The relationship between these variables may be substantively interesting, but there is a lot more to social capital at the state level than just urbanization.

There is no universal standard to judge whether a particular R^2 is "large" or "small." As such a disembodied R^2 is usually not especially interesting in its own right. In applications of regression, social scientists are often not particularly interested in R^2; the object of our analysis and theorizing is typically not to give a complete account of the behavior of y in a specific sample but rather to identify a set of factors that systematically affect y and to give reasons behind these effects. By the same token, emphasizing explanation of a particular sample of y values as the goal of social science research presents a serious threat of spurious results; even if y is "completely random," as with lottery results or roulette wheels, it is always possible to find enough covariates that correlate highly with y's behavior in a finite sample. This does not translate into real insight.

Regression and Prediction

Regression can be used not only to express relationships between variables but to predict the value of the dependent variable for any value of the covariate. A predicted or expected value of y can be obtained simply by plugging a particular value of the covariate into the regression and executing the arithmetic – that is, multiply the value of the covariate by its slope and add the intercept. Interestingly, a regression can give a prediction for y even for covariate values that are never observed in the data. That is because the data itself is used to distill an overall linear relationship between y and x, and given that linearity, we know how the function will change from any observed values of x.

Usually, theoretically guided social science research does not use regression to make prediction. We use regression to uncover relationships holding other factors fixed. However, some research, especially if used to guide decision making in organizations, may rely heavily on regression to make predictions and make more effective use of limited resources. For example, consider a city housing agency that is interested in identifying applicants who are relatively likely to fill out an invalid application for public housing that will result in a denial of benefits even if they are eligible. An agency seeking to avoid this result might use a regression to predict problematic applications based on factors that, in the agency's experience, seem to correlate with it (e.g., level of education, native language). Armed with this information the agency might be able to channel its limited resources to assist applicants who are predicted to have particular difficulty completing the application correctly. Or a city parks agency might try to predict public usage of proposed parks on the basis of their amenities and location, thus helping to prioritize new park projects.

In the sense that the conditional mean of y is the best guess of y for a particular value of x, the least squares regression already contains the information necessary to make the best possible prediction based on the relationship between x and y. A simple prediction does not require new or different machinery from what is developed earlier; rather, it implies a different emphasis in how that machinery is used.

2.3.6 Multiple Regression

The real power of linear regression is not apparent until we analyze the relationship between a dependent variable y and several covariates simultaneously. It is the ability of linear regression to accommodate this analysis that accounts for its widespread use in empirical social science research. Whereas correlation and covariance pertain to a relationship between two variables, regression can be extended to any number of covariates, to explore the relationship between y

and a number of other variables $x_1, x_1, \ldots, x_k$. Here the subscripts on x denote entirely different variables.[22] For instance, a criminologist might be interested in the relationship of some type of criminal behavior with both education and age; a political scientist might be interested in the effect of both age and education on an individual's decision to vote in an election. Sociologists and political scientists might be interested in the relationship between social capital and both urbanization and educational attainment (all measured at the level of U.S. states, for instance).

With one covariate regression is called *bivariate regression*, and with more than one covariate it is *multivariate* or *multiple regression*. A bivariate regression specifies a regression line in which the conditional mean of y is a function of x, whereas a multivariate regression specifies a regression plane in which the conditional mean of y is a function of multiple covariates. Each covariate x_j has its own slope b_j that specifies that a one-unit change in x_j is associated with a b_j unit change in y, on average, holding all other covariates besides x_j constant. There are k covariates and therefore k slope terms, but there is only one intercept, and it is the expected value of y when *every* covariate is simultaneously zero. Again, regression expresses a linear relationship between the conditional mean of y and the covariates.

The formula for multiple regression slope coefficients is more cumbersome than that for bivariate regression, unless we introduce some new notational machinery from linear algebra, which is beyond our scope at present. But the special case of two covariates is still instructive – even though it is not how regression slopes are computed with multiple covariates (a computer does that job perfectly), it still illustrates the ideas.

Before considering y, consider the relationship between x_1 and x_2. Just as y might be correlated with either or both covariates, they might be *intercorrelated* – correlated with each other. It seems likely, and is in fact true, that urbanization and educational attainment are (positively) correlated at the state level in the United States: states with higher levels of urbanization also have higher levels of educational attainment.

This relationship among the covariates can itself be simply captured in a bivariate regression of x_1 on x_2. The residuals from this bivariate regression are the portion of x_1 that is not explained by x_2. Call the collection of residuals from this regression e_1; there will be one value of e_{1i} for every value of x_{1i}. We could, of course, also regress x_2 on x_1, and the residuals from this regression – call them e_2 – is the portion of x_2 that is not explained by x_1. These residuals capture variation in one covariate that is (linearly) independent of the other covariate. By definition, e_1 has no linear relationship with x_2, but of course e_1 is still linearly related to x_1.

---

[22] Previously we used subscripts to denote different values of a given variable. We can combine these so that x_{ji} indicates the ith value of the jth variable. So there are N values of variable x_1, denoted $x_{11}, \ldots, x1N$, and N values of every other variable as well, denoted similarly.

So e_1 is what is left over in x_1 after purging it of linear association with x_2. But y might be related to x_2, and we cannot expect e_1 to capture any variation in y that is linearly related to x_2. But suppose we also run a bivariate regression of y on x_2 and call the residuals e_{2y}. These latter residuals capture the portion of y that is not explained by x_2. This unexplained-by-x_2 portion of y is fair game for e_1 to explain.

The idea of "holding constant" in multiple regression is that any relationship between y's residuals from x_2 (e_{2y}) and x_1's residuals from x_2 (e_1) is a relationship between y and x_1 that cannot possibly also be explained by variation in x_2. This is because variation in e_1 is surely variation in x_1, and variation in e_{2y} is surely variation in y – it is just variation that cannot possibly be attributed to or explained by variation in x_2. And any relationship between e_{1y} and e_2 is a relationship between y and x_2 that cannot possibly also be explained by variation in x_1. In this sense, correlation between e_{2y} and e_1 captures a relationship between y and x_1, holding constant or controlling for x_2.

Following this logic the least squares formulas for the slopes and intercept in a regression with two covariates are as follows:

$$b_1 = \frac{r_{e_{2y},e_1} \times s_{e_{2y}}}{s_{e_1}} \tag{2.13}$$

$$b_2 = \frac{r_{e_{1y},e_2} \times s_{e_{1y}}}{s_{e_2}} \tag{2.14}$$

$$a = \bar{y} - b_1\bar{x}_1 - b_2\bar{x}_2. \tag{2.15}$$

Here b_1 is the effect of x_1 on y holding x_2 constant, and b_2 is the effect of x_2 on y holding x_1 constant. In the slopes, r_{e_{jy},e_k} is the correlation coefficient between e_{jy} (residuals from the regression of y on x_j) and e_k (residuals from the regression of x_k on x_j), and s_{ek} is the standard deviation of these residuals e_k. Thus, the multiple regression slope for x_1 is obtained from a bivariate regression of the residuals e_{2y} on the residuals e_1 and similarly for the slope for x_2.

As an example, consider again state-level social capital. We saw above that it is negatively related to state urban population share, but it is easy to conjecture that other variables might also be related to it. For instance, educational attainment might also be correlated with social capital. It is tempting to aver that education has a humanizing effect and serves a social purpose of creating "good citizens." Maybe education even helps people understand social processes better so that they are more willing to participate in them. Of course, it might also be that people who are more socially connected in the first place are more likely to trust the "educational system" or, for a variety of other reasons, are likely to obtain more education. In any case, the bivariate correlation of state social capital and state educational attainment, measured by the share of the state population with at least a B.A. (from the *Statistical Abstract of the United States* for the year 2000), is indeed positive: $r = 0.33$.

The regression equation for state social capital y as a function of state urban population share x_1 and share of state population with at least a B.A. x_2 is $-0.81 - 0.03x_1 + 0.11x_2$. This regression shows a few interesting facts. First, state social capital is indeed positively related to state educational attainment measured by the share of residents with a bachelor's degree or higher. When the share of residents with a B.A. goes up by one percentage point, holding constant the urban population share, the social capital score goes up by 0.11 points. The standard deviation across states in the percent of residents with at least a bachelor's degree is about 4.3, and (as noted earlier) the standard deviation in the state-level social capital index is about .75. So when B.A. attainment increases by a typical departure from its mean, social capital goes up by more than half a standard deviation. Second, state social capital is still negatively related to state urban population share – and the effect is bigger in absolute value compared with the bivariate regression (where the slope was -0.01). When the state urban population share increases by one percentage point, holding constant the share of residents with a B.A., the social capital score goes down by 0.03 points. When state-level urbanization increases by a standard deviation, state-level social capital falls by more than half a standard deviation.

Why is the effect of urban population share on social capital affected by the inclusion of educational attainment? The reason is that educational attainment and urban population share are themselves correlated: when educational attainment in a state goes up, so does its urban population share ($r = 0.54$ in this dataset). This is itself an interesting relationship, and there are a variety of reasons it might hold; e.g., professional work in urban areas is likely to require advanced education. Whatever the reason, this correlation means that, if educational attainment is uncontrolled (as in the bivariate regression of social capital on urban population), then the states with relatively high urban population shares also have relatively high educational attainment. The urban population share "pushes" the social capital score down, but educational attainment works against this by pushing the social capital score up at the same time. In the multivariate regression, with educational attainment held constant, this "working against" does not happen. Multivariate regression essentially uses variation in urban population share by itself, isolated from variation in educational attainment, to uncover the effect of urban population on social capital. Thus in the multivariate regression with educational attainment controlled, an increase in urbanization is not simultaneously an increase in educational attainment. The ability to measure and isolate relationships between two variables, when both are correlated with a third variable, is one of the principal reasons multiple regression is useful in social science.

The foregoing explanation of "holding constant" also illustrates why there must be some independent variation in the covariates with respect to each other to identify their impact on the conditional mean of y holding the other covariate fixed. If there is no independent variation in the covariates – if x_1 always changes by about the same amount when x_2 changes by a given amount – then the covariates are highly intercorrelated, and the regression suffers from *near multicollinearity.* Collinearity is the name for the problem that occurs when covariates are strongly linearly related to each other, that is, highly correlated. One indication of this (among a vast number of others) is the R^2 from the regression of one covariate on other covariates: when this R^2 is high (e.g., above .75 or so), this covariate has little independent variation from the other covariates. This is a problem because, for a given sample size, it makes it difficult to identify the effect of x_1 on the mean of y independent of x_2 and vice versa. Unless one covariate is by definition a linear function of the other (say, degrees Fahrenheit vs. Celsius), a case of perfect multicollinearity, a collinearity problem can always be "solved" with a large enough sample. This is because, with enough sample observations, there is bound to be enough independent variation in the covariates to identify their independent effects on the mean of y.

Prediction in a multiple regression works similarly to the bivariate case, except that a value of each covariate x_j must be specified. For instance, in a multiple regression of some kind of criminal behavior on age and education, a prediction would require specifying a value of both age and education. These values are multiplied by their respective slopes, and these products summed and added to the intercept, to arrive at a predicted value of y for those values of the xs.

A slight change in reported diagnostics is necessary for multiple regression: in addition to R^2, computers will report $\bar{R}^2$, *adjusted r-squared*. It turns out that R^2 can be increased simply by adding additional variables to the regression, even if they do not add much to the overall ability of the covariates to explain variation in y. Adjusted r-squared corrects for this, and in a multiple least squares regression, is a better indication of goodness of fit than unadjusted r-squared. In the multivariate regression of state social capital on urban population share and educational attainment, $R^2 = 0.30$ and $\bar{R}^2 = 0.27$. These two covariates jointly account for about 27% of the variation in state social capital.

2.3.7 Specifying Regression Models

Covariates with Nonlinear Effects
Although linear regression imposes a straight-line relationship on y and x, it does not impose any assumption on what x actually is. A researcher can choose any variables she likes to investigate in a regression, and thus linear regression is a much more flexible tool for exploring relationships than at first meets the eye.

First, if a researcher supposes that x has a nonlinear relationship to y, it is straightforward to explore this by including a nonlinear function of x as one of the variables in the regression. For instance, suppose that a public health researcher conjectures that household income has a nonlinear effect on the birth weight of infants. She might suspect that infant birth weight increases as household income increases but at a decreasing rate. Substantively, this means that a $10,000 increase to household income has a bigger effect on birth weight when household income is, say, $20,000 than when it is $90,000. Simply put, in this situation, an extra dollar buys more neonatal nutrition when dollars are scarce than when they are more plentiful.

To explore this in a regression, let y represent infant birth weight, x represent household income, and $z = x^2$. Then $y = a + b_x x + b_z z$ is still a linear regression, the slopes and intercept of which can be obtained via least squares just as described earlier. The algorithm for obtaining these coefficients does not care how x and z are related. If the researcher's hunch is correct, she would expect to observe $b_x > 0$ and $b_z < 0$. Calculus shows that the overall "effect" of x on y in this regression is $b_x + 2b_z x$ (this is simply the first derivative of the regression equation with respect to x). If $b_z < 0$, this means that when x gets larger, the overall effect of x on y gets smaller.

A simple definition of new variables also makes it straightforward to investigate whether two covariates have an *interaction effect* on y. For instance, suppose that an analyst supposes that household income and maternal education both independently affect infant birth weight but that they also have a combined effect: household income might be associated with higher average birth weight when maternal education is held constant, but the effect of household income might be greater for higher levels of maternal education. So if the analyst has data on household income (x) and mother's years of schooling (z), she could create a new variable that is simply $w \equiv x \times z$ in her dataset.

Then to explore this idea in a linear regression, she could specify $y = a + b_x x + b_z z + b_w w$, and obtain the slopes and intercepts exactly as before. The hunch that household income x matters more when maternal education is greater translates into the expectation that $b_w > 0$. This is easy to see from the overall effect of x on y: using the definition $w \equiv x \times z$, this overall effect is $b_x + b_w z$ (again, this is the derivative of the regression equation with respect to x). When $b_w > 0$, it means that larger values of z amplify the effect of household income on the average birth weight.

Dependent Variables with Limited Range

It is also important to note that nothing in the construction of least squares regression requires or assumes that any of the variables is measured cardinally or in any other particular way. Not infrequently, social scientists are interested in multivariate relationships when one or more variables is dichotomous or multichotomous. Although interpretation of regression coefficients in these situations can require some care, least squares regression is just as applicable in these situations as any other.

To be specific, consider the case in which some variable is dichotomous. When used in a regression equation, such a variable is sometimes called a *dummy variable*. Suppose, for instance, that y is dichotomous. For instance, a political scientist might be interested in covariates of voter turnout. A sociologist of family structure might be interested in covariates of divorce, in which married couples are the unit of observation. A public management scholar might be interested in covariates of separation of an individual from public service employment. In each of these cases, y can be measured as a binary variable (1 for voting, divorcing, or separating from public service; 0 for not voting, remaining married, or remaining in public service).

When y is dichotomous, the least squares linear regression is sometimes called the *linear probability model*. In the equation $y = a + bx$, the slope b is interpreted as the change in the probability that $y = 1$ for a one-unit change in x. This is, in fact, exactly the same conditional mean interpretation as before; for a dichotomous variable, the mean value is the probability that $y = 1$, or equivalently, the proportion of cases in which $y = 1$ is the expected outcome. So the effect of x on that conditional mean is the same as the effect of x on the probability of $y = 1$. All of these points about specification can be deployed without modification in this case.

When a covariate x is a dummy variable, matters are also pretty straightforward. In the equation $y = a + bx$, b simply measures the average difference in y for $x = 0$ versus $x = 1$. For instance, if y is the annual growth rate of U.S. GDP and x is the party of the president in a given year (e.g., $x = 1$ for Republican and $x = 0$ for Democrat), then b from the bivariate regression $y = a + bx$ simply reports the difference in GDP growth rates under Republican and Democratic presidents. Bartels [2008] explored this substantive issue and many related ones, using a variety of methodological approaches.

Using least squares linear regression when y is dichotomous is sometimes a source of some consternation. Critics might suggest that linear regression is "inappropriate" in this case and that a somewhat more complicated technique (logit or probit, both discussed later) is necessary. One of the principal reasons for this is that regression may predict infeasible or absurd values of y when y is dichotomous or has a limited feasible range. For instance, in the dichotomous voter turnout example, it is possible that regression predicts that a negative percentage of people with certain (very low) levels of education vote or that more than 100% of people with a (very high) level of education vote. This occurs because of the linearity in the least squares regression function. For any value of the slope b, there are values of x such that $bx + a > 1$ or $bx + a < 0$. However, it is questionable whether this is problematic in real applications because most applications of regression in social science are not about prediction. They are about measuring the effect of x on the conditional mean of y. Whether regression is a good tool for assessing this effect in a particular case is unrelated to whether regression makes infeasible predictions of y. Thus, although it is wise to be aware of likely critiques of regression, there is no need to be excessively timid about using it.

In the end, whatever the measurement scale of the variables, regression captures the linear relationship between x (or multiple xs) and the conditional mean of y. To the extent that the behavior of y's conditional mean is interesting, a regression equation is interesting. And because least squares regression is the best linear approximation of the conditional mean function in the sense of mean squared error, it is usually interesting whenever a conditional mean itself is interesting.

Regression with Composite Indices

Speaking of measurement scales, in Section 2.1.2, we briefly discussed the construction of composite indices, as an aggregate of several variables. For instance, the measurement of state-level social capital we analyzed earlier is actually composed of 14 different subvariables. Scholars of executive power have constructed composite measures of this concept for studies in which the country is the unit of analysis. For instance, a country's level of executive power might be based on the formal powers of its executive in introducing, vetoing, and implementing legislation, as well as determining the government's budget. When researchers introduce new concepts into a literature, it is common to try to identify ways to measure them so that their importance in empirical analysis can be demonstrated, and constructing composite indices is a natural way to do that.

It is reasonably straightforward to see how these composite measures work in regression, and why they might limit the kinds of association a researcher can detect. Suppose for simplicity that a single composite index is denoted x_c, and it has two subvariables, denoted x_1 and x_2, which are added to create x_c. So $x_c = x_1 + x_2$. Suppose that a researcher wishes to explore the effect of x_c on some other variable y. The bivariate regression for this is just $y = a + bx_c$, and by definition, this is also the same as $y = a + bx_1 + bx_2$. That is, by the construction of x_c, this regression is really a multiple regression with two covariates – it's just that those covariates are forced, by the definition of x_c, to have the same slope b.

There is nothing wrong with this per se. It is a feature, not a bug, if it is what the analyst intended. But defining the composite index and using it, rather than each of its subvariables, in regression analysis forces both of the subvariables to affect y in the same way. This is useful if x_1 and x_2 really do tap into the same latent concept, but it can lead to unwitting restrictions on what the data is able to "say" if this is not probed carefully.

The analyst could always break the composite x_c into its subvariables and use them both as covariates in the regression $y = a + b_1x_1 + b_2x_2$. Now the subvariables are not constrained to have the same effect on y. If the assumption that $x_c = x_1 + x_2$ is correct, one would expect $b_1 \approx b_2$ in this multiple regression. Breaking the index apart and using its subvariables does not prevent the researcher from seeing this, but it does allow the researcher to determine whether it's credible or not.

Breaking the composite x_c into its components is not without cost. It forces the regression to "use up" more of the information in the data to establish the value of both b_1 and b_2. When the composite variable is used, only the single slope b must be determined because the assumption that x_1 and x_2 have the same effect on y adds some external information.

The composite index can also be used as a dependent variable in regression. This is analogous to what we did when using social capital as a dependent variable in regressions that explored its association with education and urbanization. Continuing the simple case $x_c = x_1 + x_2$, the regression $x_c = a + bz$ assumes that the covariate z has the same effect on both x_1 and x_2. As an alternative, the analyst could construct two regressions: $x_1 = a_1 + b_1 z$ and $x_2 = a_2 + b_2 z$. If the assumption behind using one composite index is suitable, then b_1 should be close to b_2 across these two regressions.

There is an added complication here, which is that if x_1 and x_2 really do tap the same latent dimension, then implementing two independent regressions for x_1 and x_2 throws this information away. Reintroducing this information is possible but is beyond the scope of the presentation at this point. The upshot is that two independent regressions is at least as conservative as one regression on a composite index, although again, in terms of understanding the interrelationships of these variables, it is not costless to ignore good arguments that x_1 and x_2 are tapping into the same thing.

Technical Issues

Besides these issues of specifying the nature of the relationship between y and "the xs," there are a couple of practical issues to keep in mind when trying to obtain values of intercepts and slopes in linear regression. First, a regression cannot give more coefficients than there are observations in the dataset. That is, if there are K covariates in a regression, then $K + 1 \leq N$ is necessary to obtain slope and intercept values from a computer. More precisely, it is impossible to obtain *unique* values of the slopes and intercept if $K + 1 > N$ because there are too many combinations of these values that account for the relationships among the variables. Usually, it is a good idea to have N much larger than $K + 1$; otherwise the regression algorithm "uses up" so much sample information simply to obtain values of the slopes and intercepts that it cannot use much information to pin them down precisely. The specifics of this issue are best deferred until later chapters.

Second, if two of the covariates in a multiple linear regression are perfectly correlated with each other (i.e., they have a correlation coefficient of 1), a situation called *perfect multicollinearity*, it is not possible to obtain estimates for the slopes of both. Again, there are too many combinations of these slopes that account for the patterns in the data for the computer to pick just one. Some computer software handles this situation by declining to return any coefficients at all for the regression; other software arbitrarily drops one of the offending covariates from the regression and proceeds as if it were not there. Regardless, perfect multicollinearity usually arises from a programming mistake by the analyst in defining a variable in the dataset and is not a serious substantive problem in most cases. Operationally, if x_1 and x_2 are perfectly correlated, then just one of these tells you everything that the pair of them has to say about the behavior of y, so there is no point including them both.

Finally, it is worth emphasizing again that regression can be used, and is discussed here, simply as a tool for exploring relationships in a given observed distribution. It shows us the "effect" of x on y only in the sense of a correlation. Regression does not capture any type of relationship that correlation does not also capture. Thus regression does not by itself tell us anything about a change in y caused by a change in x. Nothing about regression as a descriptive tool justifies reading the "effect" reported as a *causal* effect. Regression is a powerful tool for summarizing relationships in observed data, but it still does not do the alchemy of turning correlation into causation. We deal with this issue in greater depth in later chapters, especially Chapter 10.

2.4 CONCLUSION

Useful description of interesting data is the first step in the productive application of quantitative methods in social science. The discussion in this chapter only scratches the surface of the summaries that descriptive analysis can offer, especially on graphics and regression. Nevertheless this material covers tools that will allow for basic descriptive exploration of social science data and a wide variety of potentially interesting findings.

It is easy (in the pursuit of intellectual purity) to hew to a caricature of the interplay between theory and empirical analysis in which an analyst embargoes her data (from herself) until a complete set of theoretical deductions is obtained from first principles, and then (and only then) does she take her first peek at the data, but stops all further theorizing. Although it is true that data used to make a guess about an interesting theory cannot be used as an independent test of that theory, in real empirical research, there is often a more dynamic interplay between conceptual thinking about what relationships one should expect to observe (theorizing) and empirical analysis of actual data about relationships. It is useful to get a feel for the texture of a problem with some descriptive statistical analysis, and this can feed back into the development of expectations for further exploration.

Still, purely descriptive analysis of the data one has in hand has an inherently limited connection to theory. This is because theories in social science are about broad social or political processes, not just one specific set of observations. Instead, in theoretically oriented statistical analysis, we are usually interested in a specific set of observed data because it gives a window – albeit a partial one – into a broader social process. In other words, descriptive statistics concerns only the data that one actually observed and attempts to make no statements beyond those observations. But theory is often about something deeper: not just the specific events that were observed but all events in a particular category that might have been observed. Recognizing the connection between the events actually observed and the broader process that gave rise to those observations is, in a sense, the point of statistical inference. The next chapter takes an important step in establishing this connection and fulfilling the purpose of this book by establishing a conceptual distinction between observed data and an underlying process that gives rise to that data. In this way, the next chapter illuminates why we are uncertain about those underlying processes when we observe only part of the data to which they can give rise.

APPENDIX: DERIVATION OF REGRESSION COEFFICIENTS

In the discussion of least squares regression, a number of points were asserted: least squares regression gives a linear version of a plot of conditional means of y, minimizes the sum of squared residuals, minimizes the mean squared error of a guess about y conditioned on a value of x, maximizes the R^2 given the variables in the regression equation, and leads to residuals that are both equal to 0 on average and uncorrelated with the sample distribution of covariates. In fact, these points are all different ways of saying the same thing. This appendix demonstrates this by deriving least squares regression coefficients from scratch. This derivation is useful for applied analysts not because they must repeat it frequently (or ever) but because it allows a precise sense of what linear regression "does."

In discussing the sample mean, we noted that $\bar{x}$ is the unique value that minimizes the mean squared error (or MSE) of a guess about the value of x drawn "out of a hat." In this sense, the sample mean is the best prediction about the value of x. But this guess g could not be dependent on any other observed variable; it was just a single number.

Regression supposes a similar exercise, only now we are trying to guess the value of y drawn, and we get to condition the guess, that is, make it depend, on another variable x. The analogous version of MSE in this case is

$$\sum_i \frac{(y_i - g(x_i))^2}{N}. \tag{2.16}$$

Other than the fact that we are now guessing the value of y rather than x, the only difference between this and the previous MSE definition is that the guess g is conditioned on x. Formally, $g(x)$ expresses that the guess is a function of x.

If we were to insist that this function has to be a linear function of x, we would then have $g(x) = a + bx$. Linearity certainly compromises the ability of the guess to track all twists and turns in the behavior of y as x varies, but by the same token, it distills the relationship between x and y to a simple, easily interpreted form.

With this linear function, we can rewrite the conditional MSE as

$$\sum_i \frac{(y_i - (a + bx_i))^2}{N}. \tag{2.17}$$

If we want the best prediction of y in the sense of minimum MSE, the question we need to ask is, what values of a and b minimize this conditional MSE?

Note that the numerator of the conditional MSE is simply the sum of squared residuals. Furthermore, the denominator of the MSE does not depend on a and b. So a and b values that minimize the sum of squared residuals also minimize the MSE.

There are two things to identify, a and b, and simple calculus (namely, the chain rule) shows that this minimization boils down to finding the a and b values that solve

$$\frac{-2 \sum_i (y_i - a - bx_i)}{N} = 0 \tag{2.18}$$

$$\frac{-2 \sum_i (y_i - a - bx_i)x_i}{N} = 0. \tag{2.19}$$

Intuitively, these two equations capture how the MSE changes as a function of a and b respectively. In calculus terms, they are derivatives of MSE with respect to a and b. When the MSE is at its minimum value, for infinitesimal changes of a and b, the MSE does not change at all. So the stipulation that these derivatives both equal 0 captures the idea that at the a and b values that minimize MSE, there is no change in MSE for particularly small changes in a and b. Such a requirement for minimization, that a derivative equals 0, is called a *first-order condition*.[23]

These two equations are called the *least squares normal equations*. When solved correctly, they imply

$$a = \bar{y} - b\bar{x}$$

$$b = \frac{r s_y}{s_x}.$$

---

[23] The same argument of course applies to maximization as well, and so first-order conditions cannot distinguish between a minimum and maximum. For that, what is needed is a measure of the function's curvature at the point where the first order condition is satisfied. At a maximum, the function is shaped like a hill; at a minimum, it is shaped like a bowl with no flat spots on its bottom. The second derivative is needed to supply this information; for a minimum, the second derivative should be positive. Differentiating each first-order condition again shows this condition to be satisfied.

It is easier to see that when those values are plugged into the normal equations, the normal equations do indeed both equal 0. The normal equations have powerful implications for the properties of least squares linear regression, as some manipulation will show.

The first normal equation (Equation 2.18) is the simpler of the two. Simple algebra reduces it to $\sum_i (y_i - a - bx_i) = 0$. Because the $\sum_i$ represents addition and the order in which items are added does not affect their overall sum, this in turn implies $\sum_i y_i - \sum_i bx_i = \sum_i a$. Note that the right-hand side simply adds a to itself N times (it is the N-*fold sum of* a); this is the same as Na. The term $\sum_i bx_i$ has the same b multiplied by every x_i, so it can be factored out to give $b \sum_i x_i$. Thus we can write the same first-order condition as $\sum_i y_i - b \sum_i x_i = Na$. Of course, dividing each term by the same number will not change the equation, so we can write $\frac{\sum_i y_i}{N} - \frac{b \sum_i x_i}{N} = \frac{Na}{N}$. Using the definition of the mean and simplifying finally gives $a = \bar{y} - b\bar{x}$.

Note also that the first normal equation can also be written $\frac{\sum_i (y_i - a - bx_i)}{N} = 0$. Because $e_i = y_i - a - bx_i$ is the definition of the residual, this immediately yields that the mean value of the residuals in least squares regression is 0. This is one implication of the fact that least squares regression coefficients are obtained by minimizing the MSE.

The second normal equation (Equation 2.19) can be written $\sum_i (y_i - a - bx_i)x_i = 0$. The x_i outside of the parentheses cannot be taken outside of the $\sum_i$ because its value varies with i. But it can be distributed over the terms in the parentheses to give $\sum_i (x_i y_i - ax_i - b(x_i)^2) = 0$. Furthermore, we already know the formula for a is $\bar{y} - b\bar{x}$, so we can swap this out for the a. This is useful because it means there is only one unknown term to identify, b. So we have $\sum_i (x_i y_i - (\bar{y} - b\bar{x})(x_i) - b(x_i)^2) = 0$. Breaking the sum into pieces and factoring gives $\sum_i (x_i y_i) - \bar{y} \sum_i (x_i) + b\bar{x} \sum_i (x_i) - b \sum_i (x_i)^2 = 0$. Moving the last two terms containing b to the right-hand side, factoring out the b, and dividing each term by N, gives $\frac{\sum_i (x_i y_i)}{N} - \bar{y}(\frac{\sum_i (x_i)}{N}) = b(\frac{\sum_i (x_i)^2}{N} - \bar{x}(\frac{\sum_i (x_i)}{N}))$. Using the definition of the mean, this can in turn be written as

$$b = \frac{\frac{\sum_i (x_i y_i)}{N} - \bar{x}\bar{y}}{\frac{\sum_i (x_i)^2}{N} - \bar{x}^2}. \tag{2.20}$$

Following the discussion in the text on variance and covariance, it can be shown that the numerator is equivalent to the sample covariance of x and y, whereas the denominator is equivalent to the sample variance of x. Given the definition of the correlation coefficient, this in turn implies

$$b = \frac{r_{xy} s_x s_y}{s_x^2} = \frac{r_{xy} s_y}{s_x}. \tag{2.21}$$

The same computational formula for covariance implies that that the covariance between x and the residuals e can be expressed as $\frac{\sum_i (e_i)(x_i)}{N} - \bar{e}\bar{x}$. We already know from the first normal equation that $\bar{e} = 0$ under least squares regression, so in this case the covariance between e and x boils down to $\frac{\sum_i (e_i)(x_i)}{N}$. But given that $e_i \equiv y_i - a - bx_i$, the second normal equation implies that this too equals 0. That is, in view of the first normal equation's implication that the mean residual is 0, the second normal equation implies that the sample residuals are uncorrelated with the sample covariate x. This is simply another implication of minimizing MSE to obtain a and b.

Finally, because least squares regression coefficients are chosen to minimize the conditional MSE, assuming $g(x)$ is linear, and because the sample mean minimizes the unconditional MSE as we saw earlier in the chapter, it is apparent that regression is intimately connected to the conditional sample mean. In particular, the least squares coefficients provide the best possible linear approximation to the conditional mean of y as a function of x. We will have numerous occasions to return to results of a similar flavor later in this book.

PROBLEMS

1. Show that the sample variance of x is equivalent to $\frac{\sum x_i^2}{N-1} + \frac{N\bar{x}^2}{N-1}$. (The numerator of the second term is the square of the ordinary sample mean, times the sample size.)
2. Let σ_x denote the sample standard deviation of x. Show that for constants a and b, the sample standard deviation of $y = a + bx$ is $\sigma_y = b\sigma_x$.
3. Let σ_x^2 denote the sample variance of x; σ_y^2 the sample variance of y; and σ_{x+y}^2 the sample variance of their sum. Express σ_{x+y}^2 in terms of σ_x^2, σ_y^2, and $cov(x, y)$.
4. Go through the steps to show that Equation 2.20 is equivalent to $\frac{Cov(x,y)}{Var(x)}$.
5. Consider a dataset with N observations on each variable y and x and consider the OLS regression $y = a + bx$.
   (a) Suppose each of the y observations is multiplied by the same constant c. How does this affect a and b?
   (b) Suppose each of the x observations is multiplied by the same constant d. How does this affect a and b?
   (c) Suppose a constant g is added to each of the y observations. How does this affect a and b?
   (d) Suppose a constant h is added to each of the x observations. How does this affect a and b?
6. Consider a dataset with N observations on each variable y and x, and consider the OLS regressions $y = a + bx$ and $x = a' + b'y$. True or false, and prove your answers:
   (a) The slopes b and b' will always have the same sign.
   (b) The intercepts a and a' will always have the same sign.
   (c) The R^2 from the two regressions can be different.

(d) At most, one of the regressions can be valid, depending on the underlying theory in which either x causes y or y causes x.

(e) If all values of x are rescaled to $x' = c + dx$ where c and d are known constants, then the slope in the regression of y on x' is $c + bd$.

7. If the Republican presidential candidate's California (statewide) vote share is greater in 2016 than it was in 2012, is it necessarily true that the 2016 Republican vote share must be greater than the 20 vote share in at least one county in the state? Explain why or why not.

8. The file "endorsements.csv" available on this book's website contains data on newspaper endorsements of political candidates for governor, U.S. senator, or U.S. representative from 1940 to 2002. Each observation consists of a state-year-political office combination. The variable "d_endorse" is 1 if a given newspaper in a given year endorses a Democratic candidate for office (0 otherwise), whereas "d_incumbent" is 1 if a Democrat is the incumbent in the state-year-race (0 otherwise), and "r_incumbent" is 1 if a Republican is the incumbent in the state-year-race (0 otherwise).

(a) What is the average and standard deviation of d_endorse, d_incumbent, r_incumbent, and year? Why are the averages of the first three variables between 0 and 1? Why does their standard deviation get smaller as the average gets further from $\frac{1}{2}$? Why is the average of "year" different from the midpoint of the interval [1940, 2002]?

(b) Is a histogram informative for the distribution of d_endorse? Explain.

(c) Use a multiple regression model to assess the association of Democratic incumbency, Republican incumbency, and year with Democratic endorsements, holding the other two covariates constant. Report the regression line, R^2, and $\overline{R}^2$.

(d) Use the multiple regression model to predict the chance that a newspaper endorses a Democrat in an open-seat congressional election (i.e., no incumbent) in 2010.

9. The file "presvote.csv" available on this book's website contains data on presidential election vote shares for the party of the incumbent president from 1948 to 2004. The variables are defined in the spreadsheet to the right of the data columns.

(a) What is the average and standard deviation of the incumbent's share of the two-party popular vote, incumbent party's share of the electoral vote, percentage change in GNP in the early part of the election year, and the incumbent president's July popularity?

(b) Construct a histogram of the incumbent's share of the two-party popular vote. Does it suggest any general incumbent party advantage in presidential elections?

(c) What is the correlation between the incumbent party's popular vote share and electoral college vote share? How can you explain the difference in their standard deviations?

(d) If popular vote share were rescaled to fall between 0 and 1, how would its correlation with electoral college vote share (not rescaled) change? How would the slope change in a bivariate regression of (rescaled) popular vote share on electoral college vote share? In a bivariate regression with the x and y variables switched?[24]

(e) Use a regression model to determine the association between election year change in gross national product (GNP) and the incumbent party's two-party popular vote share. Report the regression line and R^2.

(f) How would you expect the election year change in GNP and the incumbent president's popularity in July are correlated? What is their correlation in the dataset?

(g) In a multiple regression of incumbent party popular vote share with both election year GNP change and incumbent president popularity as covariates, would you expect the effect of GNP change to be greater than, less than, or about the same as its effect in the bivariate model you estimated earlier? Explain your reasoning.

(h) Run the multiple regression model described in the previous part. Report the regression line and $\overline{R}^2$.

10. The file "smoking-short.csv" available on this book's website contains data on birth weight of infants and a variety of covariates. The codebook contains variable definitions.

(a) Give the mean, median, and standard deviation of the birth weight variable. In light of the standard deviation, identify a value of birth weight that is abnormally low.

(b) Plot a histogram of the birth weight variable.

(c) Give the mean, median, and standard deviation of the birth weight variable only for observations in which the mother smoked during pregnancy.

(d) Give the mean, median, and standard deviation of the birth weight variable only for observations in which the mother did not smoke during pregnancy.

(e) Run a linear regression of tobacco use on birth weight and interpret the coefficient. Discuss some possible problems with interpreting this relationship as causal.

(f) Give the covariances between tobacco use and birth weight, birth weight and number of prenatal visits, and number of prenatal visits and tobacco use. Given this information, what do you expect to

---

[24] You need not execute any new commands to answer this question.

happen to the coefficient on tobacco use when running a multiple regression that includes both tobacco use and number of prenatal visits? Why?

(g) Run a multiple regression that includes both number of prenatal visits and tobacco use as covariates. Interpret the coefficients.

3

Observable Data and Data-Generating Processes

Chapter 2 dealt with the summary and analysis of data that is actually observed. It is possible that a researcher or analyst has no interest in the variables or concepts being analyzed beyond the particular set of observations available to him or her. If a university wants to know whether its admissions decisions last year were less favorable to members of underrepresented groups than to others, taking as given other aspects of each application file (grade point average, entrance exam scores, etc.), it need only analyze last year's admissions data. A linear regression, purely descriptive of this data, would shed light on the question.

However, the remainder of this book covers elements of probability theory and statistical inference and modeling, which itself rests heavily on probability theory. Before launching into that treatment, it is necessary to consider why (or conditions under which) we need it.

When a theory relating two or more variables is part of the consideration, it is unusual that a researcher's interest in the variables ends with the data that happens to have been observed. Such a theory deals with the process or behaviors that give rise to the data that was observed, not just that data itself. That data helps to inform whether the theory has any drawing power in reality, but that data is not the sum total of possible observations of the social process in question.

In other words, the operating assumption in this mode of analysis is that there is a social process more fundamental than any specific set of observed cases or data. That process gives rise to observable data, and therefore observable data can help inform us about that process. The specific observed data itself is a means to a more important end of understanding the social process that created it. From the standpoint of theory in social science, the data is useful because it allows analysts to make an *inference* about the social process underlying the data.

This chapter introduces the concept of a data-generating process as an object of theoretical interest and its attendant implications for the necessity of inference on top of mere description in empirical analysis. It lays the groundwork for subsequent material on probability theory and statistical inference by elaborating reasons a data-generating process might be thought to involve some degree of random chance. Although it is informal, it serves an important purpose. Students who fail to grasp the material in this chapter will not really understand the purpose or rationale for probability models and statistical inference in empirical social science or, for that matter, the philosophical coherence of nonstatistical approaches to empirical analysis.

3.1 DATA AND DATA-GENERATING PROCESSES

For our purposes a *data-generating process* (DGP) is a rule or set of rules governing the social or political events that an analyst wishes to study and the rules by which observations of its results come to be represented in a dataset. A DGP by this definition governs how factors in a political process are related to each other.

For instance, Skocpol [1979] provided a pathbreaking account of social revolutions – fundamental alterations of a society's governmental and social structure that occurs in a short period of time. She explored three cases of social revolutions: the French Revolution beginning in the late 18th century, the Russian Revolution in the 1910s to 1930s, and the Chinese Revolution in the early 20th century culminating in the Cultural Revolution of the 1960s. Skocpol treated these cases as instances of a broader phenomenon of social revolution and used the cases to distill conditions under which social revolutions could or would occur. These conditions comprised the theoretical contribution of her book and account for much of the reason it has become so influential. The book is a landmark illustration of *comparative historical analysis* in social science: the comparison and contrast of actual historical episodes to distill necessary and/or sufficient conditions for an event to occur.

There is not a whiff of formal statistical inference or language of DGPs and so forth in Skocpol's book,[1] which might make it appear an odd lead-in for thinking about statistical modeling in social science. Nevertheless, this work illustrates that, interesting as the specific cases treated in the book may be, social scientists attempt to place them as examples or cases of a broader process. The contribution of this book is not just an erudite analysis of the time- and place-bound particularities of these specific social revolutions but of the broader concept of social revolution and of the social and political processes that give rise to it.

The conditions for social revolution that Skocpol identifies constitute (part of) a DGP in the sense defined earlier. The actual cases of France, Russia,

---

[1] For a brief re-analysis in that template see Sekhon [2004].

and China constitute the data. To be sure, the observed events she considers encompass far more texture and detail than is usually present in a "dataset" in the conventional sense of quantitative methods. Regardless of the depth and texture, however, the concepts and underlying assumptions are the same: the occurrence of social revolution follows an intelligible social process that is represented as a set of logical conditions and the social revolutions actually observed and analyzed occurred as a result of that social process when certain conditions were met.

All researchers that use empirical analysis to evaluate theory or distill a theory based on empirical observation share a common metaphysical commitment[2] that the data available for analysis is not the entire picture of the social process that gives rise to such data. Rather, the data consists of a subset of cases in which that process, the data-generating process, operated. That DGP might have generated other cases in the past that for some reason are not observable, and it might operate again in the future. This assumption about the relationship between observable data and the underlying process generating it holds whether a scholar's work follows a statistical template, a comparative-historical template, or something else that postulates an underlying social process that gives rise to specific data. All social scientists who treat data in this way share a common commitment that observed events can help us learn about more fundamental processes, and here we refer to those processes simply as the DGP.

However, there is another metaphysical fork in the road that separates research following a formal statistical template from research following (most strands of) comparative historical analysis[3] or other qualitative approaches. In any strand of research that employs statistical inference, the DGP that gives rise to observable data is assumed to involve some degree of random chance. When a DGP involves randomness, it is said to be *stochastic.* Put differently, a process is stochastic if observers of that process are uncertain of what its results will be before it operates. When a social process that generates observable data does not involve chance, it is *deterministic.*

Thus a DGP may be either stochastic or deterministic.[4] If deterministic, a DGP for some event specifies necessary and/or sufficient conditions for the event to occur (Goertz and Starr [2003]). If stochastic, a DGP specifies the probability of various possible results or events under specific conditions. Necessary and sufficient conditions generally do not make sense for stochastic DGPs; for a

[2] By "metaphysical" I mean that the validity of this commitment must be taken as given or rejected based on first principles; it cannot itself be adjudicated with reference to empirical observation.

[3] See Mahoney and Rueschemeyer [2003] for a general treatment and review of comparative historical analysis in social science.

[4] Some scholars define DGPs in terms of probability distribution (Morton and Williams [2010]), which seems to imply that DGPs must be stochastic. However, because a probability distribution can always be specified as "degenerate," or yielding certain outcomes nonprobabilistically, this is not necessarily the case.

coin flip, there are no necessary conditions for a head to occur (other than that the coin is flipped), and no sufficient ones. Stochastic DGPs consign analysts to speak of the probabilities of various events because the determination of the outcome under any given set of conditions is not certain. A stochastic DGP can specify that when a particular condition is met, a particular event is more likely to occur than if the condition is not met.

The most important presumption in this definition of a DGP is that social and political processes have governing rules in the first place, that is, that DGPs are systematic and therefore intelligible by some combination of reason and careful observation. This is true for both stochastic and deterministic DGPs. Theory in social science pertains to these governing rules themselves.

It is not possible to determine from a given set of observed data alone whether its DGP is stochastic or deterministic. This is a background assumption – a metaphysical commitment of sorts – an analyst must make to structure an inference about the DGP, and as such the DGP does not offer a test of that assumption. Even if a DGP is stochastic in the sense that its results cannot be perfectly predicted before they are obtained, it is always possible to perfectly explain any *given* set of observed results, given a large enough combination of explanatory variables. Internet sites that promise to divine future winning lottery tickets based on some combination of past results, sunspot activity, and other fantastical predictors are a testament to the human ability to see determinism in the face of chance. And when an analyst assumes a DGP is deterministic, imperfect prediction does not imply the assumption is wrong; it is simply interpreted to mean that the right explanatory variables have not been discovered yet.

For example, when a DGP for something like a social revolution is best interpreted as stochastic, it will still be possible to uncover apparently necessary and sufficient conditions for social revolutions from any specific set of cases of them. A finite set of observations, even if drawn from a stochastic DGP, can always be perfectly explained by a large enough combination of explanatory variables. But stochastic element in this DGP implies that prediction of future social revolutions will not be perfectly accurate even when these supposedly necessary or sufficient conditions are met. By the same token, a failure of prediction of the results of a previously unobserved case does not imply that the assumption of determinism in the DGP is invalid or not useful; it might simply imply that the accurate necessary and sufficient conditions were not yet uncovered. But with the new case, new conditions on the DGP can be specified so that all cases fit the pattern. Then the cycle continues again.

The DGPs on which statistical applications in social science are predicated specify that outcomes of social processes are subject to some sort of uncertainty or randomness. That is, the interesting phenomena that we want to study have a random component. This does not mean they are haphazard; we have already placed ourselves in the stream of thought that considers social processes systematic, in some part, and in that part intelligible.

When DGPs are stochastic, the social process as it unfolded and was observed yielded a particular, definite outcome. This stage of the process is ex post, after the draw of results from the DGP is made. But it could have yielded some other outcome instead, and at that ex ante stage, before the draw from the DGP is made, its result is uncertain. It follows that to understand the process, it is not sufficient to understand the observed data alone. To understand how social forces are related to each other in the DGP, it is not enough to understand how variables reflecting them are related in a specific dataset. Instead we seek to understand how they would be related in all possible datasets that could have been drawn from the process, including ones that could have been but, because of the operation of chance in the DGP, were not.

This does not imply that all interesting DGPs inherently involve uncertainty. It implies that in using tools of statistical inference – explicitly not using quantitative tools merely to summarize a collection of observed data, but to infer something about an unobserved DGP – we assume we are dealing with DGPs that involve chance.

There are (at least) three reasons to suspect that uncertainty is a part of the outcomes determined by many interesting DGPs social scientists care about, even though the observed data itself is perfectly determinate and may itself be quiet about the matter of randomness in the DGP. These reasons are explored in the next three sections.

3.2 SAMPLING UNCERTAINTY

The General Social Survey (GSS) by the National Opinion Research Center is a large, multiyear survey of Americans about a large number of attitudes, behaviors, and characteristics of Americans and their social environments (see Chapter 2 for an example of data from the GSS). It is intended to be "representative" of the American people, but it does not query them all. Political polls and opinion surveys that represent a larger whole with observation of a part all have this characteristic.

Just because the survey is representative of some larger group (e.g., American adults, likely voters in an election, possible voters who are registered as Republicans) does not mean that it is perfectly accurate in summarizing the actual state of opinions or characteristics in that group. If a thousand or so voters are surveyed as to their approval of the job performance of the president of the United States, we cannot be certain that the approval rating in the larger group of voters from which they are drawn is exactly the same as in the subset of voters that was observed (in fact, we can usually be quite certain that it is not exactly the same).

The uncertainty about the characteristics of a whole that remains after observing a part is called *sampling uncertainty*. Although the details are typically rather intricate in real surveys, the nature of the randomness in the DGP that leads to sampling uncertainty is, conceptually, relatively straightforward.

Suppose that each individual in a group has a fixed characteristic that is possible to observe with perfect accuracy, if in fact that individual is observed at all. Suppose also that an analyst has a list of all individuals in the group and has means to observe only a subset of them. The analyst can write down every person's name on a slip of paper, put all the slips in a box, shake it up, and pull out as many slips as she has the means to observe. She then makes an observation of all the people whose names were drawn from the box and records them in a dataset.

This is an idealized DGP for a survey. It specifies the entire set of possible observations (the *population*) and a rule by which possible observations actually are observed (the *sample*). The DGP is stochastic because the sample of names drawn out of the population is determined by chance. For this reason, such a sample is called a *probability sample*. Because the DGP leading to the sample is stochastic, the inferences drawn from the sample about the population are necessarily uncertain. This uncertainty is an example of sampling uncertainty.

The analyst knows the exact nature of the stochastic element of this DGP and in fact creates it on purpose. A stochastic element of this sort is the reason the sample can be said to be representative of the population. As we will see in subsequent chapters, by controlling the stochastic component of the DGP, the analyst can precisely quantify the uncertainty of inferences she is able to make about the population. Although nonstochastic DGPs for recording a sample of observations might be available in some cases, they are usually much worse than probability samples in terms of "representativeness" of the population.

3.3 THEORETICAL UNCERTAINTY

Every positive theory in social science is a simplification of the process it is designed to represent. That is part of what makes theories useful. A theory specifies *equivalence classes* of events or observations that are, in some sense, as informed by the theory, the same; it specifies other events that are not in a given equivalence class because they are, in some sense relevant to the theory, different. By the same token, the theory is a simplification; any two members of a given equivalence class supplied by a theory can surely be differentiated in *some* way, just not in a way that the theory says is relevant (otherwise they would not be in the same equivalence class according to the theory). Any theory therefore omits some factors that can connect observed happenings in different ways. That is why a theory can be useful: if it did not omit some such factors, it would simply be a full-scale recreation of reality and would not solve the predicament of the unfortunate person bewildered by a complex world who needs a theory to make sense of things in the first place.

Therefore, some factors that might influence a variable or event must necessarily be left out of a theory explaining why that variable looks the way it does in various units. That means that, when we take account of all the factors a theory *does* use to explain the outcome, some factors will inevitably be left off the table.[5] The implication is that we never fully understand the behavior of the units we are trying to understand. From the point of view of a specific theory, its behavior depends in part on unaccounted factors. Conditional on the accounted-for factors, then, the outcome must necessarily be uncertain to some degree. This is uncertainty due to theoretical incompleteness or, more succinctly, *theoretical uncertainty*.

To be concrete, suppose you experience a mysterious abdominal pain from time to time and mention it to your doctor. She tells you to pay attention to the context of the pain and try to figure out what you were doing, what you ate, your level of stress, the time of day, and so on, before the pain flares up. After doing so for a few weeks, you find nothing that reliably correlates with the pain – you cannot predict the pain or explain its occurrence based on anything you can observe. This is the same as saying that as far as you can tell, the pain occurs randomly. But the doctor thinks of abdominal organs as part of a well-understood system; the doctor has a good theory of how these organs work and when and why they hurt. After further examination and a variety of tests the doctor might determine that a buildup of some specific nutrients or their by-products is causing inflammation in an organ that results in pain. The doctor, having a more complete theory of how abdominal organs work, knows where to look to explain what is happening. You, lacking this theoretical knowledge, do not think to consider, or know how to record, the nutrient buildup that is the culprit. What seems random based on superficial observation does not seem random to your doctor.[6]

Perhaps an even clearer example from everyday life is when a computer running a buggy operating system crashes. This seems to happen at the strangest times and is often impossible to relate to anything observable in the computer's functioning or what the user is doing to it (besides perhaps working on a particularly important document that has not been saved). Yet a computer, as a finite-state machine, does not do anything that is truly random. It just looks that way to the user.

In a social science context, consider the bill sponsorship activity of a U.S. senator in a specific session of Congress. We might postulate that a senator's bill sponsorship is affected generally by length of service, committee membership, and whether his or her party is in the majority. But there's a lot more to it we cannot measure or, politically, don't even care about. Did the senator meet a constituent or donor who raised an issue the senator considered important

---

[5] See Boehmke [2006] for a constructive methodological approach for indirectly incorporating unobserved factors into models of political decision making.

[6] Of course medicine doesn't know everything about what causes abdominal pain and there are catch-all terms doctors use for "unexplained" recurrent pain – which is simply to say that it's partly random even as far as your doctor can tell. Your doctor's theory is better but not perfect.

enough to warrant a bill to deal with it? Did the senator have an illness or personal issue that precluded energetic bill sponsorship in a particular session of Congress?

A fuller account of this behavior than simply its political determinants would help to explain some otherwise idiosyncratic cases. Without this litany of extra factors, bill sponsorship will be incompletely (or less completely) explained in terms of the theory. Some senators who have the same values for all explanatory variables will still not have the same level of bill sponsorship. The difference is not intelligible in terms of the theory, and therefore, for a given theory, bill sponsorship is partly uncertain. With a more elaborate theory, some of this uncertainty would be eliminated.

With an incomplete theory, therefore, DGPs appear or are understood to be stochastic. Unobserved or neglected factors introduce randomness in decisions made by an actor, from an outside observer's point of view. The uncertainty is not due to observing only a subset of senators. Even if the population of interest is all the senators in the 110th Congress, so we can include them all in a dataset, there is some randomness in their bill-sponsorship behavior because a necessarily partial understanding of the decision maker's goals and constraints makes it impossible to predict perfectly. The variation in their behavior conditional on given circumstances, highlighted by a theory of bill sponsorship, is random from the point of view of that theory. Thus theoretical uncertainty is conceptually different from sampling uncertainty, although both amount to a stochastic DGP.

For another example, consider again the link between divided government and "legislative gridlock" in the United States. The issue is interesting even when we only look retrospectively at the (say) post–World War II history of the United States. In this particular time period, we can observe all Congresses and all major laws passed according to any operationalization. We are not taking a part of a whole; we have all the observations. The legislative experience was what it was, and we can look at it in all the detail we want as it actually did unfold in this time period.

So why would anyone think to account for random variation in any of these variables when exploring the effect of divided government? The reason is that there were random (as far as an analyst can tell) fluctuations in legislative "output" from year to year, possibly having nothing to do with the effect of divided government. Even if we had a "do-over" for 2007, would we expect everything that happened that year that affected legislative output to be the same? Could our national security situation have been different? Could some skirmishes in Iraq or Afghanistan have turned into major battles instead? Could securities markets have "imploded" sooner (or later) due to spillovers from shaky mortgage loans? And if so, could these events have diverted, or focused, Congress's attention on proposed legislation? It is not far-fetched to believe the answers to these questions could be yes, especially given the inherent unpredictability of military excursions and securities markets. And if the answers are yes, then major legislative output for the Congress seated in 2007 is in part random from the point of view of predominant theories of that concept.

If theoretical incompleteness implies only partial explanations of the events that we study, then why not simply include any and all factors in a more elaborate theory to make it "more complete"? Maybe with enough factors included in a theory of legislative output, we would understand it perfectly, and there would be no random variation left.

One reason is that wringing all random variation out of a variable's behavior is usually not the point of a theory. Many scholars find it appealing when theories explain "a lot" with "a little," and a parsimonious set of explanatory factors and account of their interaction is therefore desirable. Including every conceivable variable that might be relevant for explaining some event can make a theory cluttered and defeat the purpose of focusing on the role played by a few specific factors. Put differently, theoretical incompleteness may be desirable, notwithstanding the implication that variables we are trying to explain may appear random as a result. Another reason is that relevant variables that would reduce random variation are not measurable due to practicality, privacy, or ethical considerations. For instance, in studying labor market mobility, one might argue that expected future health problems are relevant because workers might be reluctant to forgo health insurance if they expect to be unhealthy for some reason. This could be difficult to obtain by conventional survey instruments because respondents may be reluctant to report that they expect health problems.

In summary, a theory of some event or outcome specifies a DGP for it in the sense of indicating other factors that help to explain or cause that outcome and providing reasons why. When a theory is incomplete, two cases that seem the same in terms of the explanatory factors indicated in the theory may have different outcomes. The theory itself cannot, by definition, explain this difference. It can therefore be considered random from the standpoint of the theory, so that theoretical incompleteness implies that DGPs can be thought of has having a stochastic element.

3.4 FUNDAMENTAL UNCERTAINTY

Another source of uncertainty in the processes generating observable data is the operation of human agency. This agency often means that observed data is partially random simply because the humans whose actions (at some level) generate it may be partly random in their action. Which neurons in a person's head fire, which framing of a decision problem dominates, which association with a political act is salient – all of these affect decisions and any of them may be random in any given instance. The observed data in social science is partially random not just because of a process of sampling part of a whole and not just because of an incomplete specification of behavior, but because "the" complete theory of behavior itself may imply some randomness. This can be considered *fundamental uncertainty* in the sense that the uncertainty is a fundamental part of the variable under analysis, not reducible to further explanation by some other variable or to sampling.[7]

Conceptually, fundamental uncertainty is different from theoretical uncertainty. The latter means there may be relevant factors for determining a particular variable that an analyst happens not to know. Thus, the recent personal history of a senator may impinge on his bill sponsorship, but we do not know such factors, cannot measure them, or think they are minor and idiosyncratic enough not to feature in a theory. Fundamental uncertainty, on the other hand, means that even with a complete and correct theory of a phenomenon, it may still be best thought of as random. To use an example from natural science, the theory of quantum mechanics specifies that the position of an electron in an atom is random not because we lack a complete theory of the behavior of this subatomic particle but because that is the complete theory. Even the most relentlessly reductionist account of human behavior as due entirely to physical processes (after all, energy and movement of atoms determine brain activity at some level) must acknowledge some randomness in these processes.

3.5 RANDOMNESS IN DGPs AND OBSERVATION OF SOCIAL EVENTS

When scholars frame their purpose as understanding only the specific case at hand (e.g., a specific event that actually happened at some point in history, such as a social revolution in a particular nation state) and not to generalize beyond it, their framing nullifies the importance of sampling uncertainty. There are no other cases in a larger universe of France in 1789; there is only that one case. However, this framing does not address fundamental uncertainty or theoretical uncertainty.

Fundamental uncertainty implies that if we "reran" the history of France over the relevant time period, the progress of its social revolution would not necessarily be the same as what we have in fact observed. Even France's history as such is then a realization of a random process. If we reran history, might some key participants have been afflicted with a disease? Suffered a loss of nerve? Fallen in love with some member of the ruling class? Failed to eat their spinach? Innumerable events could have turned out differently and could have materially affected the outcome. Therefore any assessment of necessary or sufficient conditions for social revolution based on France's history as it actually did unfold could conceivably be illusory. The very same conditions that France had, in its culture and history leading up to the revolutionary period, could have been associated with a different social revolutionary outcome for France.

To put it differently, using the actual realization of French history to assess necessary and sufficient conditions for French social revolutions, even with no

---

[7] King et al. [2000] introduced a related concept of fundamental uncertainty and distinguished it from "estimation" uncertainty.

ambition beyond France, is valid, strictly speaking (in the sense of accurately assessing necessary and sufficient conditions), only in case France's experience with social revolutions *could not have been different* from what has been observed, given its configuration of conditions. That is to say, we can be sure it's valid only in case French history with respect to social revolutions is a *deterministic* process, given its configuration of conditions. But if the unfolding of French history in this epoch involves random variables, there is some randomness bound up in the observed outcome of its history.

This is the exact same reason a scholar with a theory pertaining to all countries on Earth during the Cold War might nevertheless apply methods of statistical inference in a dataset that contains the relevant observations, with no noise or sampling uncertainty whatsoever in them, for all countries on Earth for the entire Cold War. The connecting thread is that, even when we have all the units to which a theory applies, we still do not have the entire population of possible observations. Their histories could have been different because of fundamental uncertainty, even though there is no possibility of sampling uncertainty. When a theory pertains to the process through which some sequence of events came about, the set of possible events, in addition to the actual ones, is relevant.

In other words, in attempting to avoid the implications of randomness for analyzing data and constructing explanations for events, it is not enough to assert that only the data at hand is important or interesting for the research question being considered. This observation – which is often perfectly sensible, as for example in research about a specific historical event – addresses only sampling uncertainty. The uncertainty of human agency and human social interaction is still present.

There is no reason to believe that these three "types" of uncertainty can be differentiated from each other in actual data. We can name the concepts, but the bases on which they differ may not be observable. Most obviously, fundamental uncertainty may be impossible to distinguish from theoretical uncertainty. Simply put, when an analyst has two cases that have all the same conditions (explanatory variables, attributes, property space location – whatever we call them) but a different outcome, we can always suspect that including more explanatory factors would have explained the difference. This would mean that the difference in the seemingly identical cases is not due to "fundamental" randomness but to an incomplete specification of its behavior. On the other hand, given a finite sample of observations and enough explanatory factors, even "fundamentally random" events can be explained perfectly ex post.

3.6 STOCHASTIC DGPs AND THE CHOICE OF EMPIRICAL METHODOLOGY

These metaphysical commitments about the nature of randomness in DGPs, or the absence of any randomness in DGPs, imply that some choices about

TABLE 3.1. *Observations for Outcome Y and Explanatory Factor X*

Case	X Attribute	Y Attribute
1	Absent	Small
2	Present	Large
3	Present	Large
4	Present	Small
5	Absent	Small

empirical research methods are sensible and others are not. Both "quantitative" and "qualitative" methods can each, at a general level at least, be reconciled with some coherent belief about the extent of randomness in DGPs.

The task for a researcher is to make sure her choice of methods matches her choice of metaphysical belief about randomness and DGPs, or else the researcher will give answers to research questions that she herself would not believe if she thought carefully about them. For instance, research in the tradition of statistical modeling assumes (or should assume) something stochastic in the DGP. Research in a qualitative-comparative tradition (see, e.g., Mahoney and Rueschemeyer [2003], Brady and Collier [2010], Goertz and Starr [2003]) often seeks to uncover necessary and/or sufficient conditions (or combinations of conditions) for particular outcomes to occur. These approaches are each capable of generating insight about DGPs under alternative assumptions about the nature of randomness in them.

To be (somewhat more) specific, suppose we are interested in explaining a social event or outcome Y that can either be "large" or "small" in value. This might be, for instance, the extent of a civil war in a group of countries. And we want to know whether some factor X that can either be "present" or "absent" helps us to explain the outcome. Suppose that the observed cases line up with the attributes in Table 3.1.

In this data we can "observe" that the presence of factor X is a necessary condition for Y to be large; Y is never large otherwise. On the other hand, the absence of factor X is sufficient for Y to be small; whenever X is absent this value of Y ensues.

This all makes perfect sense until it is revealed that X and Y are both coins. "Present" means the first one came up heads when flipped and "absent" means it came up tails; "Large" means the second one came up heads when flipped, and "small" means it came up tails. When we know the DGP and we know it is stochastic, it is transparent that methods to derive necessary and/or sufficient conditions for a particular result Y to occur are faulty. These methods can "answer" the question of what is necessary and what is sufficient (if anything), what combinations of causes are jointly sufficient, and so forth. But if the DGP is stochastic, the answers are erroneous. They can occur in a finite dataset by chance alone, but the conditions would not be expected to line up the same way if the coin were flipped again. Except for changes in the set of possible outcomes as a function of X, there are no necessary or sufficient conditions for Y to take any particular value when Y follows a stochastic DGP.

The simple act of attaching proper names of countries or the like to the cases and names of theoretical concepts to X and Y, does not change any of this: the hunt for necessary and sufficient conditions is misguided in stochastic DGPs. What's more, for a given set of observations of the outcome, a researcher seeking to explain can commence a search for explanatory factors that line up with the outcome just as necessary or sufficient conditions would, if they were possible. This exercise is not capable of producing meaning with a stochastic DGP, but a researcher committed to determinism in DGPs assumes the results are meaningful. By the same token, if the DGP really is deterministic, then researchers who assume it is stochastic are needlessly agnostic about identifying necessary and sufficient conditions empirically. In such a case researchers use up sample information estimating uncertainty and parameters that are figments of imagination, and the information would be better used identifying necessary and sufficient conditions.

Metaphysical commitments of this nature, by definition, cannot be adjudicated empirically. Despite this, or perhaps because of it, scholars occasionally hold their beliefs about this with a certain degree of intensity. These disagreements can at least make methodological choices intelligible to scholars even if they don't share the underlying metaphysical commitment.

More to the point, the purpose of enumerating these types of uncertainty is to motivate the stochastic nature of DGPs that are presumed in the remainder of this book. A metaphysical disquisition on the "type" of uncertainty present in any given case is not usually part of the template for statistical research in social science. At the same time, before launching into statistical analysis, it is usually worth reflecting on the reasons the DGP is assumed to be stochastic.

In particular, survey research and some areas of experimental research tend to be relatively careful about this because the explicit design of randomness in the DGP implies certain properties for various statistical procedures used to make inferences about the DGP. When probabilistic aspects of the DGP are introduced by the researcher explicitly and follow a known and controlled process, the selection of observations from the DGP into a dataset is said to follow *design-based sampling*. In this case, we are on relatively sure footing for understanding the effects of the stochastic component of DGPs on the uncertainty of inferences based on observed data.

On the other hand, scholars who invoke probability models as a structure for the DGP of their data often do so on the basis of assumptions about how the world works, rather than explicit control over the sampling process or introduction of randomness into the DGP by the researcher. The assumption that a DGP for some variable can be expressed according to a particular probability model, even though the researcher did not explicitly include a random component consistent with that model in the sampling process, is called *model-based sampling*. Some of the common types of probability models invoked in this approach are discussed in Chapter 6.

3.7 CONCLUSION

The assertion that observable data leaves us with uncertainty about the full list of properties of DGPs – whether due to sampling or fundamental uncertainty – simply means that the random part of the data we observe cannot be ignored in drawing conclusions about DGPs. This observation does not imply that the random part overwhelms or dominates the entire observation. To put it differently, even observations afflicted with uncertainty can be modeled as arising from a data-generating process to learn something about that process. If theories are couched as statements about those broader processes, then that modeling is how we assess theories based on observed, if noisy, data.

Sampling, theoretical, and fundamental uncertainty have far-reaching implications for the conduct of empirical research, and the conclusions a researcher can draw from data (and how they can be drawn). The central implication is that all observations in distributions of data are noisy and imperfect reflections of the underlying DGP. No one realization of events is the entire process giving rise to those events. Furthermore, any measure computed based on that noisy data will inherit some of that randomness. Therefore, the summary measures of distributions described in Chapter 2 actually do double duty in research: they summarize and distill information present in a distribution of data, but they also provide a window into the DGP. In other words, they hint at a connection between the data we can observe and the DGP we often ultimately care about.

Establishing the connection between observed data and the DGP of interest is the purpose of statistical inference. Formalizing this connection requires first formalizing the still mostly intuitive concept of a DGP. In this book, DGPs are formalized as *probability distributions*. Thus, the next three chapters develop the theory of probability and distributions in formal, mathematical terms. The first order of business, and the subject of the next chapter, is to present the central concepts of probability, random variables, and distribution functions. These functions serve as models of DGPs, and they offer a flexible framework for making precise statements with substantive theoretical content, as we see in subsequent chapters.

4

Probability Theory: Basic Properties of Data-Generating Processes

Recognizing a distinction between events that did occur and events that did not occur but might have is the point of the previous chapter. Given this distinction, we are generally uncertain, before a process unfolds, about what its outcome will be. We would like to relate the observable to the more fundamental data-generating process (DGP) behind it. But if the DGP is stochastic, we will always be uncertain about its defining features, and we need a language to express that uncertainty. Turning this around, given some stochastic DGP, we are generally uncertain about what might result from it. We need to be able to express this uncertainty explicitly and carefully.

To do so, we need some tools from the theory of probability. Probability theory is a conceptual apparatus in mathematics for expressing and evaluating uncertainty. As such, it is an important foundational component of statistical inference. But it is different from statistics. In probability theory, we start with a DGP with basic properties that we know (or assume, or pretend to know) and work out the consequences for the events that might be observed (e.g., their probabilities, how those probabilities are related to the DGP).

In (classical) statistical theory, by contrast, we start with a set of events we have observed and attempt to infer something about the properties of the stochastic DGP that generated them. In other words, probability contemplates what data will be observed from a given stochastic process. Statistics contemplates what stochastic process gave rise to the observed data. Its approach to doing so, however, draws heavily on probability. In particular, classical statistics usually turns on questions such as: "If the properties of the DGP are thus-and-so, what is the probability of seeing this data I have in my hands (or on my computer)?"

All of this means that understanding probability theory is a crucial step in getting where we want to go with our ability to engage positive theory to specify attributes of a DGP and evaluate these claims at an empirical level. In a sense, this chapter is therefore transitional. It lays out the necessary apparatus so we can turn to the relevant applications as quickly as possible. The interesting tools for applied statistics in social science come in later chapters, for the most part, but they cannot be understood without this chapter.

A brief note on the style of exposition in this chapter and use of this material in subsequent chapters: the most important material for applications begins in Section 4.3. Sections 4.1 and 4.2 lay out foundations and several important ideas that we will use later. As pertains to this chapter specifically, some of the following material is foundational for the techniques we use but not often directly used itself. But some of it is a bit more important in everyday practice. For understanding and conducting statistical modeling and inference, it is essential to know something about random variables, distribution functions, conditional distributions, and independence of random variables.

Also, some of the examples used to illustrate core concepts are, in social science terms, a bit contrived. They often have to do with coin flips or die rolls and the like. At this point, the primary goal of the exposition is simplicity rather than substantive verisimilitude. Simplicity helps to communicate and solidify the concept, and it is easier to make a contrived example simple than a realistic or substantively important one. In addition, in simple examples, students may have a (ideally, accurate) homegrown intuition that provides a base from which to develop a concept in greater generality. Where possible, I try to leverage that sort of intuition below.

4.1 SET-THEORETIC FOUNDATIONS

4.1.1 Formal Definitions

A primitive concept in probability, in the sense that cannot be further defined with reference to concepts in the field itself, is the idea of an *experiment*. An experiment is an instance of the operation of a DGP and has multiple possible outcomes. This usage of "experiment" is different from its use in most of social science in which "experiment" means controlled assignment of units to "treatments."

The set of possible outcomes of an experiment is the *sample space*, denoted simply as S. The set S is the list of everything that might happen in the experiment. A coin flip is a simple type of experiment where $S = \{H, T\}$, as is the roll of a die (where $S = \{1, 2, 3, 4, 5, 6\}$). Another experiment, in this rather sparse and formal meaning of the term, is the history of China over a time period when the unfolding and occurrence of its social revolution was still contingent and uncertain (Skocpol [1979]). This experiment cannot be repeated, but that does not matter for this definition.

A subset of the sample space is an *event*, denoted E in general. For example, if a coin is flipped twice, the set of possible outcomes is the set of outcomes on the first flip and the second flip. This is $S = \{HH, HT, TH, TT\}$. One event is

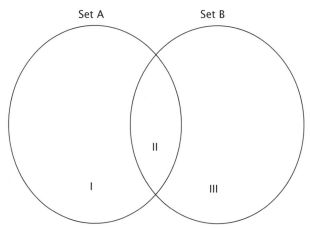

FIGURE 4.1. Union, intersection, and complement of A and B.

that the first flip comes up H: $E_1 = \{HH, HT\}$. Another is that both flips are T: $E_2 = \{TT\}$. Another is that both flips are not H: $E_3 = \{HT, TH, TT\}$. And so forth.

Note that S and the Es are *sets*, not numbers. Their members may consist of numbers, or categorical labels, or any denumerable class. But the sets themselves are not subject to algebra or arithmetic manipulations like addition or multiplication.

Sets can be combined, and the combination of two sets is the *union* of those sets. The union of E and F is denoted $E \cup F$. The union contains all elements in *either* set E *or* set F (or both). Thus the union operator is a logical "or" operator. The union operator can be extended straightforwardly to any countable collection of sets to find the union of $E_1, E_2, \ldots$, denoted $\bigcup_{i=1}^{N} E_i$. Figure 4.1 displays two sets A and B. Their union is all the area in the regions labeled I, II, and III.

The "overlap" of two sets can also be identified, and that overlap is called their *intersection*. The intersection of E and F is denoted $E \cap F$. The intersection contains all elements in *both E and F*. Thus the intersection operator is a logical "and" operator. The intersection operator can be extended straightforwardly to any countable collection of sets to find the intersection of $E_1, E_2, \ldots$, denoted $\bigcap_{i=1}^{N} E_i$.

The intersection of two sets need not have any elements: for example, the intersection of the events "the first flip is a head" and "the first flip is a tail." In this case, $E \cap F = \emptyset$, where the last symbol denotes the *empty set*, a lonely set with no members. Two sets with empty intersection are *disjoint* or *mutually exclusive*. If a collection of sets in S is mutually exclusive and exhaustive, in the sense that every member of S is contained in one of them, they form a *partition* of S. For the sets A and B shown in Figure 4.1, the intersection is the region labeled II, the (American) football-shaped region in the middle.

The set of all elements not in a particular set, or in S but not in some particular E, can be identified. This "everything but…" set is the *complement of E with respect to S*. This is denoted $S \setminus E$, or, if there is no risk of confusion about the larger set that the complement is taken with respect to, E^c or $\sim E$. The complement of a set can be taken with respect to any other set, not just the set of all possible elements S. In principle the complement of S itself can be taken with respect to itself; this would be the set of all elements not in the set of all elements: $S^c = \emptyset$. For the sets A and B in Figure 4.1, the complement of A with respect to B is the "half-moon" shaped region labeled III: the set of all elements in B not in A.

Union, intersection, and complementation are the primary mathematical operations available for sets.

As this simple discussion has implied, there are many possible events (i.e., many possible subsets of S). Those subsets of S can themselves be collected into a set. "The set of all subsets of S" is a *Borel field* on S, denoted $\mathcal{B}$. It has the properties that the complement of any member of $\mathcal{B}$ is also in $\mathcal{B}$, and the intersection of any finite number of members in $\mathcal{B}$ is also in $\mathcal{B}$. Thus the Borel field is said to be "closed under complementation and finite intersection." For a given S, this set of all subsets of S is well defined and, in principle, easy to construct. In practice, enumerating or naming all of its elements gets very complicated very quickly as S gets moderately large (e.g., if S has five elements or more).

For most of how we will use probability here, the concept of a Borel field is more or less invisible. Once we have a good understanding of random variables, in particular, it recedes quickly. But throughout, it's there in the background. It has a lot to do with how probability is defined at a formal level.

4.1.2 Probability Measures and Probability Spaces

The reason that the Borel field on S is important is because members of it are the primitive components on which probabilities are defined. For instance, in the two-coin flip experiment with its sample space $S = \{HH, HT, TH, TT\}$, a probability measure assigns a probability to every subset of S, that is, every member of the Borel field. If that were not so, the assessment of the probability of results of the experiment would be incomplete. It is not enough to give a probability to every member of S. We might specify that the probability of each member of S here is $\frac{1}{4}$ (and we will so stipulate), but it does not necessarily follow from this fact alone that the probability of either HH or TT is $\frac{1}{2}$. It is possible, and in certain experiments (including the way we usually conceptualize a two-coin flip) it is true. The point is that the assertion about how these probabilities combine is bound up with much information that is not present in the individual probabilities of H and T themselves. It must be specified or supplied from other assertions. Therefore, a complete model of probability for the experiment with sample space S has to specify (or allow to be derived) a probability for every event and collection of events that might occur.

Technically, probability is deceptively simple. A probability measure is simply a function that assigns a nonnegative number to members of the Borel field. It must also specify that the probability of *something* happening is 1, and that if two events are disjoint, the probability of one or the other happening is the sum of their individual probabilities. Formally, a *probability measure* is a function defined as follows:

$$P : \mathcal{B} \to \mathbb{R} \text{ such that}$$

1. $P(S) = 1$
2. $P(E) \geqslant 0$ for all events $E \in \mathcal{B}$
3. For two events E, F such that $E \cap F = \emptyset$, $P(E \cup F) = P(E) + P(F)$

Among other implications we consider shortly, these properties immediately imply that $0 \leqslant P(E) \leqslant 1$ for all $E \in S$. It is a straightforward property of all probabilities that they are between 0 and 1.

A *probability space* or *probability model* is a triple $(S, \mathcal{B}, P(\cdot))$, that is, a sample space, a set of events (subsets of the sample space), and a rule assigning a number between 0 and 1 to every event.

Exercises in probability are typically tricky or interesting (or both) because the probability measure is defined for some events, some structure of the experiment is specified (or implied), and the probability of other events must then be determined. We consider some simple examples here to get used to the concept of probability.

4.1.3 Ontological Interpretations of Probability

Probability is a psychologically tricky concept, and psychologists have shown that most people do not handle probabilities in mental accounting the way mathematicians handle them. But these properties all make good sense and have a natural interpretation when we reflect on them. In this section, we digress for a moment to consider the meaning and interpretation of probability.

There are two major schools of thought about the appropriate and most useful interpretation of "probability" at an ontological level. It must be stressed that the formal definitions provided earlier (and all the concepts elaborated subsequently) are consistent with both of them, and the mathematical theory of probability works the same for both conceptions. There are real differences in these schools of thought and their implications for quantitative analysis, but those differences do not crop up in the basic theoretical engine used; they crop up in how it is used.

One school of thought is the *frequentist* or *classical* school. The idea here is that probability is a "long-run frequency": the probability of an event is the fraction of times that it occurs if the experiment is repeated many, many times. There may be idiosyncratic collections of results where the outcome departs from typical behavior, but over long sequences of repetitions, these idiosyncrasies wash out. For example, in flipping a coin, a sequence of 10 flips may well have 7 heads or 8 tails. But over 10,000 flips, the fraction of times on which a head occurs is much closer to – indeed, it defines – the "true" probability of a head. Two ideas are implicit: first, that there is a "true" probability in the first place, a fixed quantity that may or may not be known but that is fixed and eternal for this experiment and its DGP; second, that it makes sense to talk about repeating the experiment under identical conditions.

The second implicit idea is apparently restrictive. What is the probability that the population of Honduras exceeded the population of Paraguay on last January 1 at 12:00 A.M. Greenwich mean time? It makes no sense to contemplate repeating that experiment, and from a frequentist standpoint, the question does not make sense: either one is larger or the other is. Yet many readers are surely uncertain about which country was more populous at this instant.[1] If the experiment cannot be repeated even in a thought experiment, it cannot have a long run frequency, which is troubling if that is our notion of probability, because any self-respecting language of uncertainty should apply to a case in which we clearly can be uncertain about the answer.

The second school of thought about the meaning of probability, the *Bayesian* school, easily handles problems like this. In the Bayesian conception, probability is "degree of belief," or "willingness to bet" on the outcome (abstracting away from any issues of risk tolerance).

For example, consider a lottery that pays \$1 if Honduras was more populous, and \$0 if Paraguay was more populous. What is the most you would be willing to pay for a ticket in this lottery?[2] Clearly, the less you pay the better, but if you are a price-taker for lottery tickets and cannot negotiate the price, what is the most you would pay?

The answer to that question *is* probability in a Bayesian sense. The maximum willingness to pay is a number between 0 and 1, and in fact, it is the "expected value" of the gamble, which in turn is simply the probability of wining the \$1 prize. An obvious result of the Bayesian viewpoint is that probability is *subjective*, and different individuals may quite reasonably have different probability assessments. Students of American policy making, for example, who are (at least as a matter of training) not well aware of the 10% or so population difference, are probably more likely to be willing to pay close to \$.50 than Latin Americanists, who, knowing that Honduras is larger, would be willing to pay closer to \$1.

This also makes for a useful interpretation of the odds quoted at sporting events or on "share prices" for political events at websites such as InTrade

---

[1] Honduras is a slightly larger country. Both have a little less than seven million people as of this writing. Yes, I had to look this up.

[2] Over this range of payoffs, it is essentially inconceivable that risk aversion is strong enough to affect the willingness to pay for the gamble.

or the Iowa Electronic Markets (IEM). InTrade and the IEM[3] have created a futures market on political events: they allow trading of contracts that pay $1 if, say, the Democratic Party controls a majority of Senate seats after the 2010 midterm elections. The price of such a contract is the market's collective judgment about the probability of the event (subject to the market maker taking a piece of the action). This is exactly the same as the $1 lottery on Honduras versus Paraguay.

It is worth noting, again, that both of these schools of thought agree on the ingredients of a probability space and on the basic "rules" of probability once a probability space is given. There are competing ontological conceptions of probability, but there are not two competing mathematical theories of it.

4.1.4 Further Properties of Probability Measures

A probability measure P is defined in terms of three simple properties: something has to happen with certainty (probability 1), nothing has negative probability, and the probability of one of two events that have no overlap is the sum of their probabilities. This third requirement is sometimes known as the *addition rule for disjoint events*.

These requirements, combined with the fact that the Borel field $\mathcal{B}$ contains any set created from other members of $\mathcal{B}$ by basic set theoretic operations, place other restrictions on the properties of a probability measure.

A first basic and useful fact is the *complement rule*: the probability of the complement of an event in $\mathcal{B}$ is one minus the probability of that event. Formally, the complement rule is $P(E^c) = 1 - P(E)$. The complement of an event is the set of all elements not in that event, and the union of an event and its complement is always the set of all possible elements. Therefore, the probability of the union of an event and its complement must be 1. Furthermore, because an event and its complement are obviously disjoint (have empty intersection), the addition rule for disjoint events applies. Therefore, the probability of the union of an event and its complement is the sum of their individual probabilities. This too must be 1, which demonstrates the complement rule. Because $P(S) = 1$ by definition of a probability measure, and $S^c = \emptyset$, it follows from the complement rule that $P(\emptyset) = 0$. Just as the probability of something is 1, the probability of nothing is 0.

A second useful and sensible fact is that if B is a superset of A, both in the Borel field (i.e., $A \subseteq B \in \mathcal{B}$), then $P(A) \leqslant P(B)$. If B contains everything in A and then some more elements, B surely cannot be less likely than A itself. As obvious and sensible as this seems, decision psychologists have accumulated good evidence that in natural social settings people violate this requirement routinely.

---

[3] The IEM did it first and is actually run by academics studying the information aggregation properties of markets.

A third useful fact is a *generalized addition rule* for events. For any two events E and F (not just disjoint ones), $P(E \cup F) = P(E) + P(F) - P(E \cap F)$. Clearly, because the last term, a probability of an intersection, is 0 for disjoint events, this simplifies to the addition rule for disjoint events in that case.

These abstract concepts of probability can be clarified in a simple type of experiment in which every element of the sample space S is equally likely. This is an experiment with *equally likely outcomes*. Although not rich in social science content, these examples do help illustrate the concepts of probability laid out above.

A simple example is a "fair die" where $S = \{1, 2, 3, 4, 5, 6\}$ and each face turns up with probability $\frac{1}{6}$. What is the probability of rolling an odd number? Intuition suggests that it is $\frac{1}{2}$, and the addition rule for disjoint events illustrates why. The event "odd number shows up" occurs whenever the die shows 1, 3, or 5. These events are disjoint, so the probability of the event "odd" is obtained by summing their probabilities, $\frac{1}{6} + \frac{1}{6} + \frac{1}{6} = \frac{1}{2}$. The probability of rolling an even number can be obtained in the same way, or by noting that the events "even" and "odd" are complements with respect to the sample space, that is, their intersection is $\emptyset$ and their union is S. So the probability of rolling an even number is $1 - \frac{1}{2} = \frac{1}{2}$. With one die, the probability of an event like "the result is odd or less than 5" is easy to compute directly – there are five possible results that meet one or the other condition: 1, 2, 3, 4, and 5. It also illustrates the generalized addition rule: $P(\text{odd} \cup \text{less than } 5) = P(\text{odd}) + P(\text{less than } 5) - [P(\text{odd} \cap \text{less than } 5)] = \frac{1}{2} + \frac{2}{3} - \frac{1}{3} = \frac{1}{2} + \frac{1}{3} = \frac{5}{6}$.

4.2 INDEPENDENCE AND CONDITIONAL PROBABILITY

At a basic level, theories in social science typically assert that the occurrence of one event has implications for the likelihood or occurrence of another. A scholar of international conflict might assert that the probability that two countries go to war with each other is affected by their type of governing regime. A student of organizations might assert that whether an organization "survives" over some interval of time is affected by its size and resources. A researcher of political participation might assert that the decision to vote is affected by knowledge of the candidates and issues in the election. A scholar of welfare state policies might assert that whether a state adopts a particular level of public benefits is affected by its ethnic or racial diversity. In probability this concept of "effect" is expressed in its simplest form as the probability of one event E, conditional on the occurrence of another event F. More compactly, this is the *conditional probability* of E given F, denoted $P(E|F)$.

To illustrate the mechanics consider a fair die, such that the probability of any given result is $\frac{1}{6}$. What is the probability that the roll is 3, given that an odd number is showing? There are three equally likely outcomes in the condition, 1, 3, and 5. "Given that an odd number is showing" means that we know for sure that one of these three outcomes has occurred. The whole sample space S

is no longer the relevant benchmark for the probability that a 3 is rolled. But all three of these odd outcomes are still equally likely. Therefore, this probability is $\frac{1}{3}$. It is a *conditional probability*, the probability of one event conditional on the occurrence of another event.

This is exactly what the definition of conditional probability produces. Formally, the conditional probability of E given F is denoted and defined as

$$P(E|F) = \frac{P(E \cap F)}{P(F)}. \tag{4.1}$$

In essence, the definition of conditional probability updates the denominator to reflect the correct benchmark for the occurrence of E – this benchmark is the conditioning event F, not the whole sample space S. For the previous example of rolling a die, the numerator is $\frac{1}{6}$ and the denominator is $\frac{1}{2}$. So the whole expression is $\frac{2}{6}$ or $\frac{1}{3}$. This matches intuition when the latter is clear, which gives us some confidence that it will make some sense when the latter is unclear.

It need not be the case that one event is informative at all about another. What is the probability that the euro is still used as the currency of Eurozone countries in 2016, given that a small meteor hits the planet Neptune in 2015? We hope it is the same as the probability that the euro is used if a small meteor does not hit Neptune; otherwise we are going to have to do some serious soul searching about European political economy. The conditional probability is the same as the unconditional probability.

When $P(E|F) = P(E)$, the events E and F are *independent* or *stochastically independent*. This is sometimes written formally as $E \perp F$. Given Definition 4.2, independence implies that $P(E \cap F) = P(E)P(F)$. This is the *multiplication rule for independent events*, and along with the complement rule, superset rule, and the addition rules, it greatly simplifies the task of computing probabilities. However, unlike the properties we covered previously, the multiplication rule only applies to independent events.

However, there is a more general multiplication rule that applies to events, whether independent or not. Under this *generalized multiplication rule*, the probability of the sequence of events E then F is $P(E \cap F) = P(E)P(F|E)$. For example, consider the four aces from a standard deck of cards: clubs, diamonds, hearts, and spades (C, D, H, S). If these cards are shuffled and two are pulled out, what is the probability of drawing the ace of clubs and then the ace of diamonds? Call this joint event $C1, D2$. Clearly, the first is $P(C1) = \frac{1}{4}$. Equally clearly, these events are not independent; the probability of drawing D on the first selection is $\frac{1}{4}$, but on the second selection, only three cards are left, and all draws are equally likely. So $P(D2|C1) = \frac{1}{3}$.[4] The generalized multiplication rule then indicates that $P(C1, D2) = P(C1)P(D2|C1) = \frac{1}{4} \times \frac{1}{3} = \frac{1}{12}$.

---

[4] This can also be obtained "mechanically" from the definition of conditional probability, of course, by enumerating all possible (12) draws of the first two cards, noting that 1 of those 12 is the event $C1, D2$, and noting that 4 of those 12 involve the event $C1$. Then $\frac{1}{12} / \frac{1}{4} = \frac{1}{3}$.

It is helpful to keep in mind for examples that the multiplication rules are usually applied for joint events and/or sequences of events (whether independent or not), whereas the addition rules are usually applied for alternative possible events (weather mutually exclusive or not). Note also that if two events are mutually exclusive, they are not independent. If $A \cap B = \emptyset$ so A and B are mutually exclusive, we know for sure that if A occurs, the probability of B is 0. The occurrence of A tells us something about the probability of B in this case, so that means A and B cannot be independent.

4.2.1 Examples and Simple Combinatorics

A canonical example of independent events is successive flips of a fair coin. In this case the probability that H occurs on Flip 2 is unaffected by whether it occurred on Flip 1. In a two-coin-flip experiment, this means that the probability of two consecutive heads is $\frac{1}{2} \times \frac{1}{2} = \frac{1}{4}$. So is the probability of H followed by T, T followed by H, and two consecutive Ts. This is the whole sample space of a two-coin-flip experiment; each element is equally likely, and their probabilities sum to 1.

Fine details of wording can matter in probability because they may change the nature of an event whose probability is sought or of a conditioning event. Consider the (not quite) mutually exclusive and (not quite) exhaustive events that a newborn is a boy or a girl suppose for simplicity that each event has probability $\frac{1}{2}$ and that these events are independent across multiple egg fertilizations. Then if a woman is pregnant with fraternal twins (so two eggs were fertilized independently), and an ultrasound reveals only that one is a girl, but not which one (the other is too hazy to tell), what is the probability that both are girls? A tempting but incorrect answer is $\frac{1}{2}$: the ultrasound reveals only that (B, B) is not the outcome. But there are still three equally likely outcomes left in S: $(B, G), (G, B), (G, G)$. So the probability that both are girls in light of this information is $\frac{1}{3}$. On the other hand, suppose in the delivery room the first twin is born and turns out to be a girl; now what is the probability both are girls? The correct answer here is $\frac{1}{2}$ by independence; the only possible elements of S are (G, G) and (G, B), and they are both equally likely.

The implications of independence can be extended to any number of repetitions or "trials" of the experiment. Just as the two-flip experiment, in which the probability of H on flip 2 is unaffected by whether it occurred on flip 1, the probability of H on flip 100 in a 100-trial experiment is unaffected by whether H occurred on each of the first 99 flips. The probability of 100 consecutive H throws is $\frac{1}{2}^{100}$, a very small number. This is the same as the probability of any other specific sequence of throws.

However, that is a different statement than asserting that 100 H is just as likely to occur as any other number of H. There is only one sequence that results in 100 H, but there are many sequences that result in, say, 50 H or 42 H. Independent "trials" of the coin-flip experiment means only that each specific sequence is equally likely. To obtain the probability of a particular result, such as 50 *H*s occur, we need to determine how many sequences result in 50 *H*. With a large number of trials, this is serious drudgery. We could get 50 *H* followed by 50 *T*, 49 *H* followed by 50 *T* followed by 1 *H*, and so forth. However, mathematicians have spent considerable effort figuring out how to count things efficiently, and this particular case turns out to have a simple structure.

The number of possible sequences of coin flips in any number of trials is straightforward. On the first trial, we can have two possible results; for each of these, we can have two on the second trial. That's four possible sequences in two trials. For each of these four, we can have two possible results on the third trial – for eight different sequences altogether up to that point – and so forth. For N trials, there are 2^N possible sequences. If we were throwing dice, with six possible results on each trial, there would be 6^N possible sequences in N trials. They are all equally likely if the individual trials are independent. Even if the trials are not independent for some reason, that is still the correct way to count the number of trials; nonindependence would mean they are not equally likely.

But to compute the probability of obtaining a particular number of H in N flips, say k heads in N flips, we need to know not only how many distinct sequences are possible but also how many of those ways result in k heads. Take for instance $k = 2$. In two trials, there is one way to get exactly two H. In three trials, there are three ways: (H, H, T), (H, T, H), (T, H, H). In four trials, there are six ways: (H, H, T, T), (H, T, H, T), (H, T, T, H), (T, H, H, T), (T, H, T, H), and (T, T, H, H). In five trials, listing all the ways is tedious and unwieldy. The number of ways grows as the number of trials grows, but not linearly and not in some kind of simple exponential fashion. It would be nice to express some underlying logic of this counting that allows it to be automated.

For four trials, we had two heads, H_1, H_2, and therefore two tails, T_1, T_2. Each trial is a "slot" into which one of these four outcomes can be placed. For the first slot, we have four choices of what to insert: one of the heads or one of the tails. Then in the second slot, we have three choices left. So there are 4×3 ways to fill these two slots. Then we have two choices left for the third slot and one for the fourth. With this group of four outcomes, we have $4 \times 3 \times 2 \times 1 \equiv 4! = 24$ ways to fill four slots.

But something seems wrong because there are only $2^4 = 16$ possible sequences, and now we have counted more ways than that to fill the slots (24). The discrepancy arises because in counting the ways to fill the four slots with four outcomes, we distinguished H_1 from H_2 as two outcomes. But in counting the sequences, (H_1, H_2, T_1, T_2) is not treated as a separate sequence from (H_2, H_1, T_1, T_2). The same is true for (H_1, H_2, T_2, T_1), (H_2, H_1, T_1, T_2), and (H_2, H_1, T_2, T_1). As long as the Hs stay in their slots, reordering H_1 and H_2 does not change the sequence, and the same is true for the Ts. Within each group, H or T, order does not matter. So we double-counted to arrive at 24.

For any allocation of the heads to the slots, either H_1 or H_2 could have gone in the first slot, and the other in the second, and the same is true for tails. So for each of the 24 slots, by distinguishing H_1 from H_2 and T_1 from T_2, we counted 2×2 ways too many. We can correct our tally of 24 by dividing by the number of ways to double count, 4. So the number of ways to choose 2 trials with H out of 4 total trials, when the ordering of the H's does not matter, is $\frac{4 \times 3 \times 2 \times 1}{(2 \times 1) \times (2 \times 1)} = \frac{4!}{2! \times 2!} = \frac{24}{4} = 6$. Because "number of ways to choose 2 trials with H out of four total trials, when the ordering of the Hs does not matter" is a lot of words, it is convenient to represent it with shorthand, and that shorthand is $\binom{4}{2}$.

Generalizing from this example,

$$\binom{N}{k} \equiv \frac{N!}{k!(N-k)!} \tag{4.2}$$

is the *binomial coefficient* for choosing k items out of N total items. This is also sometimes written as $_NC_k$ or $C(N, k)$. If that is the number of ways to get k heads in N flips, and there are 2^N equally likely sequences of N flips, then the probability of k heads in N flips of a fair coin is $\frac{\binom{N}{k}}{2^N}$.

Binomial coefficients reflect the number of *combinations* of N trials with k heads. Combinations are relevant when the ordering of the k items does not matter. If the ordering does matter, the result is a *permutation*. If for some reason we did want to distinguish H_1 from H_2 but not T_1 from T_2, the number of ways to fill the slots is $\frac{4!}{2!} = 12$; we only have to correct for double counting the tails. This is the number of permutations of two items (the heads) out of a group of four items. Thus, a permutation is an arrangement of items in slots when order matters. The number of permutations with N items and k slots is $_NP_k \equiv \frac{N!}{(N-k)!}$. Note that with $k = N$, we are counting the number of permutations of N items in N slots, so this is simply $N!$ because the denominator $0! \equiv 1$ in that case.

When we are trying to count the number of ways something can happen, and we use these devices to simplify counting with a large number of possibilities, we are dealing with *combinatorics*, of which binomial coefficients are a relatively simple example. Combinatorics is relevant in some areas of research design in social science, for example, the design of surveys or experiments. As a simple illustration, if a survey first chooses n_1 U.S. census tracts at random and then chooses n_2 households within selected census tracts, the survey will have $n_1 \times n_2$ respondents. If there are N_1 total census tracts and N_2 households per census tract on average, then the probability a given household is included in the survey is $\frac{n_1 n_2}{N_1 N_2}$. Combinatorics is also important in probability models with equally likely outcomes of the experiment; then the probability of an event is simply the number of ways the event can happen divided by the number of possible results of the experiment. Parts of the theory of statistics also rely heavily on combinatorics. But combinatorics do not crop up often in the core theory of inference presented in later chapters.

Another classic illustration of several concepts encountered so far is the "birthday problem:" suppose people are equally likely to be born on any given day of the year, so the probability that a given person was born on a given day is $\frac{1}{365}$ (so no leap year babies),[5] and birthdays are independent in a group of people (so no twins). How large does the group have to be so that the probability that at least two people share the same birthday is $\frac{1}{2}$ or more?

For a given N, the probability concepts involved in computing this probability are not difficult, but the event "at least two share a birthday" is a major hassle to deal with for even moderately large values of N: we have to consider that exactly two might share a birthday, exactly three, and so on. These events are disjoint so their probabilities can be summed to obtain the probability of at least two, but it quickly requires us to deal with a lot of individual probabilities.

However, the probability of the complement of this event is relatively simple: it is that no two individuals share a birthday. So if we have $N = 2$ people, there are 364 days on which the second person could have been born so that she would not have the same birthday as the first. There are 365 total days to choose from, so the probability that Person 2 does not share Person 1's birthday is $\frac{364}{365}$. Of course, directly finding the probability that they *do* share a birthday is no more difficult with $N = 2$: it is $\frac{1}{365}$ either way and far below the $\frac{1}{2}$ threshold we initially asked about. But continue to $N = 3$: if they all have a different birthday, Person 1 has 365 days to "choose from," and for each one of these days, Person 2 has 364 left open. The total number of ways to fill slots of the year that way is 365×364, and for each one of them, Person 3 has 363 days left open. That gives a total of $365 \times 364 \times 363$ ways to fill three distinct "slots" with three people. There are $365 \times 365 \times 365$ ways to allocate three people to days of the year, irrespective of whether two or more get the same day. So the probability that no one in the group of three shares a birthday with anyone else is $\frac{365 \times 364 \times 363}{365 \times 365 \times 365}$, and the probability that at least two share a birthday, is 1 minus this probability. A computer would tell us that although this is bigger than $\frac{1}{365}$, it is still a pretty small number: we're still not anywhere near $\frac{1}{2}$.

It is tedious and not much fun to keep iterating this in N until the probability hits $\frac{1}{2}$, but the $N = 3$ case illustrates the pattern: for any N, the probability that no two people share a birthday is $\frac{365 \times 364 \times \cdots \times 365 - (N-1)}{365^N} = \frac{365!}{365^N(365-N)!}$, and by the complement rule, the probability that at least two share a birthday is $p^* = 1 - \frac{365!}{365^N(365-N)!}$. This problem has been studied extensively and a variety of good approximations to this probability as a function of N are available, although they involve mathematics that is beyond our scope. The "easy way out" is to enter this expression as a formula in appropriate computer software and compute it for alternative values of N; a spreadsheet program does the job nicely, for example. It turns out that $p^* = 0.507$ when $N = 23$: a group only

---

[5] In reality, birthdays are not evenly spread throughout the year; in the United States, for instance, more babies are born in the summer than in other months.

needs to have about 23 people to ensure that there is at least a 50% chance that at least two share a birthday. With $N = 57$, $p^* = 0.99$.

4.2.2 Bayes's Theorem

Note that in the definition of $P(F|E)$, $\frac{P(F \cap E)}{P(E)}$, the numerator is simply $P(E \cap F)$, which is also the numerator of $P(E|F)$. $P(F|E)$ can be rearranged to yield $P(F|E)P(E) = P(E \cap F)$. This in turn can be used to re-express the probability of E given F as

$$P(E|F) = \frac{P(F|E)P(E)}{P(F)}, \tag{4.3}$$

an expression known as *Bayes's rule* or *Bayes's theorem*. In the context of Bayes's rule, the component $P(E)$ is the *prior* probability of E, and $P(E|F)$ is the *posterior* probability of E given F. Bayes's rule expresses how to update a belief about the probability of E in light of information about another event F, consistently with the definition of conditional probability.

For computational purposes, the denominator is more usefully expressed as

$$P(F) = P(F|E)P(E) + P(F|E^c)P(E^c), \tag{4.4}$$

an expression known as the *law of total probability*. This is often more useful than the compact $P(F)$, because the prior distribution of E (which has to be known for it to be updated anyway) gives the probabilities of E and E^c, and it may be relatively straightforward to assess conditional probabilities of F but not unconditional ones.

A classic application of Bayes's theorem is the "Monty Hall problem," so named because it is loosely based on the old TV game show *Let's Make a Deal*, in which Monty, the host, would let contestants see a prize behind one of three doors on stage and sometimes would ask if they wanted to forgo that prize and take whatever was behind another door – possibly a car (yay), but possibly a pile of old tires (boo). For some reason, contestants had to wear outlandish costumes which was not particularly related to the gambles, but seemed to add to the merriment.

The Monty Hall problem is a stylized version of this that works as follows: there are three doors, A, B, C. Behind two of the doors lies nothing, but behind one lies a fantastical prize. Monty tells you that the fantastical prize has been randomly placed so there is $\frac{1}{3}$ probability that it is behind any given door, and Monty knows which one. He lets you pick a door; say Door A is your choice. Monty is about to reveal what's behind Door A but then says, just for laughs, let's see what's behind Door B. He reveals that nothing is there. Monty then says, before he reveals the prize behind Door A, he'll give you one more chance to switch your choice: If you give him your Chapstick,[6] he'll let you switch to C. So the question in the Monty Hall problem is, should you switch?

Some further details on Monty's choice of Door B: If you initially guessed wrong with Door A, so the fantastical prize is behind Door B or C, Monty will not show you the door with the fantastical prize before asking if you want to switch, because then the game is obviously over, and he won't get any Chapstick that way. And if you initially guessed right, so doors B and C hide nothing, Monty can pick among them randomly – they are equivalent – and then offer you a choice to switch to whichever door he did not show you.

It would seem that you had a $\frac{1}{3}$ chance of guessing right the first time, and although Monty showed that nothing was behind Door B, Doors A and C are equally likely to be hiding the prize. So now you must have a $\frac{1}{2}$ chance of having guessed right. By that logic, there is nothing *wrong* with Door C, but it's not worth your Chapstick.

The question you want to know is, What is the probability Door A hides the prize, given that Monty showed you Door B? Let α, β, γ denote the event that the prize is behind Doors A, B, and C, respectively, and let A, B, C denote the event that Monty shows you each respective door. So the probability in question is $P(\alpha|B)$. This is a natural application of Bayes's theorem because we want to update beliefs about whether α occurred, in light of the fact that B did occur.

We know from Monty's initial description that $P(\alpha) = P(\beta) = P(\gamma) = \frac{1}{3}$; these are the priors. By Bayes's theorem, $P(\alpha|B) = \frac{P(B|\alpha)P(\alpha)}{P(B)}$. The numerator is simple: $P(\alpha)$ is known from the prior. $P(B|\alpha)$ is the probability Monty shows you Door B, given that A hides the prize; as we stipulated, Monty will randomize among B and C in this case. So $P(B|\alpha) = \frac{1}{2}$. As for the denominator, the law of total probability gives it as $P(B) = P(B|\alpha)P(\alpha) + P(B|\beta)P(\beta) + P(B|\gamma)P(\gamma)$. The first term is the same as the numerator. In the second term, $P(B|\beta)$ is the probability that Monty shows you Door B, given that Door B actually hides the prize. That probability is 0, as we specified. In the third term, $P(B|\gamma) = 1$: Monty cannot show Door C in this case because he does not show the door containing the prize. His only other choice is Door B, so he shows it for sure. And of course $P(\gamma) = \frac{1}{3}$. Putting this all together, $P(\alpha|B) = \frac{\frac{1}{2} \times \frac{1}{3}}{(\frac{1}{2} \times \frac{1}{3}) + (0 \times \frac{1}{3}) + (1 \times \frac{1}{3})} = \frac{1}{3}$. Given that $P(\beta|B) = 0$, and given that probabilities, conditional on any event, must sum to 1, $P(\gamma|B) = \frac{2}{3}$ (we could also find this directly through another application of Bayes's theorem). In fact Door C is twice as likely to be hiding the prize as Door A, given that Monty showed Door B, and it is probably worth parting with Chapstick for that.

The essential logic behind the Monty Hall problem is this: what you did in fact see, Door B, is more likely to have occurred if your initial guess was wrong than if your initial guess was right. If your initial guess was wrong, Monty's only choice is to show B, so you see B with certainty in that case. If your initial

---

[6] Assume the fantastical prize is better than partially used Chapstick.

guess was right, Monty randomizes between B and C, and you only see B with probability $\frac{1}{2}$.

The exact same logic is even easier to grasp in a simpler context. Suppose a friend tells you she has two quarters in her pocket, a double-headed quarter (i.e., heads on both sides) and a regular quarter. If she pulls one out, shows you one side only, and it's a head, would you guess that the coin is the double-headed coin or the regular one? You *always* see the head if it's the double-headed coin but only see it half the time if it's the regular coin. So your best guess is that it's the double-headed coin. What you actually saw, a head, is more likely in that case than if it's the regular coin.

Conditioning (in the sense of this section), conditional probability, and independence are some of the most important ideas that probability theory has to offer statistics and applied statistical research as well. It is most important for our purposes to understand conditioning and independence in terms of random variables (discussed next), but that itself is greatly aided by a solid understanding of conditional probabilities and independence in terms of events.

4.3 RANDOM VARIABLES

The discussion so far covers and illustrates fundamental concepts but not much of their direct relevance to social science. Concepts such as probability, conditioning, and independence may seem to have some hazy relevance to positive theory that could be interesting to social scientists, but how do we connect the descriptive summaries introduced in Chapter 2 with this material, or use it to illuminate uncertainty about a DGP? The crucial concept to make this connection is a random variable.

Formally, a *random variable* X is any real-valued function of the sample space of an experiment. This means it is a function that assigns a real number to each possible realization of the experiment.[7] We represent this with symbolic shorthand as $X : S \rightarrow \mathbb{R}$ because it is easier than writing "real valued function of the sample space" over and over. This notation means that X is a function, and it takes members of S and associates them with members of $\mathbb{R}$, the real number line. Depending on the result of the experiment, the random variable can take different values. Because the result of the experiment is random, the value taken by the random variable inherits that randomness. So, a random variable is often better thought of as a variable that has multiple values and a probability distribution over them.

The random variable (i.e., the function itself), is denoted by a capital Roman letter, such as X. The range of the random variable (i.e., the set of possible values it can assume), is denoted by the same letter in capital script, such as $\mathcal{X}$.

---

[7] "Real number" means any integer, fraction, or decimal number (repeating, finite, or otherwise); it excludes complex numbers involving $\sqrt{-1}$.

A specific value taken by the random variable in a given case (i.e., a particular member of its range) is denoted the same letter in lowercase italics, such as x. These are important distinctions because these are related but different concepts, and we will use them often. Their relationship is signified by the fact that we recognize them all as instances of the same letter, but their difference is signified by the fact that they are different versions of it.

A simple random variable results from a coin-flip experiment: an outcome of H is scored as a 1, and an outcome of T is scored as a 0. This meets all the requirements of a random variable. Of course, any experiment with two possible outcomes can be turned into a random variable in the same way: whether a given individual votes or abstains in an election – or engaged in any particular behavior, whether a country is at war in a given time period, whether an organization closes up shop, and so forth. To say that these outcomes in the latter cases are *random* variables assumes that the social processes behind them are subject to some uncertainty in determining their outcomes.

Even in a two-coin flip experiment, we can see how to build up slightly more complicated (although still pretty contrived) random variables. For example, if each flip is scored as 1 for H and 0 for T, one random variable is the sum of the results from each flip (call this X), and another random variable is the absolute value of the difference in the results from each flip (call this Y). Here $\mathcal{X} = \{0, 1, 2\}$ because either none, one, or both flips can be a 1; and $\mathcal{Y} = \{0, 1\}$ because the flips can either have the same result or a different result.

In this text, we refer to a random variable X as *discrete* if its range $\mathcal{X}$ has finitely many members *or* infinitely many that can be put into correspondence with positive integers. We refer to a random variable as *continuous* if its range has an uncountable infinity of members. Loosely, a continuous random variable is one with a range that involves a continuum of numbers or one that has at least two finite values such that there are infinitely many other values in between them. A range consisting of an interval of numbers, however wide or narrow, is the defining feature to keep in mind. A discrete random variable is some other kind: for any two finite values in the range, we can name and count all the values in between them.[8]

We will come to see that, from the standpoint of statistics, most of the variables' behavior we seek to explain in social science are considered to be random variables. This may be because we only observe a sample taken at random from a larger whole because we do not have a complete explanation of the variable's behavior or because random variation is an inherent part of the variable's behavior in principle.

---

[8] A more accurate definition of discrete and continuous random variables is given in Section 4.4.1. But for all the random variables we encounter in this text, this paragraph captures the difference adequately.

Armed with the concept of a random variable, and the distribution functions described here, the primitive experiment and sample space used to define that variable may be left in the background or not specified at all. Nevertheless, the properties of all probability statements we make, and the concepts of independence and conditioning, are fundamentally based on the material in the preceding sections.

4.4 DISTRIBUTION FUNCTIONS

The probabilistic properties of a random variable are summarized in its *probability distribution* or *distribution function*. Probability distributions are important in empirical applications of statistical inference and modeling because they serve as models of stochastic DGPs. We cover a number of distributions commonly used for modeling in Chapter 6, and starting with Chapter 7, we explore the statistical theory of how to recover attributes of a stochastic DGP from data. For now we consider the basic theory of probability distributions in somewhat general terms – a necessary building block for the apparatus we construct later in this book.

Earlier we saw that the probability measure $P(\cdot)$ in a probability model $(S, \mathcal{B}, P(\cdot))$ specifies the probability with which events in S occur. The random variable X maps these same members of S into the set of real numbers $\mathbb{R}$. Therefore, the probability measure *also* determines probability of occurrence for each number in $\mathbb{R}$, in the context of a given experiment. In a single coin flip with H scored as 1 and T scored as 0, for example, the probability measure specifies that the number 1 results with probability $\frac{1}{2}$, and the number 0 results with probability $\frac{1}{2}$. Every other number, given the definition of this random variable, occurs with probability 0; but more than that, they are impossible occurrences (there is a difference, as discussed subsequently).

The mapping of a random variable's values to the probabilities thereof is also a function. It is called the *probability distribution* of the random variable. In terms of the probability measure on S, the probability that X takes a particular value x is $\Pr[X = x | x \in \mathcal{X}] = P\{s \in S | X(s) = x\}$. This says that the probability X takes the specific value x is just the probability of drawing an element s of the sample space S for which X evaluated at that element s equals x. This does not tell us what the probability of $X = x$ is in a specific case; it just relates the probabilities over values of X to the underlying probability measure for the experiment on S. The only thing this definition conveys is that all information for the one is taken from the other. Probability distributions collect that information about $Pr[X = x]$ into a function.

We have already seen a dataset analogue to probability distributions in Chapter 2. A histogram on the density scale is a graphical representation of the probability distribution of a variable in the dataset, where the x values are grouped into discrete bins.

4.4.1 Cumulative Distribution Functions

For any random variable, discrete or continuous, its probability distribution can be represented with an important function called a *cumulative distribution function* or CDF. A CDF reports the probability that the random variable turns out to be less than some specified value $x \in \mathcal{X}$. This is a sum or accumulation of the probabilities of all values of X below this value. As x varies from the smallest possible value of X to the largest, the CDF accumulates probabilities by adding the incremental probability of new values of X to the previously accumulated values.

Formally, the CDF of a random variable is

$$F(x) = Pr[X \leq x]. \tag{4.5}$$

This is simply the probability that the random variable turns out to be less than or equal to the cutoff x. From the CDF, the probability that the random variable falls in any interval $a < X \leq b$ can be obtained as $F(b) - F(a)$. In other words, just as the CDF is obtained by summing the probabilities of individual observations below some threshold, the probability of an event between any thresholds can be obtained by differencing the CDF.

As a side note, for a continuous random variable, $F(x) = Pr[X \leq x] = Pr[X < x]$. This is because the probability of obtaining exactly x as the value of a continuous random variable is 0. The general point here is that including or excluding the end points of an interval in probability calculations for a continuous variable does not matter. But for a discrete random variable, $F(x) = Pr[X \leq x] > Pr[X < x]$, whenever x has positive probability.

Just as a probability measure $P(\cdot)$ must meet certain properties, the CDF of any random variable inherits certain properties as well. That is, a function F is a CDF for some random variable if and only if the following properties are met. Any CDF must satisfy these properties, and any function satisfying these properties is a CDF for some random variable.

First, as x gets more and more negative – unfathomably close to $-\infty$ – a CDF $F(x)$ gets closer and closer to 0. There cannot be an values of X at or below $-\infty$, so the cumulative probability at this point must be 0. CDFs are never negative. This property holds because $P(\emptyset) = 0$ in the primitive probability model from which a CDF is defined. Formally, this property reflects an important idea from calculus called a *limit*,[9] meaning that a number (x in this case) gets arbitrarily close to some threshold without hitting or crossing it. The idea of limits allow a simple expression of this property as $\lim_{x \to -\infty} F(x) = 0$.

Second and similarly, $\lim_{x \to \infty} F(x) = 1$ for any CDF. For any random variable X, as x gets closer and closer to ∞, all of the possible values of X are "used up." Just as $P(S) = 1$ for any probability model (the probability of the

---

[9] We use this idea again several times in this text, so it is useful to get the general gist of it.

entire sample space is 1), the maximum value of any CDF is 1. Because of this property, the probability that X exceeds any given value x is $1 - F(x)$.

Third, for two specific values $x, y \in \mathcal{X}$ such that $x > y$, $F(x) \geqslant F(y)$. A function with this property is *weakly increasing*. "Weakly increasing" means that as the value of x gets bigger, the CDF might get bigger or might stay the same but definitely does not get smaller. This last property results from the fact that no value of X has negative probability or density, which in turn follows from the property of the underlying probability measure that $P(E) \geq 0$ for all events E in the Borel field of S. Many commonly used CDFs in applied statistics are *strictly increasing*, so that as x gets bigger, the CDF also gets strictly bigger; it does not stay the same. A strictly increasing function is always weakly increasing but the converse is not true.

The fourth property of CDFs are stated in terms of another important concept from calculus called *continuity*. Consider a function $f(\cdot)$ and a point x in its domain. The value of the function at this point is just $f(x)$. Now think of a very small number, just a peppercorn[10] above 0, and call it ε. The function f *is continuous at x* if, for any such ε, there exists another number $\delta > 0$ such that if x changes by δ or less, the value of the function is within ε of $f(x)$. The idea is that the function can be as close to $f(x)$ as one can conceive, provided the domain value is close enough to x. A *continuous function* is one that is continuous at all of the points in its domain. The graph of a continuous function doesn't have any vertical "jumps."

Now a CDF might have some jumps. For a coin where tail $= 0$ and head $= 1$, the CDF is $F(x) = 0$ for any $x < 0$, $F(x) = \frac{1}{2}$ for any $0 \leq x < 1$, and $F(x) = 1$ for any $x \geq 1$. So at the point $x = 1$, the function F jumps from $\frac{1}{2}$ to 1 with no values in between. The point $x = 1$ is a point of discontinuity for this function. But if we approach the point of discontinuity from numbers above it, F doesn't jump. F only jumps if we approach the point of discontinuity from numbers below it. A function for which all jumps (if any) satisfy this property is *right-continuous*.[11]

That idea leads, finally, to the fourth property any CDF must satisfy: all CDFs are right-continuous. This terminology also more rigorously characterizes discrete and continuous random variables. A discrete random variable is one in which the CDF is right-continuous but not continuous; a continuous random variable is one with a continuous CDF.

4.4.2 Probability Mass and Density Functions

For a discrete random variable, we can imagine the construction of a CDF from summing up the probabilities (themselves defined in a probability measure P)

---

[10] Science has shown that a peppercorn is the smallest unit of measurement known to humankind.

[11] Left-continuity is defined analogously: all jumps occur by approaching points of discontinuity from above. A continuous function is both left- and right-continuous.

of all values of X up to (and including) a threshold x. From that CDF, we can in turn identify the probabilities of each specific value of X by taking differences of the CDF. If the M possible values of X are ordered from minimum to maximum as $x_1, x_2, \ldots, x_M$, the probability that $X = x_i$ is then denoted $f(x_i) = F(x_i) - F(x_{i-1})$.

This function f is called the *probability mass function* or PMF of the random variable X. For a given x, $f(x)$ is simply the probability that $X = x$. The PMF and CDF are intimately related; that is why we use different versions of the same letter (capital and lowercase) to denote each. The PMF is obtained by differencing the CDF at every point x, and given a PMF, the CDF can be reobtained by summing the values of the PMF below every point x.

Not just any function f can be a PMF. The CDF ensures that a PMF must satisfy certain properties (inherited for each from the probability measure P). Specifically, a PMF is a function

$$f : \mathcal{X} \to [0, 1] \text{ such that}$$

1. $0 \leqslant f(x) \leqslant 1$ for all $x \in \mathcal{X}$
2. $\sum_{x \in \mathcal{X}} f(x) = 1$
3. Given a subset of values of the random variable, $A \subset \mathcal{X}$, and letting a denote an arbitrary member of A, $\Pr[X \in A] = \sum_A f(a)$.

So the PMF maps members of the range of X into numbers in the interval from 0 to 1 inclusive – the "unit interval," denoted $[0, 1]$ with square brackets to indicate that the end points are included. Such intervals on the real number line are also called "closed sets." (Round brackets indicate that the end points are not included, e.g. $(0, 1)$. These are "open sets.")

The probability of any specific value x is between 0 and 1 (property 1), and the sum of the probabilities over the entire range of X is equal to 1 (property 2) – just as $P(S) = 1$ for the underlying probability measure. Furthermore, the probability that X lies in a specific range is the sum of the probabilities of individual members of that range (property 3). This property results because a single event in S can only give rise to one value of X by definition of a random variable, so the events that give rise to different values of X must be disjoint; therefore, the addition rule for disjoint events can be applied. *Any* function satisfying these requirements is the PMF for *some* random variable.

These definitions apply only to a discrete random variable. For a continuous random variable, taking differences of the CDF at every point x is not even conceivable because there is an uncountable infinity of them. If X lies in a continuum, what is the difference between the CDF at $X = x$, and the CDF at the next smallest value? There is no "next smallest value."

The conceptual fix requires a notion of a difference that applies over a continuum of values. This in turn invokes another important calculus idea we will use repeatedly, the idea of a *derivative*. The derivative of a function at a point x is usually understood as the "rate of change" or "instantaneous slope" of the function at that point. The idea of a slope is helpful here. For a linear function f, the slope is simply $f(x + 1) - f(x)$, and this is the same for all domain values x (that is what it means for a line to be straight). The key point is that a slope is a difference. A derivative generalizes this idea to consider what happens not just when x changes by one unit but when x changes by an infinitesimally small amount. The change in $f(x)$ when x changes by such a small amount is the derivative of f at x. This is denoted $\frac{df(x)}{dx}$ or sometimes $f'(x)$.

A function f whose derivative exists at all domain values x is *differentiable*. Note the root word "difference"; that is the important point. A derivative is a kind of difference in the value of a function. Only certain functions are differentiable; loosely speaking, their graphs look like smooth lines with no jumps, kinks, or sharp points.

Supposing a continuous CDF F is differentiable, its derivative $f(x) = \frac{dF(x)}{dx}$ is called the *probability density function* or PDF of the random variable X. For a discrete random variable, the PMF is obtained by differencing the CDF at every point; for a continuous random variable (that is differentiable), the PDF is obtained by differentiating the CDF.

To be precise, a PDF is a function[12] satisfying the following properties:

$$f : \mathcal{X} \to \mathbb{R}_+ \text{ such that}$$

1. $f(x) \geqslant 0$ for all $x \in \mathcal{X}$
2. $\int_{x \in \mathcal{X}} f(x)dx = 1$
3. For two numbers $a, b \in \mathcal{X}$, $\Pr[a \leqslant X \leqslant b] = \int_a^b f(x)dx$.

The ideas are similar to the case of the PMF, but there are some differences. Most important is that for a PMF, $f(x)$ represents probability itself; for a PDF, $f(x)$ represents density, not probability. Because a continuous variable has an uncountable infinity of values, they cannot all individually have probability greater than 0. If they did, the sum of all of their probabilities would be greater than 1, and we've already ruled that out.

We already encountered the concept of density in Chapter 2 when addressing histograms. There we defined density as the percentage per unit of the variable on the x-axis. Density means essentially the same thing here, with "percentage" replaced by "probability." The density at a given value of x is the change or difference in the probability that a variable lies below a given threshold brought about by increasing x by an infinitesimal amount. Starting at one value, say a, and accumulating these infinitesimal changes all the way up to some larger value b therefore gives the probability that the variable lies between a and b. Because these are infinitesimally small changes, there are infinitely many to accumulate, and that is what integrals do.

---

[12] The symbol $\mathbb{R}_+$ denotes nonnegative real numbers.

Put differently, density is the limiting value of the probability that X lies in an interval containing x as that interval gets infinitesimally small. Density highlights the distinction between "probability zero" and "impossible." For a continuous random variable, all the individual values in $\mathcal{X}$ have zero probability, but that does not make them impossible.

Properties 2 and 3 deal with the integral of a PDF over a range of possible values of X. An integral is essentially a sum over an uncountable infinity of elements (that is why its symbol is a stretched-out S, for sum); in that light these properties appear quite similar to the PMF case. Instead of summing over finite or countable values of elements, we are summing over uncountable infinities of elements. This is because the random variable's range is a continuum.

So just as the CDF of a discrete variable can be obtained from a PMF by summing the values of f up to a threshold x, the CDF of a continuous variable can be obtained from the PDF by integrating it up to x. In particular, for a continuous (and differentiable) random variable, the CDF is obtained from the PDF as follows:

$$\text{CDF} \quad F(x) = \int_{-\infty}^{x} f(z)dz. \qquad \text{PDF} \qquad (4.6)$$

This is simply the probability that the random variable turns out to be less than the value x. Note where x appears on each side of the $=$ sign. On the right, it is the upper limit of the integral. The notation z is used in $f(z)dz$ because x has already been taken as the specific value up to which the integral is evaluated. So we can't use that particular value again in this expression. We're still contemplating the same function $f(\cdot)$, just using a different symbol for an unspecified argument of that function.

In short, the PDF is the derivative of a CDF and the CDF is the integral of the PDF. This gives another way to think of the meaning of the density: it is the instantaneous change in the cumulative probability at any given value. Note, again, that densities need not be less than 1. The density function as a whole must integrate to 1. The CDF as a whole need not integrate to anything in particular.

An integral is a type of sum, but geometrically it is also the area under the function being integrated. In that light the CDF takes an interpretation as the "area under the curve" defined by the density or mass function (PDF or PMF). The total area under any PDF or PMF, from the minimum value of X to the maximum value, is defined to be 1. The area under the PDF when X is below some point x is some percentage less than 1: the probability that X is less than this value x. Finally, to get another handle on the concept of density, the area under the PDF when x increases by an infinitesimal amount is the density at x.

Random variables, PDFs/PMFs, and CDFs are the core formal concepts of probability distributions that we will work with from this point forward. The underlying probability space $(S, \mathcal{B}, P(\cdot))$ plays a background role. Concepts from the experiment underlying the random variable, especially independence of draws of random variables and conditioning, will continue to be important.

Probability distributions play a crucial role in theoretically oriented empirical social science. They are the instantiation of data generating processes when the process and outcomes under study are subject to uncertainty and randomness. There are several important classes of probability distributions that are used particularly often in applied quantitative research, some of which are covered in Chapter 6. For now, we can simply recognize that if most of the interesting variables in social science, from the standpoint of theory and a DGP, are random variables, the behavior of these variables is specified by a probability distribution – so that any theory of their behavior beyond the observed data at hand is a theory about a probability distribution.

4.5 MULTIPLE RANDOM VARIABLES

Statistical implementations of theories in political and social science typically explore relationships among multiple variables. A social theory is often interesting because it specifies the behavior of one random variable in terms of another or a relationship among two random variables. Multiple random variables are important in social science, because the probabilistic concepts for and statistical tools to explore relationships among random variables underpin some of the most commonly used quantitative techniques in social science. These are the probabilistic analogues of techniques for analyzing bivariate distributions from Chapter 2. Essentially every research project applying multiple regression in observational social science and policy research is dealing with multiple random variables. (Even if a variable is not "random," it can still be conceptualized as a [degenerate] random variable, and analyzed in relation to other random variables with the framework developed here.)

To fix ideas in a simple case, consider the experiment in which two fair coins are flipped. H is scored as 1 and T as 0 from each. One random variable in this experiment is the sum of the results from the coin flips. Another random variable in the same experiment is the absolute value of the difference in the results from the coin flips. Call these random variables X and Y. We can also refer to them collectively as a *multiple random variable* (X, Y). The multiple random variable maps the sample space S into the two-dimensional space of real numbers, $\mathbb{R}^2$ (read as "R-two").

The experiment has a result R_i on each flip i. These results determine the value taken by both X and Y in the experiment, because $X = R_1 + R_2$ and $Y = |R_1 - R_2|$. Since $R_i \in \{0, 1\}, i = 1, 2$, $\mathcal{X} = \{0, 1, 2\}$ and $\mathcal{Y} = \{0, 1\}$, as we noted earlier. X can be 0 if neither coin is head, 1 if one coin is a head, and 2 if both coins are heads. Y can be 0 if the coins have the same result, and 1 if the coins have different results. Clearly the definition of Y implies that it does not matter what the results of the flips are in determining the value of Y; it only matters whether they are different.

As always with these stylized examples, the purpose is not to learn about coin flips or to say that people are "like" coins in some way (although, in some respects, they arguably kind of are). Rather, it is to illustrate an idea in a case that is transparently simple, so that we can understand the identical idea in more complicated cases involving people or groups. As an example, an application with multiple random variables consists of observations of (*i*) vote choice, (*ii*) state of residence, (*iii*) household income, and (*iv*) state average income, for a collection of individuals. Gelman et al. [2004] used this information to explain a seemingly odd result that wealthy people are relatively likely to vote for the Democratic Party in American elections – odd inasmuch as Republicans are more commonly associated with public policy that is financially beneficial to the wealthy. They found that people in *wealthier states* tend to vote Democrat, but conditional on their state of residence, *wealthier people* tend to vote Republican.

4.6 MULTIVARIATE PROBABILITY DISTRIBUTIONS

Just as probability distributions specify the theoretical behavior of a random variable over its range, multivariate probability distributions specify the theoretical behavior of a multiple random variable over its range. For multiple random variables, there are three important kinds of distributions that contain different information about the behavior of the variable: the joint, marginal, and conditional distributions.

4.6.1 Joint Distributions

The full specification of the behavior two random variables X and Y is the *joint distribution of X and Y*. All information about the behavior of each random variable individually, and about their joint behavior and relationships or associations among them, is specified in the joint distribution. These are analogous to the multivariate distributions encountered in the material on descriptive statistics; the difference is that here we are dealing with a DGP, not just a distribution of observed data. Just as the probability mass function of a discrete random variable specifies the probability that the random variable equals any particular value, the joint PMF of a discrete multiple random variable specifies the probability that components of the random variable equal any particular value.

Take X and Y as defined from the coin-flip experiment. We know how the results of the experiment map into values of X and Y (from their definitions),

TABLE 4.1. *Joint Distribution for X, Y*

		X		
		0	1	2
Y	0	0.25	0	0.25
	1	0	0.5	0

and we know the probability of each result of the experiment (by simple computations). We can combine this information to determine the probability of any particular X, Y combination. These probabilities, which comprise the joint distribution of X and Y, are contained in Table 4.1. Each cell inside the table contains the probability of a specific X, Y combination. For example, the combination ($X = 0, Y = 0$) occurs with probability 0.25 in this experiment. This joint event occurs when both coins show tails – so their sum is 0, and their difference is 0 (they have the same result). But the combination ($X = 0, Y = 1$) has probability 0. If the sum (X) is 0, the flips obviously had the same result, so $Y = 1$ (which only occurs when they are different) is impossible.

The numbers in the table define a joint PMF for X and Y. That PMF as a whole (i.e., the entire function or collection of numbers) is denoted $f(X, Y)$, and an individual cell entry is denoted $f(x, y)$. Or the joint PMF may be denoted $f_{X,Y}(x, y)$. For discrete random variables X and Y, $f(x, y)$ gives $\Pr(X = x, Y = y)$, the joint probability of x, y. For continuous random variables, $f(x, y)$ gives the joint density of x, y.

The joint PDF or PMF shows, for a DGP, the same sort of information that a crosstab shows for a multivariate distribution of data.

Recall that for a PMF $f(X)$, the sum over all possible experiment results is 1. The same is true for a joint PMF $f_{X,Y}(x, y)$, as is apparent in Table 4.1 because $0.25 + 0.5 + 0.25 = 1$. Something has to happen in the experiment.

In this example, we started with the primitive experiment and sample space and definitions of the random variables in terms of the sample space. These allowed us to work out the joint PMF from the basic probability model. In applications, we do not explicitly define the experiment or sample space. We take individual vote choice, group behavior, state policy choice, and so forth as a random variable and work directly with it, rather than attempting to postulate an underlying experiment or sample space.

As for univariate random variables, the joint PDF or PMF can be reexpressed as a *joint CDF*. This is defined as

$$F(x, y) = \Pr[X \leq x, Y \leq y]$$
$$= \sum_{x_i \leq x} \sum_{y_i \leq y} f(x_i, y_i) \tag{4.7}$$

for discrete random variables. The joint CDF reflects the event that both $X \leq x$ and $Y \leq y$ (i.e., an intersection). Similarly, for continuous random variables,

$$F(x, y) = \int_{Y \leq y} \int_{X \leq x} f(s, t) ds dt. \tag{4.8}$$

This is the first appearance of a "double sum" or "double integral" in this book. Conceptually it is not so much different from the sigma or integral notation we have seen before. It occurs when two variables both vary. As written here, the "inner integral" sums over all X values for a given, single y. There is one solution to the "inner integral" for every value of Y. Then the "outer integral" sums up all these solutions, for all the possible Y values. An important basic result in multivariate calculus says that the order of integration can be changed in multiple integrals for essentially all of the functions one encounters in real life (including all the ones in this book). An integral is just a sum over an uncountable infinity of values, and as with any sum, the order in which terms are added up does not affect the result. So a joint CDF can just as well be written $\int_{X \leq x} \int_{Y \leq y} f(s, t) dt ds$.

It bears repeating that all information about the behavior of each random variable individually, and about their joint behavior and relationships or associations among them, is specified in the joint distribution. This is an important fact that it is easy to slip past. When we want to know how two random variables behave together, there is literally no more information than is available in their joint distribution. When we try to identify relationships among random variables, we are trying to identify an aspect of their joint distribution.

4.6.2 Marginal Distributions

Given a multiple random variable, each component random variable can be studied as a random variable in its own right. Similarly, in descriptive statistics, given a bivariate distribution, we could construct a histogram for any one variable in that distribution to focus on it specifically. The behavior of X abstracting away from the behavior of Y is specified by the *marginal distribution of X*. The marginal distribution specifies how X behaves over all of its values as if it were a single random variable, paying no attention to the behavior of Y. It is denoted $f(X)$ or $f_X(x)$.

The marginal $f_X(x)$ is obtained by summing over the y values for each specific value $X = x$. That is, the marginal distribution is defined as $f_X(x) = \sum_{y \in y} f_{X,Y}(x, y)$ for a discrete r.v. Analogously, for a continuous r.v., the marginal distribution is $f_X(x) = \int_y f_{X,Y}(x, y) dy$.

In concrete terms, consider again X and Y as defined from the two-coin flip experiment. The marginal distribution for X is obtained by summing up the entries vertically in each column. This procedure executes the "summing over y value" that the definition requires. That results in three numbers, 0.25, 0.5, and 0.25. That is the marginal distribution of X and specifies the probability that the sum of the flips equals 0, 1, and 2, respectively. Of course, this matches the probability distribution over X one would construct "from the ground up" in this experiment without reference to Y.

Note that the sum of $f_X(x)$ over all values in $\mathcal{X}$ is 1. This is because a marginal distribution is a distribution in its own right and follows all the usual rules of a distribution. Some value of X has to occur.

There is also a marginal distribution for Y. To sum over x values for a given y, add the numbers (all three of them) horizontally across a given row of the table. This results in two numbers, 0.5 and 0.5. That is the marginal distribution of Y, and specifies the probability that the absolute value of the difference in flips equals 0 and 1. The probability that the coins have the same result is 0.5 and that they have a different result is 0.5.

So the marginals are defined in terms of the joint. A joint distribution implies a unique collection of marginal distributions. But given a collection of marginal distributions, it is generally not possible to reconstruct an unambiguous or unique joint distribution. (This means it is possible sometimes but not all the time, i.e., not in general.) Going from marginals to joint is the problem of *ecological inference*, a long-standing issue in social science methodology. Consider a joint distribution in a single congressional district over the random variables (*i*) votes for Republican, Democratic, and third-party candidates in a race for Congress and (*ii*) population counts of Black, White, and "Other" citizens. An election typically gives the marginal distribution over the first random variable. Census information gives the marginal distribution over the second random variable. What is the joint distribution of these random variables? This is an important substantive concern because it addresses such questions as: Who are the African American voters at the district level supporting? How does this vary across districts with different levels of employment, income, and racial integration? It is "ecological" inference in the sense that aggregate information (in the marginal distributions) is used to fill in more refined information (in the joint distribution). Because it is impossible to guarantee recovery of a unique (and correct) joint distribution from an arbitrary collection of marginal distributions, the problem of ecological inference cannot be fully solved exactly. However, methodologists have devoted a lot of effort over the years to making sensible and valid statements about the joint distribution given the marginals. The most recent flurry of activity has occurred since the mid-1990s (King [1997], Freedman [2010a], Cho and Gaines [2004], Herron and Shotts [2004], King et al. [2004]).

4.6.3 Conditional Distributions

The marginal distribution of X specifies the behavior of X when Y is "averaged" over all its possible values. But the resulting distribution need not give a good picture of the behavior of X for any specific or individual value of Y; its an aggregation or average over many of them.

It is also possible to specify the behavior of X for particular values of Y. This distribution, called the *conditional distribution of X given Y*, is (like the marginals) also defined from the joint distribution. It is denoted $f(X|Y = y)$ or $f_{X|Y}(x|y)$. It specifies the probability that $X = x$ occurs, given that $Y = y$.

Formally, the conditional distribution of X at $Y = y$ is $f_{X|Y}(x|y) = \frac{f_{X,Y}(x,y)}{f_Y(y)}$. The conditional distribution is the joint distribution evaluated at (x, y) divided by the marginal distribution of Y evaluated at y. This looks a lot like the definition of conditional probability in terms of events; the logic is very much the same. We are taking as given the event that $Y = y$ occurs, and evaluating the probability of various values of X given that benchmark.

In the running example of X and Y defined from the coin-flips, consider $f_{X|Y}(0|0)$, the probability that $X = 0$ given that $Y = 0$. The joint probability that both X and Y are 0 is 0.25 (we determined this earlier). And the marginal probability that $Y = 0$ is 0.5 (we determined this earlier as well). So the definition of the conditional distribution asserts that $f_{X|Y}(0|0) = \frac{0.25}{0.5} = 0.5$. Given that the results of the coin flip are the same (i.e., $Y = 0$), either they can both be tails or both be heads. These are equally likely. Likewise, $f_{X|Y}(1|0) = 0$ and $f_{X|Y}(2|0) = 0.5$.

If we change the value of the conditioning variable in this example, X will be distributed differently over its possible values. Applying the definition, $f_{X|Y}(0|1) = 0$, $f_{X|Y}(1|1) = 1$, and $f_{X|Y}(2|1) = 0$. If the coin flips have different results so $Y = 1$, it must be that one flip was a head and one a tail, so $X = 1$. However, it need not always be the case that changing the conditioning variable changes the behavior of a conditional distribution. If it does not, X and Y are independent random variables, an important idea we cover subsequently.

Note that the sum of the conditional distribution of X given $Y = 0$ over all values in $\mathcal{X}$ is 1, i.e., $f_{X|Y}(0|0) + f_{X|Y}(1|0) + f_{X|Y}(2|0) = 1$. This will always happen for a given value of the conditioning variable. A conditional distribution is always a well-defined distribution in its own right. Given that $Y = 0$, some X value has to occur.

However, it is not the case that holding fixed a value of X and summing over all possible values of the conditioning variable Y leads to any result in particular. That is, for all $y \in \mathcal{Y}$, $\sum_{x \in \mathcal{X}} f_{X|Y}(x|y) = 1$. It is not necessarily true (and not generally true) that for all $x \in \mathcal{X}$, $\sum_{y \in \mathcal{Y}} f_{X|Y}(x|y) = 1$. Concretely, if we fix $X = 0$ and add $f_{X|Y}(0|0) + f_{X|Y}(0|1)$, we do not end up with 1.

The conditional distribution turns out to be one of the more important objects that probability theory bequeaths to positive social science. Most statistical modeling in social science explores how some aspect of a conditional distribution varies as a function of conditioning variables. Regression modeling does this, for example: it specifies that the mean of a variable's conditional distribution (i.e., its conditional mean; see Chapter 5) as a particular function of some other variables. So when social scientists execute statistical models, they are attempting to recover some parts of the conditional distribution in the DGP.

Bayes's Theorem for Distributions

After introducing conditional probability for events above in Section 4.2, we stated Bayes's theorem, a result that combines prior information and data to form a posterior probability distribution over some event. There is also a version of Bayes's theorem for distributions, derived in a similar way:

$$f_{Y|X}(y|x) = \frac{f_{X|Y}(x|y)\, f_Y(y)}{f_X(x)}. \tag{4.9}$$

The left-hand side is the *posterior distribution* of Y given X and the marginal $f_Y(y)$ is the *prior distribution*. The distribution $f_{X|Y}(x|y)$ in the numerator is the same conditional distribution we have already seen; it is sometimes called the *likelihood*.[13] The marginal of X in the denominator, $f_X(x)$, is the *data distribution*.

Bayes's theorem indicates how to combine starting information about the distribution of Y (the prior) with information about the likelihood of actual observed data, to arrive at a new distribution of Y that is updated in light of what actually occurred (the posterior).

The denominator can be reexpressed as $f_X(x) = \sum_{\tilde{y} \in \mathcal{Y}} f_{X|Y}(x|\tilde{y}) f_Y(\tilde{y})$ in a distributional version of the law of total probability. Here $\tilde{y}$ represents an arbitrary value of Y and covers all possible values of Y that might occur, not just the particular value $Y = y$ in the numerator or the posterior.

Without having introduced parametric families of probability distributions (see Chapter 6), we cannot show the operation of Bayes's theorem in any technical depth. But a simple example, although contrived, shows the mechanics and the concept.

Suppose there are two coins in a box. They are the same size and weight, but one has a head on both sides, whereas the other is an ordinary coin that, when flipped, shows head and tail with probability $\frac{1}{2}$ each. The box is shaken, and a coin is drawn out blindly and flipped. What is the probability that each type of coin was pulled out of the box, if the flip is a head?

Let $Y = 1$ denote that the coin is double headed and $Y = 0$ denote that it is the ordinary coin; let $X = 1$ denote that the flipped coin shows a head and $X = 0$ that it shows a tail. Then the question can be reexpressed as, what is $f_{Y|X}(y|1)$?

The prior is $f_Y(1) = f_Y(0) = \frac{1}{2}$: each coin has an equal chance of being drawn out of the box for a flip. For $Y = 1$, the likelihood of $X = 1$ is $f_{X|Y}(1|1) = 1$: for a double-headed coin ($Y = 1$ as the conditioning event), the coin shows head ($X = 1$) with certainty. For $Y = 0$, the likelihood of $X = 1$ is simply $f_{X|Y}(1|0) = \frac{1}{2}$. Combining these likelihoods with the prior on Y gives the data distribution for $X = 1$: $f_X(1) = \frac{1}{2} \times 1 + \frac{1}{2} \times \frac{1}{2} = \frac{3}{4}$.

---

[13] Come back to this after likelihood functions are introduced in Chapter 9: they are the same as this likelihood but, with greater context, will provide a new understanding of what Bayes's theorem does in estimation.

Combining this information according to Bayes's theorem gives the posterior distribution for Y as $f_{Y|X}(1|1) = \frac{2}{3}$ and $f_{Y|X}(0|1) = \frac{1}{3}$. The observed data $x = 1$ is more likely to occur if $Y = 1$ than if $Y = 0$, so the posterior places greater chance on $Y = 1$ than the prior does.

4.6.4 Independence of Random Variables

In the running example of the two-coin-flip experiment, the conditional distribution of $X|Y$ is different for $Y = 0$ and $Y = 1$. That is what the concept of a relationship means for multiple random variables: the (probabilistic) behavior of one depends on the value of the other. This relationship reflects *stochastic dependence* between these random variables. If there is no stochastic dependence or relationship at all, then the conditional distribution of X would be exactly the same, irrespective of the value of Y. This is a situation of *stochastic independence* or just *independence* for short.

Formally, two random variables X and Y are *independent* if and only if $f_{X,Y}(x, y) = f_X(x) f_Y(y)$, that is, if their joint distribution is the product of their marginal distributions. This fact is reminiscent of the multiplication rule for independent events, and the logic is the same. Independence of X and Y is often written formally as $X \perp Y$.

Note that by slightly rearranging the definition of independence, we can relate it to the conditional distribution. Specifically, independence implies $f_X(x) = \frac{f_{X,Y}(x,y)}{f_Y(y)}$, but the right-hand side is also the definition of $f_{X|Y}(x|y)$, the conditional distribution of X given Y. So independence of X and Y implies that $f_{X|Y}(x|y) = f_X(x)$, so the conditional distribution is simply the same as the marginal. This says that the distribution of X is not a function of the value of Y; that's what independence means for random variables. Independence also gives a special case of Bayes's theorem: the posterior distribution is the same as the prior if and only if the random variables are independent.

Independence is an important concept not only for modeling relationships but in sampling as well. If N individuals, unknown to each other, are called on the phone and asked whether they approve of how the U.S. president is handling his job, it is hard to see how the answer given by one could affect the answer given by any others. In such a case, the N yesses/nos in the sample are independent. If respondent i answers "yes" with probability p_i, then the probability of observing a "yes" from all individuals is simply $p_1 \times p_2 \times p_3 \times \cdots \times p_N \equiv \prod_{i=1}^{N} p_i$. The notation $\prod_{i=1}^{N}$ denotes a *product series*; it works for multiplication the same way that $\sum_{i=1}^{N}$ works for addition.

More generally, if $y_i = 1$ or 0 denotes individual i's answer to the question, independence implies that the probability of any entire sample can be written as $\prod_{i=1}^{N} p_i^{y_i} (1 - p_i)^{1-y_i}$. In this expression p_i the the probability that person i answers $y_i = 1$ and $1 - p_i$ is the probability that i answers $y_i = 0$. If i answers $y_i = 1$, then person i's term in the product series is simply p_i. In this case, the superscript $1 - y_i = 0$, and anything raised to the 0th power is 1, so $(1 - p_i)^{1-y_i} = 1$ and this has no effect on the whole product. Likewise, if person i answers $y_i = 0$, then person i's term in the whole product series is $(1 - p_i)$, because p_i is raised to the 0th power in this case. We use this notation in later chapters on sampling and estimation (Chapters 7 and 9), but it is useful to introduce here as an illustration of independence, as well as an introduction of what we actually do with this concept in statistical inference.

4.7 CONCLUSION

The central concepts introduced in this chapter are probability, random variable, distribution function, conditioning, and independence. We use these concepts to instantiate the types of uncertainty discussed in Chapter 3 in more precise terms. Specifically, distribution functions serve as models for DGPs. If we are interested in a population of fixed but unknown values and are able to observe specific elements of that population only probabilistically – as might occur in public opinion research – then the DGP reflects that stochastic connection between sample and population. This is sampling uncertainty. It is also possible that the object of theoretical interest is itself stochastic, and the DGP is a distribution function to model all of its possible manifestations. This is fundamental uncertainty. Either way, the contents of any observable sample are realizations of random variables.

Distribution functions of random variables can be summarized to capture their typical behavior, variability, and relationships among random variables in a joint distribution – just as distributions of observed data can be summarized (Chapter 2). These facets of distribution functions are determined by quantities called *parameters*. Typically, as explained in more detail later, substantive theoretical statements that pertain to DGPs are expressed in terms of these parameters. The next chapter defines and explores the properties of some of these key summaries of DGPs. This will sharpen our understanding of the kinds of theoretical statements we often wish to make about DGPs, and then this is fleshed out in greater detail with more specific models of DGPs in the subsequent chapter.

PROBLEMS

1. Some facts about conditional probability:
   (a) Given some event A, show that $P(\cdot|A)$ is a probability measure, provided that $P(\cdot)$ is a probability measure and $P(A) > 0$. NOTE. The notation "$\cdot$" refers to any possible argument that might appear in place of that symbol in the function. So $P(\cdot)$ is the probability of an event, which is written into that function in place of $\cdot$.
   (b) Show that $P(A|\cdot)$ is not necessarily a probability measure, even if every possible conditioning event to fill in for "$\cdot$" has positive probability and $P(\cdot)$ is a probability measure. (HINT. There is a counterexample in one of the other problems.)

2. A (continuous) uniform $[0, 1]$ random variable has the PDF $f(x) = 1$ for $x \in [0, 1]$ and $f(x) = 0$ otherwise. What is the uniform density conditional on $x \le \frac{1}{2}$? How do you know this conditional density is a PDF?

3. The exponential distribution has the PDF $f(x) = \lambda e^{-\lambda x}$ for $x \ge 0$ and $f(x) = 0$ otherwise, where λ is a fixed parameter. Derive the CDF and show your steps.

4. A discrete random variable follows a Poisson distribution with parameter λ if its PMF is $f(x) = \frac{e^{-\lambda} \lambda^x}{x!}$ for integers $x \ge 0$, and $f(x) = 0$ otherwise. It can be shown by a Taylor series expansion that for any number y, $e^y = \sum_{i=0}^{\infty} \frac{y^i}{i!}$. Show that the Poisson PMF sums to 1.

5. An organization consists of N information processing units (e.g., offices or divisions) that make recommendations about whether to adopt a single project (i.e., they all deal with the same project). Each takes independent reading of project benefits. Unit i judges the project to be "worth it" with probability F_i.

   (a) The organization has a "parallel structure" if only one of the units must judge the project worthwhile for it to be adopted by the organization as a whole (think of a job candidate who interviews at several universities). What is the probability that the organization adopts the project in a parallel system?

   (b) The organization has a "serial structure" if all of the units must judge the project worthwhile for it to be adopted by the organization as a whole (think of a tenure process within a university from department to dean to ad hoc committee to higher-ups). What is the probability that the organization adopts the project in a serial system? Comment on the differences and similarities between the systems.

6. Suppose a standardized test contains 20 questions with four possible answers each. Assume the student guesses on each question by randomly picking an answer.

   (a) What is the probability that a student gets at least 10 questions correct, given that he is guessing?

   (b) What is the probability that a student gets exactly 10 questions correct, given that he is guessing?

   (c) What is the probability that a student gets the first 10 questions correct and the next 10 questions incorrect, given that he is guessing?

   (d) What number of questions correct has the greatest probability of occurring if the student is guessing (i.e., what is the mode)?

   (e) If a student actually scores the number correct identified in the previous part, should you infer he is guessing?

5

Expectation and Moments: Summaries of Data-Generating Processes

As datasets can be usefully summarized to compress much information into small pieces (Chapter 2), probability distributions can be as well. We review some of these summaries in this chapter. These summaries of probability distributions revolve around various kinds of *expectations* of the behavior of a random variable. These expectations are important because they typically relate to the specific aspects of stochastic data-generating processes (DGPs), called *parameters*, that social scientists connect to substantive theory and attempt to uncover in empirical work. In one sense, the material in this chapter helps to explain why that is. In addition, this chapter also provides some basic familiarity with these important formal constructs that we use repeatedly in subsequent material.

One of the most important points of this chapter is to define the *regression function*, or expected value of Y as a function of X, as it exists in a DGP specified as a joint distribution function. We then proceed to establish some important properties about this DGP regression that help to motivate and justify the widespread interest in this function in empirical social science. Later chapters spend a great deal of time developing common models for this regression (and techniques to make inferences about the DGP regression from regression models fit to sample data), so it is important to get a handle on why anyone should care about it.

5.1 EXPECTATION IN UNIVARIATE DISTRIBUTIONS

The *expected value* or *expectation* of a discrete random variable is defined as

$$E(X) = \sum_{x \in \mathcal{X}} x f(x) \tag{5.1}$$

where $f(x)$ is its mass function. All three senses of "x" appear: the random variable itself (X), a placeholder for particular values of it (x), and the set of all possible values ($\mathcal{X}$). This definition implies a straightforward operation: each possible value of the random variable is multiplied or weighted by its probability, and those weighted values are all summed. The greater the probability of a single value of X, the more weight it has and the more important it is in determining the expectation of X.

The *expected value* or *expectation* of a continuous random variable is defined as

$$E(X) = \int_{x \in \mathcal{X}} x f(x) dx, \tag{5.2}$$

where $f(x)$ is its density function. This is essentially the same idea as the expectation of a discrete random variable, but we weight by the density and have to sum over a continuum. So we need an integral instead of a sum of countable elements. For a continuous random variable, we can also write $E(X) = \int_{x \in \mathcal{X}} x dF(x)$: we replace $f(x)dx$ with $dF(x)$, where $F(x)$ is the CDF. These are equivalent because $f(x) = \frac{dF(x)}{dx}$ – that is, the PDF is the derivative of the CDF – so rearranging we can write $dF(x) = f(x)dx$. The only reason for this is that $dF(x)$ takes less time to write or type.

The expectation of a random variable is sometimes called the expected value (or expectation or mean) of a random variable, and sometimes the expected value of a probability distribution. These mean the same thing because a random variable is specified in terms of its probability distribution. $E(X)$ is also called the mean of the distribution (or the random variable), but unlike the sample mean computed from a set of numbers, it is never denoted $\overline{X}$. A small point: in $E(X)$, the X is capitalized. It is the expected value of the random variable itself. $E(x)$ for any x also makes sense but is not very interesting. It is just the expected value of a single, fixed number, which is that number. For example, $E(29) = 29$. The specific values $x \in \mathcal{X}$ are weighted and used to define the expectation of X because what we want is the expectation of the random variable as a whole.

Perhaps surprisingly, there are probability distributions for which the expected value does not exist. Or, more precisely, it is not a finite number. These are not exactly daily encounters applied research, but they are interesting in probing the meaning of these definitions (and they can pop up in weird places). An example is a distribution called the Cauchy, which is useful in probability theory because it has strange properties. Its probability density function (PDF) is symmetric around 0 and bell-shaped, and the "center" of the graph of its PDF is clearly at 0, so it looks like it should have an expected value of 0. But its tails are thick, so the weight placed by its PDF on very large values of X does not decline quickly. As a result, integrating $xf(x)$ over its whole domain involves very large numbers with a large enough weight to make them "matter" in computing the integral, no matter how large they are. So the expected value is not defined.

However, this distribution does have a *median*, that is, a point $M(X)$ such that $\int_{-\infty}^{M(X)} f(x)dx \geq \frac{1}{2}$ and $\int_{M(X)}^{\infty} f(x)dx \geq \frac{1}{2}$. A median for a probability distribution expresses a similar concept as a median of a distribution of data: at least half the "possible observations" are above and at least half are below.

5.1.1 Properties of Expectation

There are several ways to think about what an expectation "means" or what it is intuitively, both analogous to ideas introduced in Chapter 2. First, an expected value is the "center of mass" in a distribution. Think of the distribution's graph as a two-dimensional object, like a histogram but where the x values are not placed into bins; they are all represented individually with their own mass or density. You can balance this graph on a pencil by placing the pencil at $E(X)$. There may only be a small range of values of X on one side of the pencil, but if they collectively have high probability, they will balance a larger range on the other side.

Second, the expected value of a random variable is in a specific sense the best predictor of the value it will take in any given draw from the DGP. That is, consider X and a single number to predict the value of X drawn in a single attempt. Suppose a predictor is "good" if it produces a small value for the square of the difference between the actual draw and the predictor itself. When the prediction is wrong by a lot, this scoring system applies a penalty that is proportionately greater than when it is wrong by a little – penalties for mistakes grow faster than the size of the mistake measured in absolute value difference (formally, the "loss function" by which "penalties" are assessed is quadratic). The mean $E(X)$ is exactly that predictor that minimizes the expected value of this squared-distance penalty.

That is, $E(X - d)^2 \geq E(X - E(X))^2$ for all predictors $d \in \mathbb{R}$ that are real numbers. More succinctly, the mean minimizes the mean square error (MSE) of a random variable. That's one way to think about what the mean *is*: it is exactly the prediction that is best in the sense of MSE. It is the best predictor in this sense even if it is wrong about the value of X with probability 1, as it must be if X is a continuous random variable.

The expectation $E(\cdot)$ has some simple properties that are used several times in future chapters. (This notation just means that we can think of the expectation as a function itself, not tied to a specific random variable X.) $E(\cdot)$ is a "linear operator," which is a way of saying that any linear operation on the random variable itself results in that same linear operation on its mean. "Linear operation" connotes adding or multiplying by constants.

So if we take a random variable X and apply a linear transformation to make it $Y = a + bX$, then $E(Y) = E(a + bX) = a + bE(X)$. The first equality follows from the definition of Y and the second is because E is a linear operator.

TABLE 5.1. *Distributions of Three Random Variables*

	$X_i = x$									
	1	2	3	4	5	6	7	8	9	10
X_1	0.2	0.3	0.3	0.2	0	0	0	0	0	0
X_2	0	0	0.2	0	0.3	0	0.3	0	0.2	0
X_3	0	0	0	0	0	0	0	0.4	0.2	0.4

Similarly, given two random variables X_1 and X_2, $E(X_1 + X_2) = E(X_1) + E(X_2)$. This is an incredibly important property of $E(X)$ that we use several times to establish some fundamental results in later chapters. The linearity of E (which is established formally in Section 5.2) occurs because it is defined as a sum or integral. Performing an operation on every term of a sum is the same as waiting until the sum is obtained and then performing that operation on the whole sum itself. Linearity depends on no properties of the random variables themselves or their joint distribution (e.g., they do not have to be independent).

Furthermore, $E(X)$ has to lie in the interior of $\mathcal{X}$. Thus, if $x_m = \min\{\mathcal{X}\}$ is the smallest value of X that has strictly positive mass or density under the distribution of X, and $x_M = \max\{\mathcal{X}\}$ is the largest value of X that has strictly positive mass or density under the distribution of X,[1] then $x_m \leq E(X) \leq x_M$. This makes a certain degree of sense. Otherwise, however, there is clearly no general restriction on where in $\mathcal{X}$ the mean $E(X)$ must lie. It need not be near the midpoint or "center" of $\mathcal{X}$, for example.

To take a simple example, consider three random variables X_1, X_2, and X_3. They all range $\mathcal{X}_i$ over integers 1 to 10 and are distributed as in Table 5.1. Note that this table is not a joint distribution over X_1, X_2, and X_3. This is easy to tell because the sum of all the numbers in the table is three. Rather, the table depicts three separate distributions, one in each row.

It is easy to compute $E(X_i)$ by direct computation, and $E(X_1) = (1)(0.2) + (2)(0.3) + (3)(0.3) + (4)(0.2) = 0.2 + 0.6 + 0.9 + 0.8 = 2.5$, $E(X_2) = 0.6 + 1.5 + 2.1 + 1.8 = 6$, and $E(X_3) = 9$.

But note also that $X_2 = 1 + 2X_1$. This means we can obtain $E(X_2)$ more simply as $E(X_2) = E(1 + 2X_1) = E(1) + E(2X_1) = 1 + 2E(X_1) = 6$, where all steps follow because of linearity.

Likewise, we can define another random variable $X_1 + X_3$. Its distribution is slightly more complicated than simply adding $f_{X_1}(x) + f_{X_2}(x)$ for all values of x (this would result in a PMF for the new random variable that sums to 2). But if all we want to know is the mean of the new random variable, we

---

[1] Actually the minimum and maximum values may not be members of the range, e.g., if the distribution of a continuous random variable puts positive density on all real numbers. This is a minor issue because then we use $x_I = \inf\{\mathcal{X}\}$ (the infimum) and $x_S = \sup\{\mathcal{X}\}$ (the supremum) instead of x_m and x_M.

TABLE 5.2. *Distribution of a Random Variable*

	$X_i = x$									
	1	2	3	4	5	6	7	8	9	10
X_1	0.2	0.3	0.3	0.2	0	0	0	0	0	0

can bypass such complications because $E(X_1 + X_3) = E(X_1) + E(X_3) = 11.5$. How X_1 and X_3 are related has no bearing on this.

Finally, note where the values of $E(X_i)$ fall relative to the strictly positive (nonzero) entries in each distribution.

5.1.2 Variance

Formally, the *variance* of a random variable (or a probability distribution) is defined as

$$Var(X) = E(X - E(X))^2, \tag{5.3}$$

where $E(X)$ is the expected value of the same random variable. The $E(\cdot)$ on the whole expression on the right-hand side works just as the expectations defined in Equations 5.1 and 5.2. So it is a sum for a discrete random variable and an integral for a continuous one.

Thus the mean itself is involved in computing the variance. The variance is the expected squared departure of a random variable from the mean. The variance is a special case of the mean squared error of a guess g about X, when $g = E(X)$.

In the earlier simple example of X_1, the distribution is given in Table 5.2. The variance is $Var(X_1) = (0.2)(1 - 2.5)^2 + (0.3)(2 - 2.5)^2 + (0.3)(3 - 2.5)^2 + (0.2)(4 - 2.5)^2 = (0.2)(2.25) + (0.3)(0.25) + (0.3)(0.25) + (0.2)(2.25)$, or 1.05.

An equivalent, and often clearer and more useful, version of variance is

$$Var(X) = E(X^2) - E(X)^2. \tag{5.4}$$

This is the expectation of the square minus the square of the expectation. These are not the same quantity. The function applied to the square of a variable is not the same as the square of the function applied to the variable. So this alternative definition requires one to know the expected value of the square of the random variable, as well as its expected value.

$Var(X)$ is always a nonnegative number. It is only 0 in case the distribution is degenerate, that is, places probability 1 on a single value. So for a fixed number, the variance is 0; e.g., $Var(29) = 0$.

The units for variance are the square of the units for the mean and the random variable itself. To put the quantity back into the same units as the data and expected value, one can compute the standard deviation as the square root of the variance.

The variance of sums of random variables plays an important role in several later chapters. If the variables are stochastically independent, the variance of their sum is the sum of their variances, or $Var(X + Y) = Var(X) + Var(Y)$. Otherwise, this is not generally true.[2] Note the difference between the linearity of variance and the linearity of the expectation: for variance, linearity requires the random variables to be independent (more precisely, uncorrelated; a formal definition of this for random variables is given later). For expectation, linearity does not require this.

Another general result that has important uses in future chapters has to do with the variance of a linear transformation of a random variable. Specifically, for real numbers a, b, $Var(a + bX) = b^2 Var(X)$ – similar to a fact noted in Chapter 2. So adding constants to a random variable does not change the variance at all. This makes sense: the variance is a measure of spread around the mean, and if we add a single constant to every draw of a random variable, we change where the mean is but not the spread of the distribution relative to that mean. But multiplying a random variable by a constant has a greater-than-linear effect on the variance. This multiplication is a change in scale of the random variable not just its location. Intuitively this is not surprising; the daily variation in air temperatures denominated in Fahrenheit is greater than the daily variation of the same temperatures denominated in Celsius. By comparison, as noted earlier $E(a + bX) = a + bE(X)$. The expectation is a linear operator, but the variance is not.

The mean and variance of a distribution are both *moments* of that distribution. The mean is the "first moment" of a distribution, and the variance is the "second central moment" or "second moment about the mean." Generally speaking, a distribution can have infinitely many moments $1, 2, 3, \ldots$, but most of them are not readily interpretable or important in social science research.

However, the third and fourth central moments are sometimes referred to by name: the third central moment is the *skew* of the distribution. It is a measure of how symmetric the distribution is or how long one tail is relative to the other. It is not unlike the concept of skew mentioned in Chapter 2. The fourth central moment is the *kurtosis* of the distribution. It is a measure of the thickness of the tails of the distribution. A distribution with thicker tails than some benchmark (usually a standard normal distribution; see Chapter 6) is said to be "leptokurtic" or to have "leptokurtosis."

---

[2] What is really required for additivity of variance is *linear* independence, not necessarily complete independence; i.e., X and Y must be uncorrelated, although other relationships besides a linear one in their joint distribution are possible.

5.1.3 The Chebyshev and Markov Inequalities

Variance reflects how "spread out" a probability distribution is. There are limits to how spread out a distribution can be relative to its mean and still have the mean exist as a finite number. This limit is reflected in *Chebyshev's inequality*. Let μ denote the (finite) expected value of a distribution and σ the square root of its (finite) variance, and let k be any positive real number. For probability distributions with finite mean and variance, Chebyshev's inequality asserts

$$\Pr(|X - \mu| \geq k\sigma) \leq \frac{1}{k^2}. \qquad (5.5)$$

On the left-hand side, $|X - \mu|$ measures the distance between X and its mean. The absolute value means we are considering distance of X above μ or below. $|X - \mu| \geq k\sigma$ is the event that the distance of X from its mean is at least some multiple k of its standard deviation. So the left-hand side represents the probability of this event. The inequality guarantees that this probability cannot exceed $\frac{1}{k^2}$. So the inequality is informative for values of $k > 1$; for these values, the right-hand side is less than 1.

This inequality applies to any conceivable probability distribution with finite mean and variance. For instance, there is no probability distribution (with a finite mean and variance) that gives more than $\frac{1}{4}$ chance of drawing an observation at least two standard deviations from its mean (obtained by setting $k = 2$). To put more weight of the distribution further from the mean than this would violate the constraint that the area under the PDF is 1. As we will see later, for some common distributions the bounds are much tighter than this.

What Chebyshev's inequality shows is that there is a limit to how much of a distribution's cumulative probability can be far away from its mean (provided that its mean exists), where "far away" is measured in terms of standard deviation. In general terms this is not just a special property of commonly used distributions; it is a property of any distribution with μ and $\sigma^2 < \infty$.

Chebyshev's inequality can also be used to show that the median of a probability distribution is no more than one standard deviation away from its mean, when the latter exists. In other words, the mean does not have to be at the "center" of the distribution, but a value cannot be the mean if it is too far off the center or if the distribution places too much weight on one side of it. Chebyshev's inequality is used in theoretical statistics to prove some important theorems that social science applications rely on to justify common procedures, but here it is interesting simply because it shows some implications of what it means to be a mean and the limits on how widely spread out a distribution can be.

Chebyshev's inequality is a special case of the *Markov inequality*, which states that for any $a > 0$, $\Pr(|X| \geq a) \leq \frac{E(|X|)}{a}$. Like Chebyshev's inequality, this inequality places a bound on how much weight a probability distribution can place above or below any particular value. The larger the mean of the absolute value of X, the larger this bound; but for a given mean of $|X|$, the bound gets smaller as the value of a gets larger. So a distribution with finite mean of $|X|$ cannot place more weight above 50 and below -50 than it places above 5 and below -5. This is particularly obvious for a distribution with only positive values of X; then any weight above 50 is also weight above 5, so $\Pr(X > 50)$ cannot exceed $\Pr(X > 5)$. Furthermore, the only way to have $EX < 50$ for a random variable with $X \geq 0$ is for the distribution to place sufficient mass or density below 50 that $\Pr(X > 50) < \Pr(X > 5)$.

5.1.4 Expectation of a Function of X

We saw earlier how to evaluate $E(a + bX)$ from the expectation of X. It is not necessary to apply $g(x) = a + bx$ to every value of x, obtain a new distribution of $g(X)$, and evaluate its expectation (although this would certainly do the job); we can just apply $g(\cdot)$ directly to $E(X)$ and get the same answer: $E(g(X)) = g(E(X))$ in this case. This is a special case because g is linear; if g is not linear it is not valid to obtain $E(g(X))$ simply by computing $g(E(X))$. For a general function $g(x)$ and a discrete random variable with PMF $f(x)$,

$$E(g(X)) = \sum_x g(x) f(x). \tag{5.6}$$

Expectation of a function of X comes up often in both the theory of statistics and in some theoretical paradigms in social science (e.g., expected utility theory). For instance, we saw above that $Var(X) = E(X^2) - E(X)^2$. The second term on the right-hand side is obtained directly from $E(X)$ by squaring it. But in the first term $E(X^2)$ is an expectation of a function of X. Can we be sure that $E(X^2) > E(X)^2$, so as to ensure that this expression of $Var(X)$ is nonnegative? Yes we can!

The function $g(X) = X^2$ is a member of a class called *convex functions*. What convex functions share in common is that their graphs look like a bowl (and if there are no flat spots on the bowl, it is strictly convex). For X^2, the (unique) "bottom" of the bowl is at 0. The right side of the bowl is a curve traced out as x increases above 0, and the left side is a curve traced out as x decreases below 0.

The function is called "convex" because the set of points above its curve forms a *convex set*: for any two points in the set, any point on the line joining them is also in the set. In calculus terms, a simple characterization of convex functions that are differentiable (at least twice) is that the second derivative is positive: $\frac{d^2 g(x)}{dx^2} > 0$. A derivative is a rate of change in a function at a point; this is a derivative applied to a derivative. The first derivative reflects how the function changes as x changes: the rate of change in the function. The second derivative reflects how the first derivative changes as x changes: the rate of change in the rate of change. If a function is increasing, so $\frac{dg(x)}{dx} > 0$, then $\frac{d^2g(x)}{dx^2} > 0$ means the function is increasing at an increasing rate. For X^2, the second derivative is simply 2, so it does fit the criterion. Squares, functions with even-numbered powers, and exponential functions are commonly encountered examples of convex functions.

A result called *Jensen's inequality* asserts that, when $g(\cdot)$ is convex,

$$E(g(X)) \geq g(E(X)). \tag{5.7}$$

Thus the mean of a convex function of X is never less than that convex function of the mean of X. As a special case, $E(X^2) \geq E(X)^2$.

The negative of a convex function is a *concave function*, a similar but different class. Concave functions look like upside-down bowls. For a concave function, the set of points below its curve forms a convex set. For a twice-differentiable concave function, $\frac{d^2 f(x)}{dx^2} < 0$, so a decreasing concave function is decreasing at a decreasing rate. Square roots, functions raised to a power less than 1, and logarithmic functions are commonly encountered examples of concave functions. Applied to concave functions, Jensen's inequality implies that $E(g(X)) \leq g(E(X))$.

In expected utility theory, decision makers who are *risk averse* are modeled with preferences over money (or some valuable resource the disposition of which is analyzed in a model) reflected in a concave function: they prefer more of the resource to less of it, but the extra utility from a given increment decreases as they obtain more. *Risk-seeking* decision makers have convex preferences over the resource. *Risk-neutral* decision makers have linear preferences. If the utility function is $u(X)$, then $E(u(X))$ is the expected utility obtained from any risky proposition where amounts of X won are determined by chance. Jensen's inequality shows one way to think about how these different risk postures evaluate taking a gamble versus taking its expected value with certainty. Take, for instance, the simple gamble in which a fair coin is flipped and you win \$100 if it comes up heads but lose \$100 if it comes up tails. The expected value of this gamble is \$0. Jensen's inequality says that for a risk-averse person, the utility of \$0 is higher than the expected utility obtained by taking the gamble ($u(E(X)) \geq E(u(X))$ because u is concave); for a risk-seeking person, the expected utility of the gamble is higher; a risk-neutral person attaches the same utility to both.

5.2 EXPECTATION IN MULTIVARIATE DISTRIBUTIONS

Recall from Chapter 4 that multivariate distributions describe how multiple random variables are jointly distributed over their possible values. Any one of the variables in a multivariate distribution can be analyzed as a random variable in its own right – for example, in a joint distribution $f(x, y)$ of the random variables X and Y, we can analyze the behavior of either X or Y in isolation from the other variable.

As we saw in that chapter, the marginal distribution of X, $f_X(x)$, describes how X is distributed over its possible values, irrespective of Y. For a joint PMF, it is obtained by summing the probability $f(x, y)$ for each value of Y and repeating this sum for each value of X. For a joint PDF, it is obtained by integrating the density $f(x, y)$ with respect to y, and repeating for each value of X.

The expectation of X in this joint distribution is then the expectation of the marginal of X, that is,

$$E(X) = \sum_x x f_X(x) \tag{5.8}$$

when X is discrete, and

$$E(X) = \int_x x f_X(x) dx \tag{5.9}$$

when X is continuous. Again we have all three uses of "x" in this definition: the random variable itself (X), a particular value of the random variable (x), and the set of possible values $(\mathcal{X})$. Likewise, the variance of X can be obtained from the marginal distribution.

Another way to see the definition of $E(X)$ in a multivariate distribution comes from thinking again about exactly what a marginal distribution is: $f_X(x) = \sum_y f(x, y)$ from Chapter 4. Using this in the definition of $E(X)$ for a discrete random variable gives $E(X) = \sum_x x \sum_y f(x, y) = \sum_x \sum_y x f(x, y)$. Because $\sum_y f(x, y)$ is constant for a given x, that x can be freely moved into or out of that sum. So $E(X)$ can be expressed equally well in terms of a marginal distribution over X alone or a joint distribution over a larger group of random variables.

For a continuous random variable, the analogous expression is $E(X) = \int_x \int_y x f(x, y) dy dx$. (Just as changing the order of summation in a sum does not affect the result, it does not matter if the first integral is with respect to x or with respect to y: an integral is simply a sum over an uncountable infinity of items.) Thus the expectation of X can be obtained directly from the joint distribution by multiplying each value of X by its density for each value of Y, summed over all possible values of X and Y. The same is true for variance: it can be obtained directly from the joint distribution of X and Y or by first obtaining the marginal distribution of X.

The definition of $E(X) = \int_x \int_y x f(x, y) dy dx$ allows us to see transparently that $E(X + Y) = E(X) + E(Y)$ for *any* random variables X and Y provided their individual means exist; that is, expectation is a *linear operator*. By definition, $E(X + Y) = \int_x \int_y (x + y) f(x, y) dy dx = \int_x \int_y x f(x, y) dy dx + \int_x \int_y y f(x, y) dy dx = E(X) + E(Y)$. The crucial equation is the second one, which is valid because an integral is a sum, so it can be broken apart into sub sums that are added back up at will. These steps make no assumptions about the joint distribution of X and Y other than that their individual means exist; for instance, it does not require that X and Y are independent. In later material, we have many occasions to take the expected value of a sum, so this result is important.

5.2.1 Conditional Mean and Variance

As noted in Chapter 4, the conditional distribution of one random variable given another is one of the most important objects that probability theory gives to quantitative social science. Likewise, summary measures of conditional distributions, particularly conditional mean and variance, are critically important as well. This is because the mainstay of quantitative empirical research, regression modeling, is a technique for modeling the conditional mean of one variable as a function some others. Moreover, the behavior of the conditional variance has a crucial effect on the quality of any application of regression modeling. (Readers who have seen some type of regression or coursework before know this as the assumption of "homoskedasticity," or constant conditional variance as a function of any independent variables.)

These conditional moments of a distribution are deceptively simple to define. The conditional distribution $f_{Y|X}(Y|X = x)$ is a well-defined probability distribution in its own right. To this distribution we can apply the definitions of expectation and variance from above (Equations 5.2 and 5.3).

Thus, the *conditional mean* of a discrete random variable Y given $X = x$ is

$$E(Y|x) = \sum_{y \in \mathcal{Y}} y f_{Y|X}(y|x). \tag{5.10}$$

This is read as "the expectation of Y given $X = x$." The notation $E(Y|x)$ denotes the use of a conditional distribution to arrive at the conditional expectation. The variance of Y conditional on $X = x$ is

$$Var(Y|x) = E((Y - E(Y|x))^2|x). \tag{5.11}$$

These expressions have capital Y and lowercase x because they define an expectation of one random variable Y given that another random variable X equals a specific value x. As $E(Y)$ is just a number, once we know the range of Y and the distribution, so $E(Y|x)$ is just a number. Same for the variance and conditional variance.

For a simple example, return to the random variables defined from the sum and difference of two-coin flips from Chapter 4. The joint distribution of these random variables is in Table 5.3. Conditioning on $Y = 0$ defines a distribution over values of X. This distribution is obtained by dividing entries in the top row of the table by 0.25. The mean of this conditional distribution, a.k.a. the conditional mean of X given $Y = 0$, is $E(X|Y = 0) = (0.5)(0) + (0.5)(2) = 1$. The variance of this conditional distribution, a.k.a. the conditional variance

TABLE 5.3. *Joint Distribution of X, Y*

		X		
		0	1	2
Y	0	0.25	0	0.25
	1	0	0.5	0

of X given $Y = 0$, is $Var(X|Y = 0) = (0.5)(0 - 1)^2 + (0.5)(2 - 1)^2 = 1$. Conditioning on $Y = 1$ defines another distribution over values of X, a degenerate distribution that places probability 1 on $X = 1$. Thus $E(X|Y = 1) = 1$ and $Var(X|Y = 1) = 0$.

It is also possible to explore how $E(Y|x)$ behaves as x changes. This is a collection of numbers, one for each x. It specifies the conditional mean of Y in terms of the value of X. The conditional mean of Y expressed as a function of X is denoted $E(Y|X)$ and is the *regression* of Y on X in the DGP. For emphasis we often refer to this as the *DGP regression* or *conditional mean function*; these are synonyms. For students familiar with regression from prior coursework, it might be more informative to say that $E(Y|X)$ is *the* regression of Y on X. Note that if we know the true DGP/joint distribution $f(x, y)$, then $E(Y|X)$ is not "modeled" in the sense of postulating an analytically simple construct to represent an interesting but more complicated form. With the joint distribution in hand, no such modeling is necessary. Note that $E(Y|x)$ is a number, whereas $E(Y|X)$ is a random variable. In particular, it is a function of X, but it is not a function of Y.

The conditional mean function captures important information about the relationship among these variables. If X and Y are independent, then the conditional mean of Y will not vary at all with X. In other words, if Y and X are independent, the regression $E(Y|X)$ is flat or constant as a function of X. Thus a theory asserting that Y is related to or stochastically dependent on X is an assertion that the regression is not a constant function of X. This is why, in applied settings, so much attention is focused on the conjecture that the regression *is* a constant function of X. This is the conjecture that an analyst claiming a relationship between X and Y wants to disprove. We see much more of this in future chapters.

The regression of Y on X gets a lot of attention also because, in a specific sense, it is the best guess about Y that can be conditioned on a covariate X. We return to this point and state it formally later, after introducing some additional concepts and results.

5.2.2 The Law of Iterated Expectations

Because $E(Y|X)$ is a random variable, we can also explore its expected value. This expected value is denoted $E(E(Y|X))$. However, the E inside the brackets is with respect to Y, whereas the E outside the brackets is with respect to X. This is because $E(Y|X)$ is a function of X only; the "inner" expectation averages out the effect of Y. This can be precisely denoted by writing $E(E(Y|X))$ as $E_X(E_Y(Y|X))$, but the former version is more common because it is unambiguous once we internalize that $E(Y|X)$ is a function of X. Given that fact, the only sensible expectation of $E(Y|X)$ is with respect to X.

The *law of iterated expectations* asserts that $E(E(Y|X))$ takes a particularly simple form. It says that for any random variable Y, the expected value of Y can be expressed as the expected value of the conditional mean function.

$$E(E(Y|X)) = E(Y). \qquad (5.12)$$

Intuitively, if we "average out" the behavior of X, we are left with no particular information about X to use in predicting the value of Y. In that case, the average value of Y is simply $E(Y)$, its unconditional mean.

The formal logic behind the law of iterated expectations is not difficult if we consider that $E(Y|X)$ is a function of X. For a continuous random variable, we already saw that $E(g(X)) = \int_X g(x) f(x) dx$, where $g(X)$ is some function of X and $f(x)$ is its PDF. Setting $E(Y|X) = g(X)$, this means that $E(E(Y|X)) = \int_X E(Y|x) f(x) dx$. In this expression, $E(Y|x)$ can also be replaced with its definition to obtain $\int_X E(Y|x) f(x) dx = \int_X [\int_y y f(y|x) dy] f(x) dx$, where $f(y|x)$ is the conditional PDF of Y given $X = x$. Furthermore, in this expression, $[\int_y y f(y|x) dy] f(x) dx$ is the same as $[\int_y y f(y|x) f(x) dy dx]$: when every element of a sum or integral is multiplied by the same constant (here $f(x)$, which is constant with respect to y for a given value of x – it's just the density of x), we can either multiply every element by that constant and sum the results or sum every element and multiply by that constant. Making this replacement gives $\int_X [\int_y y f(y|x) dy] f(x) dx = \int_X \int_y y f(y|x) f(x) dy dx$. Now look at the last part of the right hand side: from the definition of the conditional distribution $f(y|x)$, $f(y|x) f(x) = f(y, x)$. The probability of $Y = y$ given $X = x$, times the probability that $X = x$, is the joint probability that $Y = y$ and $X = x$, the shorthand of which we already know as $f(y, x)$ from the joint distribution. So now we have $\int_X \int_y y f(y|x) f(x) dy dx = \int_X \int_y y f(y, x) dy dx$, and this is simply $E(Y)$. We started with $E(E(Y|X))$ and used results we already know are true to show that the iterated expectation is $E(Y)$.

We will use this result several times to establish important properties of the conditional mean function $E(Y|X)$, but first we need to introduce some additional concepts about expectation in joint distributions.

5.2.3 Covariance

Association among variables in data and DGPs plays a crucial role in quantitative research in the social sciences. This is another way to see the technique of regression modeling, and indeed, in Chapter 2, the least squares best fit line was presented as a way to summarize association in bivariate data. Covariance and correlation are two basic measures of association in data distributions, and their analogues for probability distributions serve the same purpose for DGPs.

The *covariance* of two random variables X, Y is defined as

$$\text{Cov}(X, Y) = E[(Y - E(Y))(X - E(X))], \tag{5.13}$$

that is: the expectation of the product of the differences between the random variable's and their respective expectations. A little inspection shows that $\text{Cov}(X, Y) = \text{Cov}(Y, X)$. One consequence of this is that Y can be called by fiat a "dependent variable" and X an "independent variable," with Y interpreted as being dependent on X and X understood as driving, perhaps even causing, the changes in Y. But covariance does not care about these interpretive aspirations and causal fantasies. If we had said that Y does the causing and X is dependent on it, $\text{Cov}(X, Y)$ would be exactly the same. This is basically another version of the fact that correlation (or association) does not imply causation. Note that if $X = Y$ so we really have only one random variable, this definition collapses to Definition 5.3; the covariance of a random variable with itself is simply its variance.

A more intuitively and often computationally useful formulation of covariance is

$$\text{Cov}(X, Y) = E(XY) - E(X)E(Y), \tag{5.14}$$

so that the covariance of two variables is the expectation of their product minus the product of their expectations. Straightforward algebraic manipulation of the first definition of covariance, combined with the fact that $E(\cdot)$ is a linear operator, leads to this second definition.

It is worth going through a simple example because it reveals something about what the covariance is. In this case, it also reveals an important point about relationships between random variables in general versus their measurement through covariance. Take again the random variables defined from the sum and difference of two-coin flips. The joint distribution is a table of six cells. Chapter 4 derived the marginal distributions of X and Y, which we need for the covariance. The marginals yield $E(X) = 1$ and $E(Y) = 0.5$.

Now make another table of six cells, each cell containing $(x - E(X))(y - E(Y))$, as in Table 5.4. To obtain the covariance, multiply cell i, j of the joint distribution (Table 5.3) by the corresponding cell in Table 5.4, and add up all the resulting products. This gives $\text{Cov}(X, Y) = (0.25)(0.5) + (0.5)(0) + (0.25)(-0.5) = 0$. No matter how complicated the distributions of X or Y, this same basic idea is always behind their covariance.

The important point this reveals about covariance is that two random variables can be related (in the sense of not being statistically independent) even if their covariance is 0. That is exactly the situation here: a straightforward computation showed 0 covariance. But another straightforward computation showed that (for example) the conditional distribution of X changes as a function of Y. By definition that means the variables are not independent. It seems

TABLE 5.4. *An Intermediate Result for the Covariance of X and Y*

		X		
		0	1	2
Y	0	$(-1)(-0.5)$	$(0)(-0.5)$	$(1)(-0.5)$
	1	$(-1)(0.5)$	$(0)(0.5)$	$(1)(0.5)$

that the covariance is telling us there is no relationship between X and Y, while the conditional distributions are telling us that there is. What is going on here?

This occurs because covariance measures a *linear relationship*, and linear relationships work through changes in the conditional means. It was noted in the previous section that $E(X|Y=0) = E(X|Y=1) = 1$ in this example. The conditional means are the same for the different values of Y; the effect of Y on the conditional distribution of X shows up in the conditional variance of X, $Var(X|Y)$. This was not the same for $Y=0$ and $Y=1$, as noted in the previous section.

The point is that covariance measures a particular kind of relationship between X and Y, a linear relationship affecting the conditional mean of one random variable given the other. There are other kinds of relationships out there. Covariance, correlation, and regression models focus on one kind of relationship. Those techniques are a lot easier to work with than the full joint distribution, and for most kinds of relationships, they are sufficient to capture what is interesting.

Nevertheless, when quantitative social science focuses on covariance and conditional mean functions (i.e., regression functions), it thereby focuses on only one type of relationship. The upshot is that just because two variables appear unrelated as measured by their covariance does not mean they are independent and does not mean that one random variable has no effect on the behavior (i.e., conditional distribution of) the other. Put differently, if you limit yourself to studying relationships with covariance- and regression-based techniques, you might be leaving out parts of the relationship between two random variables. However, you will not be leaving out how a change in one variable affects the expected value of the other.

5.2.4 Correlation

The covariance $Cov(X, Y)$ is a number, given a joint distribution over X and Y. It can be any number at all. Covariance in probability distributions suffers from all the defects of covariance in data distributions: it is scale-dependent and not readily comparable across DGPs because of this and the fact that it has no limits.

To overcome these limits, we can define the *correlation* of X and Y as

$$Corr(X, Y) = \frac{Cov(X, Y)}{\sqrt{Var(X)}\sqrt{Var(Y)}}, \tag{5.15}$$

where the denominator is the product of the standard deviations. As with covariance, $Corr(X, Y) = Corr(Y, X)$. This is obvious, because correlation inherits all its information about the relationship between X and Y from covariance. For example, $Corr(X, Y) = 0$ if and only if $Cov(X, Y) = 0$. Correlation is simply a scaled version of covariance.

But that rescaling is useful because $-1 \leqslant Corr(X, Y) \leqslant 1$. This can be shown from the *Cauchy-Schwartz inequality*, which holds that $|E(WZ)|^2 = E(W^2)E(Z^2)$. Taking $W \equiv (X - E(X))$ and $Z \equiv (Y - E(Y))$, squaring the covariance, and working out some algebra implies that $|Cov(X, Y)|^2 \leq Var(X)Var(Y)$, which implies that $|Corr(X, Y)| \leq 1$.

Correlation measures the strength and direction of a bivariate relationship in a scale-independent fashion. If X is rescaled, it will affect the covariance, but it will affect the square root of the variance in exactly the same way. So any such scale changes cancel out when computing correlation.

Covariance and Independence

Put succinctly, the point is worth remembering: statistical independence of two random variables (defined in Chapter 4) implies that their covariance (and correlation) is 0, but zero covariance does not imply statistical independence. More obviously, independence implies linear independence but the converse is not true.

In fact this point is often made more strikingly by showing that the covariance of X and X^2 is 0 as long as the support of X is $\mathbb{R}$ (or, in fact, symmetric around 0). (If, say, $X > 0$, then X and X^2 are obviously strongly correlated: when one gets bigger the other one does too.) Obviously these random variables are related, but it is a quadratic, not linear, relationship. However, this particular fact is only sort of dramatic because there are well known and easy ways to measure quadratic relationships using linear association techniques such as covariance and regression. An example is presented in Chapter 6, and analogues were already presented in Chapter 2.

An important point highlighted by this alternative formulation of the covariance is that covariance does not require knowledge of the entire joint distribution between X and Y. It requires knowledge of their individual (marginal) distributions, to evaluate $E(X)$ and $E(Y)$, and the distribution of their product, to evaluate $E(XY)$. That is less information than is contained in the entire joint distribution. Thus the covariance between X and Y contains less information about two random variables and their relationship than the joint distribution does. By extension, any measure of association computed from covariance and the moments of X and Y also contains less information about the relationship than the joint distribution does. This applies to correlation and linear regression modeling. This is really just another way of seeing the point made above: that covariance captures one kind of relationship between two random variables, but there may be other relationships among them as well. The joint distribution contains all of that information.

Another important point in this formulation is what has to happen for $Cov(X, Y) = 0$. Namely, $E(XY) = E(X)E(Y)$ so the expectation of the product equals the product of the expectations. Independence of X and Y is a sufficient condition for this equality to hold. In that case, $E(\cdot)$ can be passed through a product. Otherwise, $E(\cdot)$ cannot be passed through a product. Although it is true that $E(X + Y) = E(X) + E(Y)$ regardless of how the random variables are related, $E(XY) = E(X)E(Y)$ only if X and Y are independent. Linear operators can be passed through sums but not in general through products (or only in special cases).

Important Properties of the DGP Regression

Regressions occupy a great deal of attention in social science applications of statistical methods. It is important to understand why, so that one understands why quantitative analysis often looks the way it does. On the basis of the law of iterated expectations and other concepts introduced in this chapter, we can establish several properties of the DGP regression or conditional mean function that help to explain its importance. These properties also provide an opportunity to see how expectations can be manipulated to deduce conceptually useful properties.

First, when random variables are independent, knowing the value of one provides no information to use in making a guess about the other.

$$X \perp\!\!\!\perp Y \Rightarrow E(Y|X) = E(Y), \forall x \in \mathcal{X}. \tag{5.16}$$

(Recall that "$\perp\!\!\!\perp$" denotes stochastic independence.) The variables are unrelated so the regression of Y on X is necessarily "flat," that is, not a function of X at all. In turn, $E(Y|X) = E(Y)$ for all x implies $Cov(X, Y) = 0$. These are two formulations of a condition that is used often to establish properties of a least squares regression coefficient, as explored further in Chapter 7.

Second, every random variable Y can be decomposed into its regression[3] and an "error" or departure of Y from that regression, and the error has some special properties itself. We refer to this as the *regression decomposition property*.

Formally, for a random variable Y, we can write

$$Y = E(Y|X) + \varepsilon, \tag{5.17}$$

where $E(\varepsilon) = 0$, $E(\varepsilon|X) = 0$, and $Cov(h(X), \varepsilon) = 0$ for any function $h(\cdot)$.

---

[3] Provided $E(Y|x)$ is finite for every $x \in \mathcal{X}$.

$E(\varepsilon) = 0$ is easy to establish: $E(\varepsilon) = E(Y - E(Y|X))$ by rearranging the decomposition to isolate ε, and this in turn is $E(Y) - E(E(Y|X))$ by the linearity of E. By the law of iterated expectations, $E(E(Y|X)) = E(Y)$, so $E(Y) - E(E(Y|X)) = 0$. So if we use the regression of Y on X as a guess of Y, on average the error in this guess is 0.

$E(\varepsilon|X) = 0$ is actually no more involved: $E(\varepsilon|X) = E(Y - E(Y|X)|X) = E(Y|X) - E(Y|X) = 0$. Here we have used the fact that $E((Y|X)|X) = E(Y|X)$; once we condition on X, conditioning on it again changes nothing.[4] So if we regress ε on the covariate X, the regression is flat. In the DGP, the regressor X and regression error ε necessarily have no linear relationship.

We can go further and show that $Cov(h(X), \varepsilon) = 0$ for any function of $h(X)$ (and so, per force, $Cov(X, \varepsilon) = 0$). Formally, using the shortcut $Cov(Z, W) = E(ZW) - E(Z)E(W)$, we have $Cov(h(X), \varepsilon) = E[h(X)\varepsilon] - E(h(X))E(\varepsilon)$. We already know that $E(\varepsilon) = 0$, so we are left with $E[h(X)\varepsilon] = E[h(X)(Y - E(Y|X))] = E[h(X)Y] - E[h(X)E(Y|X)]$.

At this point, it is helpful to write the Es longhand as integrals. We have $\int_X \int_Y h(x)y\,dy\,dx$ and $\int_X h(x)(\int_Y yf(y|x)dy) f(x)dx$. This second integral is exactly like the one encountered to establish the law of iterated expectations, and it can be written as $\int_X \int_Y yf(y|x) f(x)dy\,dx = \int_X(\int_Y h(x)yf(x, y)dy\,dx = E[h(X)Y]$ for the same reason as shown there. In other words, by the law of iterated expectations, $E[h(X)E(Y|X)] = E[h(X)Y]$. Thus $Cov(h(X), \varepsilon) = 0$.

So the covariate X and the regression error ε necessarily have 0 covariance. As we will see in Chapter 7, covariance between a covariate and the regression error plays a fundamental role in evaluating the "quality" of least squares regression coefficients. So it is interesting to note that if $f(x, y)$ truly is the joint distribution of X and Y, then the covariate X is necessarily not linearly related to the regression error. For properly interpreting this fact in light of results on regression theory we cover later, note that the regression for which this claim holds is $E(Y|X)$ – the actual regression, not a linear model or approximation of it.

Because ε has the characteristics just show, it can also be shown that $Cov(X, E(Y|X)) = Cov(X, Y)$. In other words, if we care about the linear relationship between X and Y, it is sufficient to analyze the regression $E(Y|X)$ as a function of X; there is no other information of interest about this relationship.

Altogether, the regression decomposition property and its implications for the regression error ε go a fair distance to show why regressions occupy so much interest in applied social science research. If we want to understand the behavior of a random variable Y – such as the onset of war between nations, the survival of organizations, the degree of polarization in a legislature, the transition of states from autocracy to democracy, a region's economic development, and soon – we can do so by focusing on a regression. The regression does not

---

[4] This is straightforward to establish by writing out E long-hand as an integral, which is left as an exercise.

give a perfect encapsulation of the variable Y; there is some error ε. But the regression is "correct" on average (overall and for every value of x), and the error is unrelated to the regression, so that there are no systematic distortions in our understanding of Y induced by focusing on $E(Y|X)$.

A third and equally important property of the regression $E(Y|X)$ is that it is, in a sense, the best possible guess of Y we can make, accounting for the information in X. Specifically, consider a guess about Y that can be based on a covariate X. For example, we might consider whether a member of Congress voted for or against the Patient Protection and Affordable Care Act ("Obamacare") as Y, and the member's party as X. Then $g(X)$ is a guess of Y that is based on X. We would obviously guess that Democrats in Congress were more likely to vote in favor than Republicans. But how should the guess $g(X)$ be related to the regression?

The regression is "best guess" in that it minimizes $E[(Y - g(X))^2]$. This is the *mean squared error* or MSE of the guess: the error is $Y - g(X)$, and the squared error is $(Y - g(X))^2$. The MSE of the guess is the expected value or mean of the squared error. Just as the mean EY is the best (in the sense of MSE) guess of Y that is just a single number, not conditioned on X, the regression or conditional mean $E(Y|X)$ is the best guess of Y that can be conditioned on X. This is the *minimum mean squared error* or MMSE property of regression.

The proof of this fact illustrates how we can manipulate the expectation operator $E(\cdot)$ using simple algebra and the fact that $E(\cdot)$ is linear. The "trick" of the proof is to add and subtract $E(Y|X)$ to the MSE, which obviously changes nothing but allows useful regrouping of terms.[5]

Using this trick, $E(Y - g(X))^2 = E\{[Y - E(Y|X)] + [E(Y|X) - g(X)]\}^2 = E[Y - E(Y|X)^2 + 2(Y - E(Y|X))(E(Y|X) - g(X)) + (E(Y|X) - g(X))^2]$. The last expression follows from expanding the square in the previous expression. Because $E(\cdot)$ is linear, it can distributed over the three parts of this sum to yield $E[Y - E(Y|X)^2] + E[2(E(Y|X) - g(X))(Y - E(Y|X))] + E[(E(Y|X) - g(X))^2]$ as the MSE.

The first term, $E(Y - E(Y|X)^2)$, is not a function of $g(X)$. So no choice of $g(X)$ can affect this part of the MSE. To dispose of the second term, note that it can be written $E[h(X)(Y - E(Y|X))] = E[h(X)\varepsilon]$. This is the same ε from the regression decomposition property above, where we showed that $E[h(X)\varepsilon] = 0$ for any function $h(X)$. So this second term always disappears. The third term of the MSE, $E[(E(Y|X) - g(X))^2]$, is never negative because it is a square, and is 0 if and only if $g(X) = E(Y|X)$. Therefore $g(X) = E(Y|X)$ minimizes the MSE when a guess of Y can be conditioned on X.

---

[5] The same trick can be used to prove that $E(Y)$ minimizes MSE when the guess cannot be conditioned on X, as was claimed earlier as a result for univariate distributions. Indeed we used it in Chapter 2 already, but it may not have been completely clear then, so it bears repeating.

Note that this result applies to the regression $E(Y|X)$, whatever it is. This does not imply that a formulation of the regression as a linear function of X is a good or useful or approximately correct specification, although it is common to make this assumption in applied work because it allows such a simple depiction of a relationship.

Given that a linear approximation to the regression is invoked, we should still want to use the "best" possible one, and that means we should focus on the line that minimizes the MSE of the regression. The proof in the appendix to Chapter 2 applies here as well to identify what this line is. When applied to a DGP, the terms of this line depend on the covariance of two random variables, which is defined previously. Again, this proof simply identifies the best linear approximation to the conditional mean of Y as a function of X; it does not imply that a linear approximation, best or otherwise, is any good.

It bears emphasis, for reasons that become clear in later material on regression theory, that the properties of the DGP regression discussed here do not necessarily hold if the DGP regression $E(Y|X)$ is modeled as a linear function of X. That is, they are always true for the actual regression but need not be true for linear approximations of it. Linear approximations are what we typically use in applied research because they are simple to express and interpret. The degree to which the foregoing properties hold true for such linear models of the DGP regression is a significant focus of critique of regression results in applied research.

5.3 CONCLUSION

Chapters 4 and 5 comprise our treatment of fundamental tools and concepts of probability theory. This theory gives us a coherent framework for analyzing and evaluating uncertainty, which is inherent in the DGPs assumed or designed in applied statistical research. It gives us a tool for modeling DGPs with results that have some degree of uncertainty in them: we can model these as probability distributions and the outcomes of those social processes (which constitute observable sample data) as random variables. And as shown in this chapter, probability theory gives us concepts for summarizing the properties of DGPs themselves, including their central tendency, dispersion, and behavior conditional on some other random variable. We need these tools in theoretically oriented empirical research because, although we can observe data and use it to draw conclusions, the data we observe is often generated by a partially random process (cf. Chapter 3), and the conclusions we want to draw are about the DGP itself not just the data drawn from it.

In the next chapter, we complete our discussion of probability theory as such by exploring several canonical probability distributions that are widely used as models for DGPs in a variety if social processes. We also discuss in more detail the connection between positive theories in social science and the properties of DGPs. In particular, we explore how parameters of DGPs can be expressed or *modeled* in terms of explanatory factors. This modeling represents a clear, as well as common, approach to connecting substantive theories about social processes with the formal apparatus of probability theory.

Because the next chapter develops models in terms of DGP properties themselves, no statistical inference is actually involved at this point. That is taken up in the subsequent three chapters (Chapters 7, 8, and 9). These discuss methods for drawing connections between data and DGP. That is exactly what the theory of statistical inference is about, and these three chapters comprise our core treatment of it. At that point, with a link between positive theory and stochastic DGP, and a link between observable data and a DGP of interest, we will have established a link between observable data and positive theory. This is basically the rationale for statistical modeling, based on observable data, as a tool for theory exploration in social science.

PROBLEMS

1. Show that the bounds in Chebyshev's theorem cannot be improved on. That is, provide a distribution that satisfies the bounds exactly for $k \geq 1$, show that it satisfies the bounds exactly, and draw its PMF. Then explain why, logically, this is the same as providing that the bounds cannot be improved on.
2. Prove the law of iterated expectations for discrete random variables.
3. Show that $Var(X) = E(X^2) - (EX)^2$.
4. For a random variable X and constant a, show that $Var(aX) = a^2 Var(X)$.
5. Show that $Cov(X, Y) = E(XY) - E(X)E(Y)$.
6. Show that $Var(X + Y) = Var X + Var Y + 2Cov(X, Y)$.
7. What is $Cov(X, X)$?
8. For random variables X and Y and constants a and b, show $Cov(aX, bY) = ab Cov(X, Y)$.
9. For three random variables X, Y, Z, show that $Cov(X + Y, Z) = Cov(X, Z) + Cov(Y, Z)$.
10. Show that $E[(Y|X)|X] = E(Y|X)$.
11. Show that $Cov(X, E(Y|X)) = Cov(X, Y)$.
12. Prove the "analysis of variance" or "ANOVA" theorem: $Var(Y) = Var(E(Y|X)) + E(Var(Y|X))$. HINT. Use the fact that $E(Y|X)$ and ε are uncorrelated, as shown in the regression decomposition property.
13. Look at the random variables in Table 5.3.
   (a) What is $E(Y|X)$?
   (b) Use the definition of covariance to find $Cov(X, E(Y|X))$.
   (c) Use the definition of covariance to find $Cov(X, Y - E(Y|X))$.

6

Probability and Models: Linking Positive Theories and Data-Generating Processes

info. derived from logical/mathematical treatments is the exclusive source of all authoritative knowledge

Positive theories in social science assert characteristics of data-generating processes (DGPs). This connection is a fundamental one in linking positive theories with statistical research. It links observable data (our window into the world) and positive theories (models of how the world works) as per the following schematic:

$$\text{Positive Theory} \rightleftarrows \text{DGP} \rightleftarrows \text{Data} \tag{6.1}$$

It is important for theoretically oriented empirical research that both sets of arrows are bidirectional. Positive theory implies features of a DGP, which in turn implies something about the observable data that is likely to be observed in fact. The arrow pointing from "data" back to "DGP" is exactly what statistical inference, developed in subsequent chapters, is designed to establish. This chapter addresses the links between the positive theory of ultimate interest in research with DGPs. Altogether these links therefore connect positive theory to the observable data.

This chapter focuses particularly on the expression of positive theories in terms of statistical models of DGPs, and the interpretation of more or less common families of models. The emphasis is on the way in which models reflect and help to evaluate the ability of theories to explain observed events. Because all the discussion is in terms of models of DGPs, there is nothing in this chapter on how to *estimate* the various components of the models discussed from observed data. That is a statistical problem taken up later in the book, especially in Chapters 7, 8, and 9. The problem of estimation is of course central to doing research using statistical models. But there is a more basic problem: that of simply understanding the substantive content of the estimates one encounters in reading, or that one explains in writing about, empirical research. Pedagogically, the reason to separate model development and connection to substantively oriented, positive theory (this chapter) and model estimation (later chapters) is that a social scientist must understand how a model is meaningful in substantive terms before it will seem worthwhile to spend time on approaches to estimating components of models from data.

In addition, this is the natural place in the text to present common families of probability distributions. Dealing with models in terms of DGPs allows for a substantively useful presentation of these families, in the sense in which they actually appear in empirical research. In addition to those distributions presented in the text of this chapter, several others – more technically involved, some less common in applied research, but important for theoretical development – are presented in the online appendix to this chapter at the book's website.

6.1 DGPs AND THEORIES OF SOCIAL PHENOMENA

In general terms, the task of positive theorizing in social science is to explain how interesting or important social outcomes come to look the way they do. Such an explanation usually entails an argument that the outcome is the result of other social forces or events that serve as *explanatory factors*. The thing to explain, then, is how the DGP of an event or outcome can be related to or shown to depend on the explanatory factors. Examining relationships between a social outcome to be explained and explanatory factors is the first order of business in that case.

6.1.1 Statistical Models

Consider a simple caricature of a theory contending that one outcome Y depends on one explanatory factor X. Real theories are more complicated than this, most obviously in that they entail multiple explanatory factors and possibly interactions between them. But this schematic captures the relevant issues for modeling DGPs. For example, a theory might assert that a country's degree of democratization in its political system is a function of the per capita income in that country.

The theory asserts a relationship in terms of DGPs. The joint distribution of X, Y is the most complete specification we have of that DGP. The most elementary theoretical claim would assert that X and Y are not stochastically independent for some reason. From the definitions of independence and conditional distribution in Chapter 4, it is apparent that such a theory asserts, at minimum, that the conditional distribution of Y is not the same for every value of X.

Theories usually imply more than this (and more is demanded if the current participants in a literature on some topic are expected to take notice). A researcher advancing a theory must explain *how* the conditional distribution of Y depends on X. This can be done verbally or it can be done formally, but the theory explains what changes to Y's conditional distribution are expected to occur for given changes in X.

Probably the most common case is one in which a theory asserts that as X gets bigger, the conditional distribution of Y is ordered in some way. Theories about DGPs in social science, verbal or formal, often do not specify any more about Y's behavior than its general tendency as a function of X. So as a country's per capita income grows, so does its "tendency" to democratize, or the "typical degree" of democratic-ness (this is, in effect, the *modernization* thesis, e.g. Lipset [1959]). Or as a person's household income increases, her "tendency" to support income redistribution decreases (Meltzer and Richard [1981]).

As we have seen several times, a natural way to judge "tendency" and "typical" is with the mean, so claims of this nature can be translated into claims about conditional means without doing them much interpretive harm. Conditioning the distribution of Y on X is an essential part of these theories; that is how dependence of one variable on another is expressed for stochastic DGPs (see Chapter 4).

Again, these are simple examples, not intended as factual statements nor as full-fledged schools of thought on these topics. What they indicate is that, according to the theory, the conditional mean of Y (democratization, votes for income redistribution) is ordered by X (per capita income, household income). Concretely, as X grows, the conditional mean of Y should grow in the first case (democratization) and decline in the second (voting for redistribution).

There are two ingredients rolling around here. First is the joint DGP of X and Y. At the very least, if Y's behavior is stochastic, this DGP is a joint probability distribution. Perhaps little will be said in theoretical discussions about the nature of this DGP, but there must be a set of joint distributions to which it belongs, even if it is just the entire set of conceivable probability distributions. Second is the link from the value of X to that joint distribution. A theory that orders the conditional mean of Y as a function of X is just one example of this link, and if that makes more concrete sense, it is fine to think in those terms.

These two ingredients define a *statistical model*.[1] It is statistical in the sense that Y's behavior is understood as stochastic and represented by a DGP. It is a model in two senses: first, the DGP for Y may be assumed to take a more or less idealized form; second, the joint distribution over X and Y is specified to change in certain ways as X changes.

It is possible to be much more specific about both components of a statistical model – the joint DGP for Y and X and the exact link from the joint distribution (or the conditional of Y) to the value of X. As is usually the case,

---

[1] For formal definitions of statistical model, see McCoullagh [2002] and citations therein. Canonical formal definitions are isomorphic to the one used here because the link with X will be understood to pin down parameter values of the DGP of Y.

this specificity has both costs and benefits. On the plus side, it allows for much sharper specifications of relationships, as well as much sharper inference from data to DGP. On the negative side, greater specificity on these components is often assumed without firm justification and in some cases may obscure more about relationships and the behavior of Y than it reveals. There is no theorem indicating when the benefits outweigh the costs or vice versa; it is a matter of judgment and, to some extent, taste.

The purpose of this chapter is to explain some of the leading examples of this specificity, both in terms of the form of the DGP and in terms of the link from the DGP to the value of explanatory factors. Formally, this chapter is where I introduce parametric families of probability distributions, which are often used as models of DGPs. Because most social scientists do not have much interest in families of probability distributions in their own right, they are introduced in conjunction with common links of the parameters of those families with explanatory factors.

6.1.2 Parametric Families of DGPs

Probability theory has many families of models for DGPs of random variables, models that social scientists, by both theory and convention, have found useful for particular situations and types of data. These probability distributions have been studied and used widely enough to have acquired specific names. We encounter a number of specific examples in this Chapter.

What distinguishes the members of a family of DGPs or probability distributions from each other are their *parameters*. Parameters are quantities that are fixed for a particular distribution, but vary from one distribution to the next. A *parametric family* of probability distributions is identical except for the parameters of its members. The family has a *functional form* common to all members of the family. The functional form specifies the probability distribution up to these parameters; the parameters complete the specification of the distribution.

When an analyst assumes the DGP to be a member of a particular parametric family of probability distributions, the resulting statistical model is a *parametric model*. The DGP behind the data is assumed to be a member of a that parametric family, and all that is left to do is figure out what those parameters are.

Sometimes the process of sampling itself justifies the use of a particular parametric model, because the analyst has introduced a known form of randomness into the DGP. This is the case of *design-based sampling*. The central limit theorem, an important result covered in Chapter 7, is another example of how to justify the use of a particular family of DGPs.

Another justification of a particular parametric model of a DGP is the assumption of *model-based sampling*. This is the assumption that the process by which the data came to be available to the analyst is a member of the conjectured parametric family, which is known except for the specific parameter values. Why is this assumption any good or even acceptable? In the best-case scenario, assuming the data was generated by some member of a specific parametric family can be rigorously justified in theoretical terms. This is occasionally the case with, for example, the normal, Poisson, Bernoulli, and exponential distributions, of which we see more later. In reality, however, such rigorous justification of a specific parametric model assumed in model-based sampling is rarely sought or offered.

One common reason to invoke model-based sampling assumptions is that the range of a DGP matches the range of the data the analyst is dealing with. We refer to this as *range matching*. For instance, if a dependent variable in a theory is an event count – the number of times some event happened in a specific interval of time – analysts often assume it to follow a Poisson or negative binomial probability distribution (discussed later), for no other reason than that these distributions assign positive probability to nonnegative integers, which is also the range of any variable that is a count or tally.

Range matching is important in and of itself to the extent that one wants a model to assign positive probability only to values of a variable that are actually feasible. The impulse behind it is to avoid the critique of least squares regression applied to binary dependent variables, noted in Chapter 2, that the model might predict values that are not actually feasible. However, because we usually use these models to identify and estimate relationships between a dependent variable and some covariates implied by a theory, the importance of range matching is often minimal and makes for a weak justification. As we discuss further in Chapter 9, range matching can lead analysts to favor "fragile" statistical procedures over more robust ones, all to solve a problem (infeasible predicted values) that is marginally relevant or irrelevant given our usual reason for using models (identifying relationships).

Besides theoretical justification that a DGP belongs to a parametric family (rare in applied work) and range matching of the data and the DGP (common in applied work), analysts can fall back on the flexibility of the parametric family as a justification for assuming it. The argument here is that a given parametric family might have many members with many kinds of shapes. Therefore, imposing the structure of that parametric family on the DGP is not actually all that constraining or restrictive. The beta distribution, for random variables in a closed interval of points, is a prime example: for various parameters, it can be skewed left or right, symmetric, unimodal, bimodal, for example. But other families are not actually so flexible; the Poisson is always skewed right, although the skew disappears as the mean increases and the Poisson collapses to a normal distribution. The normal distribution is always bell shaped. The exponential is always shaped like a ski slope. And so on. So this flexibility justification – which is more of an excuse that the parametric assumption has low costs, not high benefits – only goes so far.

Plenty of quantitative analysts doubt or dispute the blithe assumption of model-based sampling. Even researchers who use it do not dispute that it would be nice to draw conclusions that are not heavily dependent on specific parametric assumptions; when conclusions are so dependent, one has to wonder whether they are tapping into the real DGP of interest, or whether our view of that DGP is excessively structured by the assumption that it follows a particular model.

Avoiding this dependence on parametric assumptions is rationale behind *nonparametric* statistics. Several nonparametric inference procedures are presented briefly in Chapter 8. The trade-off for less model dependence, not surprisingly, is inferences that are often less sharp. With a specific parametric family assumed for the DGP, the observed data only has to be used to identify the unknown parameters of the particular member that happens to be the DGP for this specific data. That is typically "easier" for the data to "do" than to identify an entire functional form. So the fact remains that in many social science applications, particularly outside of survey research traditions where explicit control over randomness in sampling can (sometimes) allow for rigorous and careful selection of models of DGPs, quantitative analysts work and communicate in model-based terms.[2]

To that end, the next sections introduce several widely used parametric families of probability distributions. We discuss their properties and features and potential uses. We also pay particular attention to how the parameters of a DGP might be *modeled* as a function of explanatory variables and how such a model might be interpreted. That is, in the end, the ultimate purpose of these probability distributions for social science: we take them as models for a dependent variable, and we wish to link the systematic part of that dependent variable to other (explanatory) variables. This presentation is, by design, completely separate from issues of *estimation* of parameters of those models form data. The most important thing to understand about a logit model, Poisson model, and so on, is how it expresses dependencies among variables, and that is what is covered here.

6.2 THE BERNOULLI AND BINOMIAL DISTRIBUTION: BINARY EVENTS

Many important variables in social science can be expressed as binary or dichotomous outcomes: a state is either at war or not at war; a person either engages in a particular behavior or does not; a political system either has certain characteristics or it does not. This distribution is one that brings categorical, dichotomous events within the ambit of statistical methods.

A natural distributional choice for binary random variables is the *Bernoulli* distribution. This is the canonical distribution for a single flip of a coin that has probability p of coming up heads. We can think individual decisions to vote in an election as draws of Bernoulli random variables for each individual. In fact,

---

[2] *Semiparametric* models, as the name implies, occupy a middle ground between fully parametric, functional form-based models and fully nonparametric models. See Keele [2008].

it is hard to think of another sensible choice for the DGP here. The random variable Y in this case is either 0 (a person does not cast a ballot) or 1 (a person does cast a ballot).

The probability mass function (PMF) of a Bernoulli(p) random variable Y is as follows:

$$\Pr(Y = 1) = p; \ \Pr(Y = 0) = 1 - p, \qquad (6.2)$$

$$\text{given } p \in [0, 1], \mathcal{Y} = \{0, 1\}.$$

The probability p is the *parameter* of the Bernoulli distribution. So this is our first example of a parametric family; all Bernoulli distributions have a PMF with the above functional form, and all that distinguishes members of this family from each other is the value of the parameter p. Everything systematic about the behavior of a Bernoulli random variable Y is determined by p. Sometimes p is called the probability of "success" and $q \equiv 1 - p$ the probability of "failure." Obviously this is a naming convention with no substantive or normative significance.

The Bernoulli is a "one-parameter family" of distributions. The parameter p fully determines the mean, the variance, and all other moments of Y. When p changes, we get a different distribution from the Bernoulli family. For a fixed value of p, variation in Y in successive observations is entirely random. The name "parameter" connotes something in between a variable and a constant: for charting out the distribution of a given variable, the parameter is fixed. But the parameter can change and give a new distribution in this family.

For a Bernoulli random variable, $E(Y) = 1p + 0(1 - p) = p$, and $Var(Y) = p(1 - p)$. So the expected value of Y is simply the probability that $Y = 1$. This is analogous to the case of a dichotomous 0-1 variable in Chapter 2, where the mean was the share of observations for which the variable equals 1. Note that $Var(Y) = 0$ for $p = 0$ or $p = 1$: in these polar cases, the "coin" will definitely either be head or tail. There is no variation around this expectation. For $p = .5$, $Var(Y)$ takes its maximum possible value of .25. The standard deviation of Y in this case is then $\sqrt{.25} = .5$. Intuitively this makes a lot of sense: the variable is either 0 or 1, so it is always .5 away from its expected value, $p = .5$. The standard deviation, as always, is simply the "typical" departure of the variable from its mean, and for $p = .5$ that departure is always just .5.

Taking N independent draws from a given Bernoulli distribution defines a *binomial distribution* with parameters (N, p). If Z is binomial, $EZ = Np$ and $Var(Z) = N(p)(1 - p)$. The binomial is the natural distribution to count the number of successes in N trials, for example the number of times a person turns out to vote in N elections. Note, though, that if voting is thought to be "habit forming," or if the costs of voting in later elections go down (e.g., because a voter figures out where his polling place is), then a plain-vanilla binomial distribution is not appropriate, because the sequence of draws is not independent.

Any dichotomous random variable observed one time in isolation necessarily follows a Bernoulli distribution. So this is a fairly general model of the DGP of Y when Y is dichotomous. This covers the first ingredient of a statistical model for a binary variable – specifying the DGP from which the variable is drawn.

The second ingredient of a statistical model, the link between the DGP of Y and some explanatory factors, is where things can get more interesting with the Bernoulli. What a social scientist wants to do with a theory is to explain why the variable Y takes the value 1 sometimes and 0 other times, that is, explain the variation in Y across units, individuals, or cases. This is what positive theory in social science is about.

Such a theory of Y explains its behavior in terms of some other variables. One might theorize that voter turnout is a function of the voter's level of education, age, and competitiveness of the election: the dichotomous outcome variable, vote or don't vote, is related to or asserted to depend on some covariates: the voter's education level and age and the election's competitiveness.

Because Y is a random variable, we cannot explain everything about its variation from case to case. In the case of a Bernoulli random variable, the scope for explaining Y's behavior is simple: we can try to explain why p is big for some people and small for others, and thus why some people are more likely to vote than others. Put differently, p captures the systematic part of a Bernoulli random variable, and once p is specified, all variation in Y is random chance. Thus our ability to explain Y boils down to our ability to explain its parameter p.

6.2.1 Introducing a Covariate

A positive theory asserts $p = p(X)$, that the parameter p is a function of other covariates X. More education and more competitive races increase the value of p, making it more likely that the voter will vote under those conditions. A theory of a random variable Y means that we confine attention to its systematic part, its parameters. It does not assert that all individuals with "more" education vote and those with "less" education do not vote; even conditional on education, there is unexplained – random – variation in Y from person to person. The theory specifies one component of a statistical model – how the parameters of Y's DGP are related to covariates.

Such a model allows different individuals to have different turnout probabilities (more generally, different probabilities that $Y_i = 1$ for different units or individuals i). The parameter p is a function of covariates X, and so different values of X generally imply different values of p. Thus, fixing an age and level of competitiveness in an election, person i with a college degree is supposed to have one probability of voting; person j without a degree is supposed to have another. A theory that education tends to increase turnout asserts that the former is bigger than the latter.

By the same token, given a model $p = p(X)$, two individuals with the same covariates are asserted to have the same probability of voting. Once the covariates are set at specific values, no more explanation of Y's behavior is possible other than that it follows a Bernoulli distribution. That does not mean two voters with the same Xs actually do make the same decision to vote or not; it means they have the same probability of making a given decision, and the theory offers no further explanation of the difference. Somebody else, with a new theory, could try to explain it, and for a given dataset, that would require new covariates.

Note that for a Bernoulli random variable, $p(X) = E(Y|X)$: just as p is the expected value of Y, p as a function of X is the expected value of Y given X. In other words, in modeling a dichotomous variable's systematic behavior, we are specifying a relationship between its conditional mean and the explanatory variables. This is a type of *regression model*: $E(Y|X)$ is the regression of Y on X, as noted in Chapter 5, and a theory of how p varies is therefore a model of the regression of Y.

In common usage, statistical modeling usually comes with a more specific link between p and the explanatory factors, in the form of a mathematical function expressing this relationship. In fact, in my experience, many scholars would not consider a link between parameter and covariates to be a model at all until it specifies that link according to a specific mathematical function.

By far the most common function to establish this link is a linear one. With a specification of the class of DGPs to which Y's DGP belongs, such a link specifies a *linear model*. In Chapter 2, we saw some of the virtues of linear functions for expressing relationships; those benefits carry over here as well. Linear models express the dependence of Y's parameters on X in a very sharp, easily interpretable fashion. That is why linear models are so common. The word "linear" should almost always be followed by "model" to remind us that this is just a simplification imposed on the DGP's link to the covariate to make it easy to interpret.

In terms of the Bernoulli DGP, a linear model of the regression with one covariate is $p(X) \equiv E(Y|X) = \alpha + \beta X$. Note again that the conditional mean function of X is the same as the probability that $Y = 1$ for a given value of X; that is what the "$\equiv$" means. Because this is a linear model of the probability that a binary variable is 1, this linear regression model is called a *linear probability model*.

A linear probability model poses an obvious potential problem. The systematic part we are modeling is $p \in [0, 1]$, a probability. But for *any* values of α and β, it would be possible to find values of X such that $\alpha + \beta X \notin [0, 1]$. This is a *range-matching* problem: the range of the dependent variable Y (binary) is not equal to the range of a linear model (in principle, all real numbers). Of course, whether this alone invalidates a linear model of $E(Y|X)$ is open to question.

If a linear model of $p(X) = E(Y|X)$ cannot be defended, a small trick helps us out: although $p \in [0, 1]$, note that $\frac{p}{1-p}$ can be any positive number. This fraction is called the *odds on* the event $Y = 1$: the probability it happens divided by the probability it does not. If p is small, $\frac{p}{1-p}$ is small too. If p is a peppercorn shy of 1, $\frac{p}{1-p}$ approaches infinity (as the denominator gets smaller the fraction gets bigger). And, really, dealing with $\frac{p}{1-p}$ instead of just p is not asking for more information; once we know p, we know $\frac{p}{1-p}$ as well. So now we have a transformation of the systematic part that is a little more forgiving in terms of the range it can occupy. It cannot be negative, but at least we have convinced it to allow us to specify it as anything positive.

Of course, that's only part of the problem: $\alpha + \beta X < 0$ is always positive for some values of X. So this linear function of X is not a suitable specification for the odds $\frac{p}{1-p}$. But a second small trick is also helpful to deal with this: $e^{\alpha+\beta X}$ can also only take on nonnegative values, just like $\frac{p}{1-p}$.

So instead of a linear model of the regression, we can use the model $\frac{p}{1-p} = e^{\alpha+\beta X}$. Here we have a specification that captures the systematic part of Y and can relate to a function of the regressors X in a way that satisfies the range restriction on p in a Bernoulli distribution. The left- and right-hand sides of the $=$ sign have the same range, all positive numbers.

So for Y following a Bernoulli distribution, we can say

$$\frac{p}{1-p} = e^{\alpha+\beta X}. \tag{6.3}$$

A third small trick makes the model even easier to deal with: in Equation 6.3, take the natural log (ln) of both sides to give

$$\ln\left(\frac{p}{1-p}\right) = \alpha + \beta X. \tag{6.4}$$

The left-hand side of this is the "log odds" or "logit," and this is a *logit model*, also known as *logistic regression*. Thus, this is still a linear model – not of the regression $E(Y|X)$ but of the logit of $\frac{p}{1-p}$. This expression is handy in that the right-hand side does not involve any powers; instead it is a linear function of the covariate. And it's still a model of Y's regression; $E(Y|X)$ is clearly specified by this model. But it is not a linear model of the regression. It is a *generalized linear model*: a nonlinear, invertible function of the model parameter is expressed as a linear function of the covariate(s). The logit model is perhaps the leading case of a statistical model when the dependent variable is binary.

The logit model can be easily extended to any number of covariates. With two of them, X_1 and X_2, entered additively, it looks like this:

$$\ln\left(\frac{p}{1-p}\right) = \alpha + \beta_1 X_1 + \beta_2 X_2. \tag{6.5}$$

The basics are easier to internalize with just one, so we'll stick with that case for now. Later in this chapter (Section 6.7), we turn back to a few issues

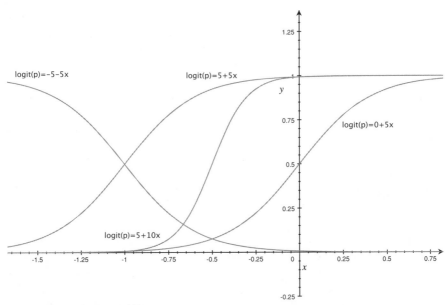

FIGURE 6.1. Examples of logistic curves.

about including multiple covariates that are common to all generalized linear models.

Because the logit of p is a linear function of X in this model, and p is a nonlinear function of its logit, the regression $p(X)$ is obviously expressed as a nonlinear function of X. Rather, p is related to X through a *logistic curve*. The logistic curve relating p and X looks like a rightward-stretched "S." Several examples of logistic curves are shown in Figure 6.1. "logit(p)" refers to the function $\ln \frac{p(x)}{1-p(x)}$. A larger value of β makes the curve steeper, meaning that for intermediate values of x, a small change in x produces a large change in $p(x)$. For $\beta < 0$, increases in x lead to decreases in $p(x)$. In all cases, when x is relatively extreme (high or low), even a large change in x has a very small effect on $p(x)$. A change in α shifts the whole curve to the left or right without changing how steep it is.

It bears noting that this is not a model of Y itself. It is a model of a parameter of the DGP of Y. A value of X determines the parameter p according to the model in equation 6.4. Then that value of p determines the probability $Y = 1$, according to the Bernoulli DGP postulated for Y. The statistical model comprises these two components – the family to which the DGP belongs and the function relating its parameter to X. Once p and the DGP are determined, all remaining variation in Y is inexplicable noise. The model is only about the systematic part of Y, that is, its parameter and DGP, not the inexplicable noise.

Extending the logit to include more covariates is straightforward. They just enter the right-hand side additively (or in some other function the researcher specifies), and each covariate gets its own slope. The latter feature is what makes the right-hand side linear; it is *linear in parameters*. The variables can be any function the researcher chooses of the data on her computer. So the right-hand side does not have to be *linear in variables*.

The parameters α and β determine, for any value of X, the effect of a change in X on $p = E(Y|X)$. When X is measured cardinally, the quantity we are interested in here is a derivative: the change in the regression $E(Y|X)$ for an infinitesimal change in X. The *marginal effect* of X on the systematic part of Y is

$$\frac{dE(Y|X)}{dX} = \beta[\Pr(Y = 1|X)][1 - \Pr(Y = 1|X)]. \tag{6.6}$$

When a researcher feeds N observations of a binary Y variable and some covariates into a computer and asks a statistics software package to fit a logit model to the data, the computer will return its best guess of β for each covariate X. So it is important to know how to interpret this substantively, and that is what a marginal effect is about.

In this part of the text, we are only examining the interpretation of the guess about β returned by the computer and its connection to substantive theory of how y varies or is determined. When reading, writing about, and doing research with an eye to substantive implications, that is the first order of business. But there is also an important matter of how statistics programs go about obtaining "best guesses" of β in the first place. What makes a guess the "best" one? How is it determined from the data? How stable is that guess under slight changes in the data? How much would we expect that "best guess" to change, if a new sample of N observations were drawn from the same DGP? These are core issues in the theory of statistical inference, and they are covered later in the book. The loose idea behind the "best guess" about β is that it is the value of β that makes the observed sample as likely as it can possibly be. That is the idea behind *maximum likelihood estimation*, an approach to estimation covered in more detail in Chapter 9. The typical variation in that guess about β across samples is captured by the *standard error* of β, a concept covered in great detail in Chapters 7 and 9. Although these issues are important, they are not actually necessary to understand model building and substantive interpretation at the level of DGPs, the issue on the table now.

Note the difference between the marginal effect in this case and a linear model of the regression itself (i.e., a linear probability model). In the latter case, the marginal effect of X on $E(Y|X)$ was simply β itself, so X had a linear effect on the systematic part of Y. Here the effect of X is nonlinear, because $[\Pr(Y = 1|X)][1 - \Pr(Y = 1|X)]$ is a nonlinear function of X. However, because $\Pr(Y = 1|X)$ is between 0 and 1, the *sign* of the marginal effect is determined entirely by the sign of β. So the sign of β is enough to specify the direction of the effect of X on $E(Y|X)$ but not its size.

In addition to the effect of X on $E(Y|X)$, the logit model also specifies the probability of $Y = 1$ for any value of X. Specifically, given β and some value x_i, we can plug these into Equation 6.3 and rearrange a little to find

$$p_i = \Pr(Y_i = 1) = \frac{e^{\alpha + \beta x_i}}{1 + e^{\alpha + \beta x_i}} \tag{6.7}$$

$$1 - p_i = \Pr(Y_i = 0) = \frac{1}{1 + e^{\alpha + \beta x_i}}. \tag{6.8}$$

Therefore, p_i is always between 0 and 1 in this model.[3]

In short, when we try to understand the systematic component of dichotomous random variables using some positive theory, we wind up really wanting to understand the probability that Y takes the value 1 (and therefore, of course, the probability of 0). So having specified p as a linear function of X by way of α and β, we have as before specified a conditional expectation. The parameter of the DGP p has been reexpressed in terms of the parameters α and β combined with the covariate X.

A PMF closely related to the Bernoulli(p) distribution is the Binomial(n, p). The Binomial is simply a sequence of n independent Bernoulli(p) trials. For a random variable that is dichotomous on each trial, the binomial specifies the probability of any specific number of 1s in n trials. If X denotes that number of 1s, its expected value is $E(X) = np$ and variance is $Var(X) = np(1 - p)$.

A closely related alternative to the logit model, applicable to data with a binary dependent variable, is called the *probit* model. This replaces the logistic CDF in equation 6.8 with the normal CDF. The normal CDF does not have a "closed form" expression that does not involve an integral of the normal PDF, so it cannot be written in a clean form as the logit can. The idea is the same; the curve that relates X to p is slightly different. In particular, the normal CDF (discussed further later) also looks like a stretched-out S.[4]

6.2.2 Other Flavors of Logit and Probit

The "ordinary logit" and "ordinary probit" models just laid out apply to dichotomous dependent variables. But the same logic can be extended to apply to dependent variables with any number of categories. A variable of this nature is *multichotomous*. For instance, a voter in a parliamentary election can usually vote for one of several political parties, and there is not necessarily a natural

---

[3] The logistic curve is a probability distribution in its own right, and its CDF at $x_i \beta$ is given in Equation 6.8. The logistic distribution is a bell-shaped distribution and looks a lot like the normal, but its tails are slightly thicker (although not as thick as the pathological and beguiling Cauchy) and it has a much simpler functional form.

[4] The analytical simplicity of the logit model partly accounts for its popularity. When computing power was scarce, giving the software a closed-form expression to evaluate according to a known formula was often preferable to the probit model, which requires numerical simulations to identify parameters. Nowadays, this doesn't much matter.

ordering of the Social Democrats, Christian Democrats, Green Party, and so on.

The extensions of logit and probit to this type of dependent variable are *multinomial logit* and *multinomial probit*, respectively. The statistical model postulates a *multinomial distribution* for the dependent variable. If Y's possible values are 0, 1, and 2, the multinomial distribution, the multinomial is a two-parameter family specifying $\Pr[Y = 0] = p, \Pr[Y = 1] = q, \Pr[Y = 2] = 1 - p - q$, where $p \in [0, 1]$ and $q \in [0, 1]$. The multinomial logit links these parameters to covariates just as the ordinary logit does; the multinomial probit also works for each parameter as the ordinary probit does.

The idea in multinomial logit is that one of the outcomes is a "baseline" category; suppose the baseline is $Y = 0$ (it does not matter which this is; it is up to the researcher to specify). Multinomial logit consists of two separate but linked logit models. The first specifies the effect of each covariate on the probability of $Y = 1$ versus $Y = 0$. The second specifies the effect of each covariate on the probability of $Y = 2$ versus $Y = 0$. Each covariate enters in each of these two logit models. So a covariate X has two β_X values associated with it: one reflecting its effect on changing from the baseline to the first alternative, the other reflecting its effect on changing from the baseline to the second alternative.

These two logits are linked in the sense that the implied probability of each value of Y, for any given value of X, must add up to 1. Because of this, multinomial logit is different than breaking a multichotomous variable into a collection of dichotomous variables and running ordinary logit on each one; these ordinary logits would not satisfy the adding-up constraint. The multinomial logit uses the information that the DGP is multinomial, whereas the individual ordinary logits would not.

Like ordinary logit and probit, multinomial logit and probit are similar, except for one aspect of the multinomial logit that the multinomial probit does not have. Specifically, multinomial logit implies a property known as *independence of irrelevant alternatives*. This is sometimes known as the "red bus–blue bus problem." Suppose there are three alternative modes of transportation to get from point A to point B: taking a red bus, taking a blue bus that uses the same route on the same schedule, and taking a car. Suppose that p is the probability of taking a red bus. Then if that option is suddenly deleted, multinomial logit implies that the probability of each of the remaining two options increases by $\frac{p}{2}$. But because the red and blue bus options are so similar, one would expect the probability of taking the red bus would increase by a lot, and the probability of taking a car would increase only a little, if at all. Because of this problem, multinomial logit is best used in cases where none of the alternative categories are close substitutes for each other. In any case, multinomial probit does not have this issue.

Another extension of the ordinary logit/probit framework addresses dependent variables that are *ordinal*: for instance, an individual may drop out of high school, complete high school, complete some college, or complete a college degree; a government safety regulator can respond to a violation either with a warning, a warning and a fine, or with legal action against the violator; a voter may identify her attachment to a political party as strong, moderate, or weak. In all of these cases, a positive theory deals with the effect of covariates on where the dependent variable falls in these orderings.

Ordinal logit and *ordinal probit* models are designed to deal with ordered dependent variables. Suppose that there are J possible categories of Y, and category j is "bigger" than category $j - 1$. For each covariate in an ordered logit or probit, β describes the effect of a change in that covariate on the probability that Y falls in category j versus $j - 1$. Both ordered logit and probit assume that this effect is constant across all categories of Y. This is assumption is known as *parallel regression* or *proportional odds*.[5] So ordinal logit/probit models specify one coefficient β for each covariate.

Ordered probit is further addressed in Section 6.9.1, which reviews an application from recent literature in detail.

6.3 THE POISSON DISTRIBUTION: EVENT COUNTS

A lot of outcomes of interesting or important political outcomes can be measured just (or only) by counting them. How many countries in a particular region are experiencing civil wars in a given year? How many voting fraud challenges are sustained in the U.S. states in a given year? How many criminal convictions does a person experience? How many political parties are "competitive" by some specific definition in a collection of countries? In all these cases, the dependent variable is a nonnegative integer: a tally of the number of occurrences of some event in a given interval of time.

All of these measurements involve counts of things. There are a few parametric families that, across fairly wide experience, have come to be seen as useful models of random variables that are counts. One important and simple family for event counts is the *Poisson distribution*. The Poisson assigns positive probability to nonnegative integers. Tallies or counts of how many times an event occurred have this feature as well, and that alone is enough to make the Poisson a compelling DGP when the dependent variable is a count variable.

A random variable Y following a Poisson distribution has a PMF

$$f(y) = \frac{e^{-\lambda}\lambda^y}{y!},$$

given $\lambda > 0$, $\mathcal{Y} = \{0, 1, 2, 3, \ldots\}$.

(6.9)

---

[5] The parallel regression assumption can be formally tested and relaxed if necessary, but the extended versions are beyond our scope here.

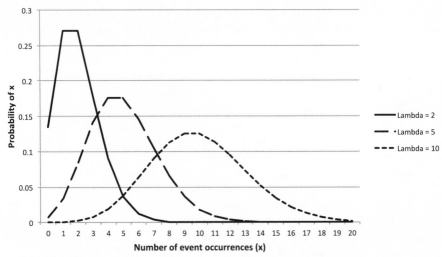

FIGURE 6.2. Three members of the Poisson family.

For $Y \sim \text{Poisson}(\lambda)$, $E(Y) = Var(Y) = \lambda$. All members of the Poisson family have this functional form; what distinguishes one from another is the parameter λ. The Poisson is a one-parameter family, and λ is the parameter. It specifies both the mean and the variance, which are the same. The range of possible values is all nonnegative integers. So λ is the expected number of occurrences of whatever event is being counted.

Thus the Poisson distribution specifies a probability for each nonnegative integer, which is the probability that the count in question assumes that specific value. The PMF is right-skewed. Three examples of the PMF for different parameters are shown in Figure 6.2.

A positive theory explaining the behavior of some event count is a specification of other variables that are related to or affect the event count, and how. The theory will assert a particular relationship between explanatory variable(s) X and the event count Y. It might say, for example, that a senator tends to sponsor more bills as his level of seniority increases, as he becomes better "networked" among legislators in some observable sense (say, mutual campaign donations), when he is in the majority party, and so forth.

Of course, no collection of factors can perfectly explain the event count across senators. Bill sponsorship activity can be considered a random variable for each senator. It is always possible, for example, that unobserved events in the senator's home state divert his attention from bill-sponsorship activity. Or that a senator takes an idiosyncratic personal stake in an issue and introduces a slew of bills on it. At the level of an individual senator, we can regard this as either theoretical or fundamental uncertainty.

Once we've specified that Y is a $\text{Poisson}(\lambda)$ random variable, the only possible way for explanatory variables X to affect Y systematically is by somehow affecting λ. That is the only systematic part of the value Y takes in this model. Once λ is specified, all variation in the value of the dependent variable is given up to random variation, which we cannot explain from observation to observation by definition. So given that Y is a Poisson variable, a positive theory must tell us something about how λ depends on some explanatory factor X.

Because $E(Y) = \lambda$ in the Poisson family, modeling $\lambda(X)$ as a function of X means we are once again turning our attention to a conditional mean – the expected value of Y given X. For the same reasons laid out earlier, a linear model of this conditional mean is sometimes useful. Assuming a Poisson DGP for Y and a linear model of λ as a function of X completes a specification of a statistical model – one that is both parametric and linear.

But as with a Bernoulli DGP for Y, a simple linear model of λ as a function of X does not satisfy the restriction $\lambda(X) > 0$ for all possible values of X, no matter the values of α, β. By using the following specification rather than a linear one, we can still model the conditional mean while respecting the limited range of its values:

$$\lambda(X) \equiv E(Y|X) = e^{\alpha + \beta X}. \tag{6.10}$$

Both sides of this can be any positive number. By taking the natural log of both sides, we wind up with a linear model of the natural log of the regression $\lambda(X)$, rather than a linear model of the regression itself. That is not a much more complicated link from parameter to covariate, and it captures the range restriction that $\lambda > 0$. Combined with the assumption that the DGP is Poisson, this equation defines the canonical *Poisson model*.[6] As with the logit model and other models described later, it is straightforward to extend this to include other covariates on the right-hand side; each covariate gets its own slope term.

In this model, we let the parameter β determine the effect that a change in X has on Y. Note that this determination of λ still allows it to differ from individual to individual whenever they have different values of X. Once we have a value of β, which *is* the same for every individual i, then a value of x_i for individual i produces a specific value of λ_i.

Again, an important aspect of this DGP is how large an effect X has on the systematic part of Y. For the Poisson model as specified here, the marginal effect is

$$\frac{dE(Y|X)}{dX} = \beta e^{\alpha + \beta X}. \tag{6.11}$$

This is simply the derivative of Equation 6.10 with respect to x, for the calculus-minded. When a researcher feeds N observations of some event count Y and covariates X into a computer and asks a statistics package to fit a Poisson model, the computer will report its best guess about the β for each covariate,

---

[6] Although the exponential function is the default form for Poisson models, any invertible function that is always nonnegative will do.

as well as a number of other numbers. The key issue at this point is interpreting what the estimated β values say about the effect of X on $E(Y|X)$.

This marginal effect itself depends on the value X takes the first place, meaning it is nonlinear in X. This is as in the logit model for dichotomous Y, but unlike the (normal) linear model. As with other marginal effects, this is an important feature of a Poisson model. It is not enough to simply know some estimate of β to get an accurate sense of the effect of X on the value of Y in expectation. But if one only needs to know the sign of the effect of X on $E(Y|X)$, β alone is enough to determine that.

One important feature of Poisson event counts is that the waiting time between them is exponentially distributed (discussed later) and the *hazard rate* associated with that waiting time – the probability a new instance at time t given that no new instances have occurred since the last one – is constant over time. This may or may not be a suitable assumption for the DGP, but once the Poisson is invoked, there is no way around it.

Suppose for instance that Y is the number of violent conflicts between two nation-states in a particular period of time. If engaging in violent conflict takes resources from a finite pool, a spell of many instances may need to be followed by a regrouping period. But this implies an increasing hazard rate: the probability of violent conflict at instant t goes up if many instants have elapsed since the last conflict, because groups will have had time to replenish resources.

On the other hand, we could also imagine that conflict would breed more conflict as it leads to a weakening of social order and institutions for nonviolent settlement of political disputes, as well as a development of aggression and desires for retribution. This would produce a decreasing hazard rate; going through a quiet spell removes all these causes of violence and lowers its probability. Either one of these could be true, and more to the point, it would be surprising in light of these competing explanations if a constant hazard were exactly true. Although the hazard can't be both decreasing and increasing, these stories cast doubt on the suitability of the Poisson model in some applications. Other parametric families discussed later are more flexible than the Poisson in this respect and can be useful when it is unsuitable to make these assumptions about the DGP.

Besides its implicit assumptions about the hazard rate, the restriction in the Poisson distribution that $E(Y) = Var(Y)$ is often untenable. There are DGPs that retain the desirable features of the Poisson (namely, defining Y over positive integers, natural for event counts) without imposing this restriction. The negative binomial model, in particular, is actually more commonly used in applications as a DGP for event count data because of this. It is a more complicated family than the Poisson and, for our purposes right now, not more illuminating. Usually, analysts start event-count models by testing the Poisson assumption that $E(Y|X) = Var(Y|X)$, then reject it, then work with a negative binomial model instead.

6.4 DGPs FOR DURATIONS

Social scientists often find themselves wanting to know the determinants of how long a social event lasts. Why do some wars end earlier than others? Why do some strikes last a long time? Why do some leaders of autocratic governments get deposed quickly while others stay in power for decades? Why do some political protests persist for weeks or months, while others fizzle after a weekend? A social scientist studying any of these issues makes progress by relating the duration to some explanatory factors. Duration of protests might be related to a country's degree of economic malaise and availability of other channels for expressing dissatisfaction with the ruling elites. An autocrat's time in power might be affected by their distribution of economic rents to leaders of key political or ethnic factions (Bueno de Mesquita et al. [2003]).

In all of these cases, the dependent variable is a positive number and reflects the amount of time for which some event lasted. The units of time are of course up to the analyst and depend on the problem at hand. For modeling the duration of protests, days or weeks would probably be natural; for modeling the duration of a parliament, presumably years would be appropriate.

6.4.1 Exponential Distribution

We can deal with these issues by specifying a *duration model*. Duration modeling is also known as *event history analysis, survival analysis*, or *failure time analysis*. When researchers specify parametric models of durations, there are a few especially common DGPs. The simplest is the exponential. The exponential distribution, like other parametric models of durations, is a continuous distribution that assigns positive density to all nonnegative numbers. Durations have that property too; that is one of the principal reasons this distribution is useful for modeling durations. The cumulative distribution function $F(y)$ indicates the probability that an event starting at some initial time 0 lasts up to time y and then stops.

The exponential density is

$$f(y) = \frac{e^{-y/\theta}}{\theta}, \tag{6.12}$$

given $\theta > 0$, $y > 0$.

For an exponential random variable, $E(Y) = \theta$ and $Var(Y) = \theta^2$. If this distribution is understood as a DGP for a duration, θ is the expected amount of time the duration lasts. Different values of θ give different members of the exponential family, but they all have this same general functional form. The parameter θ is a "scale" parameter. It determines how one particular shape is spread out. Three exponential PDF's are displayed in Figure 6.3.

The exponential distribution is "memoryless." Consider two numbers s and t, with $s < t$. Given that Y exceeds the threshold s, the probability that Y also

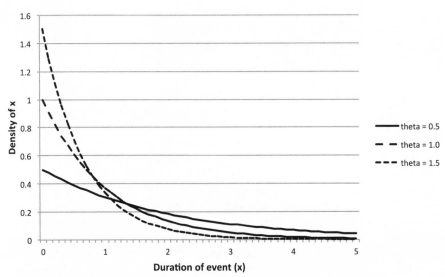

FIGURE 6.3. Members of the exponential family.

exceeds the threshold t is always equal to the unconditional probability that Y exceeds the threshold $t - s$.

In concrete terms, consider the event that a governing coalition collapses in a parliamentary democracy. For statistical modeling, we would consider this event a random variable. Suppose further that we assume it is exponentially distributed. This implies that the probability of coalition collapse some time after $y = 3$ years, given that it has not collapsed after $y = 2$ years, is exactly the same as the probability of collapse some time after $3 - 2 = 1$ year, unconditionally and starting from the date of coalition formation ($y = 0$).

To put this differently, the conditional exponential distribution defined only over Y values above some point y is exactly a miniature version of the whole (unconditional) exponential distribution. In the conditional case, the ratio of the density at any point $r > y$ to the density at y is exactly the same as the ratio of the density at $r - y$ to the density at 0. On the one hand, this makes the exponential distribution simple to work with; on the other hand, it makes it unsuitable as a model for a lot of interesting durations in social science.

It turns out that there is a close connection between the exponential DGP for durations and the Poisson model of event counts. If an event count random variable follows a Poisson distribution, the waiting time between occurrences of the event follows an exponential distribution (Casella and Berger [2002]). This may help to give some sense of the suitability of the Poisson as a model for some event count of interest. For example, if the waiting time between two events is not likely to be memoryless, then the count of events per time period is not likely to be Poisson.

6.4.2 Exponential Hazard Rate Model

Usually duration models actually focus not on the duration of event itself, but a related quantity known as the *hazard rate*. The hazard rate gives the probability that an event terminates at some time y, given that it has not terminated before y. In other words, the hazard of event at time y is the conditional probability or density of the event ending at y, given that it has not ended prior to y. Formally, the hazard rate is

$$h(y) = \frac{f(y)}{1 - F(y)}. \tag{6.13}$$

Because the CDF $F(y)$ reflects the probability that the event ends at or before time y, $1 - F(y)$ reflects the probability that it has not ended by time y. The numerator is the density function, which captures the instantaneous change in the probability that the event ends at y.

It turns out that for exponentially distributed durations, the hazard rate is simply $\frac{1}{\theta}$, where θ is the scale parameter of the PDF. This is constant over time: the probability of termination at time y does not go up or down as time passes. This is exactly because of the exponential distribution is memoryless. Suppose, for example, that a researcher is studying the duration of peace between warring factions in some area. If a researcher is willing to assume that, in the DGP, wars don't become more likely just because there hasn't been one for a while, the exponential duration-constant hazard might be appropriate.

Note that the hazard rate can be any positive number. In the exponential case, when y is very close to 0, the density $f(y)$ in the numerator is very large, and the denominator is close to 1. So the hazard rate is very large too. A linear hazard model $h(y|X) = \frac{1}{\theta(X)} \equiv E(Y|X) = \alpha + \beta X$ would be undesirable inasmuch as the implied value of $h(y)$ could be negative for some values of X.

We encountered this same problem when modeling the Poisson regression, and addressed it by specifying the right-hand side as an exponential rather than linear function. That is, $h(y|X) = e^{\alpha + \beta X}$. This can also be rewritten $\ln h(y|X) = \alpha + \beta X$, because the natural log function is the inverse of the exponential.

Because the link from parameters to covariates is the same as in the Poisson model, the marginal effect of X on $h(y|X)$ is also the same as in that model. In particular,

$$\frac{dh(y|X)}{dX} = \beta e^{\alpha + \beta X}. \tag{6.14}$$

Sometimes a constant hazard doesn't make sense. For instance, if a period of peace allows for buildup of military resources and a longer period of peace allows for more buildup, it is possible that the hazard rate of peace goes up as its duration increases. That is, the probability that the peace ends, given that it has lasted for a given amount of time, increases as the amount of time it has lasted increases.

In such a case, a duration or waiting time modeled by the exponential distribution is not appropriate, but other parametric families can handle this possibility. They are more complicated but also less restrictive in their assumptions about the distribution of durations. This is a common trade-off in statistical modeling; the simplest distributions may be inflexible about some properties for which a researcher does not wish to make a firm assumption. We saw the same trade-off earlier with the simple but restrictive Poisson distribution versus the more complicated but more flexible negative binomial.

6.4.3 Weibull Distribution

One such distribution that may be more appropriate for studying durations in politics, and one that is more commonly used for this purpose, is the Weibull distribution. The PDF of the Weibull is

$$f(y) = \left(\frac{\gamma}{\theta}\right) y^{\gamma-1} e^{-y^{\gamma}/\theta}, \text{ for } y > 0, \theta > 0, \gamma > 0. \tag{6.15}$$

This is clearly more complicated than the exponential PDF, and the Weibull's mean and variance are as well. They both involve something called the "gamma function." The details are presented in this chapter's online appendix; for now we can simply note that the gamma function is not unlike the idea of factorials, except it operates on any positive number while factorials apply only to integers.

Again θ and γ are parameters determining a specific member of the Weibull family. Note that if $\gamma = 1$, the Weibull collapses to an exponential distribution with parameter θ: the latter is a special case of the former. Alternatively, if Y is distributed exponentially, then $X = Y^{1/\gamma}$ is Weibull distributed.

The Weibull distribution, although messier than the exponential, is useful for modeling hazard rates that either increase or decrease with time. The Weibull hazard rate is

$$h(y) = \left(\frac{\gamma}{\theta}\right) y^{\gamma-1}. \tag{6.16}$$

So the Weibull hazard is a function of time y. Hazard rates that are either increasing or decreasing with time can result depending on the Weibull's parameter values. If the substantive question at hand requires this, something like the Weibull can be useful. For example, in modeling the duration of unemployment spells (and, say, how they depend on benefits and the political backdrop), we might want to take account of the fact that the longer someone's been on unemployment, the more likely their spell is to end at any moment. This is an increasing hazard.

Specifying a hazard rate that follows from a parametric DGP such as the exponential or Weibull is one approach to modeling durations. There are other widely used models for durations that do not make any assumptions at all about the functional form of the DGP (or its hazard rate). The leading example is the *Cox proportional hazards model*, which assumes that assume that a "baseline" or unconditional hazard $h_0(y)$ is proportional to an exponential function of covariates. A simple Cox proportional hazards model with one covariate X is

$$h(y|X) = h_0(y)e^{\alpha+\beta X}. \tag{6.17}$$

The "baseline" hazard function $h_0(y)$ can be estimated from empirical data and may depend on the duration y. The parameter β structures how the covariate X changes the hazard rate, in proportion to the baseline hazard $h_0(y)$. This is a *semiparametric* model: it does not assume a specific parametric family for the duration's DGP $f(y)$ but does assume a parametric link between the hazard rate and covariates. The Weibull hazard model is the special (fully parametric) case of this model in which the baseline hazard $h_0(y)$ is the Weibull hazard rate, as given in Equation 6.16. As noted earlier, an exponential hazard model is $h(y|X) = e^{\alpha+\beta X}$, so it is simply a special case of a proportional hazards model in which the baseline hazard is constant over time.

These issues, although interesting, are beyond the scope of a basic treatment. More focused treatments such as Box-Steffensmeier and Jones [2004] and Cameron and Trivedi [2005] start basic and go into considerable depth. The material in this subsection should at least give students a starting point to delve into this material.

6.5 THE UNIFORM DISTRIBUTION: EQUALLY LIKELY OUTCOMES

When analyzing probability measures in Chapter 4, we found it useful to consider the special case in which all events have equally likely outcomes – not because of the descriptive accuracy of this case but because of its simplicity. A similar situation arises with random variables in which all outcomes are equally likely. These variables are defined by *uniform distributions*. The uniform is a useful choice when a random variable has definite (if possibly unknown) maximum and minimum values, and there is no basis for assuming that any range of its values is more likely than any other range of the same size.

The uniform has discrete and continuous versions. The continuous version[7] describes a random variable X that lies in the range $[a, b]$. All subsets of that interval with equal width have equal probability under the uniform(a, b) distribution. In this sense, it is a distribution of equally likely outcomes over an

---

[7] The continuous uniform distribution is a special case of the beta distribution; see the online appendix to this chapter.

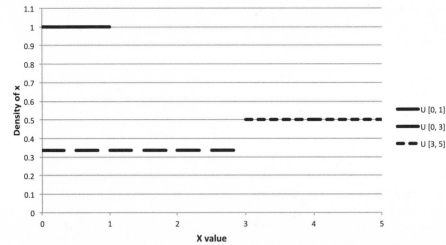

FIGURE 6.4. Uniform probability density function.

interval. Its PDF is simple:

$$f(x) = \frac{1}{b-a}, \tag{6.18}$$

given $a < x < b$, $a \in \mathbb{R}$, $b \in \mathbb{R}$.

The parameters are a and b. For a uniform(a, b) random variable, $E(X) = \frac{a+b}{2}$ and $Var(X) = \frac{(b-a)^2}{12}$. The expected value is simply the midpoint of the range of X values. It is slightly odd to see such a conspicuous number as 12 in a general specification of a moment, but there it is. A wider spread in a uniform distribution does not necessarily affect its mean, but increases its variance. This pushes the density down vertically, so that it always integrates to 1.

So the PDF is simply a flat line, constant in X. Three members of the (continuous) uniform family are shown in Figure 6.4. The height of the PDF is inversely related to the width of the set of X values. The CDF, by the same token, is also simple: $F(X) = \frac{x-a}{b-a}$. In the uniform $(0, 1)$, the PDF is simply 1, and the CDF is simply x. The probability that $X < x$ is drawn is simply x itself in this case.

6.6 THE NORMAL DISTRIBUTION: WHEN ALL ELSE FAILS

Sometimes a researcher wishes to develop a parametric model, but the dependent variable lacks distinguishing features that usually lead researchers to DGPs such as the Poisson, Bernoulli, or exponential. When the dependent variable can take any conceivable range, and the analyst lacks any good basis to choose another DGP, or simply when all else fails, the normal distribution is a suitable, or at least common, catch-all family.

There are, it turns out, situations in which a normal DGP can be rigorously justified, at least as an approximation. Because of the manner in which many statistical estimators are computed, the normal distribution plays an important role in statistical inference, whether or not a lot of parametric structure is assumed about Y's DGP, and in some approaches, even if the DGP of Y is assumed to follow some other specific parametric family. We encounter these points in later chapters (Chapters 7 and 9), and when you encounter the phrases "central limit theorem" and "maximum likelihood sampling distribution," remember this passage.

Therefore, for a variety of reasons beyond choosing a model for Y's DGP, the normal distribution is important in statistical inference. Here we introduce it and analyze its properties primarily as a parametric family that might be invoked for the DGP of a dependent variable in a statistical model.

6.6.1 Normal Density

The *normal density function* is defined as follows:

$$f(x) = \frac{1}{\sigma\sqrt{2\pi}} e^{\frac{-(x-\mu)^2}{\sigma^2}}, \tag{6.19}$$

given $\mu \in \mathbb{R}, \sigma > 0, \mathcal{X} = \mathbb{R}$.

The normal is a two-parameter family of distributions, with $E(X) = \mu \in \mathbb{R}$ and $Var(X) = \sigma^2 > 0$. The only difference between members of the normal family is these parameters. Except for them, all normal distributions are identical. A normal density defines a "bell-shaped" curve (several other densities do as well, including the logistic). The PDFs of several members of the family are shown in Figure 6.5.

Some key properties of the normal distribution can be identified by inspecting the mathematical definition carefully. In the normal PDF, all terms in the fraction $\frac{1}{\sigma\sqrt{2\pi}}$ are positive (π is just the familiar constant 3.14159 etc.). The exponential term $e^{\frac{-(x-\mu)^2}{\sigma^2}}$ is also always positive because any positive number ($e = 2.7182\ldots$ – Euler's number (not to be confused with Euler's constant)) raised to a power is positive. Thus the density is positive for all real numbers x (as it must be). But the exponent itself, $\frac{-(x-\mu)^2}{\sigma^2}$, has a maximum value of 0, which occurs when $x = \mu$; in that case the normal density is $f(\mu) = \frac{1}{\sigma\sqrt{2\pi}}$ because $e^0 \equiv 1$.

Furthermore, the exponent gets smaller as x gets further from μ, so that the density of a value x far from the mean μ quickly gets very small. The exponent changes in the same way as x departs from μ, whether x is above or below; because the exponent is the only part that is a function of x, the density is *symmetric* around μ in x. This means that its graph to the left of μ is the mirror image of its graph to the right of μ.

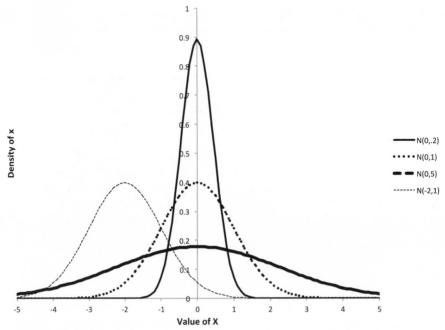

FIGURE 6.5. Members of the normal family.

Finally, as x departs from μ in either direction, the density first decreases at a decreasing rate up to $x = \mu \pm \sigma$; that is, it is concave for $x \in [\mu \pm \sigma]$. But for $x \notin [\mu \pm \sigma]$, the density decreases at an increasing rate; that is, it is convex in these regions. Thus $\mu \pm \sigma$, points where the function changes from concave to convex (the second derivative changes signs), are *inflection points* of the normal. The normal CDF, obtained by integrating the PDF up to any given value x, does not have a *closed form solution*, that is, the CDF involves an integral that cannot be evaluated to any simpler function. However, the normal CDF's graph looks like an S stretched to the right. This is intuitive because the density of very small values is very small, so the cumulative probability below those values is small. The density picks up steam around $\mu - \sigma$, and cumulative probability changes quickly from here up to $\mu + \sigma$, marking the "more vertical" part of the S. Above $\mu + \sigma$, the density again changes slowly as x increases, so the additional cumulative probability from increasing x in this region is small – marking a return to a "flatter" part of the S.

The mean μ is a "location" parameter. Changes in it shift the entire bell curve left or right but do not change the relative densities of points a given distance from each other. The variance σ^2 for a normal is a "scale" parameter. Changes in it change the height of the peak relative to the tails but do not change the location of the peak. Different choices of these parameters define a different member of the normal family. The notation $X \sim N(\mu, \sigma^2)$ means that X is a normally distributed random variable with mean μ and variance σ^2.

An important characteristic of normal distributions is that any sum of independent, normally distributed random variables is also normally distributed. More specifically, if $X \sim N(\mu_x, \sigma_x)$ and $Y \sim N(\mu_y, \sigma_y)$, and X and Y are independent, then $(X + Y) \sim N(\mu_x + \mu_y, \sigma_x + \sigma_y)$. And, because any rescaled normal random variable is also normal, it follows that any linear combination of independent normal random variables is also normal: if X and Y are normally distributed and independent, then $(a + bX) + (c + dY)$ is normally distributed for any constants a, b, c, d.

In fact, this special property that a sum of normal variables is also normal applies only to the normal distribution. Specifically, if a *finite* sum of random variables is exactly normally distributed, then each random variable in the sum is exactly normal. This is sometimes called *Cramér's theorem*, after the mathematician who first proved it. In Chapter 7, we have occasion to consider the distribution of sums of random variables in some detail, so the fact that sums of random variables from a given parametric family do not generally belong to that same family is important.

The theoretical behavior of normal random variables was first established in the 18th century. The normal distribution shows up in many places in statistics, as reflected in later chapters – so much so that it can seem kind of eerie that this rather intricate function seems to provide so much underlying order. The reason it appears so often is that a lot of what happens in statistical inference is the summation of pieces of information that each deviate from some underlying trait by "white noise." Because this same aggregation process occurs over and over in statistics, it is reasonably understandable that the probability distribution of "errors" in it will have the same basic structure regardless of the application.

6.6.2 Z Scores and the Standard Normal Distribution

Normal distributions have some well-understood properties, two of which are used often in statistical inference. First is the "1-2-3" rule, which specifies the probability that a normal random variable falls less than one, two, or three standard deviations away from its mean. For *any* normal density, about 68% of the area under the curve lies in the range $\mu \pm \sigma$; about 95% of the area under the curve lies in the range $\mu \pm 2\sigma$ (actually $\mu \pm 1.96\sigma$ is a more precise specification of the 95% cutoff); and about 99.7% of the area under the curve lies in the range $\mu \pm 3\sigma$.[8] Thus, normal random variables essentially never fall, say, four or more standard deviations away from their expected value. Such observations have positive density, and any range of them has strictly positive probability, but it is very, very small. The normal density is necessarily positive for all real numbers x.

---

[8] Compare the probabilities at these σ cutoffs to the probabilities obtained at the same cutoffs from Chebyshev's inequality (Chapter 5): the bounds for the normal curve are much tighter than the general bounds.

More generally, for all normal distributions specified by particular values of μ and σ, and any value of $k \geq 0$, $\Pr[\mu - k\sigma \leq \mu \leq \mu + k\sigma] = p$: this probability p is the same no matter what the values of μ, σ, and $k \geq 0$. Many statistics textbooks contain "normal tables" that report values of p for a very large number of possible values of k; given ubiquitous computer software, it is generally more important to know the common property and the value of p for a few key values of k (discussed further in Chapter 8) than to use a normal table as such. The common property that all normal distributions share is that what determines the density of any value of x is how many standard deviations it is away from its mean.

For this reason, a particularly important member of the normal family is the *standard normal* or $N(0, 1)$ distribution. A standard normal random variable has a mean of 0 and variance (and standard deviation) of 1. Any normal random variable can be transformed into a standard normal random variable by (appropriately enough) standardizing it: dividing the difference between any normal random variable and its expected value by its standard deviation produces a standard normal random variable. That is, if $X \sim N(\mu, \sigma^2)$, then $Z = \frac{X-\mu}{\sigma} \sim N(0, 1)$. It is standard to use Z to denote a standardized normal random variable, and for any value of X, this is called the *z score* of a random variable. A *z* score measures the number of standard deviations the random variable is away from its mean. Note that by the 68-95-99.7 rule, the probability that a *z* score is less than 3 in absolute value is about 99.7.

6.6.3 Models with a Normal DGP

Suppose an analyst has a theory about a social process that explains the behavior of a normal random variable Y in terms of or as an effect of a covariate X. Given that Y is normal, once μ and σ are specified, we have no further explanation for why some value of y occurred rather than another, other than the workings of chance itself. The theoretical task of explaining Y's behavior in terms of other social factors is limited in scope to Y's systematic part – μ and σ in a normal distribution.

The task of a positive theory explaining the behavior of Y in terms of other factors, which we denote X, is to express these parameters – usually μ because it captures central tendency – as a function of the explanatory factors. This reflects a dependence of μ on X, which is captured in the expression $E(Y|X) \equiv \mu(X) = g(X)$. The content of such a positive theory of Y specifies the contents of " X."

Because any real number is a feasible value of μ for a normal distribution, there are no range-matching problems from stipulating that g is a linear function, that is, that the conditional mean is itself linearly related to covariates. Unlike the previous models we've considered, no manipulations of this link are necessary to make the range of the left-hand side match the range of the right-hand side.

Because of this, as well as its simplicity and flexibility (see Section 6.7), a linear model of the regression is by far the most common approach with normal DGPs. If a collection of observed Ys are assumed to be independently distributed according to normal DGPs with the same variance, the result is more specifically the *classical normal linear regression model*.

The bivariate linear regression model is specified simply as follows:

$$\mu(X) = E(Y|X) = \alpha + \beta X. \tag{6.20}$$

Note that a linear specification of $E(Y|X)$ can be made regardless of the DGP of Y. The linear regression model does not become a normal linear regression model until Y's DGP is assumed to belong to this parametric family.

In the normal family, μ is a parameter. In the linear regression model it has been stated in terms of α, β, and X. The terms α and β are also called parameters because they govern the DGP's behavior for given X.

In short, we now have two conceptually distinct parametric assumptions, albeit ones that often appear together in social science applications. First, we have the assumption that Y's DGP is a normal distribution. Second, we have the assumption that its conditional mean is a linear function of a covariate X. Together these two assumptions specify a statistical model.

An important aspect of the DGP in substantive terms is how large an effect X has on Y or, at the very least, its sign. When assessing whether the political party of the U.S. president affects the growth rate in gross domestic product (Hibbs [1977], Bartels [2008]), this is what research is driving at. In a linear regression of economic growth on the party of the president, the sign of the slope tells us whether growth tends to be bigger under one party than the other, and the magnitude tells us how much bigger. This again is the issue of a marginal effect.

In the foregoing models, marginal effects were expressed as derivatives. This is a generalization of the idea of a slope, expressing the change in the value of a function for an infinitesimal change in the domain variable. In the linear regression model the marginal effect is

$$\frac{dE(Y|X)}{dX} = \frac{d(\alpha + \beta X)}{dX} = \beta, \tag{6.21}$$

which is simply the line's slope. No matter how big X is in this model, an incremental change in it has the same effect on the systematic part of Y. This is exactly the same as saying that $E(Y|X)$ is a linear function of X. If the model has more covariates, and they are considered additively as independent influences on $E(Y|X)$, each one of them gets its own slope term, and the marginal effect of covariate X^j is its slope β^j.

All of this has assumed that the outcome of some interesting social process was a normal random variable. It is not so difficult to accept that it's a random variable of some sort, but how do we come by the knowledge that it is specifically a normally distributed one? Usually a hazy reference to the normal distribution is all we have.

We have also assumed that the conditional mean of Y is a linear function of X. In most applications of a linear model to a DGP, this is an optimistic or convenient approximation rather than a literal truth. The hope is that nonlinearities are not so pronounced, at least over the observed range of the covariates X, that conclusions based on a linear model are qualitatively false. For a critique of naive assumptions of linearity in regression and the problems it can create, see Achen [2002]. For a spirited defense, see Angrist and Pischke [2008]. In bumper-sticker form, the defense is that linearity is more flexible than meets the eye (as will be elaborated later in this chapter), and DGPs rarely imply any particular function to use as a link between $E(Y|X)$ and covariates. Another arbitrary choice of this link would not necessarily be any better than a linear one and may be more fragile. We happen to focus a lot more on the defensibility of linearity assumptions because linear specifications are so common.

6.6.4 Bivariate Normal Distribution

However, there is one special case in which the linearity of $E(Y|X)$ in X follows from the DGP itself, specifically, if the joint distribution of X, Y is *bivariate normal* or *joint normal*. That is, both X and Y are random variables and their joint PDF is

$$f(x, y) = \frac{1}{2\pi \sigma_x \sigma_y \sqrt{1 - \rho^2}} e^{\left\{ \frac{1}{2(1-\rho^2)} \left(\frac{(x-\mu_x)^2}{\sigma_x^2} + \frac{2\rho(x-\mu_x)(y-\mu_y)}{\sigma_x \sigma_y} + \frac{(y-\mu_y)^2}{\sigma_y^2} \right) \right\}}, \qquad (6.22)$$

given $\mu_x \in \mathbb{R}, \mu_y \in \mathbb{R}, \sigma_x > 0, \sigma_y > 0, \rho \in [-1, 1], \mathcal{X} = \mathbb{R}, \mathcal{Y} = \mathbb{R}.$

This is a somewhat intricate expression, but on inspection its similarities to the univariate normal PDF (Equation 6.19) emerge. For the bivariate normal distribution, μ_x and σ_x are the mean and standard deviation of X, μ_y and σ_y are the mean and standard deviation of Y, and ρ is the correlation between X and Y. So the bivariate normal distribution is a five-parameter family. For the bivariate normal, $\rho = 0$ implies X and Y are independent; here correlation captures not just a linear relationship but any stochastic relationship.

The bivariate normal is an interesting benchmark for statistical models because of an important feature of the conditional PDF of Y given $X = x$. Specifically, conditional on $X = x$ it can be shown that $Y \sim N(\mu_y + \frac{\rho \sigma_y}{\sigma_x}(x - \mu_x), (1 - \rho^2)\sigma_y^2)$. This notation means that given $X = x$, Y is normally distributed with mean $\mu_{y|x} = \mu_y + \frac{\rho \sigma_y}{\sigma_x}(x - \mu_x)$. Distributing the factor over $(x - \mu_x)$, this can also be written as

$$E(Y|X = x) \equiv \mu_{y|x}(x) = \mu_y - \frac{\rho \sigma_y}{\sigma_x}\mu_x + \frac{\rho \sigma_y}{\sigma_x}x. \qquad (6.23)$$

Look carefully at this expression for the conditional mean: it contains the unconditional mean of Y; some parameters times the unconditional mean of X; and a function of parameters that does not depend on x, times x. Therefore, in a bivariate normal DGP, *the mean of Y conditional on x is a linear function of x*. Linearity of the regression $E(Y|X)$ need not be *assumed* in this case; it follows from the DGP. In other words, once this joint distribution is invoked as a model for the DGP of (X, Y), the functional form linking X to the parameters of Y's conditional DGP follows "for free."

This linear function matches up with the form we've used before if we define $\beta \equiv \frac{\rho \sigma_y}{\sigma_x}$ and $\alpha = \mu_y - \frac{\rho \sigma_y}{\sigma_x} \mu_x$. Then Equation 6.23 can be written more compactly as $E(Y|X) = \alpha + \beta X$, an already familiar version.

Now look a little more at those Greek letters in β: $\frac{\rho \sigma_y}{\sigma_x}$. This is the correlation between X and Y, times the standard deviation of Y, over the standard deviation of X. We have seen a similar quantity before in the context of linear regression, in Chapter 2: $b = \frac{r s_y}{s_x}$ is the least squares bivariate regression coefficient. The slope b is computed based on sample quantities; the slope β just replaces these with analogues from the DGP.

The reason OLS estimates of linear regression coefficients match up with the coefficients in the bivariate normal case is not because OLS applied as a descriptive tool implicitly assumes bivariate normality; it does not, and we needed no model of Y's DGP (or the concept of a DGP at all) when introducing regression in Chapter 2. Rather, the reason for the similarity is that, as we saw in Chapters 2 and 5, the regression necessarily minimizes the mean squared error of any guess about Y that can be conditioned on X. OLS gives the linear approximation to a regression that has the smallest MSE, and for the bivariate normal distribution, the regression is exactly linear already. So these functions each minimize an MSE, for the sample and DGP respectively and that is the reason they are analogous.

The variance of the conditional distribution of Y is also worth a brief note. It is $(1 - \rho^2)\sigma_y^2$. For one thing, it is not a function of X: it is constant for all values of the covariate. This is a condition called *homoscedasticity*, or constant conditional variance. Second, the conditional variance is increasing in the unconditional variance σ_y^2, which makes a fair degree of sense: as Y is unconditionally more variable, it is more variable conditional on any value of X as well. Third, the conditional variance is negatively related to the absolute value of the correlation between X and Y: if $\rho = 1$, the conditional variance is 0. This is because knowledge of X is perfectly informative about the value of Y in this limiting case, so conditional on x we have a perfect guess of Y with no variation of possible values around that guess.

The bivariate normal DGP is an interesting benchmark not because it is especially common in social science modeling applications but because it is a case in which the linear regression model is exactly right. If N mutually independent observations are taken from a joint normal DGP, the classical normal linear regression model is automatically implied.

6.7 SPECIFYING LINEAR MODELS

Many of the models we dealt with earlier involve a linear specification of some function of a conditional mean. For the normal and bivariate normal models, this is a linear function of the regression $E(Y|X)$ itself. In the logit model for the Bernoulli/binomial distribution, this is a linear function of the logit $\ln(\frac{p}{1-p})$. For the Poisson model, this is a linear function of the natural log of the regression $\ln(\lambda(X))$. Linearity comes with real restrictions as to the kinds of relationships that are usually explored in these models. On the other hand, linearity is less restrictive than meets the eye, so that if a researcher knows where to look, a wide variety of relationships can be specified under this structure. In this section, we reprise the discussion of specifying regression models in Chapter 2 to show how these points carry over to the linear models commonly used for DGPs.

To do this, we'll use $g(E(Y|X))$ to represent some function of the conditional mean. For a linear regression model, this function g is linear; for the Poisson, g is the natural log function; for the logit, it is the natural log of $E(Y|X)$ over $1 - E(Y|X)$. This formulation encapsulates all of these examples as special cases of a *generalized linear model* or GLM, where some invertible function of the regression is assumed to be a linear function of the covariates.

6.7.1 Interaction Effects

One type of theoretical relationship these specifications need to be able to capture to represent the types of considerations that social scientists bring to their modeling occurs when the effect of one factor on $g(E(Y|X))$ depends on the presence or size of another factor. For instance, Boix [2003] and Acemoglu and Robinson [2005] have argued that income inequality within a country impedes its democratization – but more so when the sources of income and wealth cannot be easily moved from that country's borders. The idea (in simplified terms) is that, compared with autocratic government, democracy grants more power to the middle class, who have an interest in enacting policies that redistribute wealth from the rich to themselves. The rich, in turn, can either repress democratization or allow it to happen. The rich face relatively small costs of allowing democratization if they can move the sources of their income abroad to avoid domestic redistribution, but they face larger costs if they cannot move the sources of their income – for example, if a large share of their income derives from natural resource stocks within the country's borders. Greater income inequality implies that the rich have more to lose under redistribution, but they will only actually lose it if they cannot move their income sources abroad. Operationally, these scholars have argued that natural resource wealth is a good way to measure the ability of the rich to move their income abroad. So the theory implies that income inequality has a negative effect on democratization but more so (or only in) countries with relatively large shares of income deriving from natural resources.

Under this theory, the covariates have a multiplicative or interactive effect on a country's propensity to democratize. Supposing a binary measure of whether a country democratizes or not, we can reflect this theoretical claim in the statistical model by including an *interaction term*:

$$g(E(Y|X_1, X_2)) = \alpha + \beta_1 X_1 + \beta_2 X_2 + \beta_3 X_1 X_2. \tag{6.24}$$

Here X_1 could be income inequality and X_2 the share of national income derived from natural resources. The last term is the interaction term. It is simply the product of the two explanatory variables: they enter the model of the conditional mean additively and separately but also multiplicatively. This is still a linear model of $g(E(Y|X))$, however, in the sense that each explaining factor affects $g(E(Y|X))$ in a linear fashion.

The interaction of the explanatory variables is best seen in the marginal effect of one of them, say X_1, which is given by

$$\frac{\partial g(E(Y|X_1, X_2))}{\partial X_1} = \beta_1 + \beta_3 X_2. \tag{6.25}$$

Thus X_1 has its own effect (i.e., β_1) but also another effect that depends on the size of X_2 (i.e., $\beta_3 X_2$). Here we are dealing with a partial derivative because several variables affect the conditional expectation, and the marginal effect of X_1 is only asking about one of them.[9]

The theory in question claims that income inequality decreases the tendency to democratize, when resource income is relatively large. So as X_2 gets larger, the effect of X_1 on $g(E(Y|X))$ should become (more) negative. Thus regardless of the value of β_1, this implies $\beta_3 < 0$.

Note that this marginal effect is on $g(E(Y|X))$, not on $E(Y|X)$ itself. We should not lose sight of the fact that $E(Y|X)$ is actually the theoretically interesting quantity. Obtaining the marginal effects on $E(Y|X)$ itself takes a little more calculus. Concretely, we could apply the inverse function g^{-1} (which exists, because g is strictly increasing) to both sides of the model, which leaves $E(Y|X)$ by itself on the left-hand side, and then use the chain rule to differentiate $g^{-1}(\alpha + \beta_1 X_1 + \beta_2 X_2 + \beta_3 X_1 X_2)$ with respect to X_1 or X_2. The marginal effect of the interaction term is then $\frac{\partial^2 g^{-1}(\cdot)}{\partial X_1 \partial X_2}$, i.e., the cross-partial. Care is required because this need not have the same sign as β_3.

In nonlinear models, that is, where $g(E(Y|X))$ is not linear, the function $g(\cdot)$ automatically "builds in" an interaction effect of the covariates on $E(Y|X)$. This is most apparent in the marginal effects in simple models like the logit or Poisson. For instance, for a Poisson model with two covariates $E(Y|X) = \alpha + \beta_X X + \beta_Z Z$, the marginal effect of X on $E(Y|X)$ is $\beta_X e^{\alpha + \beta_X X + \beta_Z Z}$. This is a simple extension of Equation 6.11 to allow two covariates. The point is that the entire model is part of the marginal effect of any one variable: $g(\cdot)$ is not linear, so the terms besides X do not drop out when $E(Y|X)$ is differentiated

---

[9] See Brambor et al. [2006] on interpretation of interaction terms and common mistakes that stem from this.

with respect to X. So as the value of Z changes, the effect of X on $E(Y|X)$ changes too. That is what an interaction effect is all about: the effect of one covariate depends on the value of another.

In general, in GLMs it is impossible to avoid these "built-in" interaction effects. But this is not usually what people are talking about when they refer to "interaction terms" in the model; instead this conventionally means a specification along the lines of Equation 6.24. These models of interaction effects are much more flexible than the built-in interaction effects in any GLM. For instance, in a Poisson model with two covariates where $\beta_1 > 0$ and $\beta_2 > 0$, the built-in interaction effect means that a larger value of Z always amplifies the effect of X on $E(Y|X)$. If a researcher is interested in the possibility that a larger value of Z instead mitigates the effect of X on $E(Y|X)$, an interaction term to account for that must be explicitly included in the model.

6.7.2 Exponential Effects

Exponential effects of a covariate are also easy to represent in GLMs, because any nonlinear function of a covariate can itself be linearly related to the dependent variable. So in fact linear models allow for an extremely wide range of "shapes of the relationship" between X and Y.

Suppose for instance that in the case of social capital, a researcher conjectures that more state-level education leads to more social capital but that increases in education from a low baseline matter more than increases from a high baseline – for example, a change from 0 years of college to 4 years of college matters more for social trust and connectivity than the change from 4 years of college to 8 years. Clearly, this postulates a nonlinear effect of education on social capital: a given increment in education does not have a constant effect on social capital.

To model such an effect we can specify

$$E(Y|X) = \alpha + \beta_1 X + \beta_2 X^2. \tag{6.26}$$

Here X enters as a linear term weighted by β_1, and the same variable enters as a quadratic term weighted by β_2. The marginal effect of X on $E(Y|X)$ is $\beta_1 + 2\beta_2 X$. The theory asserts $\beta_1 > 0$ – more education increases social capital. However, it also asserts $\beta_2 < 0$ – the effect of education gets smaller when the level of education is larger.

So this model postulates that the conditional mean of Y is related to both X and the square of X.[10] This model is still linear – in X and X^2. This is all the linearity that a "linear model" of the regression requires. We could

---

[10] Unless X contains both positive and negative numbers, X and X^2 will be highly correlated, which can make it difficult to estimate their independent effects on $E(Y|X)$ in a sample. But this does not present any conceptual problems on the modeling side; it presents some technical problems on the estimation side, which we address later.

simply think of X^2 as an altogether new covariate $Z \equiv X^2$, and the model $\alpha + \beta_1 X + \beta_2 Z$ is clearly linear. As long as the slope and intercept terms enter as real numbers with no nonlinear transformations, the model is still linear in those terms.

There is only one covariate in this model, and its marginal effect on the conditional mean of Y is

$$\frac{\partial E(Y|X)}{\partial X} = \beta_1 + 2\beta_2 X. \tag{6.27}$$

Thus, if $\beta_2 > 0$, then the effect of X on $E(Y|X)$ increases as X increases, as in a convex function. If $\beta_2 < 0$, the effect of X on $E(Y|X)$ decreases as X increases, as in a concave function.

Including a power of X or the natural log of X as well as X itself allows for a huge variety of "scale effects" or nonlinearities to be captured in a linear regression model. The only caveat is that the decision to include them requires some thought about the social process by which Y is related to X. Including nonlinear effects in this way is not a default assumption in linear models, and capturing these effects requires a conscious and purposeful decision.

6.7.3 Saturated Models

In fact, it is straightforward in principle to develop a model that is linear in the sense used here, but yet implies nothing at all about the shape of the relationship between $g(E(Y|X))$ and X. In particular, consider a bivariate model relating $g(E(Y|X))$ to one covariate X. Suppose there are k possible values of X, and these values are denoted $X_1, \ldots, X_k$. For instance, if X is binary, then $k = 2$. This is the case when the political party of the U.S. president is used to explain the growth rates of GDP in the United States.

Given these k possible values, let $X^j = 1$ if $X = X_j$, and $X^j = 0$ otherwise. Thus instead of one variable with k different *values*, we wind up with k different *variables*, each of which is a binary *dummy variable* or *indicator variable* about the covariate X.

We can put all these variables into the regression

$$E(Y|X) = \beta_1 X^1 + \beta_2 X^2 + \cdots + \beta_k X^k, \tag{6.28}$$

which is called a *fully saturated* regression model. In this model, every possible value of the covariate is associated with a unique parameter reflecting $E(Y|X)$ under that possible value. For the simple case where X is binary, the fully saturated model collapses to $E(Y|X) = \beta_1 X^1$ for the smaller value of X (say $X = 0$), and collapses to $E(Y|X) = \beta_2 X^2$ for the larger value of X.

In a fully saturated model, there is no single parameter β that structures how X in general can be related to $E(Y|X)$. Instead X is broken into each of its possible values, each of which can be associated with a unique value of

$E(Y|X)$. Because of this, a fully saturated regression model simply amounts to a collection of k different values of $E(Y|X)$, one for each value of X.

This, in turn, implies that a fully saturated regression model, although it is linear and although the conditional mean itself is on the left-hand side, is not restrictive in any way. Once a DGP for Y and its covariate X is specified, a fully saturated regression model gives linearity "for free." In practice, fully saturated models require a large number of observations of Y for each value of X to provide precise estimates of the β_j terms. Thus, they are informationally intensive. In that sense, although linearity may be "free" or unrestrictive, it is only realistically available in large datasets. And the more values of X there are, the larger the dataset must be. In other words, in statistical models, nothing is really free.

Two last notes on fully saturated regression models. First, note that Equation 6.28 does not have an intercept α. This is because it would be redundant to include one. Once the k values of X are broken into individual variables and included in this way, the model gives the fullest specification conceivable for $E(Y|X)$. An intercept α would have nothing to do. It is always possible to rewrite Equation 6.28 so that an intercept is included: $E(Y|X) = \alpha + \beta_1 X^1 + \cdots + \beta_{k-1} X^{k-1}$. But note that this version drops the dummy X_k for the final value of X and the associated slope. Having included the intercept and the other $k-1$ values of X with their slopes, α necessarily equals $E(Y|X = x_k)$ in this specification. For empirical purposes, the number of slope/intercept parameters to establish is the same in either case, so the informational/data demands are identical.

Second, with multiple covariates, the logic of a fully saturated model is not any more difficult than that given earlier, but the number of variables and slope terms grows quickly. With two covariates X and Z, a new variable must be defined for each unique *combination* of X and Z values. So if X and Z are both binary, a fully saturated model entails four variables and β parameters. If X and Z can each take three possible values, a fully saturated model entails nine variables and β parameters.

6.8 BEYOND THE MEANS: COMPARISONS OF DGPs

Each of the models we explored thus for links the mean of Y's conditional DGP to explanatory factors. This link may entail relating a nonlinear function of Y's conditional mean to covariates, as in the logit, Poisson, and exponential models, but the point remains that these models relate the conditional DGP to covariates through the mean of the conditional DGP.

Part of the reason for this is a mean, as a typical value in the sense of mean squared error, is an interesting quantity. Without doubt, it obscures variation and difference, but focusing on means does capture an important part of the question: are two DGPs different in their typical behavior? Another part of the reason means are so often used in comparing DGPs is that they are relatively easy aspects of a DGP to work with and to link to sample information. We focus more on this tractability in Chapter 7. When a quantity is both interesting and tractable to estimate it tends to get a lot of attention.

Yet there is no reason why DGP comparisons must be phrased in terms of the means. Sometimes comparison of means is so ingrained in how social scientists approach quantitative data that other aspects of DGPs are neglected, or social scientists get confused about how to handle them using tools designed to compare means. But the substantive focus of a theory may be on some aspect of a DGP besides its mean, such as its spread; or there may be much stronger DGP comparisons available than means alone can substantiate.

6.8.1 DGP Comparisons by First-Order Stochastic Dominance

Taking the second case first, a common structure of positive arguments is that the DGP of Y tends to get bigger as some explanatory factor gets bigger. Myriad examples fit into this template, some of which we have considered already in this chapter. The theoretical claim of "tends" can be translated into a statement about the conditional mean, but stronger statements are possible. A stronger statement about the relative "size" of two random variables relates to *first-order stochastic dominance* or FOSD.

Let X be a random variable with CDF $F_X(x)$, and Y be a random variable with CDF $F_Y(y)$. X first order stochastically dominates Y, written $X \succeq_1 Y$, if and only if $F_X(a) \leq F_Y(a), \forall a \in \mathcal{X}, \mathcal{Y}$. $X \succeq_1 Y$ means that X is bigger than Y in the sense that for every specific value $\tilde{v}$ the random variables might take, X assigns more weight than Y does to values higher than $\tilde{v}$. This is the reason for the possibly counterintuitive definition $F_X(a) \leq F_Y(a)$: that's how we say that Y has "used up" more of its total or cumulative probability by the time the value of a rolls around, and that is true for every a. In this sense, first-order stochastic dominance is a pointwise comparison of two functions (the CDFs): it says that at every point in the domain of each function, one of them lies below the other one.

On the other hand, $E(X) \geq E(Y)$ simply means that X is bigger than Y in expectation. There may be relatively large values of the random variable where Y has higher probability of producing that value than X, but the "best guess" about the value of X is higher than the best guess about the value of Y.

If $X \succeq_1 Y$, then $E(X) \geq E(Y)$, but the converse is not true in general for random variables (it is true for some specific and important ones). $X \succeq_1 Y$ means that for every possible value $\tilde{v}$ of the random variables, X has more weight on the values greater than $\tilde{v}$ than Y does. Think in particular of $E(Y)$ as a possible value that both random variables can take: first-order stochastic dominance means that X places less weight than Y does on values below this one and more weight than Y does on values higher than this one. Placing more weight on higher values pulls up a mean because it is simply a weighted sum of values the random variable can take, so this means $E(X) > E(Y)$.

Normally distributed random variables are an important case for which $E(X) \geq E(Y)$ implies $X \succeq_1 Y$, that is, a ranking of means implies FOSD. Fixing σ, the normal distribution with the higher mean μ first-order stochastically dominates the other. Fixing variance or the scale parameter, a normal spreads out the observations on each side of its mean in the same way for any value of the mean. So moving the mean k units to the right moves every percentile k units to the right as well. This means that at every point, the distribution with the further right mean has not yet reached the percentile reached by the distribution with the further left mean. That's exactly the same as FOSD.

First-order stochastic dominance is a more conservative comparison of random variables than a comparison of means (in general) and by that fact more compelling when it happens. There are cases in which the means can be ranked but the random variable with the higher mean does not FOSD the other; there are no cases where FOSD holds and the means cannot be ordered the same way. FOSD of course need not hold at all; for any pair of distributions it is not true that one must FOSD the other.

So if a theory implies that a random variable "gets bigger" in some vague sense as a covariate increases, then conditional mean comparisons are usually an adequate approach to evaluating this, but FOSD is even stronger. FOSD conveys more information about "bigness" of a random variable because it implies bigness not only at the centers of mass, but everywhere.

In empirical work, it is usually easier to determine which of two conditional distributions has a larger mean than which of them is larger in the sense of FOSD. To compare means, all the information in a dataset can be focused on pinning down just those quantities, but to evaluate FOSD, much of the information in the data is required to pin down aspects of the distribution over the entire range of X. That allows for less information to be used in pinning down any one particular point in the distribution, so FOSD comparisons are usually less precise. In other words, there are many distributions for which means can be ranked empirically but for which FOSD is ambiguous. This is the main reason why FOSD is seen a lot less as the basis for comparing DGPs. Nevertheless, it is good to remember that means are only one way to compare the "size" of random variables and not the most informative way.

6.8.2 DGP Comparisons by Variance and Second-Order Stochastic Dominance

Although all the theoretical arguments sketched out thus far suggest that Y tends to get bigger (or smaller) as X changes, there is nothing about statistical modeling that requires theoretical effects to work through the typical magnitude or general tendency of a random variable at all. Instead, for instance, a theory might imply that the *spread* of Y grows as X grows. As claims about "typical magnitude" or "general tendency" are naturally (although not necessarily, as the previous subsection noted) expressed in terms of conditional DGP means, claims about "spread" are naturally expressed in terms of the variance of the conditional DGP.

For instance, Alvarez and Brehm [2002] analyze individual responses to political survey questions as a function of the certainty and intensity of their attitudes. In particular, they contend that individuals who experience cognitive dissonance of attitudes that impinge on their answer should be expected to exhibit greater variance in their survey responses. The idea is the cognitive dissonance vitiates the individual's uncertainty of belief about which response is the "right" one given their attitudes and leads to greater variation in response.

As another example, consider the propagation of behavior or traits in social networks. Whether individuals form networks on the basis of similar characteristics (*homophily*) or whether observance of behavior in their network causes changes in their own behavior, network-based theories often assert that some attribute or behavior should have lower variance among members of a network than among members of an entire population. For instance, Christakis and Fowler [2007] showed that obesity seems to propagate through social networks. Whether obesity is "contagious" (in the sense that obese people induce a "spread" of obesity in their social networks) or whether individuals form networks on the basis of traits correlated with obesity in the first place, this propagation implies that individuals in a particular social network should have lower variance in their obesity levels than any random subset of the same size from the population as a whole.

In principle, statistical models for variance can be developed along the same lines as the models for conditional means we have laid out thus far. Christakis and Fowler [2006] laid out some general theoretical issues that lead naturally to implications for variance rather than means of the conditional DGP (as well as attendant subtleties of causal inference in such cases, but we defer discussions of such issues until later). What is required for such a model is a DGP to begin with and a specification of how covariates affect its parameters which in turn affect its variance. Range restrictions are common for parameters that determine variance, and due account would be necessary for this when linking the conditional DGP of Y to the covariates. Indeed, when the parameters of a DGP are modeled as a function of covariates, it sometimes happens that the model already implies how covariates affect the conditional variance, whether researchers are always conscious of this or not.

Just as with mean comparisons versus first-order stochastic dominance in the previous subsection, there are stronger statements about comparison of spread than can be made on the basis of variance alone. An analogous property to FOSD for spread is *second-order stochastic dominance* or SOSD.

Let X be a random variable with CDF $F_X(x)$, and Y be a random variable with CDF $F_Y(y)$. X second-order stochastically dominates Y, written $X \succeq_2 Y$, if and only if $\int_{-\infty}^{a} [F_Y(z) - F_X(z)]dz \geq 0$, $\forall a \in \mathcal{X}, \mathcal{Y}$. Intuitively, SOSD formalizes the idea of a *mean preserving spread*: imagine taking the distribution of X and squashing it so that its center of mass stays the same but its mass or density spreads out on both sides of this. This resulting distribution is the distribution of Y, and it is a mean preserving spread of the distribution of X. This means $X \succeq_2 Y$.

As with FOSD and mean comparisons, $X \succeq_1 Y$ implies that X has smaller variance than Y, but the converse is not true in all cases. Thus, SOSD allows for stronger statements about the spread of one distribution compared to another. Also like FOSD, establishing SOSD is more difficult empirically than establishing a comparison of variances, because much information in data must be used to pin down the entire shape of a distribution rather than just a small number of parameters.

6.9 EXAMPLES

In this section, we explore in detail the model specifications that have been used to investigate important questions in recent research. In this section, we focus only on the assumptions about the DGP used in these models and how they are connected to the substantive theories that occupied the authors of the research in question. We also discuss the interpretation of results of the models as if they reflect the DGP itself. But for the moment, we set aside issues of how those results were obtained from the observed sample data and on the evaluation of the inferences that can be drawn from these results about the DGP. These are issues of statistical inference – estimation and hypothesis testing, respectively – that we address (with respect to these same examples) in Chapter 9.

6.9.1 Attitudes toward High- and Low-Skilled Immigration

Immigration has been a major policy issue in the United States and many other "Northern" democracies in recent years, and its importance promises to continue given the state of global demographics. Therefore it is important for both scholars and policy makers to understand the determinants of attitudes to immigration among residents in "receiving" countries.

One widely held perspective asserts that these determinants are largely based on the effect of immigration on one's own personal economic circumstances. Although there are a variety of channels by which immigration can affect the economy of the receiving country, research and public discourse often centers on the labor market implications. By adding more potential workers in various occupations, immigration can affect the supply of labor in the receiving country, which in turn can affect the earnings of "natives" (read: residents already established) in the receiving country's labor market. For instance, if immigrants are primarily highly skilled professionals, allowing more of them into a country will increase labor market competition of highly skilled natives. This can drive down labor market earnings of highly skilled natives, which might in turn make them opposed to immigration. Similarly, immigrants who are low-skilled workers impose greater labor market competition on lower-skilled natives, which can drive down their wages and in turn make low-skilled natives opposed to immigration.

Before turning to any model specifications or estimates, note that this already presents an illustration of an important theme in this book. The theory is described as a logical relation among assumptions (economic motivations of natives in receiving countries), conditions (the skill match of immigrants and natives), and results (attitudes of natives toward immigration). The theory is not about specific groups of people in specific places in specific times; rather, it is an assertion of results that occur, for specific reasons, when the assumptions and the conditions hold. In other words, the theory specifies aspects of a DGP.

The explanatory power of this theory (and others) was explored in an interesting recent paper by Hainmueller and Hiscox [2010] in the *American Political Science Review*. The authors conducted a *survey experiment* to investigate them. Specifically, they asked each person in a sample of 1,601 Americans one of the following questions:

1. Do you agree or disagree that the United States should allow more highly skilled immigrants from other countries to come and live here?
2. Do you agree or disagree that the United States should allow more low-skilled immigrants from other countries to come and live here?

One of these two questions was assigned at random to each survey respondent. For each question, the responses were from the set "strongly disagree (1), somewhat disagree (2), neither agree nor disagree (3), somewhat agree (4), strongly agree (5)." The random assignment of questions to survey respondents makes this a survey experiment: randomization ensures that the respondents who face one question are not systematically different from the respondents that face the other question. This is important but not for our purposes now.

This variable is an operationalization of the abstract concept of an "attitude toward immigration." It is the dependent variable, variation in which is explained by the economic theories. It is an ordinal variable: the values are categories, and their ordering is informative. For this reason, Hainmueller and Hiscox specified an ordinal probit model of Y.

Formally, this model starts with another variable, Y^*, called an *index* or *latent* variable. In ordered probit, Y^* is distributed normally with mean μ_i and variance σ^2. I introduce covariates soon; for now the subscript on μ simply denotes that different observations are allowed to have different means of the latent variable Y^*. Thus Y^* can be written $Y^* = \mu + \varepsilon$ where ϵ is normally distributed with mean 0. Y is built from Y^* as follows:

$$Y = \begin{cases} 1, & \text{if } Y^* \le u_1 \\ 2, & \text{if } Y^* \in (u_1, u_2] \\ 3, & \text{if } Y^* \in (u_2, u_3] \\ 4, & \text{if } Y^* \in (u_3, u_4] \\ 5, & \text{if } Y^* > u_4. \end{cases} \tag{6.29}$$

The u_l values are DGP parameters that define which Y value is observed for a given Y^* value. The idea is that Y^* represents a continuous, latent degree of "warmth" or "positivity" that a survey respondent feels about immigration. If this latent warmth crosses a threshold parameter u_l, the respondent answers $l + 1$ on the observable, discrete opinion scale. Warmer (continuous) attitudes correspond to greater (discrete) survey responses.

Although ordinal probit is a "natural" choice for this variable at some level, a further comment is useful to explain why that is. Other statistical models are possible. For example, both the ordered and multinomial probit models are suitable for a dependent variable that takes multiple categorical values. Even a linear model of $E(Y|X)$ would "work," in the sense of producing results for parameters linking Y to the covariates, although it would not satisfy the "range-matching" requirement for Y.

The ordinal probit (or logit) model has the advantage over other possibilities by explicitly building the information about the ordering of Y's category values into the model. A multinomial model is agnostic about ordering among the values. In general, any information that a researcher knows for certain about the DGP of a dependent variable should be built into the model; to ignore this is to "leave money on the table." The specific reason has to do with the precision of statistical estimation, which we do not explore until later (Chapters 7 and 9). For the moment, we simply assert without further explanation that failing to include known features of the DGP leads to estimates of model parameters from sample data that are less precise than they could be and thus fail to exploit all the available information in the sample. It goes (almost) without saying that it is perfectly possible for researchers to "know" things about the DGP that are not in fact true, build them into a model, and reach erroneous or erroneously strong conclusions as a result.

Although the ordinal structure of Y suggests that some type of ordered model is useful, there is nothing about the data or sampling process that implies a normal distribution of the index model's random disturbance ε (which is what makes this specifically an ordered probit model). The normality assumption is necessary to specify the model completely and is typically invoked without formal justification. On the other hand, other specifications of the distribution of ε usually lead to similar substantive and statistical results, and it would be unusual for this assumption alone to drive the results in applications such as this.

Note also that while the 1,601 survey respondents are drawn at random from the U.S. population and the questions are assigned at random to the respondents, neither of these randomizations necessarily implies that Y^* is random in the DGP and therefore that Y is random. In an ordinal probit model, we assume the "warmth" an individual feels toward immigration of a given skill type depends on a "systematic" part μ_i and an idiosyncratic part ε_i. Different individuals i may have different values of μ_i; ordinal probit is just like other models we've considered in that this parameter will be expressed as a function of some covariates. All randomness in the "warmth" individuals feel (Y^*) and therefore opinions they express (Y) lives in ε. The ordered probit model itself is agnostic about whether this randomness arises from sampling, theoretical, or fundamental uncertainty, in the language of Chapter 3. Two people with the μ_i may express different attitudes. The difference may be due to other factors the researchers have not specified or do not know (theoretical uncertainty). Even if these factors are fixed and a given respondent's answer is deterministic, random selection of survey respondents from the U.S. population implies that observed responses are a random draw from a larger collection of possible responses (sampling uncertainty). In addition, it is also possible that a single respondent gives stochastic answers, so ε_i is a random variable for each individual respondent (fundamental uncertainty).

In any case, the ordinal structure of Y allows specification of one part of a statistical model: the functional form of the DGP of Y. The substance of the labor competition theory allows specification of the other part: the link between the DGP's parameter μ_i and the covariates. Hainmueller and Hiscox constructed this on the basis of two primary components.

First, the labor competition theory focuses on the effect of natives' skill levels. To measure this, Hainmueller and Hiscox also obtained reports from survey respondents about their own education levels. These education levels are taken as an indicator of a respondent's skill level in the labor market; more highly educated people have (one hopes) greater skills to deploy in the labor market. Education levels, specifically the highest level of education attained, are reported as "some high school (1), high school graduate (2), some college (3), college graduate or higher (4)." Denote this variable as X_1.

Second, the labor competition theory turns on the match between native and immigrant skill. Thus Hainmueller and Hiscox construct a dummy variable to indicate whether the respondent saw question 1 about highly skilled immigrants (dummy = 1) or questions 2 about low-skilled immigrants (dummy = 0). Denote this variable as X_2.

In addition, Hainmueller and Hiscox recorded several demographic characteristics or respondents to use as control variables. Refer to these collectively as Z. With these covariates, Hainmueller and Hiscox specify the following regression function for the ordered probit model:

$$E(Y^*|X_1, X_2, Z) \equiv \mu = \alpha + \beta_1 X_1 + \beta_2 X_2 + \beta_3 X_1 X_2 + \beta_4 Z. \qquad (6.30)$$

Recall that μ is the conditional mean of Y^*, the continuous latent variable in the model. This feeds into the ordinal structure of the observable, discrete response variable Y as defined in Equation 6.29. Equations 6.29 and 6.30, and the assumption that Y^* is normally distributed, jointly define the statistical model, which is another variant of a generalized linear model of the regression of Y.

The labor competition theory has implications for β_2 and β_3. Hainmueller and Hiscox expected low-skilled ($X_1 = 1$) respondents to have more positive attitudes toward immigration toward the highly skilled ($X_2 = 1$), so that

$\beta_2 + \beta_3 > 0$. But they expect highly skilled ($X_1 = 4$) respondents to have more negative attitudes toward immigration by the highly skilled ($X_2 = 1$), so that $\beta_2 + 4\beta_3 < 0$. These expressions imply $-\beta_2 < \beta_3 < -\frac{\beta_2}{4}$, and also $\beta_3 < 0$.[11]

Apart from the labor competition theory, β_1 and β_2 are of independent interest. They reflect (respectively) whether more highly educated people are more favorable about immigration and whether respondents are more supportive of high-versus low-skilled immigration, all else constant. These parameters could shed light on other sociocultural determinants of attitudes toward immigration, above and beyond the labor competition theory.

From their observed sample, Hainmueller and Hiscox estimated that $\beta_1 = 0.27$, $\beta_2 = 0.73$, and $\beta_3 = -0.07$. In Chapter 9, we address how these estimates are obtained; for now we analyze what they mean as if they reflect the actual DGP.

First, in terms of parameter magnitudes alone, the labor competition theory achieves mixed results. As expected under that theory, $\beta_3 < 0$ and $\beta_2 + \beta_3 > 0$. But the effect of the skill match on the effect of education (the interaction effect) is small: $-\frac{\beta_2}{4} = -18.25$, and β_3 is less than half of this amount. In addition, we have not yet considered the degree of uncertainty in these estimates of β's, a topic we address (in general and about this particular study) in Chapter 9. When that uncertainty is considered, the ability of the labor competition theory to explain the results is considerably weakened, as we will see.

Second, all else constant, attitudes toward immigration by the highly skilled are much more positive than attitudes toward immigration by low-skilled workers. This is reflected in the positive and (relative to other magnitudes) large value of β_2. Third, irrespective of immigrants' skill levels and labor market competition, more highly educated respondents express more positive attitudes toward immigration, as reflected in the positive value of β_1. Together, these coefficients indicate that there are other important sociocultural determinants of attitudes toward immigration that do not boil down to its effect on one's own economic prospects.

Hainmueller and Hiscox explored much more than this specification of μ. They analyzed other specifications that relax the assumption that respondent skill has a linear effect on attitudes or on the effect of facing the highly skilled immigration question. They also explore another economic theory about the effect of immigration on respondents' likely tax burden (this theory also does a poor job of explaining attitudes toward immigration). Although we have explored only a small piece of this paper, the extended detail hopefully provides some insight about what is going on in this model, how is connects to theory, and what in principle can be learned from it.

---

[11] The unconditional negative interaction parameter β_3 is explained as follows. When $X_2 = 1$, greater education X_1 indicates a greater match between respondent and immigrant skills – and thus greater exposure to labor market competition. These respondents should be less supportive of this type of immigration. Thus the theory implies $\beta_3 < 0$, all else constant.

6.9.2 Protest Movements in the Former Soviet Union

The effect of social behavior such as protest movements on the stability of political regimes is of great interest to both political scientists and sociologists. It is also of considerable importance for public policy. The Soviet Union may be long gone as a political regime, but because it seemed rock-solid just a couple years before its demise, it is an interesting case to analyze the effect of social movements on regime stability.

Beissinger [2002] analyzed protest behavior by various nationalities in the Soviet Union from the years 1987 to 1991, the period coinciding with the glasnost reforms toward greater openness and transparency in government and the ultimate disintegration of the USSR. Beissinger developed a statistical model of the number of protests consisting of 100 or more persons, by each of 47 non-Russian nationalities over this period. He began with a set of 5,067 protest events and coded 2,840 of these as involving "ethnonationalist claims." Thus the dataset consists of 47 rows, one of each nationality. The columns of the dataset record the variables, the dependent variable being the number of protest events. As for the covariates, Beissinger was interested in both institutional and sociocultural determinants of protest activities across nationalities. The explanatory variables reflect this interest and are further detailed later.

Given that the dependent variable is a tally of the number of protest events, Beissinger analyzed the relationship between the dependent and explanatory variables in a count model similar to the Poisson model laid out in Section 6.3. To get the idea, start with the Poisson model itself: we assume that the number of protest events Y follows a Poisson distribution for every nationality. The substantive theory is reflected in the expression of the parameter of that distribution, λ, as a function of institutional and sociocultural covariates. Different nationalities then have different numbers of protests for two reasons: first, because they have (generally) different covariates; second, because of random chance conditional on the values of those covariates. The specification of the DGP family for Y and the link of its parameter to covariates constitutes the statistical model in this case.

In terms of "types" of uncertainty discussed in Chapter 3, the randomness in this DGP is not due to sampling uncertainty. Beissinger observed all ethnic groups that recorded an observable ethnonationalist protest event, not a sample of them, and he recorded all protest events with 100 or more persons over this time period, not a sample. Nevertheless, because the DGP is assumed to be a specific probability distribution, it is definitely assumed to have a stochastic element. The randomness that operates to generate observable data can come from either theoretical uncertainty or fundamental uncertainty. Either is a valid interpretation of the nature of the uncertainty and neither is explored or ruled out. First, protest events may depend on factors that are not measured or recorded in this dataset, so that two ethnicities with the same recorded covariates may have different numbers of protest events. The determination of protest events may actually be deterministic on this interpretation, but because we do not have access to all the relevant determining factors, it would nevertheless appear random (i.e., varying from case to case with no apparent explanation) to an observer. Second, protest events may be partly random in the sense of fundamental uncertainty, so that the complete and true theory does involve random variation. Individuals may have incentives to randomize their participation in protest events, which makes the occurrence and size of the protest also random. Either way, invoking a Poisson (or related) count model to describe these processes requires an optimistic assumption that "nature" is cooperative in generating the observations from a well know, tractable DGP. It is, in other words, an example of model-based sampling. Beissinger did note that a normal distribution is not a good match for this dependent variable because it assigns positive density to all real numbers, both negative (impossible for county data) and very large (not observed in count data). Beyond this, as is common in applications of count models and parametric models in general, there is no specific justification for the functional form of the DGP that is invoked.

As noted earlier, the Poisson has the special feature that, conditional on covariates, the mean and variance are the same. Denoting the covariate vector generally as X, this assumption is that $\lambda(X) = E(Y|X) = Var(Y|X)$. It is possible to investigate whether this is approximately true in the observed data, and we explore how (in this same example) in Chapter 9. As is almost always the case in applications of count models, Beissinger found that this assumption is not a credible description of his DGP. When the conditional mean and variance are not the same, usually the conditional variance is greater. This is referred to as *overdispersion*.

Therefore, as is also almost always the case in applications of count models, Beissinger turned to a related but more general DGP called the *negative binomial*. The negative binomial distribution has more parameters than the Poisson; one must estimate not only the mean of Y conditional on X but also the conditional variance because it is not the same. These differences notwithstanding, in a negative binomial model, the canonical (and default in most computer software) specification of the regression is $E(Y|X) = e^{\alpha+\beta X}$. This is exactly like the link of the regression to the covariates in the Poisson model. Thus the interpretation of coefficients is similar. In addition, the implementation of the negative binomial model in computer software is no more difficult than the Poisson: one imports the dataset into the software of choice and directs it to estimate a negative binomial regression model rather than a Poisson regression model. Unless otherwise directed, the software will assume that the mean of the negative binomial and the covariates are related through the exponential function just specified.

Beissinger actually compiled a large number of datasets and investigated a wide variety of statistical models to ensure that his key substantive conclusions hold up under various specifications of the regression and of the DGP of Y.

TABLE 6.1. *Determinants of Number of Ethnonationalist Protests in Former USSR, by Nationality*

Variable	$\widehat{\beta}$	$e^{\widehat{\beta}}$
Population size, 1,000s (natural log)	0.658	1.931
Linguistic assimilation	−0.072	0.930
Urbanization	0.066	1.068
Number of protests, 1965–1986	0.057	1.059
Communist party membership per 1,000	−0.003	0.997
Dummy for Islamic culture	−0.328	0.720

The explanatory variables and estimated parameter values from one of these are displayed in Table 6.1.

The covariates in this model reflect demographic factors pertaining to each nationality (population size, linguistic assimilation, urbanization, and whether its people are predominantly from a traditionally Islamic culture), its institutional connection to the USSR (Communist party membership), and its history of participation (number of protests in preceding decades). As in a Poisson model, the parameter estimates have meaningful signs; these indicate the direction of the effect of an increase in the covariate on the conditional mean. They also give a rough sense of relative magnitudes of effects, although because the covariates are all measured in different units, this is not particularly meaningful from a substantive standpoint. But the magnitudes themselves are not really what we want to know. They indicate how each covariate affects the natural log of the conditional mean, not the conditional mean itself – which is what we care about.

In Section 6.3, we discussed the marginal effects of each covariate in the Poisson model on its conditional mean, which are substantively meaningful. Beissinger took a similar but slightly different approach to reporting useful quantities: he reported the *incident rate ratio* (*IRR*) of each parameter estimate. This is obtained simply by exponentiating each coefficient, and the results are in the third column. *IRR* −1 indicates the percentage increase in *Y* for a 1-unit change in *X*. Thus positive parameter estimates correspond to *IRR*s above 1, and negative parameter estimates correspond to *IRR*s below 1. These quantities are calculated in the same way as in a standard Poisson model.

Although the parameter estimates are interesting, it is hazardous to read too much into them. They are estimates, not the parameters themselves. To adequately interpret them, we must develop a method for capturing how uncertain we are about the actual DGP parameters based on these estimates. This development occurs in later chapters, primarily 7 and 9. We return to this example in Chapter 9, where we can present estimates of this uncertainty and get a fuller picture of what these results say about the DGP. For now, the important point is to see how a count model is applied in real research, what it implies about the randomness in the DGP, and how it is connected to substantive considerations about the dependent variable.

6.10 CONCLUSION

This chapter has defined a statistical model as consisting of two components: (*i*) a specification of the DGP of Y, and (*ii*) a link from the parameters of that DGP to some explanatory factors. In principle, the first part may consist of any specification, from simply observing that Y's DGP conditional on X is stochastic and not layering any more assumptions on it, all the way up to invoking a specific parametric family as the DGP for Y (or a specific family as governing the joint DGP of Y and X). In practice, it is common for analysts to impose some degree of parametric assumptions on the DGP used in the model, resulting in a parametric model.

It is possible that explicit mathematical theorizing about Y or knowledge of the process by which Y is sampled (see Chapter 7) justifies these parametric assumptions. But it is also common for analysts to invoke parametric assumptions out of convenience or convention. It is a good idea to keep an eye on where these assumptions come from in any application because they do a lot of work to structure our understanding of the behavior of Y and its relationship to explanatory factors. If these parametric assumptions are faulty, they can easily lead to conclusions that are false, for example, that some explanatory variable has an "important" effect on a dependent variable in the DGP when it actually does not. When conclusions are driven by the parametric model rather than the data, the model has effectively obscured rather than illuminated the process under study.

The second component of the definition of a statistical model has to offer something specific about how the explanatory factors affect the DGP of Y. To say "Y has a DGP and there are also some covariates that may affect its conditional distribution in some way" is not much of a theory. The typical approach in statistical modeling in social science is to contend that the conditional distribution of Y, or even more specifically its mean $E(Y|X)$, changes in a particular way as covariates change. This simple framing encapsulates a wide array of substantive arguments about social phenomena.

More particularly, statistical modeling usually specifies an explicit mathematical link between the parameters of Y's DGP and explanatory factors. In a linear regression model, the regression $E(Y|X)$ itself is assumed to be a linear function of covariates. In a GLM, some function of the regression is assumed to be a linear function of covariates. Because the regression $E(Y|X)$ is governed in some way by the parameters of Y's DGP, these specifications link the parameters to the covariates.

This link is the right focal point of theorizing about the systematic behavior of Y, because the DGP's parameters specify the systematic behavior of Y. Once the parameters of a DGP are determined, the remaining variation in Y

is random. In parametric models, it is assumed to follow a specific probability distribution, but that random variation from case to case is not in itself explainable.

This chapter has deliberately separated the conceptual issues of modeling and interpreting the parameters of a model from estimation of those parameters on the basis of data. Modeling is part of the theoretical enterprise in empirical research; a model is separate from the techniques used to estimate its parameters from data. Armed with this material, students can begin translating their own theoretical arguments into models and can interpret at least the estimated values of model parameters that are obtained from data. Actually doing the estimation and understanding the uncertainty about those estimates is still to come in the subsequent chapters.

As a whole, the remaining chapters analyze how to establish is a link between a DGP and observable data. This link cannot be taken for granted, in light of the discussion in Chapter 3. Establishing and probing the extent of that link is what statistical inference is about, and the remaining chapters constitute our coverage of this field as such. The next chapter, in particular, considers the implications of the fact that observable sample quantities are random variables drawn from a DGP. It shows how that randomness transmits to quantitative summaries of observable data, and how these summaries (sample means, variances, regression coefficients, etc.) are therefore also random variables. The most important new concept in that chapter is the *sampling distribution*, which is a distribution function of a statistic. The chapter then shows how parameters of sampling distributions are related to parameters of the DGP that gave rise to the data.

PROBLEMS

1. Consider a logit model $\ln(\frac{p}{1-p}) = \alpha + \beta_1 X_1 + \beta_2 X_2$.
   (a) What is the regression of Y on X_1 and X_2 in this model?
   (b) Does X_2 affect the effect of X_1 on $g(E(Y|X))$? On $E(Y|X)$?
2. A researcher is investigating the decision of a public welfare agency to deny or grant benefits to individual applicants. He postulates that both the applicant's race and gender may separately affect denial of benefits but also that the effect of race may differ by gender. Assume these are the only covariates. Express this in a statistical model.
3. An individual's performance on a task is measured on a scale $Y \in \mathbb{R}$. Measured performance is an additive function of the unit's "skill" ϕ, its "effort" ξ, and a mean-zero random variable ε (all scalars). Y_i can be observed on multiple iterations of the task, but neither ϕ_i nor ξ_i nor ε_i can be observed. Assume that ε_i is independent of ε_j for all $i \neq j$ and that $\phi_i = \phi_j$ for all i, j (thus "skill" is fixed and not under the individual's control). An observer gives the individual some fixed reward or praise (e.g., a dollar, a lollipop, a warm handshake) on any iteration of the

task where Y_i exceeds some fixed threshold $\tilde{Y}$ and gives some fixed penalty or criticism (e.g., a stern glare, a rap on the knuckles) whenever Y_i does not exceed $\tilde{Y}$. After many iterations the observer realizes that, on average, Y declines in any iteration after praise is applied, and Y increases on average in any iteration after the penalty is applied. The observer concludes that praise causes the unit to "slack off" and reduce its effort ξ after it is praised but to work hard and increase effort after it is penalized. Is this conclusion justified by the findings? If not, what accounts for the change in the individual's performance in successive periods?

4. (a) Using a computer software package, draw 10,000 samples of five independent draws from an exponential distribution with parameter $\theta = 20$. For each sample, compute the mean and then plot the histogram of sample means from all 10,000 samples. Compare the histogram to a normal distribution.

   (b) Repeat for 10,000 samples of 50, then 5,000 independent draws, and compare those histograms of sample means to a normal distribution.

7

Sampling Distributions: Linking Data-Generating Processes and Observable Data

In Chapter 6, we saw a variety of examples of data-generating processes (DGPs) that are common in statistical models, which consist of a DGP for the data and a link from its parameters to explanatory factors. Although the parametric family of the DGP may be assumed, the specific parameters of the DGP that gave rise to data we have available are generally not known. The whole point of empirical analysis is to use observable data to learn something about those parameters. A theory may assert that the conditional mean of Y increases as X increases, for instance, but in empirical analysis, we wish to determine how credible this assertion actually is. That is the point of statistical inference, which is the subject of the rest of this book.

To understand how we can use data to inform ourselves about parameters of DGPs when they are unknown, it is useful to see what happens when we pretend these parameters are known. If we have data drawn from a known DGP with known parameters, we can see how summaries and statistics computed from that observed data are related to those parameters. That is the subject of the present chapter. Here we study how summaries and statistics computed exclusively from observable data are related to the DGP, given a collection of observations from the DGP.

The process of drawing observations from the DGP is *sampling*. We will see that sampling allows for a precise statement of the connection between the DGP and summaries of observable sample data. That connection is what this chapter is actually about. The term "sampling" might suggest that we are constructing methods to identify respondents for a survey, and that is indeed part of the theory of sampling. But that is not what we are doing here, and it is not an essential part of the toolkit for research on statistical models with observational data. Rather, we are interested in whether and how the properties of a DGP are inherited by summaries that can be computed based on data drawn, or sampled, from that DGP.

A brief note on terminology: Thus far we have used the term "data-generating process" to describe the fundamental social and political process underlying some event, regardless of observation of that event. But the process of generating data literally also has to involve making (some) results of that fundamental process observable in a dataset. So sampling too is an important part of the DGP. Indeed, in some schools of thought, the "DGP" as we have used it before this chapter pertains to deterministic events, and the only stochastic element is in selecting a random subset of those events for observation. In other words, it is possible for a DGP to be stochastic only due to sampling uncertainty (Chapter 3), not to fundamental or theoretical uncertainty, and some approaches to statistics assume this. Obviously this book is not limited to that view.

7.1 RANDOM SAMPLING AND IID DRAWS FROM A DGP

The idea in sampling theory is that a DGP is operated in a sequence of trials to generate observable results. These results form a dataset. The dataset can be analyzed by a variety of techniques, many covered in Chapter 2.

The sampling process may involve correlation across observations or omission of some variables or observations from the observed data. This can arise from strategic behavior or individual optimizing behavior, for example, sometimes people or units do not want to be observed by an analyst or the behavior of a unit on one trial in the sample can affect the behavior of units on other trials. The canonical benchmark for the theory of statistical inference puts these complications aside and starts with a sampling process with sequential, independent operations of a single DGP to generate the observable data.

In a *simple random sample* of size N, each member in the sample is an independent draw from a common population of elements or DGP. That is, the sample consists of N random variables, $X_1, X_2, \ldots, X_N$, which are all mutually independent and identically distributed. The assumption of *independence and identical distribution* of draws from the DGP is so commonly invoked in the basic theory of sampling that it is referred to as simply the iid (independent and identically distributed) assumption.

The PDF or PMF of X_i, the ith element of the sample, can be denoted $f_i(x)$. This distribution is simply called either the DGP of the random variable (sometimes *parent DGP* to emphasize its existence logically before the sample) or the *population distribution*. Assume the *population mean* or *DGP mean* is finite (i.e., $\infty < EX_i \equiv \mu < \infty$) and *population variance* or *DGP variance* is finite (i.e., $Var X_i \equiv \sigma^2 < \infty$). In other words, we use μ as a symbol to denote the mean of the distribution and σ^2 to denote the variance.[1] These are both called *parameters* of the population or parent distribution.

---

[1] Finite mean is not a completely unrestrictive assumption. For example, the Cauchy distribution (encountered in the online appendix to Chapter 6), which has a bell-shaped density with tails

The sequence of observations in the sample is itself a joint random variable. As such it has a joint distribution of its own. If $\mathbf{X}$ is just shorthand for the entire sequence $X_1, X_2, \ldots, X_N$, then the probability or density of a specific set of observations in the sample is $f^s(x_1, x_2, \ldots, x_N) \equiv f^s(\mathbf{x}) = \prod_{i=1}^{n} f_i(x_i)$. Here we have already used the assumption of independence: because the sample random variables are all independent of each other, we can multiply their marginal distributions to get their joint distribution.

The sample of the data at hand is a random variable, and thus any quantity computed from it or based on it is also a random variable. Now, obviously, for a *given* dataset (i.e., a given draw from $f^s(\mathbf{x})$), repeated application of a certain formula will of course give the same result every time. That is not the point. The point is that a new dataset could be drawn at random from $f^s(\mathbf{x})$ (or we can conceptualize such a draw), and in general some of the values in it would change in random fashion compared to a previous draw. Therefore an application of any formula to the new dataset would produce a result different from the application in the previous dataset. The difference is due to random variation in the datasets drawn from the parent DGP.

This simple idea is foundational in the classical or frequentist theory of statistics: the summaries we compute from a dataset are simply draws of a random variable. As such, they too have probability distributions, which are called *sampling distributions*. This idea is presented here simply to plant the seed of the concept for the presentation below, where the idea is covered much more fully. The next three sections explore the implications of this idea for three important quantities computable from sample data: the sample mean, sample variance, and sample regression coefficients.

7.2 SAMPLE MEAN WITH IID DRAWS

Consider the simple probability distribution of X in Table 7.1. Clearly, $E(X) = 2.5$. Now consider an iid sample of five elements from this parent DGP. One such sample is $2, 2, 4, 1, 4$. Because the draws are independent, we can easily determine that the probability of drawing these five elements in this order from this DGP is $0.3 \times 0.3 \times 0.2 \times 0.2 \times 0.2 = 0.00072$. That is a small number, but the most likely iid sample – any five-tuple of twos and threes – has probability $0.3^5 = 0.00243$. That's only about 3.5 times larger. No *particular* sequence of five random draws is especially likely.

In any case, in the sample $2, 2, 4, 1, 4$, the sample mean is $\overline{x} = \frac{13}{5} = 2.6$. Seems "in the ballpark" of 2.5, but that kind of naked-eye comparison is hazardous, and we will learn to distrust it fiercely.

---

thicker than the normal distribution's, does not have a mean (and thus no variance, skewness, kurtosis, or higher moments either). So what follows does not apply to samples drawn from literally any distribution. But it applies to essentially all of the distributions encountered in applied quantitative research.

TABLE 7.1. *Distribution of a Random Variable*

	\multicolumn{4}{c}{$X = x$}			
	1	2	3	4
$f(x)$	0.2	0.3	0.3	0.2

Suppose we drew another iid sample of five elements from this parent DGP, and this time we come out with $4, 3, 1, 2, 2$. For what it's worth, the probability of drawing this sample is 0.00108. In this sample, the mean is $\overline{x} = \frac{12}{5} = 2.4$.

So we took two samples and their sample means bracketed the population mean. Note that we applied the same formula to both samples but got a different answer the second time. This is because by random chance, we drew new elements in the sample, and so a deterministic formula applied to those new elements will produce a new result. As the sample data itself is random, so the sample mean computed from that data is random.

The sample mean, in short, is a random variable. The sample itself is random in the sense that if we repeated the sampling process by drawing N more observations from the DGP, we would generally get different observations in the second sample than in the first. The sample mean is random in the exact same sense: if we drew a new sample from the DGP, the sample mean would change because the observations on which it is computed change.

When we deal with the sample mean as a random variable, we use the capital letter designation $\overline{X}$. When we deal with the mean in any specific dataset, merely a garden-variety number, we use the notation $\overline{x}$.

As a random variable, $\overline{X}$ inherits the properties of any random variable. It has a probability distribution, for one thing. That distribution is called a *sampling distribution* to mark how special it is. More generally, any quantity computed from a random sample is a *statistic*, and any statistic is a random variable. The probability distribution of a statistic is known as a sampling distribution.

7.2.1 Expectation of the Sample Mean

When we try to learn about DGPs, the reason the sample mean is interesting is because it helps us to do that. When a quantity from a sample T is used to learn about a quantity in the DGP or population θ, that sample quantity T is called an *estimator* of θ. We encounter a more formal definition of estimator and various properties of estimators in Chapter 9. For now, this idea is enough.

What can we say about the sampling distribution of $\overline{X}$ in general, and in particular, its connection to the DGP? The simplest and first cut at exploring this is to consider the expected value of $\overline{X}$.

The idea of "the mean of the sample mean" and "the standard deviation of the sample mean" takes some getting used to. But because the sample mean is a random variable and it has a (sampling) distribution, we can explore the mean of the sample mean using the tools of Chapter 5, just the same as we can for any probability distribution. So "the mean of the sample mean" really means $E(\overline{X})$. The math is pretty clear even though the English is a little odd.

This expectation turns out to be rather straightforward. The reason is that $E(\cdot)$ is linear, as stressed in Chapter 5. Using that fact and simply applying the definition of $\overline{X}$ from Chapter 2, $E(\overline{X}) = E(\frac{\sum X_i}{N}) = \frac{E(\sum X_i)}{N} = \frac{\sum E(X_i)}{N} = \frac{\sum \mu}{N} = \frac{N\mu}{N} = \mu$. The last quantity μ is none other than the mean of the parent DGP/population distribution. In short,

$$E(\overline{X}) = \mu. \tag{7.1}$$

The fact that $E(\overline{X}) = \mu$ means that $\overline{X}$ is an *unbiased estimator* of the DGP mean μ. Unbiasedness means that the expected value of the statistic equals the population quantity it is used to estimate. Invoking the meaning of expectation discussed in Chapter 5, this implies that the single best guess of the value of $\overline{X}$ (in the sense of MSE) is μ. (We return to estimators and bias of them in greater detail in Chapter 9.)

Now, in examples so far we have started with a known DGP, so having a good estimator of its parameters is no great achievement. We know those parameters exactly, so estimating them is not that interesting. The profound importance of this simple result is that when we take these tools out into the wild, we do not know the DGPs nature gives us, or even if we know (or postulate) functional forms for them (see Chapter 6), we do not know all of their important parameters. That is why we apply statistical tools to datasets – to learn something about the DGP that generated them. Because the sample mean is an unbiased estimator of the DGP mean, we can be sure that even when we do not know the DGP, the sample mean of a dataset drawn from it is on average equal to the mean of the DGP itself. That is the where we stop doing probability and start doing statistics.

Note that the proof of $E(\overline{X}) = \mu$ does not assume independence in random sampling. The sequence of steps used to prove this invoked the definition of $\overline{X}$, the linearity of $E(\cdot)$, some arithmetic, and the assumption that all X_is in the sample have the same mean μ (identical distribution), but not independence. The key point is that the linearity of $E(\cdot)$ does not depend on independence of the sample elements. Any correlation among the sample elements still gives a sample mean that is unbiased for μ. For example, if a draw of a large value early in the sample makes it more likely to get a large draw later (say, survey respondents see earlier responses and are subject to peer pressure) or a small draw early makes it more likely to get a small draw later (a condition of *positive autocorrelation* or *serial correlation*), the sample mean is still unbiased for μ.

This proof of unbiasedness of $\overline{X}$ also does not depend on the sample size N. The sample mean equals the population mean in expectation *no matter how small the sample is*. Because the best predictor of a random variable in the sense of mean squared error (MSE) is its expected value, this implies that $\overline{X}$ is the best predictor of μ for any sample size.[2]

7.2.2 The Standard Error of $\overline{X}$: Standard Deviation of the Sample Mean

Because $\overline{X}$ is an unbiased estimator of μ, we know it is on average equal to this DGP parameter. But how "good of a guess" does it provide about the value of μ? What is the typical size of the error we will make by asserting $\mu = \bar{x}$ in a given sample? The bias of the sample mean addresses only the central tendency of the sample mean as a random variable. As always, the central tendency of a distribution is only a partial picture of it; we also need to know the variability of the distribution or its spread over its possible values.

For the sampling distribution of a statistic, the standard deviation is known as the *standard error*. Determining the standard error, or equivalently $Var(\overline{X})$, requires more assumptions than determining $E(\overline{X})$.

Specifically, and relying crucially on the assumptions of independent and identically distributed sample observations, $Var(\overline{X}) = Var(\frac{\sum X_i}{N}) = \frac{Var(\sum X_i)}{N^2} = \frac{\sum Var(X_i)}{N^2} = \frac{\sum \sigma^2}{N^2} = \frac{N\sigma^2}{N^2} = \frac{\sigma^2}{N}$. This is none other than the variance of the population distribution over the sample size. The square root of this is the standard error of the mean, or

$$SE(\overline{X}) = \frac{\sigma}{\sqrt{N}}. \tag{7.2}$$

This is an important expression in statistics, and it is a good idea to commit it to memory now. More generally, standard errors are an essential building block in statistical inference. The standard error has the same interpretation that any standard deviation has, relative to the mean of the distribution of its random variable. In particular, it is a measure of the typical deviation of a random variable from its expected value. So when learning about DGPs from observed data, standard errors are important because they tell us how certain or uncertain are the conclusions about the DGP that we base on the sample. Understanding the uncertainty in one's best estimates is essential for understanding what one learns about the DGP.

Note how $SE(\overline{X})$ is related to N. First, it's an inverse relationship. The bigger is N, the smaller is $SE(\overline{X})$. So the sample mean is a better, more precise, more accurate estimator of μ in bigger samples than in smaller ones, in the sense that this measure of the typical deviation of $\overline{X}$ from $E(\overline{X}) = \mu$ gets smaller as

---

[2] Needless to say, a suboptimal predictor in a large sample from a DGP may be a better predictor than the sample mean in a small sample from the same DGP. But computing all predictors from a sample fixed at size N, none is better than the sample mean in the sense of MSE.

N grows. In fact, as $N \to \infty$, $SE(\overline{X}) \to 0$, so in an infinitely large sample, the sample mean is a spike located at the population mean.

Second, $SE(\overline{X})$ decreases slower than linearly with N. That means that an increase in N has less effect on $SE(\overline{X})$ when N is large than when N is small. The sample mean gets more precise as an estimator of μ as N grows, but the precision does not grow as fast as N. In contrast, $SE(\overline{X})$ is linearly related to σ. If you could spend \$1 to decrease σ or increase N, you'd get more SE-bang for the buck by spending it on σ.

This is the first appearance in this book of any benefit from the mythical "large N," as statistical approaches are called in some social science disciplines. Given that this whole school of thought is sometimes called "large N methods," that bears noting. The point is that so-called large N methods are not justified fundamentally by the sample size. They are justified (or not justified) depending on a theory of the nature of DGPs. The justification or necessity of a particular approach to inference depends not on the attributes of the sample (its size or what have you) but on the nature of the information to be learned. If there is a DGP and it is stochastic, statistical methods and models are appropriate whether N is large or small. We may not learn as much with small N as with large N, but we will learn even less (and perhaps literally nothing at best) by applying methods suited to deterministic DGPs in the context of stochastic ones.

Now that we do have some clear benefit of large N, though, it may seem that the prescription is "go forth and get large samples." But with the first reference to a benefit of big samples comes the first caveat. Larger N is only good as long as the sampling process is understood or as long as it conforms to the same sampling process as in a smaller sample on which one might want to improve. In particular, if it is necessary to violate either the i (independence) or id (identically distributed) in order to increase N, it may introduce much deeper, more fundamental, and less easily recognized problems than it solves. The reason is that data do not tell you when they fail iid. It is sometimes possible and practical to test for failures of iid, but often this assumption is invoked at an analyst's discretion. Even when it is possible to execute tests for failures of iid, the remedies are not pleasant and may cause more problems than they solve. The purpose of quantitative methods is to learn something from the N you have, not make you commit all manner of substantive flaws by aggregating observations that are not (at least conditional on covariates) drawn from the same distribution.

Note what the standard error of $\overline{X}$ does *not* depend on: the size of a sample relative to the "size" of a population. This is particularly relevant for surveys and polls with respondents drawn at random from a population of potential respondents. The number of respondents in the sample relative to the number of potential respondents does not factor into the standard error of $\overline{X}$. Thus surveys do not need to draw more respondents from California than from Wyoming to achieve a given desired level of precision about μ for the state based on $\overline{X}$ for the state.

The implicit condition for this is that the sample size N is a small fraction, say 1%, of the population size N_{pop} (Freedman et al. [2007]). When this condition is met, the "removal" of the N sample elements from the N_{pop} population elements has a small effect on the aggregate characteristics of the units left in the population, so $\frac{N}{N_{pop}}$ has no effect on the accuracy of $\overline{X}$. This condition is necessary because, in practice, surveys do not take strictly iid draws from the population. Once a respondent is selected to be included as observation i, they are removed from the population from which other observations besides i are selected. So when a respondent is removed, the remaining population changes slightly. If N is a very small fraction of N_{pop}, this change is so slight it can be ignored. When model-based sampling is assumed, this issue is not relevant because there is no "population size"; there is simply an assumed DGP from which N draws were taken.

It is important to be able to spot the use of the independence assumption in the reasoning and derivations just discussed. This is because in some applications, the first "i" in iid (to say nothing of the second) is not credible. This is in fact a pretty common state of affairs in some applications. So understanding how independence factors into the definition of $SE(\overline{X})$ is necessary to understand where basic formulas for "average error in the mean" go wrong and need modification when independence fails. Such modification can be complicated, but it is worth it to avoid making incredible assumptions about a sampling process.[3]

Specifically, we used independence here when the variance of a sum of random variables is equated with the sum of their individual variances. This is valid only if their covariance is equal to zero (Y may be correlated with X, but successive Ys are not correlated with each other), for which independence is a sufficient condition. The assumption of identical distribution also plays a crucial role and is used to replace the sum of individual variances with n times a single variance.

7.2.3 The Shape of the Sampling Distribution of $\overline{X}$

So far we know that the sample mean equals the population mean in expectation, for any sample size. And we know that the quality of that prediction in the sense of the standard error gets better as the sample size grows. So we know the mean and variance of the sampling distribution of $\overline{X}$ and how they depend on N.

To get a sense of how we use these facts in statistical inference, consider a sample drawn from a DGP with an unknown mean. If we have a conjecture or

---

[3] This is an important point about the practice of quantitative research. Generally speaking, techniques get more complicated as they are designed to prevent invalid applications of more basic techniques. Nobody wants to glorify in complicated techniques themselves, but we want even less to be consigned to inappropriate ones.

guess or a theory about the unknown value of μ, we can compute $\bar{x}$ and use the standard error of $\overline{X}$ to determine whether the observed $\bar{x}$ differs from μ by more or less than a typical amount (which is what the SE tells us). In this way we can roughly evaluate whether the conjecture about μ is reasonable or not. We will develop this logic in much further detail in future chapters (that is what statistical hypothesis testing is all about).

But it would also be useful to know not just the expected value of the sampling distribution of $\overline{X}$, and not just its standard deviation (the SE of $\overline{X}$) but also its entire shape. That is, if we know the entire probability distribution from which $\overline{X}$ is drawn, we can evaluate not only whether any particular $\overline{X}$ from a sample differs from a guess about μ by more or less than typical but also the probability of observing a sample mean "like" $\bar{x}$ if the guess about μ is in fact correct. That allows for a much more precise evaluation of the reasonableness of the guess than simply using the SE of $\overline{X}$ alone.

When the parent DGP of the sample is a normal distribution and the sample observations are independently drawn from that parent DGP, the shape of the sampling distribution of $\overline{X}$ is straightforward. Sums of independent normal random variables are themselves exactly normal, as noted in Chapter 6. Because the sample mean is a sum of the variables in the sample, it too must follow a normal distribution if the parent DGP is normal. Thus for a normal parent DGP, we know the expected value, standard deviation, and exact parametric family of the sampling distribution of $\overline{X}$.

When the DGP is not normal, things are not so straightforward. Obviously, the shape of the parent DGP has some effect on the shape of the distribution of $\overline{X}$, at least for small samples. For instance, suppose we take a sample of $N = 1$ from a Uniform[0,1] distribution, where $\mu = .5$. That is, we take one draw from the distribution and call it a "sample," so $\bar{x}$ is simply the value of the one observation we drew. So the sampling distribution of $\overline{X}$ for $N = 1$ is also exactly uniform.[4] The expected value of $\overline{X}$ is still $\mu = .5$, of course, but the sampling distribution of $\overline{X}$ does not concentrate its values around μ any more than the parent DGP does.

What if the DGP is Uniform[0,1] and we take $N = 2$ independent draws? The only way to get a very small value of $\bar{x}$ (close to 0) is to draw two very low values from the DGP, and the only way to get a very large value of $\bar{x}$ is to draw two very large values from the DGP. Two intermediate values drawn from the DGP will produce an intermediate value of $\bar{x}$ – but so will a sample with a very large and a very small value.

Under a uniform DGP, all of these types of samples are equally likely by assumption, and with $N = 2$, more possible samples lead to intermediate values of $\bar{x}$ than lead to extreme values of $\bar{x}$. So the probability of an intermediate value of $\bar{x}$ exceeds the probability of an extreme value of $\bar{x}$. Even though the

---

[4] The same is true for a sample of $N = 1$ from any other DGP; the sampling distribution of $\overline{X}$ when $N = 1$ is simply the parent DGP exactly.

parent DGP is not peaked near $\mu = .5$, the sampling distribution of $\overline{X}$ for $N = 2$ is. Now the sampling distribution of $\overline{X}$ is not uniform, it is tent-shaped. The distribution of $\overline{X}$ is more concentrated around μ than the parent DGP for either observation. (Put differently, the sampling distribution of $\overline{X}$ second-order stochastically dominates the parent DGP; see Chapter 6.)

The shape of the sampling distribution of $\overline{X}$ gets even more interesting as the sample size N continues to grow: remarkably, it gets closer and closer to a normal distribution. Also remarkably, the parent distribution of X has no effect on this fact, and we need not know anything about that parent to ensure it, other than that its mean and variance are finite. As the number N of iid observations in the sample gets larger, the sampling distribution of $\overline{X}$ gets closer to normal.

This is the key point of the *central limit theorem* (CLT), which we discuss in further detail later. This theorem is one of the most widely known, applied, celebrated, and probably misunderstood results in statistics. Because data analysts so often deal with sample means as estimators, this theorem helps to justify the widespread use of the normal distribution in applied research.

7.2.4 Sampling Distribution of a Difference in Means from Two Samples

Theoretical, policy, and substantive considerations often focus attention on comparisons (and specifically, differences) of means across DGPs. Is student achievement higher on average under literacy program A or B? Do Democratic presidents preside over higher or lower (or about the same) economic growth, on average, as Republican presidents? Are religious people more likely to vote than the nonreligious? Do leaders of authoritarian governments stay in power longer on average than leaders of Democratic governments? Is child poverty higher or lower on average under Temporary Assistance to Needy Families than Aid to Families with Dependent Children?

Although these DGP comparisons are limited to means only, they are important. In policy terms, it is difficult to recommend an intervention that typically does not help in some identifiable way. In theoretical terms, we usually do not try to explain all of what we take to be random or idiosyncratic variation from case to case; we try to explain regularities, tendencies, and typical behaviors. In each case, comparison of means is a natural statistical interpretation of the substantive concern.

It is therefore fortunate that, considering two samples 1 and 2, taken independently of each other from possibly different DGPs, the sampling distribution of $\overline{X}_1 - \overline{X}_2$ is not in principle much more complicated than the sampling distribution of $\overline{X}$ by itself. This is not too surprising because a difference in means is a kind of sum, so results that are true for the distribution of $\overline{X}$ are also true for $\overline{X}_1 - \overline{X}_2$.

In particular, suppose sample 1 consists of N_1 iid draws from a normal (μ_1, σ_1) DGP, and sample 2 consists of N_2 iid draws from a normal (μ_2, σ_2)

DGP. And suppose that sample 1 is independent of sample 2. Because $E(\cdot)$ is linear and $\overline{X}$ is unbiased,

$$E(\overline{X}_1 - \overline{X}_2) = \mu_1 - \mu_2. \tag{7.3}$$

And because sums of independent normal random variables are normal, $\overline{X}_1 - \overline{X}_2$ is exactly normal. More generally, by the CLT, the distribution of $\overline{X}_1 - \overline{X}_2$ converges to normal as the sample sizes increase, no matter what DGP the samples come from.

The only minor issue is the standard error of the difference. Because the samples are independent, the variance of the sum is the sum of the variances – and so is the variance of the difference. This is a straightforward implication of the definition of $Var(\overline{X}_1 - \overline{X}_2) = E((\overline{X}_1 - \overline{X}_2) - (\mu_1 - \mu_2))^2$.

It follows that $Var(\overline{X}_1 - \overline{X}_2) = \frac{\sigma_1^2}{N_1} + \frac{\sigma_2^2}{N_2}$, so the standard error of the difference in means is

$$SE_D = \sqrt{\frac{\sigma_1^2}{N_1} + \frac{\sigma_2^2}{N_2}}. \tag{7.4}$$

As either DGP becomes more variable, holding the other one fixed, it is easier to obtain a sample sequence that puts $\overline{X}_1 - \overline{X}_2$ far away from its average. And as either sample size increases, we learn more and more about the mean of the DGP of that sample, so there is less variability of the sample mean around that DGP mean.

7.3 SUMS OF RANDOM VARIABLES AND THE CLT

The CLT applies to more than just the sample mean $\overline{X}$. It applies to any sum of iid random variables from any parent DGP satisfying mild conditions – specifically, the parent DGP must have finite mean and variance. Given such a parent, any sum of N iid random variables is approximately normally distributed, and the approximation gets better and better as N gets larger and larger. That is the idea of the CLT.

With the CLT, we know that $\overline{X}$ is approximately distributed $N(\mu, \frac{\sigma}{\sqrt{N}})$. Because it is approximately normal, and the normal is a two-parameter family, and we know those two parameters for the sample mean (or at least we know how they are related to DGP parameters), that means we know approximately everything there is to know about the sampling distribution of the sample mean in large samples, almost irrespective of the parent DGP. This is a remarkable fact and useful for using the sample mean to make inferences about the DGP mean. We start to develop tools for this in Chapter 8.

To see the idea of of this convergence to a normal distribution, consider the following simulation: flip a coin N times and denote the proportion of heads (i.e., the sample mean) in the sample as p_H. Repeat this experiment 10,000 times for the same N. Plot the proportion of times out of 10,000

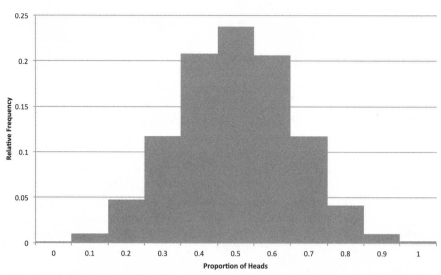

FIGURE 7.1. Proportion of heads in 10 flips: 10,000 simulations.

that p_H was observed, for each possible value of p_H. Figures 7.1 through 7.3 illustrate this from computerized simulations, a rudimentary kind of *Monte Carlo* simulation.[5] They each show histograms of p_H from the simulations for $N = 10, 20$, and 100.

Because the proportion of heads in N flips is a type of sum, and flips are iid, the central limit theorem applies. The proportion of heads in each sample is approximately normal and centered at 0.5. Furthermore, the approximation to the normal distribution in the histogram of p_H improves as N grows. In the figures for all N, the modal proportion of heads for each figure is located around 0.5, and the histograms are approximately bell shaped. The approximations do indeed get closer to normal as N increases.

Each one of these figures shows a simulated sampling distribution. For any statistic that is a sum of N sample observations, there is a different sampling distribution for each value of N. The "real" sampling distribution for any given N is what results if we take not 10,000 samples from the DGP but ∞ samples.[6] That of course is impossible, and for these purposes, 10,000 samples is large

[5] The idea is to repeat each experiment, with a fixed N, some "large" number of times so that the actual results of the simulation can approximate the sampling distribution for that value of N; 10,000 is understood here to be "large enough," but it's rather small for actual Monte Carlo simulations.

[6] Simulations like those presented in Figures 7.1–7.3 are sometimes confusing because there are "two Ns" and it is sometimes not clear which is the relevant one for the convergence result. In these figures, there is N for the number of flips of the coin ($N = 10, 20$, or 100), and there is also the number of iterations of the sample. Denote this as T – equal to 10,000 in all three figures. The convergence result of the CLT applies to increasing N, not increasing T. The key is that

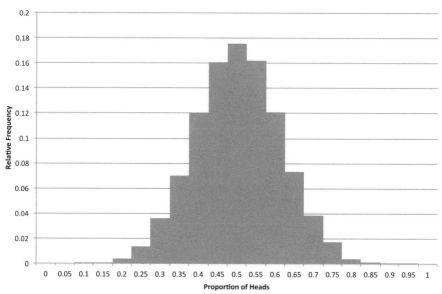

FIGURE 7.2. Number of heads in 20 flips: 10,000 simulations.

enough to make the histogram for each N look a lot like the real sampling distribution for that N.[7]

When $N = 1$, so we take just one draw from the DGP (one coin flip, one roll of a die, one person sampled from the voting age population, etc.), the sampling distribution of any sum of sample elements is simply the DGP itself.

For $N = 2$, the sample has two observations drawn from the same DGP, Y_1 and Y_2. The sum of these two random variables is called a *convolution* of the random variables. Even for $N = 2$, the sampling distribution for any sum of iid random variables loads more weight on the mean of the DGP than the DGP itself does. The idea is simple: if both draws are near the DGP mean, then the average of the draws is as well. If one of the draws is very large and the other is very small, the mean of their sum is still near the overall mean of the DGP – because the very large result counterbalances the very small one. Only if both draws are very small can the mean of the sum be far below the DGP mean,

the histogram looks "more normal" in the figure with $N = 100$ than the one with $N = 10$. The relevant comparison is across figures.

[7] The number of iterations of the sampling, T, is fixed at some large number so that the histogram in each panel looks like the real sampling distribution for that case. T should be large enough that every possible "type" of sample is observed with a relative frequency about equal to its actual probability under the DGP. In other words, the purpose of large T is to make the set of observed samples in the simulation look approximately identical to the set of possible samples under the DGP. Therefore, the histogram of sample averages for a given sample size N looks like the actual sampling distribution for the sample average for that N.

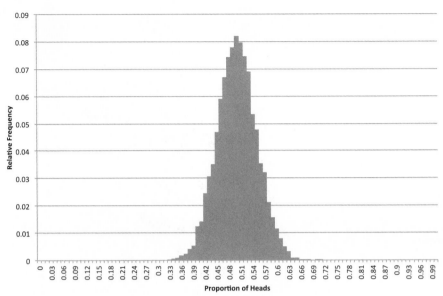

FIGURE 7.3. Number of heads in 100 flips: 10,000 simulations.

and only if both are very large can the mean of the sum be far above the DGP mean. But neither of these cases is likely.

This logic carries through for $N = 3$, only more strongly. To obtain a sample mean far below the DGP mean for $N = 3$ requires three consecutive draws that are all far below the mean. But any one very small draw can be counterbalanced by two moderately large draws to give a sample mean close to the DGP mean or by one moderate draw and one large draw. So as N increases, the sampling distribution of any sum will be more and more peaked, and the average of the sample elements in the sum will be closer and closer to the DGP mean.

The logic behind the CLT is this: when we take N iid draws from a distribution $F(x)$, each of the N draws departs from their common mean μ by some independent, mean-0 error. These errors are all "white noise": they create a background fuzz but do not have a systematic bias on average, and they do not snowball through correlation with each other. And for μ to be a mean, it must be possible for the white noise errors to be both positive and negative.

Now, no matter the parent DGP (as long as μ exists), a sample mean generated from N draws is the DGP mean μ, plus the accumulated white noise errors from each observation. Accumulating that white noise to push $\overline{X}$ above μ requires that the most of the white noise errors turn out to be positive, larger than their average. If there are a lot of these independent errors in the accumulation, that is unusual. When many errors are accumulated, is even unusual when the DGP is highly asymmetric (puts very little mass or density above the mean). So it is less likely to obtain this sort of accumulation of a large number

of white noise errors than a collection of errors in which their acc
closer to their average. Accumulating white noise errors to push
μ requires that all the white noise errors are very large, which i_ _
unusual. So it is even less likely and becomes more so as N increases.

So the CLT says that as $N \to \infty$, the sampling distribution for any sum
of independent random variables drawn from a DGP with finite mean and
variance converges to a normal distribution.

Using a Bernoulli or binomial distribution to illustrate the CLT is clear
enough but does not really reveal the full power of the theorem. The normal
distribution was in fact *invented* as a continuous approximation to the number
of successes in a binomial distribution (Stigler [1986]), so it is no real surprise
that the number of heads follows an approximately normal curve.

The real power of the theorem is that it holds true regardless of how the
parent DGP is shaped – skewed, bimodal, irregular, whatever. It may take more
sample observations N for the mean of a sample drawn from a strange DGP
to be approximately normally distributed, but sooner or later it will be.

The normal distribution is simply the distribution that results when a large
number of more or less independent white noise errors are accumulated. The
mean of the resulting normal distribution is the mean around which those white
noise errors are drawn. So it is actually not deeply magical that the sampling
distribution of sums converges to normal per se because the normal is simply
the definition we give to the distribution that results from the random process in
accumulating white noise (independent, mean-0) errors from any distribution.
In this sense, the CLT is powerful because it points out that no matter what
parent distribution we start with, the process of accumulating a large number
of white noise errors from draws from that distribution is always, in some
sense, the same.

The CLT concerns the behavior of sums of iid draws as the number of draws
N approaches ∞. This is a *convergence* result, in that it asserts that the distribution of $\overline{X}$ or any other sum converges to a particular *limiting distribution* as
N grows larger and larger. It deals with the convergence of the entire sampling
distribution of the statistic, an idea referred to as *convergence in distribution*.

To understand this concept, think about the sampling distribution of a sum
or average for any sample size N – such as one of the histograms above for 10,
20, or 100 coin flips. Now imagine an exact normal distribution overlaid on top
of that histogram. At each value on the horizontal axis, there is some difference
between the sampling distribution and the exact normal distribution on the
vertical axis. And among all these vertical differences between the sampling
distribution for given N and the exact normal, one will be at least as large as
all the others.

Convergence in distribution means that this maximum vertical difference
can be made as small as one could possibly want, if N is large enough. More
precisely, let d_N denote the maximum vertical distance between the exact normal distribution and the sampling distribution of a sum of a sample of size N.

For any real number $\varepsilon > 0$, no matter how small, there is a value of $\widetilde{N}$ such that $d_N < \varepsilon$ for any sample size $N \geq \widetilde{N}$.

There are actually several versions of the CLT. They vary in how much independence they require in the iid sample and some technicalities; it turns out that some degree of correlation among sample elements can occur without breaking the result. The important point is that each random component of a sum cannot contribute "too much" to the overall total; if that condition holds, then a variant of the CLT will hold as well.

The problem created by correlation among sample elements is easy to see in the limiting case of perfect correlation. Then once a single observation is drawn from the DGP, all the remaining observations are equal to it because they are perfectly correlated. So the sample mean is immediately pinned down to that one observation. More observations cannot smooth out the sampling distribution of the sample mean as N grows.

Versions of the CLT also vary to some extent in the conditions they impose on the parent DGP, but in all cases, these are fairly mild. It is not impossible to find a parent DGP that fails the conditions of the CLT (e.g., the Cauchy has no mean), so that the sampling distribution of its sample mean would not be assured by the theorem to be approximately normal, but it is uncommon to find one in applied research.

The importance and use of knowing the sampling distribution of a sample quantity cannot be overstated. The reason is that we can assess the density or probability of a value of the sample quantity in specific cases. Such probability statements are based on conjectures about unknown DGP parameters, and if the sampling distribution assigns very low probability or density to an observed value of a sample quantity, it suggests that the conjecture about the unknown DGP parameters is not very good. We develop this logic further in Chapter 8. In this and the next few sections, we simply note the sampling distribution of several sample quantities.

Central Limit Theorem: Application
In addition to its importance for pinning down sampling distributions, which plays a crucial role in hypothesis testing and estimation as covered in Chapters 8 and 9, the CLT is directly useful because of the approximate probabilities it provides quickly. For instance, consider the issue of "missing girls" in countries where some large subpopulations have a preference for male children.

Demographers have established that the probability of a female birth among humans is about 0.487, a fact that is stable across time and demographic groups.[8] In India in 2009, approximately 47% of the roughly 15 million babies

---

[8] Interestingly, however, it does not take long for the number of females in a given age cohort to reach parity with the males, because males are more likely to die than females at any given age, conditional on surviving to that age – a fact that is also stable across time and demographic groups.

born were girls. Assuming that birth genders are independent across mothers and that a woman has at most one baby per year, this was approximately 15 million "flips of a coin." Is it fair to assume, based on 47% "heads" in the sample of 15 million, that the distribution for India in 2009 matched the general human distribution?

The CLT allows a quick answer to this question. The number of girls born in that group of 15 million is a sum. Assuming that the probability of a female birth in India in 2009 was the same as for the general human population implies $\mu = 0.487$ and the standard error of $\overline{X} = \frac{0.5}{\sqrt{15 \text{ million}}} \approx .0001$. This means that the *observed* $\overline{X} = 0.47$ is more than 100 SE's from its expected value.

So far none of this actually involves the CLT; these are properties of the sample mean under random sampling. But by the CLT, we also know that $\overline{X}$ is approximately normally distributed, and with a sum of 15 million independent draws from the distribution, the approximation is good. With a normal distribution, we can see that drawing a sample with a mean 100 SEs away from the DGP mean is an incomprehensibly rare event.

The bounds implied by Chebyshev's theorem (Chapter 5) for any conceivable distribution would suggest that this is a 1 in 10,000 event; invoking a normal distribution from the CLT suggests it is essentially impossible. If there were a single green grain of sand on Earth, we'd have a far better chance of picking that one grain at random out of a pile containing every single grain of sand in the world than of drawing a sample from a normal DGP with a mean 100 SEs away from the DGP mean.

Of course, the CLT can tell us that there is a discrepancy but not why it exists. In particular, the CLT cannot tell us how many of the "missing girls," compared with how many there "should" be, are missing because of female infanticide, hepatitis B among mothers (which tends to raise the probability of a male birth (Oster [2003])), or any other conjectured cause. The CLT can tell us with great certainty that something worth investigating is going on.

7.4 SAMPLE VARIANCE WITH IID DRAWS

Of course, substantive considerations may lead to interest not only in the mean or conditional mean of a DGP but also its spread. For instance, in the study of the U.S. Congress, a researcher may be interested to know whether electoral institutions such as partisan primaries or direct election of senators affect the degree of ideological heterogeneity within a political party. If primaries and the structure of campaign financing allow national party elites to exert greater control over the selection of candidates for office, we might expect intraparty heterogeneity to decline. One interpretation of this is that the standard deviation of ideological positions within a party declines. As another example, if globalization and the rise of supranational institutions leads to a convergence of institutional structures across nation-states, we might expect the standard deviation of some measure of institutional differences across nation-states to decline.

These types of questions focus attention on the standard deviation or variance of a DGP and what we can infer about it from a collection of observed values. So the sampling distribution for sample standard deviation or variance is useful to know.

Note a terminological subtlety of this compared what we have already seen. We have already dealt with the variance of a sampling distribution – but it was the sampling distribution of the sample mean. And we have already seen how the DGP variance σ^2 plays into that – it is the numerator of the variance in the sample mean across repeated samples. But neither of these cases is the same as what we address now: the behavior of S^2, the sample variance, across repeated samples. We can think about the variance of the sampling distribution of any statistic; now we are addressing the sampling distribution of the sample variance.

7.4.1 Expected Value of Sample Variance S^2

The sample variance is a random variable defined by $S^2 = \frac{\sum_i (X_i - \overline{X})^2}{N-1}$. The $N-1$ rather than N in the denominator has always been a little curious. We have stories about "using up pieces of information" in computing $\overline{X}$, degrees of freedom, and the like, and those stories are true. But $N-1$ rather than N is necessary to ensure that $E(S^2) = \sigma^2$. As we saw with the sample mean, unbiasedness of the sample variance does not depend on independence in the sample and does not depend on the parent DGP in any way except that the DGP must have finite mean and variance.

Showing $E(S^2) = \sigma^2$ is a bit more involved than showing unbiasedness of $\overline{X}$ or deriving the standard error of $\overline{X}$.

To begin, note again that our assumption about the DGP is $E(X) = \mu$ and $Var(X) = \sigma^2$, both finite. Further note that the definition of S^2 implies $(N-1)S^2 = \sum(X - \overline{X})^2$, or $\sum(X^2 - 2X\overline{X} + \overline{X}^2)$. This in turn equals $\sum X^2 - \sum 2X\overline{X} + \sum \overline{X}^2$, or $\sum X^2 - 2\overline{X}\sum X + \sum \overline{X}^2$.

We can make two replacements in this expression. Because $\sum X = N\overline{X}$, the second term is just $2N\overline{X}^2$. And because $\sum_{i=1}^{N} 1 = N$, the third term is $N\overline{X}^2$. Making these replacements, we have $\sum X^2 - 2N\overline{X}^2 + N\overline{X}^2$. Simplifying this, we wind up with $(N-1)S^2 = \sum X^2 - N\overline{X}^2$. (This is just the "computational formula" for S^2 that was mentioned offhandedly in Chapter 2.)

Therefore, taking the expectation gives $E((N-1)S^2) = E(\sum X^2) - E(N\overline{X}^2) = \sum E(X^2) - NE(\overline{X}^2)$. Now, by the definition of $Var(X)$, it follows that $E(X^2) = Var(X) + E(X)^2$, and $E(\overline{X}^2) = Var(\overline{X}) + E(\overline{X})^2$. We have stipulated that $E(X) = \mu$ and $Var(X) = \sigma^2$, and we have seen above in this chapter that $E(\overline{X}) = \mu$ and $Var(\overline{X}) = \frac{\sigma^2}{N}$ (the last result holding true under iid draws). Making substitutions accordingly, we have $E((N-1)S^2) = \sum(\sigma^2 + \mu^2) - N(\frac{\sigma^2}{N} + \mu^2)$, or $N\sigma^2 + N\mu^2 - \sigma^2 - N\mu^2$. This in turn simplifies to $(N-1)\sigma^2$.

In short, $E((N-1)S^2) = (N-1)\sigma^2$. Because $E((N-1)S^2) = (N-1)E(S^2)$, we have

$$E(S^2) = \sigma^2. \tag{7.5}$$

So the sample variance is unbiased. Unlike the proof that $E(\overline{X}) = \mu$, the proof that $E(S^2) = \sigma^2$ does rely on the assumption that the N sample observations are independent of each other.

Note that because S^2 is unbiased, it cannot be that $\widehat{\sigma}^2 \equiv \frac{\sum(X_i - \overline{X})^2}{N}$ is unbiased. In particular, $E(\widehat{\sigma}^2) = \frac{N-1}{N}\sigma^2$, so $\widehat{\sigma}^2$ systematically underestimates σ^2. However, the degree of the underestimate is very small if N is relatively large.

7.4.2 Sampling from a Normal Distribution and the χ^2 Distribution

So we have established the expected value of S^2; what about the shape of its sampling distribution? We have seen that the sampling distribution of the sample mean $\overline{X}$ is either approximately or exactly normal. This is because sample means are sums of the sample observations. Because weighted sums of independent normal random variables are exactly normal, the sample mean is exactly normally distributed if the sample observations themselves are normal. And because sums of independent random variables from *any* DGP or population have a limiting normal distribution as the sample size approaches ∞ (the CLT), the sample mean is at least approximately normally distributed in "large" samples.

Sample variance S^2 is also a sum of independent random variables: if X_i is independent of X_j for all $i \neq j$ in the sample, then $(X_i - \overline{X})^2$ is independent[9] of $(X_j - \overline{X})^2$. So the CLT applies to $S^2 = \frac{\sum(X_i - \overline{X})^2}{N-1}$ as well. For any DGP, S^2 is approximately normally distributed in large samples.

But even if the sample observations X_i are exactly normal, $(X_i - \overline{X})^2$ cannot be exactly normal. The square means that negative values are impossible, hence they have zero density. But the normal distribution places strictly positive density on all real numbers, positive and negative. So S^2 cannot be a sum of independent normal random variables, even if the DGP of the sample X_i's is normal. This means that S^2 cannot be exactly normal in a finite sample, no matter what the DGP of the sample observations is.

However, we can say a bit more about the shape of the sampling distribution of S^2. Whereas $(X_i - \overline{X})^2$ should be "small" in expectation, because $E(X_i) = E(\overline{X}) = \mu$, the expectation of the squared deviation from the sample mean

---

[9] More generally, if X_1 is independent of X_2, then $f(X_1)$ is independent of $f(X_2)$ for any function f.

must be positive. In addition, progressively more extreme values of X_i above or below $\overline{X}$ map into the same value of $(X_i - \overline{X})^2$, and by Chebyshev's theorem the likelihood of these values must eventually decline as X_i gets far enough away from $\overline{X}$, no matter what the DGP of the sample is (provided it has finite mean). So in small samples, the sampling distribution of S^2 must have some right skew, when sampling from any DGP. In general, it is hard to say more than that.

In the benchmark case of sample observations drawn from a normal DGP, we can specify the exact distribution of S^2 for any sample size. *If* the individual X_is in a sample $X_1, X_2, \ldots, X_N$ are iid normal, then (*i*) $\overline{X}$ and S^2 are stochastically independent random variables; (*ii*) the random variable $\frac{(N-1)S^2}{\sigma^2}$ follows a χ^2 distribution (here χ is the Greek letter chi) with $N - 1$ *degrees of freedom* (df's).

The χ^2 distribution governs a continuous random variable. It has a right-skewed PDF, defined for nonnegative values of a random variable. The PDF assigns strictly positive density to all nonnegative numbers, and 0 density to all negative numbers. The χ^2 is a one-parameter family and the number of df's $N - 1$ is the parameter.

The expected value of the distribution is simply $N - 1$, and the variance is $2N - 2$. The functional form of the PDF is messy, but the graph of the PDF is more intuitively useful. Several members of the χ^2 family are shown in Figure 7.4. The χ^2 is indexed for df's to note that the estimate of σ^2 given by S^2 becomes more precise as the sample size and df's grow.[10]

That $\frac{(N-1)S^2}{\sigma^2}$ follows a χ^2 distribution under normal sampling follows from two basic facts about the χ^2 distribution. These facts are asserted without proof (see Casella and Berger [2002]), and we will only look at a sketch of how they combine to give the χ^2 result. First, a squared standard normal random variable has a χ^2 distribution with 1 df. Second, a sum of independent χ^2 random variables is also χ^2, with df's equal to the sum of the df's from the random variables in the sum.

The first fact allows us to pin down the distribution of S^2 in the not-very-interesting case of a sample with $N = 2$ observations. Specifically, for this case, $S^2 = (X_1 - \frac{X_1+X_2}{2})^2 + (X_2 - \frac{X_1+X_2}{2})^2 = \frac{(X_2-X_1)^2}{2}$. It can be shown that $\frac{X_1-X_2}{\sqrt{2}}$ is standard normal, so for $N = 2$, S^2 is the square of a standard normal random variable and, hence, has a χ^2 distribution with 1 df.

Although the $N = 2$ case is not useful by itself, it is a useful starting point. Because the second fact about the χ^2 distribution allows us to show that if $\frac{(N-1)S^2}{\sigma^2}$ follows a χ^2 in a sample of size k, it must follow a χ^2 for a sample of size $k + 1$ as well.

So the derivation of the χ^2 distribution as the exact distribution of $\frac{(N-1)S^2}{\sigma^2}$ under normal sampling follows from *mathematical induction*. We know the

---

[10] In fact, the limit of the χ^2 distribution in an infinitely large sample is actually normal. But the χ^2 converges to normal very slowly.

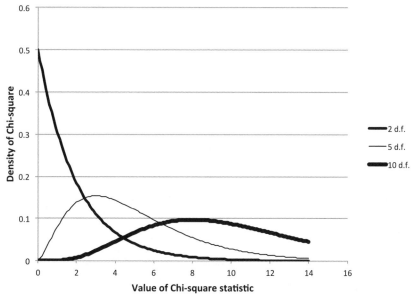

FIGURE 7.4. χ^2 distributions for various dfs.

result is true for $N = 2$. The "true for $k \to$ true for $k + 1$" result therefore implies that the result must also be true for $N = 3$. In turn it must therefore be true for $N = 4$ as well, and so forth for any possible value of N.

7.5 SAMPLE REGRESSION COEFFICIENTS WITH IID DRAWS

The idea that $\bar{x}$ or s^2 varies randomly from one sample to the next takes some getting used to, but simple cases such as coin flips help to make the point. The implication of random variation in sampling from a DGP is that any quantity computed from a sample is a random variable. This holds true even if the sample is a bivariate distribution and even if the quantities computed from the sample data are regression coefficients. Even regression coefficients are random variables, and they too have probability distributions.

To take a simple example, suppose we take a sample of size five from a bivariate distribution where X is a coin flip (0 or 1) and Y is the result of the roll of a die. We have a fair coin and a fair die; we flip the one and roll the other five times and record the results. Now suppose we regress Y on X. Plainly, in the DGP, the coin flip will convey no information about the die roll, so the regression slope β is 0. This is not a random variable. It is a property of the DGP as specified in this probability model.

But suppose the sample of five flips and five rolls works out as in Table 7.2. We could compute the ordinary least squares (OLS) coefficient from the linear regression of y on x as we could in any other sample and as we saw in Chapter 2.

TABLE 7.2. *Coin Flips (X) and Die Rolls (Y)*

Obs.	X	Y
1	1	4
2	1	6
3	0	4
4	1	5
5	0	1
Mean	0.6	4

In this particular, case the OLS regression coefficient happens to be simple: it is $\widehat{\beta} = 5 - 2.5 = 2.5$.[11] Any time there is only one covariate and it is dichotomous, the OLS regression coefficient is simply the difference in the mean of y given $x = 1$ and the mean of y given $x = 0$ (i.e., this regression model is fully saturated by default; see Chapter 6). This is nothing other than the change in the conditional mean of y as x changes by 1 unit, which is always what a regression coefficient means.

In this sample, when x changes by 1 unit, y grows by 2.5 units on average. There is definitely a linear relationship between y and x in this sample. But we know that $\beta = 0$ in the population. What has happened here is that a relationship appears in the sample by idiosyncratic chance, even though there is no relationship in the DGP. The sample OLS coefficient $\widehat{\beta}$ is a random variable: as the sample members drawn from the DGP change by chance, the quantity computed from the sample as $\widehat{\beta}$ changes by random chance too. The computed quantity inherits the random variation across samples inherent in the sample members themselves.

7.5.1 Expected Value of the OLS Regression Coefficient

In this respect, the OLS regression coefficient $\widehat{\beta}$ computed from a sample is no different from the sample mean. And, just as for the sample mean, this random variation naturally presents a question: how "good of a guess" does $\widehat{\beta}$ provide about β, on average? It would be useful if, just as $E(\overline{X}) = \mu$, so also $E(\widehat{\beta}) = \beta$. As laid out in Chapter 6, our substantive theories as social scientists are about β, but our observations in empirical research are about $\widehat{\beta}$. Ideally, when we use empirical techniques such as OLS regression, there is a close connection between the two, and what we see in data speaks clearly to our theoretical concerns.

An important part of answering this is to ask: What is the mean of the sampling distribution of $\widehat{\beta}$?

---

[11] Here the OLS slope is denoted $\widehat{\beta}$ instead of just b to reflect its connection to the DGP slope β.

Suppose specifically that $E(Y|X) = \alpha + \beta X$ is the DGP regression, of the regression and X really is linear in the DGP. This is a strong assumpu̇. but it allows for a sharp result as we will see. Y is a random variable with (unconditional) mean μ_Y and conditional variance $Var(Y|X) = \sigma^2$. Note that the conditional variance is the same for all values of X – this is sometimes called *homoscedasticity* or constant conditional variance.

This linear regression is equivalent to asserting $Y = \alpha + \beta X + \varepsilon$, where ε is a *random error* or *disturbance* with $E(\varepsilon) = 0$ and $Var(\varepsilon|X) = \sigma^2$. This disturbance or error is different from the residual defined in Chapter 2. The residual is the observed difference in the sample between the regression and the actual value of y. The error is a random variable with a DGP and not in and of itself observed in a dataset.

Note that for the linear specification of $E(Y|X)$, we have imposed no assumptions on the parametric family of the distribution of Y or ε, e.g., we have not assumed it is normal.[12] Thus none of what follows depends on the parametric family of Y or ε.

We can let X be a random variable too with mean μ_X and variance σ_X^2, but its distribution does not concern us a great deal because, in a regression, we condition on the X values.

A simple random sample from this DGP is a sequence of independent random variables $(X_1, Y_1), (X_2, Y_2), \ldots, (X_N, Y_N)$. Each pair of observations is independent of each other pair of observations, but X_i and Y_i may or may not be independent from each other in the DGP that generates the observations. If X and Y are uncorrelated in the DGP, $\beta = 0$.

To make some headway on the sampling distribution of $\widehat{\beta}$, recall the definition of the OLS regression coefficient from Chapter 2, with X and Y now written as random variables: $\widehat{\beta} = \frac{\widehat{Cov}(X,Y)}{S_X^2}$, where $\widehat{Cov}(X, Y)$ signifies that this quantity is the covariance as computed in the sample, rather than the DGP covariance as given by the joint distribution of X and Y.

To reduce the clutter in what follows, where $\widehat{Cov}(X, Y)$ and S_X^2 is written out longhand, it is also useful to write $\frac{(X_i - \overline{X})}{\sum (X_i - \overline{X})^2}$ simply as W_i. This redefinition does not change anything mathematically because each i gets its own W value, just as for the longer expression that W_i replaces. This makes it easier to see how we are manipulating the expressions.

Note that the numerator of W_i depends on i but the denominator does not. The denominator is simply the sum of squared deviations of sample X_i's from $\overline{X}$, and in any sample, this is constant and the same no matter what observation i we are dealing with (it is also itself the numerator of the sample variance, which

---

[12] However, the DGP of the disturbance ε will only be the same as the DGP of $Y|X$ if the DGP is normal (Cameron and Trivedi [2005]). For example, if the DGP of $Y|X$ is Poisson, the DGP of ε in the random error formulation is not Poisson. But if the DGP of $Y|X$ is normal, the DGP of ε is normal as well.

is obviously the same for all sample observations because it is a property of a sample, not an observation). Note further that $\sum W_i \equiv \frac{\sum(X_i - \overline{X})}{\sum(X_i - \overline{X})^2} \equiv 0$ because the numerator of this sum is the sum of deviations from a mean – which is always 0 (see Chapter 2).

To identify a connection between $\widehat{\beta}$ and β, we need to rewrite the definition of the former so that it depends on some way on the latter. This takes some algebra, but we will get there.

Given W_i defined earlier, and because the descriptive statistics $cov(x, y)$ and s_x^2 have the same denominator, the coefficient $\widehat{\beta}$ can also be written

$$\widehat{\beta} = \sum W_i(Y_i - \overline{Y})$$
$$= \sum W_i Y_i - \sum W_i \overline{Y}$$
$$= \sum W_i Y_i - \overline{Y} \sum W_i$$
$$= \sum W_i Y_i. \tag{7.6}$$

This is simple algebra for sums, but Equation 7.6 is a useful result in its own right. The OLS slope coefficient in a bivariate model can always be written as a weighted sum of the values of the dependent variable. The weight for observation i in OLS is just W_i: the difference between X_i and $\overline{X}$, divided by the numerator of the variance of X. We will use this form of $\widehat{\beta}$ again, so it is useful to keep it handy.

Continuing, we know also by the linearity assumption for the DGP regression that we can write $Y_i = \alpha + \beta X_i + \varepsilon_i$ for any observation. So we can replace Y_i in Equation 7.6 with this definition of Y_i. This is important because it begins to show how $\widehat{\beta}$ is related to β. We end up with

$$\widehat{\beta} = \sum W_i(\alpha + \beta X_i + \varepsilon_i)$$
$$= \sum \alpha W_i + \sum \beta W_i X_i + \sum W_i \varepsilon_i$$
$$= \alpha \sum W_i + \beta \sum W_i X_i + \sum W_i \varepsilon_i. \tag{7.7}$$

Here we have simply done more algebra, breaking an overall sum into smaller sums to be added up and factoring constants out of those smaller sums. We end up with Equation 7.7, a sum of three terms; consider each one carefully.

The first term is always 0 because $\sum W_i = 0$.

The second term contains the expression $\sum W_i X_i$. Comparing this to Equation 7.6, we can see that this turns out to be simply the slope coefficient in an OLS regression of X on itself. Intuitively, that coefficient seems like it ought to be 1, and it is. One of the exercises in this chapter calls for a demonstration of this.

The third term is $\sum W_i \varepsilon_i$. Comparing this to Equation 7.6, we can see that this is simply the coefficient in an OLS regression of the error ε on the regressor X.[13] And we know that, as an OLS regression coefficient, this can be written as $\frac{\widehat{Cov}(X,\varepsilon)}{S_X^2}$, where again $\widehat{Cov}$ indicates a sample covariance between two random variables.

All considered, we have a new way to express the sample regression coefficient:

$$\widehat{\beta} = \beta + \frac{\widehat{Cov}(X,\varepsilon)}{S_X^2}. \tag{7.8}$$

To get here, we leaned heavily on the assumption that the DGP regression is linear, that is, $Y = \alpha + \beta X + \varepsilon$. We cannot determine the value of $\widehat{Cov}(X,\varepsilon)$ from algebra alone, but we can see that it plays a critical role in determining the value of $\widehat{\beta}$. In essence, this expression tells us that the observable quantity $\widehat{\beta}$ equals the quantity we wish to ascertain, β, plus a quantity that depends on the relationship between the regressor and the error term.

Given this, $E(\widehat{\beta}) = E(\beta) + E(\widehat{Cov}(X,\varepsilon))$. Because β is a DGP quantity, not a random variable, $E(\beta) = \beta$. So $E(\widehat{\beta}) = \beta + E(\widehat{Cov}(X,\varepsilon))$.

Thus we need to establish something about $E(\widehat{Cov}(X,\varepsilon))$. That is, what is the expected value of the sample covariance between X and ε? It turns out that this is simply the DGP covariance, $Cov(X,\varepsilon)$. A sufficient condition for $E(\widehat{Cov}(X,\varepsilon)) = 0$ is that $E(\varepsilon|x) = 0, \forall x \in \mathcal{X}$, which is established as follows.

Because the denominator of sample covariance is a constant $N-1$ for a given sample, the key lies in the numerator. This is $\sum(X_i - \overline{X})(\varepsilon_i - E(\varepsilon))$. Because $E(\varepsilon) = 0$ by definition and $\overline{X}$ is a constant, this is $\sum X_i \varepsilon_i - \overline{X} \sum \varepsilon_i$.

Taking the expected value of this expression, the second term drops out because $E(\sum \varepsilon_i) = \sum E(\varepsilon_i) = 0$. So we are left with $E(\sum X_i \varepsilon_i)$. If $E(\varepsilon|x) = 0, \forall x \in \mathcal{X}$, then $E(\sum X_i \varepsilon_i) = E(\sum X_i \times 0) = 0$. If $E(\varepsilon|x) \neq 0$ for at least one $x \neq 0 \in \mathcal{X}$, then $E(\sum X_i \varepsilon_i) \neq 0$. We already know $E(\varepsilon) = 0$ in the DGP by the definition of ε, but $E(\varepsilon|x) = 0$ says much more. It says that the mean value of the error is 0 for *every* value of the regressor – a much more stringent condition, and not necessarily true, as we shall see.

In short, if $E(\varepsilon|x) = 0, \forall x \in \mathcal{X}$, then $E(\widehat{Cov}(X,\varepsilon)) = 0$. If this holds and the DGP regression is linear, then

$$E(\widehat{\beta}) = \beta. \tag{7.9}$$

That is, given linearity in the DGP regression, *if the covariate and the random error are uncorrelated in the DGP, the OLS regression coefficient equals the*

---

[13] Here we see the crucial difference between the error ε and the regression residuals we encountered in Chapter 2. In the appendix to that chapter, we saw that OLS coefficients are constructed so that the regressor and the residual are necessarily uncorrelated (the second least squares normal equation implies this). But that does not mean that the regressor and the error term are uncorrelated. The residual is a sample quantity, but the error is a DGP quantity.

DGP regression coefficient on average. In other words, the OLS regression slope from a sample is unbiased.

The reason that $Cov(X, \varepsilon)$ matters so much is that $\widehat{\beta}$ "attempts" to pick up the influence of X, and anything besides X that is not explicitly included as a covariate. So if some factor left out of the model is correlated with X, it shows up as correlation between X and the unexplained part of Y (i.e., ε). So then $\widehat{\beta}$ will pick up the actual effect of X, β, but also the effect of omitted factors that are correlated with X. These factors cause bias in $\widehat{\beta}$. But if these factors are explicitly included as covariates instead of omitted from the regression, they do not cause bias. As we saw in Chapter 2 on multiple regression, OLS estimates $\widehat{\beta}$ by taking the part of X that other covariates cannot explain in a regression model and using this "residualized X" to explain the part of Y that other covariates cannot explain. So for covariates included in the model, their association with both X and Y is purged to estimate the effect of X on Y.

Note that the result did not use the assumption of independence of sample observations anywhere. As the unbiasedness of $\overline{X}$ does not depend on independence in sampling, so the unbiasedness of $\widehat{\beta}$ does not either. And we did not assume that the dependent variable or the random error is normally distributed or follows any other particular distribution.

We did use the assumption that sample observations are identically distributed, conditional on covariates; this is why we assumed that α and β are the same for all Y_i. However, the conditional variance of Y given X does not factor into unbiasedness. Homoscedasticity can fail and still gives unbiased sample regression coefficients.

And, again, we leaned heavily on the assumption that $E(Y|X)$ is a linear function of X. That is why we could decompose $\widehat{\beta}$ into the three terms analyzed earlier – for a nonlinear model of $E(Y|X)$, this would not hold. But the restrictiveness of the linearity assumption is a matter of judgment. For a saturated model (Chapter 6), we have a linear DGP regression by construction. Beyond the saturated case, even in nonlinear regression models (such as the generalized linear models covered in Chapter 6), $E(Y|X)$ is approximately linear for small changes in X (i.e., $E(Y|X)$ is *locally linear*), and problems due to nonlinearities such as the feasible range of predicted values may be tolerable. In other words, even if the link from the DGP regression $E(Y|X)$ to covariates is not exactly linear, it will often be "close enough" that unbiasedness of the OLS $\widehat{\beta}$, at least in a neighborhood of the mean of X, is on the mark.

So linearity in the DGP regression can be relaxed somewhat. The one assumption we used that cannot be emphasized enough is $Cov(X, \varepsilon) = 0$.

7.5.2 Exogeneity of Covariates

The condition $Cov(X, \varepsilon) = 0$ is implied by $E(\varepsilon|x) = 0, \forall x \in \mathcal{X}$ – the former says the DGP covariance is zero, the latter says the regression in the DGP is flat as a function of X (and it must pass through 0, the unconditional mean of ε by assumption). The condition that $E(\varepsilon|x) = 0, \forall x$ is one of *exogeneity of regressors*. If the condition holds, X is an *exogenous regressor*. If the assumption fails, the regressor X is *endogenous*.

Exogeneity is *not* merely a technical condition. It is a feature of the social process an analyst is modeling and is a deeply substantive concept. It is not, in a narrow sense, a part of the process of collecting or observing data, and it deeply affects the sampling distribution of $\widehat{\beta}$, so it is useful to introduce it here.

A compelling illustration is one of the most celebrated examples of endogeneity in political science. It concerns the relationship between campaign spending by incumbents in U.S. congressional elections and their vote shares in the elections. All manner of reason and good sense suggests that campaign spending is a means to an end of a strong campaign. More money allows candidates to get their message out in a variety of media, to obtain better polling and information about the "pulse" of the district and craft a suitable message, and to host high-quality events. To be sure, the link from money to a good campaign is not automatic, but money certainly helps. And a good campaign, in these respects, should translate into votes. So in the DGP governing incumbent campaign spending and incumbent vote share, we expect a positive relationship: the conditional mean of vote share should increase with incumbent expenditures in the DGP, all else constant.

Stunningly, Jacobson [1978] did not find this – instead he found that as incumbents spent more money on their campaigns, their vote share changed very little, or even went down. The regression coefficient $\widehat{\beta}$ estimated from a sample of data was in fact negative. Thinking about $Cov(X, \varepsilon)$ provides a clue as to why, and it is not because the assumption that $\beta > 0$ in the DGP is wrong.

Specifically, suppose that $Y = \alpha + \beta X + \varepsilon$ is the DGP model,[14] where Y is incumbent vote share and X is incumbent campaign spending. Now incumbent members of Congress, as (mostly) career politicians attuned to political intelligence (especially about themselves), can be expected to have a sense of when their reelection campaigns are in trouble. When they are in trouble, the incumbent anticipates doing worse at the polls than might be expected, given his or her spending (and perhaps other covariates such as length of tenure). "Doing worse than expected" in turn translates into $\varepsilon < 0$: this must accompany any case whose performance is below its conditional mean.

Precisely because money can translate into votes (i.e., because $\beta > 0$), this realization of $\varepsilon < 0$ could cause an incumbent to raise his level of campaign spending X. Therefore, $Cov(X, \varepsilon) < 0$: as the incumbent anticipates poorer

---

[14] The style of analysis is important here. We do not need to maintain an empirical commitment that this regression function is, in fact, "the right one." Rather, we wish to show that even if it were, we would still obtain the odd pattern of data that Jacobson uncovered. What we learn is that Jacobson's empirical findings alone do not invalidate this model, due to the possibility of endogeneity. Put differently, this highlights that endogeneity concerns are fundamentally about an inability to distinguish which of two DGPs is "correct" based on observable data; under endogeneity, at least two DGPs are *observationally equivalent*.

performance (ε shrinks), he raises campaign spending to compensate (X increases). So even if $\beta > 0$, if $Cov(X, \varepsilon)$ is strong enough in absolute value, we would have $E(\widehat{\beta}) < 0$. If the endogeneity of the regressor is strong enough (i.e., the correlation of X and ε is high enough), it not only fails to equal β in expectation, it does not even have the same sign in expectation.

Exogeneity is rightly one of the major sources of questions that researchers always face when assessing relationships in observational data. Making an argument that a regressor is endogenous is a good way to critique research because it means that the magnitude or even sign of OLS regression coefficients in samples may be wrong. And although we have seen the importance of exogeneity demonstrated formally for OLS, the importance of this point holds much more generally in statistical modeling.

Critiques based on endogeneity are especially compelling because, once the data is collected and the paper is written, these critiques amount to theoretical claims that are hard for a researcher to defend against on the basis of the data alone. Technical conditions of statistical modeling often warrant critique – for example, iid sampling is assumed when independence is actually questionable, an exponential distribution is used to model durations that do not have a constant hazard rate – and they can certainly affect the substantive conclusions drawn from a model. But a reasonable account by which a regressor is endogenous usually trumps all other concerns in seriousness and gravity. Endogeneity can instantly eviscerate an entire research design – alternative statistical assumptions almost never are able to make the problem go away.

Because of their importance for making data analysis meaningful about DGPs, endogeneity critiques are common in applied research. This is the critique faced by every scholar of social networks who argues that members of the same network affect each other. Here the endogeneity critique shows up as an argument of *homophily*: maybe the behaviors or attributes of members of the same network are similar because they sorted into their network on that basis in the first place. For instance, if married couples tend to exhibit similar political values and behaviors – and they do (Stoker and Jennings [1995]) – is that because of persuasion within the marriage, or because people only marry other people who are similar to themselves on attributes they find important? Attempts to head off endogeneity critiques also help to account for the dramatic rise of experiments for generating data in social science, as discussed more in Chapter 10.

The ability of critics to invent endogeneity critiques should not be underestimated. They are essentially impossible to overcome definitively with a given set of observational data. Nevertheless, to get a sense of how much to worry before heading back to the drawing board, it is worthwhile to peruse graphs of the regression residuals as a function of covariates. Plot a given covariate on the horizontal axis, and the residuals for all y_i associated with that covariate on the vertical. If there is a clear pattern here of the average residual changing as a function of X, it suggests that exogeneity is a sketchy assumption. These are just the residuals e_i computed from data against the observed x_i's, not the disturbance ε and the entire set of X, which is the real issue in exogeneity. So this sort of exercise (supposing the residuals show no clear pattern with the x's) will not offer dispositive proof of exogeneity in the face of a clever critic. But it is a start.

7.5.3 Omitted Variable Bias

One common source of endogeneity occurs when relevant variables in the DGP of Y are omitted from a regression model. If these omitted variables are correlated with both Y and the other variables that are included in the regression, they give rise to *omitted variable bias*.

Suppose that in the DGP, $E(Y|X, Z) = \alpha + \beta_X X + \beta_Z Z$. But a researcher only has data on Y and X, so estimates the regression model $E(Y|X) = \alpha + \beta_X X$ by OLS. For instance, suppose Y is the victory margin of an incumbent member of the U.S. House of Representatives running for reelection, X is the amount of money he spends on his campaign, and Z is the "quality" of the challenger he is facing in an election.

Clearly, we would expect $\beta_X > 0$ and $\beta_Z < 0$. Holding challenger quality fixed, more campaign spending should lead to a larger margin of victory. But holding campaign spending fixed, a higher-quality challenger should lead to a lower (possibly negative, if they're good enough) margin of victory.

One would also suppose that incumbent politicians are good at sizing up the quality of their challengers and would spend more money on their campaigns when they think challenger quality is high. So X and Z should be positively correlated in the DGP too. Suppose that in the DGP, $E(Z|X) = \gamma + \delta X$. So we'd expect $\delta > 0$.

Supposing the linear model for $E(Y|X, Z)$ is absolutely the right one, and there are no further omitted variables or endogeneity issues, we'd have $Cov(X, \varepsilon) = Cov(Z, \varepsilon) = 0$. But if Z is not observed by a researcher or otherwise not included in the model, it does not cease to matter for determining $E(Y)$ – it is simply forced into the disturbance of the model that is actually estimated. In other words, the model $E(Y|X) = \alpha + \beta_X X$ has an error term of $u = \beta_Z Z + \varepsilon$. Although X is not correlated with ε, it is correlated with this composite error term u because it is correlated with Z.

In particular, if we regress Z on X, the coefficient it δ as we assumed earlier. But the composite error u contains not just Z, but $\beta_Z Z$. So if we regress the composite error u on X, the coefficient is $\beta_Z \delta$.

So working this through Equation 7.8 for the expected value of $\widehat{\beta}_X$, it follows that with an omitted variable,

$$E(\widehat{\beta}_X) = \beta_X + \beta_Z \delta. \tag{7.10}$$

As long as $\beta_Z \neq 0$ and $\delta \neq 0$, $E(\widehat{\beta}_X) \neq \beta_X$. Note how the requirements that Z is related to both X and Y enter into this. If X and Z are unrelated, $\delta = 0$, so the bias in $\widehat{\beta}_X$ goes away. If Y and Z are unrelated, $\beta_Z = 0$, so the bias in $\widehat{\beta}_X$ goes away again. But if β_Z is negative enough and/or X and Z are correlated strongly enough, relative to the magnitude of β_X, then $\widehat{\beta}_X$ will not only be biased, it will not even have the same sign as β_X. Thus omitted variable bias can make us think that two variables are negatively related when they are actually positively related in the DGP (or vice versa).

It may seem that the upshot of this is to control for everything in sight to avoid even the possibility of omitted variable bias. This strategy is also unwise because adding variables into a regression model when they are not actually related to Y simply adds noise to it and reduces the information that estimates of, say, β_X, are able to convey about its actual value. In other words, the issue is that including irrelevant covariates increases the standard errors of the relevant ones. We turn to the issue of the standard error of OLS slopes in general shortly.

7.5.4 Sample Selection Bias from "Selecting on the Dependent Variable"

When analysts wish to study a particular event, it occasionally seems natural at some level to look at cases in which the event happens. This is a sampling process in which units are excluded from analysis unless they have particular values of the dependent variable. It is sometimes called *selecting on the dependent variable*. Sometimes this is unavoidable: for example, when studying the effect of various factors on vote choice, we cannot explore the effect these covariates would have had on nonvoters because they are excluded from the sample. Sometimes selection on the dependent variable is done on purpose. This sampling process is sometimes used in qualitative comparative research in political science and sociology (see, e.g., King et al. [1994] and Brady and Collier [2010] for discussions of the issue and examples).

For simple analytics, suppose that $E(Y|X) = \alpha + \beta X$ is the DGP regression and Y is symmetrically distributed (e.g., normal) conditional on X. Suppose also that $\beta > 0$ (the case isn't any better with $\beta < 0$ but some of the changes sketched out below go the other direction). Then suppose that a researcher collects a sample of observations that meet the condition $y > y_c$, that is, he will only observe cases in which the observed value of Y exceeds some cutoff. This sample is *truncated* at y_c: neither X nor Y values of observations below that cutoff are observed.[15]

Now think about the value of X – call it x_c – such that $E(Y|X = x_c) = y_c$. This is the X value associated with observations for which the Y value is near the cutoff for observation. At x_c, there will be several values of Y above and

---

[15] Truncation is simlar to *censoring*. In censored data, Y values are not observed beyond some cutoff y_c, but X values are observed for units with unobserved Y values. This sometimes makes it possible to *impute* the missing values of Y by using the other observations to construct a model of Y based on observable Xs (Rubin [1976], King et al. [1995], Gelman et al. [2004]). With truncation, this is not possible.

below y_c because Y is symmetrically distributed conditional on X. There is, in other words, a vertical spread around the DGP regression line at this specific value of X.

Truncation implies that at x_c, only those Ys that lie above the DGP regression line are observed in the sample; the rest are below y_c. Because of this, the average value of the ys *observed in the sample* exceeds $y_c \equiv E(Y|X = x_c)$. In other words, the errors for Y around the DGP regression for those observations in the sample are all positive at x_c. As X increases a little above x_c, there can be a few observations in the sample with negative errors for Y around the DGP regression, but they still tend to be positive. As X increases relatively far above x_c, the regression errors in Y around $E(Y|X)$ will tend to be mostly symmetric for observations in the sample, just as in the DGP.

The issue is that truncation creates a correlation between DGP regression errors and the covariate X for observations in the sample. This creates a bias in $\widehat{\beta}$, the OLS estimate of β. In particular, if $\beta > 0$, $\widehat{E(\beta)} < \beta$. The nature of this bias is, at one level, exactly the same as that already presented: it is a correlation between the (DGP) regression error and the regressor. But here the bias resulted from the process of selecting observations for the sample. For this reason, a bias from this source is sometimes called *sample selection bias*. It bears noting, relative to Chapter 3, that this bias can only occur if the DGP for Y is stochastic. If it is not, there are no random errors around the DGP regression.

The problem is especially acute if there are only a few values of Y, for example it is dichotomous (a civil war either happens or not, etc.). With little or no variation on Y and a stochastic DGP, it is essentially impossible to rule out any DGP relation between Y and covariates (Ashworth et al. [2008]). If Y's DGP is deterministic, then even if there is no variation in Y, it is at least possible to identify necessary conditions for Y take its sole observed value. Whether these conditions are of substantive interest is another matter (it will usually be possible to identify the necessary condition that the event occurred on earth). If Y's DGP is stochastic, even this is not possible without variation in Y, or, put differently, an analyst can mistakenly identify conditions as necessary even though they are not (cf. Chapter 3).

7.5.5 Standard Error of $\widehat{\beta}$ under Random Sampling

Although $E(\widehat{\beta}) = \beta$ with exogenous covariates is a useful and informative property, to get a fuller sense of what we learn about β from $\widehat{\beta}$, we also need a sense of how $\widehat{\beta}$ changes from sample to sample. This variation is captured in the standard error of $\widehat{\beta}$.

In redefining $\widehat{\beta}$ in Equation 7.6, we arrived at $\widehat{\beta} = \frac{\sum (X_i - \overline{X}) Y_i}{\sum (X_i - \overline{X})^2}$. We also saw that this can be written as $\widehat{\beta} = \sum W_i Y_i$ where $W_i \equiv \frac{(X_i - \overline{X})}{\sum (X_i - \overline{X})^2}$. This tells us that the OLS coefficient can be thought of as a weighted sum of the y_is, where the weight is the deviation of X from the mean of X for observation i, over the sum of squared deviations of the X_is from $\overline{X}$.

With this formulation we can see that

$$Var(\widehat{\beta}) = Var(\sum W_i Y_i)$$

$$= \sum Var(W_i Y_i) \text{ (by independence of } Y_i\text{'s)}$$

$$= \sum W_i^2 Var(Y_i) \text{ (by properties of variance)}$$

$$= \sum W_i^2 \sigma^2 \text{ (by homoskedasticity)}$$

$$= \sigma^2 \sum W_i^2 \text{ (since } \sigma^2 \text{ is constant for all } i\text{).} \qquad (7.11)$$

Now go back to the W_i weights. Equation 7.11 tells us to square each weight and sum the results across i to obtain the variance of $\widehat{\beta}$. This gives us the sum of squared deviations of the X_is from $\overline{X}$ in the numerator, over the square of that same quantity in the denominator. So $\sum W_i^2 = \frac{1}{\sum (X_i - \overline{X})^2}$. The denominator of that is in turn the numerator of the sample variance (see Chapter 2), so altogether we have $\sum W_i^2 = \frac{1}{(N-1)s_X^2}$.

In short, $Var(\widehat{\beta}) = \frac{\sigma^2}{(N-1)s_X^2}$, so the standard error of $\widehat{\beta}$ is

$$SE_{\widehat{\beta}} = \frac{\sigma}{\sqrt{N-1}s_X}. \qquad (7.12)$$

Unlike the demonstration that $E(\widehat{\beta}) = \beta$, this derivation crucially relies on both independence and constant conditional variance of Y. If either of these assumptions fails, as they often do in applied regression modeling, this standard error is not accurate. The role of independence and identical variance in deriving $E(\widehat{\beta})$ and $SE_{\widehat{\beta}}$ exactly parallels the use of these assumptions in deriving the expected value and standard error of the sample mean $\overline{Y}$.

In the benchmark iid case, as the dependent variable Y becomes more variable (so the numerator σ increases), the slope coefficient estimated in the sample becomes more variable from one sample to another. As Y varies more over its possible values in the DGP, a wider range of values for any x will be observed in samples, and there is a greater chance of drawing a sample that gives an idiosyncratic picture of how Y changes on average as x changes. Furthermore, as the sample size N increases, the denominator of SE grows (but not as fast as N), so the SE falls. As N increases the sample gets a little closer to tracing out the full DGP, so the sample gives a more accurate picture of what happens in the DGP.

The denominator of SE contains another component, the standard deviation of x in the sample. As sample variation in X increases, the sample contains a wider range of x values against which idiosyncratic changes in $E(Y|x)$ for small changes in x can be smoothed out. So more variation in the covariate actually improves the accuracy of the sample OLS estimate as a picture of the DGP quantity β. From a research design standpoint, it is useful to plan for as much variation in x as possible, provided linearity of $E(Y|X)$ over the range of Xs is still reasonable.

For instance, consider an experiment on the effects of political information exposure on participation in an election. Here β reflects the size of the effect of the treatment on the outcome in the DGP, and suppose the experimenter will estimate β with a linear model. For a fixed sample size (e.g., number of subjects times participation decisions per subject), a design with two information conditions, "high" and "low," is better than a design with "high," "intermediate," and "low" information conditions from the standpoint of precisely estimating β. Because β is going to be estimated by a linear model, the latter design only adds noise to the information contained in the former.

The fact that $\widehat{\beta} = \sum W_i Y_i$ means that the OLS regression coefficient is a *linear estimator* of β. That is, each value of Y_i is multiplied by a constant (for that i), and the resulting products are all added up to obtain the estimator. There are many other linear estimators of β; any choice of new weights z_i instead of W_i defines a new one.

In Chapter 9, we encounter a result called the *Gauss-Markov theorem*, which asserts that, under homoskedasticity and holding all the regressors fixed, OLS is the *best linear unbiased estimator* or *BLUE*. In this context "best" means "minimum variance." So among all linear unbiased estimators, OLS has the smallest variance. If you were picking from the set of "LUEs," it's hard to think of a better one to pick than the one with smallest variance. That way, we not only get the simplicity of linearity and the average accuracy of unbiasedness; we also get the most precise guess possible from a given sample that satisifies L and U.

7.5.6 The CLT and the Sampling Distribution of $\widehat{\beta}$ under Random Sampling

So far we have established the expected value and standard deviation of β, under specific assumptions about the sampling process (that it is iid) and DGP (that its regression is a linear function of covariates, and X is exogenous). So if we have a theory that β is some specific value β_0, we can use $SE(\widehat{\beta})$ to compare it to the value of $\widehat{\beta}$ computed from observable data. If $\widehat{\beta}$ and β_0 are far apart, we can conclude that the observed data is unusual if indeed this theory about β is correct.

We do not yet know the shape of that sampling distribution. Just as we noted for $\overline{X}$, that is useful for establishing just how usual or unusual the observed data is, in light of the value β in the DGP.

We can use $\widehat{\beta} = \frac{\sum(X_i - \overline{X})Y_i}{\sum(X_i - \overline{X})^2} \equiv \sum W_i Y_i$ from Equation 7.6 one more time. This expression highlights that $\widehat{\beta}$ is a weighted sum of the realizations of the random variables Y_i. Because the Y_is are independent and identically distributed, the CLT tells us that this sum is approximately normally distributed in large samples, and the larger the sample, the better the approximation to normality.

That is, as the sample size N increases, the sampling distribution of $\widehat{\beta}$ converges in distribution to a normal distribution with mean β and variance $\frac{\sigma^2}{(N-1)s_x^2}$. So in a reasonably large sample (and in practice N of a several dozen is often sufficient to get pretty close), $\widehat{\beta}$ computed from a random sample is itself a draw from a normal distribution.

There is no assumptions about the parametric family of Y's DGP behind this result. We assumed independence (twice: to invoke the CLT and to derive the variance of $\widehat{\beta}$). We assumed identical distribution in the sense that (*i*) α and β are the same for all Y_i and (*ii*) the conditional variance of Y is not a function of x (three times, for the mean and variance and to invoke the CLT). We assumed linearity of $E(Y|X)$ as a function of covariates in the DGP. And we assumed exogeneity of X and ε to establish $E(\widehat{\beta}) = \beta$. But we did not assume that Y or equivalently the error ε follows any particular probability distribution.

If we do, in addition, assume that Y is normally distributed – as in the conditional normal linear model or the bivariate normal model from Chapter 6 – then $\widehat{\beta}$ is a weighted sum of exactly normally distributed random variables. In these particular cases, $\widehat{\beta}$ itself is therefore exactly normally distributed. Conversely, if $\widehat{\beta}$ is exactly normally distributed in a finite sample, then by Cramér's theorem the Y_is must be exactly normal as well.

7.6 DERIVED DISTRIBUTIONS: SAMPLING FROM NORMAL DGPs WHEN σ^2 MUST BE ESTIMATED

Thus far we have studied the sampling distributions of three important statistics – the sample mean, sample variance, and sample regression coefficients – on the assumption of iid sampling from a DGP. That was important because it tied the sampling distributions to the parameters.

But the parameters of these sampling distributions depend on the parameters of the DGP, and we are engaged in this line of work because we do not know those. For example, the standard error of $\overline{X}$, that is, the average spread of $\overline{X}$ around its expected value μ, involves the unknown parameter σ. So does $SE(\widehat{\beta})$. What can we say we know about the spread of a random variable that depends crucially on an unknown quantity?

In this section, we analyze what happens to the properties of sampling distributions of these statistics when they depend on other DGP parameters that also must be estimated from data. The general theme is that if we assume Y's DGP belongs to a specific parametric family, we can still say a fair bit about the sampling distributions of statistics.

7.6.1 Student's *t* Distribution

Although we may not know σ^2 from the DGP of X, we do have an unbiased estimator of it in $S_X^2 \equiv [\sum_{i=1}^{n}(X_i - \overline{X})^2]/[N - 1]$, the sample variance. So taking the sample mean, we can make headway on establishing the sampling distribution of $\overline{X}$ if we simply replace σ^2 with S_X^2.

In turn, we can use the square root of this to approximate the standard error of $\overline{X}$ as $\frac{S_X}{\sqrt{N}}$. This "approximate standard error of $\overline{X}$" is based entirely on quantities from the sample. Replacing a required but unknown DGP quantity with a known sample estimate is called *bootstrapping*, and

$$\widehat{SE}(\overline{X}) = \frac{S_X}{\sqrt{N}} \qquad \text{\textit{bootstrapping.}} \qquad \frac{\sigma \leftarrow S_X}{\sqrt{N}} \tag{7.13}$$

is the *bootstrapped standard error* of $\overline{X}$.[16] Here $\widehat{SE}$ indicates that we are estimating the actual standard error, which involves the generally unknown σ from the DGP.

Bootstrapping is in fact much more general, powerful, and flexible than this small use of it. It is the subject of a large literature in statistics starting with Efron [1979] (see, e.g., Chernick [2007] for a recent treatment). It has been established as a useful way to pin down properties of a sampling distribution while making few assumptions about the parent DGP – radically fewer than we are making here. A fuller exploration of it is beyond the scope of a basic treatment, but it is worth a mental sticky note that there is a lot of depth here.

With $\frac{\sigma}{\sqrt{N}}$ approximated by $\frac{S_X}{\sqrt{N}}$, we can get a sense of how far $\overline{X}$ is from any conjectured mean μ by measuring the distance between the two in bootstrapped standard error terms. That is, because $\overline{X}$ is approximately normal, and therefore $z = \frac{\overline{X}-\mu}{\sigma/\sqrt{N}}$ is approximately *standard* normal, then

$$t = \frac{\overline{X} - \mu}{S_X/\sqrt{N}} \tag{7.14}$$

is "approximately" approximately standard normal.

It's only "'approximately' approximately," because both $\overline{X}$ and S_X both introduce random error into the quantity we can compute. We already recognize the sampling error wrapped up in $\overline{X}$; S_X introduces another source. Put differently, $t = \frac{\overline{X}-\mu}{S_X/\sqrt{N}}$ is a ratio of two random variables – one in the numerator and one in the denominator.

If the DGP of the sample observations is normal, then not only do the numerator and denominator of t both contain random variables, but they ($\overline{X}$ and S_X^2) are also stochastically independent. This means that the white

---

[16] The idea is that, faced with a problem requiring an unknown DGP quantity, we solve it by "pulling ourselves up by our bootstraps" and using only the information we have available in the sample.

noise separating $\overline{X}$ from μ is not fundamentally changed by the bootstrapped standard error. The basic "bell shape" of the distribution of $\overline{X}$ around μ is preserved, but the addition of independent random variation in $S_{\overline{X}}^2$ makes it a little "noisier." So for a normal DGP generating the sample, the quantity t is essentially a z statistic with a little more variance.

The probability distribution of t is called *Student's t distribution* – so named because its discoverer published under the pseudonym Student.[17] The t distribution is symmetric and bell shaped. It looks roughly like the normal in medium-sized samples but has thicker tails – this is because of the greater variance than a standard normal inherited from random variation in $S_{\overline{X}}^2$.

In larger and larger samples, this source of sampling error diminishes in importance. As a result, Student's t converges in distribution to the standard normal distribution as sample size N increases. Even for samples with $N = 30$ or more, the difference between the t and the standard normal is basically irrelevant for applied purposes.

Implicit in all of this is that the quality of the approximation for σ depends on N. The t distribution is a family with many members – indexed by *degrees of freedom*. In particular, in a sample of N independent $N(\mu, \sigma^2)$ observations, $t = \frac{\overline{X} - \mu}{S_X/\sqrt{N}}$ follows a t distribution with $N - 1$ degrees of freedom.

The t distribution is a one-parameter family, and the number of df's $N - 1$ is the parameter. The PDF assigns positive density to all real numbers, as the normal distribution does. The expectation of a t distribution is always 0 provided $N \geq 2$ and the variance is $\frac{N-1}{N-3}$ provided $N > 3$.[18] The function for the PDF of the t distribution is rather homely; however, graphs of different members of the t family are readily interpretable.

A collection is shown in Figure 7.5. Overlaid in the figure is the standard normal distribution; it has the tallest peak and the thinnest tails. But even a dozen or two degrees of freedom, Student't t is close to normal. For more than a couple dozen df's, the difference is essentially zero as far as applied research is concerned.

"Degrees of freedom" means, loosely, "pieces of information." The idea is that, given a sample mean, the sample has $N - 1$ more observations that are linearly unconstrained – pieces of information through which to learn about some other quantity. The mean involves a sum of sample elements, which is a restriction or constraint on the values that can actually exist in the sample. In particular, once the sum of the sample elements is known, and $N - 1$ of them

---

[17] The discoverer was one William Gossett, who discovered it (with help from Karl Pearson) in 1908 while working as an agronomist for the Guiness brewery. Guiness didn't want proprietary information to leak out, so it didn't let employees publish the results of any research. So Pearson had Gossett's paper published anonymously in the journal *Biometrika*, a famous, still published journal of statistics and applications in life sciences. See Freedman et al. [2007].

[18] For $N = 2$, Student's t is equivalent to a Cauchy distribution, which has an undefined mean. This is because the ratio of two standard normal variables follows a Cauchy distribution.

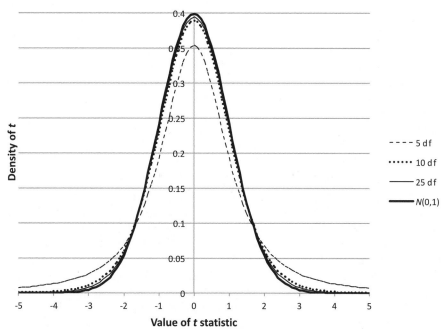

FIGURE 7.5. Student's t distribution for various dfs.

have known values, the value of the Nth is tied down by the fact that they have to sum up to a known value. The Nth can't be just any value: it can only be the one that makes the other $N - 1$ plus the Nth sum to the known value. So computing a mean "uses up" some of the sample information.

It can be shown that the ratio of a standard normal random variable and the square root of a χ^2 random variable follows Student's t distribution. Formally, the derivation of Student's t then follows because

$$t = \frac{\overline{X} - \mu}{S_X/\sqrt{N}} = \frac{(\overline{X} - \mu)/\frac{\sigma}{\sqrt{N}}}{\sqrt{\frac{S_X^2}{\sigma^2}}}. \tag{7.15}$$

The numerator of the last term is exactly standard normal when sampling from a normal DGP, and the denominator is exactly χ^2 when sampling from a normal DGP.[19]

Although $\frac{\overline{X}-\mu}{\sigma/\sqrt{N}}$ is approximately standard normal for *any* parent distribution over the X_i's (by the CLT), the random variable $t = \frac{\overline{X}-\mu}{S_X/\sqrt{N}}$ exactly follows Student's t only for iid normal sample observations.

---

[19] Note that this does not mean that the denominator is also standard normal. It was noted earlier that the square of a standard normal is χ^2 with 1 df, so the square root of a χ_1^2 is standard normal. But the denominator is χ_{N-1}^2, not χ_1^2, so its square root is not standard normal.

That said, inference about μ using $\overline{X}$ based on the t distribution is relatively robust to departures from normality in the DGP (Casella and Berger [2002]; this is not true for the χ^2 and F distributions discussed later; they are more sensitive to the assumption that the DGP is actually normal) – so much so that researchers often "forget" that theoretically, a normal distribution in the population is required for the derivation of Student's t. The reason is that although $\overline{X}$ and $S_{\overline{X}}^2$ may not be exactly independent when sampling from DGPs other than normal, the correlation is often not excessively large, so the random noise introduced by the random variables in the numerator and denominator of t are not strongly correlated. So the same logic laid out earlier about $S_{\overline{X}}^2$ adding largely independent noise to the bell shape of the distribution of $\overline{X}$ around μ (a shape that follows from the CLT for any parent DGP) still holds.

We have seen that the sampling distribution of a difference in sample means is a straightforward extension of the sampling distribution of a sample mean. Matters are not that straightforward when σ_1 and σ_2 for the DGPs from which those two samples are drawn must both be bootstrapped. The short version is that under some conditions, a difference in means still approximately follows Student's t distribution when both σ_1 and σ_2 must be bootstrapped, but this result is not automatic as it was for the normal distribution when σ is known. We return to this in greater detail in Chapter 8.

The situation for estimating $SE(\widehat{\beta})$ when we don't know $Var(\varepsilon|X) = \sigma^2$ is similar to that for estimating $SE(\overline{X})$. We need a sample quantity, computable only from what we can observe, that stands in for the σ^2 we cannot. The natural choice is the variance of the residuals e_i. Recall from Chapter 2 that the residual for observation i is the difference between the observed y_i and the regression for that observation, $\widehat{\alpha} + \widehat{\beta}x_i$. The variance of the residuals is $S_e^2 = \frac{\sum e_i^2}{N-1}$ because the mean residual is 0 by definition for OLS (see Chapter 2 Appendix).

Slipping S_e^2 into the OLS standard error, Equation 7.12, gives

$$\widehat{SE}(\widehat{\beta}) = \frac{S_e}{\sqrt{N-1}\,S_x} \tag{7.16}$$

as the bootstrapped standard error for the OLS slope term. If the DGP of Y is normal, $\widehat{SE}(\widehat{\beta})$ follows Student's t distribution. Here, however, the t distribution has $N - k$ df's, where k the number of covariates plus 1. A df is "lost" for every parameter estimated, and that includes one slope for each covariate plus the intercept. As with the t distribution for $\overline{X}$, in practice the t is invoked for $\widehat{\beta}$ with a bootstrapped SE without much regard for how close the parent DGP of Y is to normal.

7.6.2 The F Distribution

Thus far we have identified the sampling distribution of $\overline{X}$, $\overline{X}_1 - \overline{X}_2$, $\widehat{\beta}$, and S^2. We are interested in these sampling distributions because they relate the distribution of what we can observe in samples to important facets of DGPs. Thus they will allow us to make inferences, evaluate conjectures, and make comparisons about DGPs.

As noted in Chapter 6, there is also a wide array of substantive questions that focus attention on comparisons of the variance of two DGPs (or conditional variances of a DGP as a covariate changes; these mean the same thing). There is a known sampling distribution to facilitate these comparisons based on sample variances in some cases. Establishing this requires that the DGP for the samples from which the variances are drawn are normal.

In particular, if we have N_1 independent draws from one normal DGP, and N_2 independent draws from a possibly different normal DGP, and these samples are independent of one another, then

$$F = \frac{S_1^2}{\sigma_1^2} / \frac{S_2^2}{\sigma_2^2} \qquad (7.17)$$

follows the *F distribution* with $N_1 - 1$, $N_2 - 1$ df.[20] So a pair of df's has to be specified, one from each group from which a variance is computed. The order in which the df's are written matters for the shape of the F distribution. This random variable is often simply called an F statistic.

Like the χ^2 distribution, the F distribution is also right skewed, with a lower bound at zero. It is more strongly "peaked" than the χ^2. The F distribution is a two-parameter family and the parameters are $N_1 - 1$ and $N_2 - 1$. The PDF assigns strictly positive density to all nonnegative numbers and 0 density to all negative numbers. Its expected value is $\frac{N_2 - 1}{N_2 - 3}$ and its variance is a mess. Like the t and χ^2 distributions, the F distribution's functional form is not easily interpretable, but it is useful to see graphs of members of the F family. Several are shown in Figure 7.6. As the df's increase, the right skew disappears and the F distribution slowly becomes more sharply peaked and symmetric around its mode.

So the ratio of two χ^2 random variables follows an F distribution. Additionally, the square of a Student's t random variable with v df's follows an F distribution with $1, v$ df's. The F has the somewhat unusual property that the inverse of an F random variable with u, v df's also has an F distribution, with v, u df's.

Like Student's t and the χ^2 distributions, the F distribution exactly follows only when sampling from normal DGPs. However, if the parent DGPs of the samples are reasonably symmetric but not exactly normal, and samples are independent, the F statistic still approximately follows an F distribution.

---

[20] The F distribution is named for R. A. Fisher, a major figure in the development of statistics who, among other things, first figured out just exactly how broadly applicable the t distribution was (some time after it was published). It is also sometimes called Snedecor's F distribution or the Fisher-Snedecor distribution, after the statistician George Snedecor who did seminal work on it. See Casella and Berger [2002].

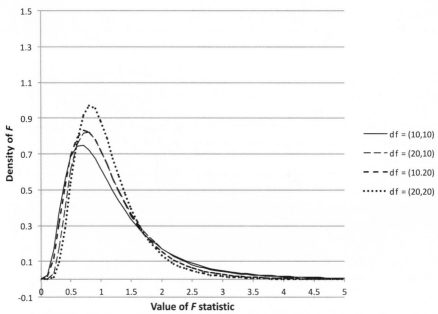

FIGURE 7.6. *F* distributions for various dfs.

7.7 FAILURES OF IID IN SAMPLING

Many of the properties of statistics derived thus far assume iid sampling, or independent draws from a DGP that is the same for all observations, up to possibly different covariates. As noted several times, it is not at all unusual for a sampling process to fail independence, identical distribution, or both.

These failures of iid can arise for reasons closely connected to the social process in question or because of how an analyst identifies and collects observations to study. Non-independence in a sample means that the random variable in one position in a sample is correlated with a random variable at another position. That is, when the random variable takes a large (or small) value for one observation, it affects the expected value of the random variable in another observation. Failure of identical distribution means that the random variable in one position is drawn from a different distribution (either a different parametric family or a different member of the same parametric family).

For a case of nonindependent sampling, consider that if two economies are linked by trade, they may both have above average or below average economic performance at the same time. We have a different expectation of the economic performance in country j when country i has above average performance than when it has below average performance. That is exactly what correlation means. Or consider military conflicts in a large region: if a conflict starts in one place, it may raise the likelihood of a conflict starting in a nearby place. This can happen because of interlocking alliances among regional political groups, for example. For a third example, suppose individuals give survey responses observable to other respondents, and later respondents are subject to peer effects or desire to conform to earlier ones. This will also induce correlation across observations: the value of one affects the value of others. All of these examples are cases of *spatial correlation*.[21] The correlation is across individual units.

Another common type of correlation across observations in samples is *temporal correlation*, more commonly known as *serial correlation* or simply *autocorrelation*. This is correlation across time in observations of a single unit. The margins of victory of a member of Congress in sequential elections might show autocorrelation. For instance, a wide margin of victory in election t may deter strong challengers from bothering in election $t + 1$, because they do not want to "waste" a candidacy in a race they are unlikely to win. Or a wide margin of victory may signal simply that the member is a good campaigner in some ways we cannot exactly measure. Because strong challengers are deterred, the incumbent's margin of victory in $t + 1$ may be wide as a result. The correlation exists because the result at time t affects the expected result at $t + 1$.

All of these examples are failures of independence across observations from a DGP. Nonindependence in each case follows from a story of the social process. Independence is not merely a technical condition; it is a substantive statement about the social process reflected in the DGP. Sometimes a sampling technique may be able to suppress nonindependence (e.g., for survey respondents subject to peer pressure, by making the answers anonymous), but when a researcher does not control the sampling process, these remedies are not available. By the same token, recognizing and addressing nonindependence requires substantive understanding of the problem one is facing. Specifying a model of the correlation among sample observations is an issue rich in substantive considerations.

Detecting serial or spatial correlation is the subject of a variety of formal statistical tests (see Cameron and Trivedi [2005], Greene [2011]). One can often get a clue of its presence in a linear regression model by perusing a graph of the residuals in successive observations. On the horizontal axis plot the index of the observation from 1 (the first observation) to N; on the vertical axis plot the residual for each observation. If there seem to be trends in this graph, serial correlation is a likely suspect.

7.7.1 Expectation and Standard Error of $\overline{X}$ and $\hat{\beta}$ under Nonindependent Sampling

Nonindependence is unproblematic if we look only at the expected values of the familiar statistics $\overline{X}$ and $\hat{\beta}$. It was already noted that unbiasedness for both of these cases does not depend on independence in sampling from the

---

[21] See Cho [2003] and Franzese and Hays [2007] for recent treatments of estimation issues in the presence of spatial interdependence.

DGP. So, for example, spatial correlation and autocorrelation do not throw off $E(\widehat{\beta}) = \beta$. We have already seen this.

Independence among draws from the DGP is important for the standard errors of these statistics. The main point is that if sample members are positively correlated, then the actual standard error is greater than the standard error computed under the assumption of independence. So if an analyst applies the usual formula for $SE(\overline{X})$ assuming *iid* observations, he will believe that the standard error of $\overline{X}$ is smaller, and the precision of $\overline{X}$ as an estimator of $E(X)$ greater, than it really is.

Why this occurs is easy to see in a simple case for $\overline{X}$. Recall how the standard error was derived: we assumed an iid sample, so the variance of the sum of the sample is the sum of the variance of each individual member. This equivalence only happens when the observations are independent. The variance is not a linear operator, so in general the sum of the variances is not the variance of the sum.

Consider a sample with two random variables, that is, a sample of size $N = 2$. In general, $Var(X_1 + X_2) = Var(X_1) + Var(X_2) + 2Cov(X_1, X_2)$. Under independence, the covariance is 0 so drops out of this equation. If the variables are positively correlated, then $Cov(X_1, X_2) > 0$ and $Var(X_1 + X_2) > Var(X_1) + Var(X_2)$.

When the variables are identically distributed, $Var(X_1) = Var(X_2) = \sigma^2$. So if the sample members are correlated but identically distributed, the variance of the sample mean is $Var(\overline{X}) = \frac{N\sigma^2 + Cov(X_1, X_2)}{N^2} = \frac{\sigma^2}{N} + 2\frac{Cov(X_1, X_2)}{N^2}$, where $N = 2$. If an unsuspecting analyst computes the sample mean and wants to know the "average error" in this estimate, she may pull the formula $Var(\overline{X}) = \frac{\sigma^2}{N}$ off the shelf and apply it to this data. But if $Cov(X_1, X_2) > 0$ the standard error is underestimated by the usual formula. The analyst would conclude that the sample is more informative about μ than it actually is, and this may lead to erroneous inferences.

Of course, if $Cov(X_1, X_2) < 0$, a situation of negative autocorrelation or negative spatial correlation among sample elements, the situation is reversed. The usual formula for the standard error overstates the estimation error. The analyst may fail to draw conclusions that are in fact warranted by the data.

The situation is only computationally more complicated when $N > 2$. It is not conceptually different. In particular, the covariance of each pair of sample members appears in the variance of their mean (or any sum). Other than that the ideas are the same.

The ideas are also the same for the standard error of $\widehat{\beta}$. When the Y_i members of the sample are positively correlated (e.g., positive autocorrelation), the average error in the sample coefficient $\widehat{\beta}$ as an estimator of β is understated. An analyst may again draw conclusions that are unwarranted by the actual attributes of the DGP.

We return to these problems in Chapter 8 and get a better sense of what erroneous conclusions can be drawn. For now, the important point is to grasp how the expected values and standard errors of these statistics are affected by correlation among the sample members, and why.

7.7.2 Heteroskedasticity and Issues for Regression Modeling

Easily the most common failure of identical distribution that quantitative social scientists recognize is *heteroskedasticity* of sample members. Heteroskedasticity occurs when the random variables comprising the sample have different variances but otherwise follow the same distribution. In social science applications, heteroskedasticity is almost always discussed in the context of regression modeling and will occupies considerable attention in classes dedicated to that topic.

Consider a sample $(Y_1, X_1), \ldots, (Y_N, X_N)$ drawn from a bivariate distribution, where the regression is $E(Y|X) = \alpha + \beta X$, where each Y is normally distributed conditional on X. Heteroskedasticity occurs when different observations i have different conditional variance, so $Var(Y_i|X_i) \neq Var(Y_j|X_j)$ for some i, j. However, all observations still have the same conditional mean function (i.e., the same α and β map X into $E(Y|X)$ for all sample observations i). They are just draws from different members of the family of normal distributions because they have different conditional variance.

As with serial correlation, detecting heteroskedasticity is the subject of a large battery of formal statistical tests. We will not go into detail about these. In linear regression models, a clue about the presence of heteroskedasticity can sometimes be gleaned from a plot of the residuals as a function of the covariates. On the horizontal axis plot the covariate and on the vertical plot the residuals for each value of the covariate. The cloud of points should have about the same vertical spread around various X values. If the cloud of points "fans out" as X gets bigger, it suggests that the conditional variance of Y grows with X. If the cloud of points "funnels down" as X gets bigger, it suggests that the conditional variance of Y shrinks with X. Each case reflects heteroskedasticity.

Whereas autocorrelation is a failure of independence, heteroskedasticity is a failure of identical distribution. With heteroskedastic observations, the demonstration that $E(\widehat{\beta}) = \beta$ is still valid. The reason is that they have the same conditional mean function; identical conditional variance did not play a role in demonstrating unbiasedness.

However, as with autocorrelation, heteroskedasticity does invalidate the derivation of the standard error of $\widehat{\beta}$. Replacing the sum of the variances of the N observations with N times their common variance is invalid in this case.

Furthermore, even when a linear specification of $E(Y|X)$ holds in the DGP, OLS is not BLUE under heteroskedasticity. In particular, the "B" part (best, or minimum variance among all linear unbiased estimators) no longer holds. Simply put, if Y_i has larger variance when X_i is large than when X_i is small, the larger X_is convey less information about the regression slope than the smaller ones. But OLS considers them both equally important. It "ignores" the information that some observations are noisier/less informative than others.

The point about unbiasedness of the estimator of β under heteroskedasticity does not carry over to other statistical models laid out in Chapter 6. For instance, in a logit model heteroskedasticity can cause make estimates of β parameters biased and therefore systematically misleading about the relationship between X and Y.

7.7.3 OLS with "Robust" Standard Errors

To summarize the previous two subsections, under correlated observations or under heteroskedasticity, OLS retains some desirable properties for estimating the unknown βs based on data. It is mainly the standard errors of OLS that go awry. So theoreticians of statistical modeling have developed a number of approaches that allow for "fixes" to OLS standard errors, but retain the OLS approach to estimating β itself. Sometimes these standard errors are generally known as *robust* standard errors because they are supposed to be accurate estimates of the SE of the OLS slope even under specific departures from iid draws.

Perhaps the best known in this family of "robust" SEs is one for dealing with heteroskedasticity. This SE has a variety of names, including the *Huber-White, Eicker, sandwich,* or *heteroskedasticity consistent standard error*. The proper names refer to the scholars that (independently) developed this estimate of the OLS SE (Huber [1967], White [1980]); the term "sandwich" refers to the mathematical expression of this SE in terms of matrix algebra, where one term is "sandwiched" in between two other identical ones.

In the homoskedasticity case, all Y_is, or equivalently all disturbances ε_i, have the same variance, σ^2. When observations are homoskedastic but σ^2 is unknown, we estimate it with the variance of the residuals e_i computed in the sample. So the estimated variance of $\widehat{\beta}$ is $\frac{s_e^2}{(N-1)s_x^2}$, where s_e^2 is the variance of the residuals in the sample.

But under heteroskedasticity, the observed residuals cannot be pooled together to estimate the common variance of Y because there isn't one. The idea in heteroskedasticity-consistent standard errors is to use the residual of each observation to estimate its own, observation-specific conditional variance of Y_i. Because $E(\varepsilon_i|X) = 0$ is still a maintained assumption, the estimated variance of Y_i for each observation is just e_i^2, its squared residual.

We can take this estimate of $Var(Y_i)$ back up to Equation 7.11, right before the point where we invoked homoskedasticity. Inserting e_i^2 in place of $Var(Y_i)$ in this expression gives us $Var(\widehat{\beta}) = \sum W_i^2 e_i^2$, where our old friend $W_i \equiv \frac{(X_i - \overline{X})}{\sum (X_i - \overline{X})^2}$ appears again. Thus the heteroskedasticity-consistent variance of $\widehat{\beta}$ is

$$Var_{HC}(\widehat{\beta}) = \frac{\sum ((X_i - \overline{X})e_i)^2}{((N-1)S_X^2)^2} \qquad (7.18)$$

and the Huber-White standard error is the square root of Equation 7.18. This does not have the clean and reasonably intuitive form of the SE of $\hat{\beta}$ under homoskedasticity, but that is the price to pay for relaxing assumptions.

The Huber-White SE is suitable no matter how the variance of Y_i changes over its observations. In particular, it does not depend on any model of how Y_is conditional variance is related to covariates. This makes it relatively useful because no additional assumptions about the structure of heteroskedasticity need to be maintained.

The purpose of going through this trouble is that the SE computed assuming homoskedasticity is incorrect, so it gives a misleading gauge of the distance between the OLS slope $\hat{\beta}$ and any theoretical conjecture about β. With the heteroskedasticity-consistent standard error, we can be on more secure footing to make these comparisons.

Similar innovations have been made for the case of serial correlation, where *Newey-West standard errors* are the leading case of corrections to the OLS standard error that allow for any degree of serial correlation (as well as heteroskedasticity; Whitney and West [1987], Cameron and Trivedi [2005]). For panel data, which may exhibit serial correlation, spatial correlation, and/or heteroskedasticity, Beck and Katz [1995] have developed *panel corrected standard errors*. As with Huber-White standard errors, these SEs leave the OLS estimator of β alone and deal directly with the problems caused for the SEs by failures of iid.

In some computer statistics packages, Huber-White, Newey-West, and panel-corrected SEs are easy to invoke with a simple option in the command to estimate a regression model. In addition, there are typically several alternative ways to implement each one of these "robust" SEs. These kinds of options can get inexperienced analysts into trouble because it is easy to do things one does not understand. But there is no reason to be timid about implementing these specifications. A reasoned justification for doing so, in terms of concerns about iid in the social process generating the data, goes a long way to fending off criticism. In addition, the brief coverage of these issues here is at least a starting point to exploration of them in more specific treatments. What is essential is that a researcher does not keep poking around at alternative specifications until the desired answer according to some pet theory pops out.

Interestingly, some statistical software packages allow for "robust" standard errors of β estimates even in generalized linear models such as the logit and Poisson. But as noted, if heteroskedasticity is present in these models, canonical estimates of β can exhibit bias. So in these cases it is not clear that "robust" standard errors solve the real problem. They leave the canonical estimator of the model's βs in place and change only its SEs. But heteroskedasticity in these generalized linear models means that the researcher should be suspicious of those canonical estimators of the βs in the first place. In other words, to invoke "robust" commands in these contexts is to acknowledge a potentially serious problem with the model itself due to heteroskedasticity, and changing the SE is not going to solve it. It just puts us on a fast train to the wrong station. See Freedman [2010c] for a formal demonstration of this point. Heteroskedasticity in these contexts requires an explicit alteration of the model to deal with it. For instance, see the development of a heteroskedastic probit model in Alvarez and Brehm [2002].

7.7.4 OLS versus Generalized Least Squares

Bear in mind again that the aim of these approaches is to "fix" the standard errors of OLS but to leave the OLS estimator of β alone. OLS still has some desirable properties; in particular, it is still unbiased. Retaining OLS as the estimator of β and changing only the SEs represents a sort of "first, do no harm" ethos.

If we knew the exact conditional variance of Y for each observation, we could use that information to get an even better estimator than OLS through an approach called *weighted least squares* or WLS, also sometimes referred to as *generalized least squares* or GLS. In brief, WLS weights each observation when computing $\widehat{\beta}$ according to the inverse of the conditional variance of Y_i for that observation. So observations with high conditional variance get relatively less weight in determining $\widehat{\beta}$, whereas the opposite is true for observations with relatively low conditional variance.

Because it weights each observation exactly in accord with its relative information content about the regression slope, WLS is BLUE. Under homoskedasticity, WLS collapses to OLS automatically. If all observations have the same conditional variance of Y, all observations get the same weight. OLS is BLUE in this case (Gauss-Markov), and WLS is identical to it, so WLS is BLUE too. But under heteroskedasticity, WLS changes the estimator from OLS by changing the weights of each observation in computing the estimate of β.

Although WLS attains BLUEness, it requires the rather mythical information about the exact conditional variance for each observation. Because we do not generally know this aspect of the DGP with certainty, WLS as such is not feasible on the basis of data alone.

It might seem reasonable to estimate a model of how the conditional variance of Y depends on X from the data and use that model to provide weights for a WLS-like procedure. This approach is called *feasible generalized least squares* or FGLS. The FGLS approach models $Var(Y|X)$ as a linear function of covariates and then treats the model estimates of $Var(Y|X)$ as true enough to use in weighting the observations in the estimator of β.

The FGLS estimator of β has some nice properties if this model of $Var(Y|X)$ is exactly right, but it is fragile in the sense that those properties can go completely haywire if the model is not exactly right. In particular, an incorrect model of $Var(Y|X)$ can cause bias in the FGLS estimate of β that never goes away no matter how large the sample size.

Most researchers have little confidence in our ability to model the conditional variance exactly right within the constraints of the FGLS approach. For one thing, FGLS models assume that heteroskedasticity is a specific function of X, whereas Huber-White standard errors make no assumption about any particular relationship between $Var(Y|X)$ and X; they allow for arbitrary changes in $Var(Y|X)$ as X changes. In that light, using FGLS rather than OLS with some correction to the standard errors seems like throwing the baby (OLS unbiasedness) out with the bathwater (OLS's failure to be BLUE under heteroskedasticity). This undesirable trade-off is what has led most researchers to favor use of OLS with SE corrections over the FGLS approach in the past couple decades.

7.8 CONCLUSION

This chapter is the first to cover statistical inference as such. It establishes a formal connection between DGPs and (statistical summaries of) observable sample data. As Chapter 6 argued, in many cases, what is theoretically interesting is the DGP behind any observable data. Because we can only work with what is observable, it is important to link the observable and the interesting. This chapter gives some insight into how we can do that. It shows how various quantities computed from observable sample data, and first introduced as tools of descriptive statistics (see Chapter 2), link up to the DGP that generated the data. It also introduced the crucially important concept of the sampling distribution, which is the foundation of much of classical statistical inference (the kind presented in this book, and as distinct from Bayesian statistics, which bases all of its theory and techniques on the posterior distribution of a parameter; see Chapter 4). Particularly important results are available for sample means and regression coefficients, for which we saw the entire sampling distribution, and sample standard deviation.

The following two chapters build on this one. In the next, we develop techniques to assess and quantify the weight of evidence that observed samples give to conjectures about the DGP. When one advances a theory asserting that some parameter of a DGP has a specific value or lies in a specific range of values, one must convince skeptics in one's research community that this is a reasonable or useful way to interpret how the world works. To do that, it is useful to adopt, contrary to one's own belief, the posture that the skeptics are right and that one's own theory is wrong. This skeptical posture can often be boiled down to a specific conjecture about the DGP. If one can show that this conjecture about the DGP is hard to reconcile with actually observed data, then one has the beginnings of a compelling argument against that skeptical posture. This is the basic idea of *hypothesis testing* in classical statistical inference, and this reasoning illustrates why this technique is so commonly employed in theoretically oriented empirical research. Chapter 8 explains the theory of hypothesis testing in reasonably general terms and explores applications to convey the flavor of its use in social science research.

1. Show that $\sum_{i=1}^{N} W_i X_i = 1$, where X_i is a random variable observed in N draws and $W_i = \frac{(X_i - \bar{X})}{\sum (X_i - \bar{X})^2}$.

2. A professor on his department's Ph.D. admissions committee decries the oppressive hegemonization of GRE scores in admissions decisions. He gathers GRE scores of matriculating students and their performance in the first year of the Ph.D. program measured by some standard metric Y. He estimates the regression model $Y = \alpha + \beta X + \varepsilon$ where X is $V + Q$ GRE score, finds that $\widehat{\beta} \approx 0$, and tells his colleagues that GRE scores are therefore uninformative and should be ignored.

   (a) Assume that the committee evaluates students' "potential" as $\tilde{Y} = X + Z$, where X is $V + Q$ GRE score and Z is the student's *je ne sais quois*, and admits students only if $\tilde{Y}$ exceeds some cutoff value $\tilde{Y}_C$. Given this constraint, if X falls, what do you expect to happen to Z for admitted students?

   (b) Assume that $Y = \tilde{Y} + \omega$, where ω is a random variable with $E(\omega) = 0$ and $Cov(X, \omega) = Cov(Z, \omega) = 0$. What can you say about $Cov(X, \varepsilon)$ in the DGP the professor is dealing with for his regression? How does this affect $E(\widehat{\beta})$ and therefore his conclusion that GRE scores are uninformative?

3. The following problems require you to download and analyze data in the file "major-laws.xls," a Microsoft Excel spreadsheet on the book's website. The exercise is about political determinants of the number of major laws passed by Congress and signed by the president, in a given Congress. The unit of observation is a single Congress, which spans a 2-year period. "N Laws" specifies a tally of the number of major laws passed in a Congress. "Unified government" $= 1$ whenever the House, Senate, and presidency are all controlled by the same party, and $= 0$ otherwise (a condition of "divided government"). "Public mood" is based on an amalgamation of public opinion research; $= 1$ when the public was considered to be in an "activist mood" and $= 0$ otherwise. "Budgetary" is an ordinal variable indicating the size of budget deficits relative to government spending; negative numbers indicate larger deficits.

   (a) What is the average, median, and standard deviation of the number of major laws passed in a given session of Congress? Does this distribution appear to be skewed or relatively symmetric?

   (b) What is the average number of major laws passed under unified government? What is the average under divided government?

(c) Is the difference in the number of major laws passed under divided and unified government statistically significant? Identify and execute a hypothesis test to answer this question.

(d) Does unified government affect the number of major laws passed, controlling for public mood and budgetary conditions? Estimate a multiple regression model to find out. Report the magnitude and standard errors of the coefficients. Discuss the magnitude and significance of the coefficients.

(e) Explain why the results on divided versus unified government are different in parts (C) and (D). Which one do you believe more?

(f) Is heteroscedasticity a reasonable concern with respect to the model in part (D)? Explain why or why not. Regardless of your answer, estimate the model in part (D) with "heteroscedasticity-robust" (a.k.a. "Huber-White") standard errors. Do the coefficients change? Do any of the significance judgments change?

(g) Estimate the effects in part (D) with a Poisson regression model rather than a multiple regression model. Report the magnitude and standard errors of the coefficients. Interpret the marginal effects from this model compared to those from part (D). Do any of the significance results for the coefficients change compared to part (D)? Finally, explain why anyone would ever bother with a Poisson model in this problem.

4. Using a computer software package, draw 10,000 samples of 30 independent draws from a standard normal distribution. For each sample, compute the variance s^2 and $\frac{(N-1)s^2}{\sigma^2}$. Plot a histogram for the latter quantity and compare it to the PDF of a χ^2 distribution with $N-1$ degrees of freedom.

5. Draw 10,000 samples of 30 independent draws from a (continuous) uniform distribution on the interval $[-3, 3]$. For each sample compute the variance s^2 and $\frac{(N-1)s^2}{\sigma^2}$. Plot a histogram for the latter quantity and compare it to the PDF of a χ^2 distribution with $N-1$ degrees of freedom.

6. In each of your 10,000 normal samples, compute $t = \frac{\bar{x}-\mu}{s/\sqrt{N}}$. Plot a histogram of the 10,000 values of t and compare to the PDF of Student's t distribution with $N-1$ degrees of freedom.

7. In each of your 10,000 uniform samples, compute $t = \frac{\bar{x}-\mu}{s/\sqrt{N}}$. Plot a histogram of the 10,000 values of t and compare to the PDF of Student's t distribution with $N-1$ degrees of freedom.

8

Hypothesis Testing: Assessing Claims about the Data-Generating Process

Positive theories in social science assert relationships among concepts. An example is that the number of police officers on the beat leads to a drop in crime or that monolingual education in linguistically diverse schools leads to stronger attachments of group members to their own ethnic identity. Postulating a statistical model – (some aspects of) a data-generating process (DGP) for the data and (some aspects of) a link from its parameters to covariates – is how we translate theories into statements about stochastic DGPs. Often, as we have seen (Chapter 6), these translations relate to the conditional mean of Y given some explanatory factors. For instance, a (very simple) theory might assert that the mean of the DGP (generating crime levels conditional on beat cops) is higher when there are "few" beat cops than when there are "many." This can also be stated in terms of the slope coefficients in a regression model; for example, in a linear model for the conditional mean of turnout levels given voters' information, saying the former is positively related to the latter is the same as saying the slope term on information levels is positive.

Sampling distributions of the sort covered in Chapter 7 provide a basis for evaluating theoretical claims about the DGP based on evidence from a collection of draws from that DGP (i.e., a sample). This is the subject of *hypothesis testing*, which provides a set of statistical techniques for evaluating the strength of sample evidence supporting specific conjectures about the DGP.

Hypothesis testing is a full-throated exercise in statistical inference, the process of working from observed data back to DGP. Statistical inference is relevant when some facet of the DGP – from specific parameters to the entire functional form – is unknown, but a collection of draws from the DGP is observable and can help us learn about the unknown facets of the DGP.

Thus although statistical inference makes extensive use of results from previous chapters, the perspective is different. In the theory of sampling and sampling distributions in Chapter 7 (as well as in probability theory), we assumed

236

a known DGP and asked what kinds of properties are inherited by samples or statistical summaries of samples. In statistical inference, we go the other direction, asking about the properties of a DGP that generated any sample we happen to be working with. The assumption of an unknown (but extant) DGP means that the world works according to some intelligible (although stochastic) process, but we have to figure it out rather than assume knowledge of it.

The unifying idea in classical hypothesis testing is simple. First we make a guess about some aspect of a statistical model – unknown parameters of a DGP or their link to covariates. Then we find a way to estimate those unknown aspects of the DGP (e.g., with a sample mean or OLS regression coefficients) and obtain the sampling distributions of those estimators. Finally we use that sampling distribution to figure out exactly how likely the specific sample in front of us would be if our guess about the DGP were actually correct. If the data actually observed is unlikely given that the guess about the DGP is correct, the data casts doubt on the guess. If the data actually observed is reasonably likely given that the guess is correct, the data supports the guess. Hypothesis testing formalizes this process of conjecturing and establishing conditional probabilities given the conjecture. In this sense, hypothesis tests assess the weight of the sample evidence in favor of a guess about the DGP's unknown parameters.

Although clear in their logic and simple in their basics, classical hypothesis test results are often mangled in their presentation. Most important, classical hypothesis tests never allow assessment of the probability that the conjecture about the DGP is true. Rather, they allow assessment of the probability of observing what was in fact observed, conditional on the truth of the conjecture about the DGP. Classical tests never allow us to say that we are $p\%$ sure that the DGP parameter lies in a certain region or interval. The DGP parameter is what it is; it is unknown, but it is not a random variable. So probability statements about it, in classical frequentist terms, make no sense.[1] The sample, not the DGP, is the random quantity, and therefore so is any quantity computed from the sample. That randomness is what prevents us from ever obtaining perfect information about the DGP parameters based on any finite sample.

8.1 A CONTRIVED EXAMPLE

This section presents a simple stylized example of a hypothesis test to communicate the ideas in concrete terms. The example is somewhat unusual compared with the typical routines of hypothesis testing encountered in introductory material. The hope is that the example will therefore convey concepts rather than present hypothesis testing as a rote procedure or mystical incantation.

---

[1] Bayesian approaches to hypothesis testing do allow for probabilistic statements about parameter values because posterior distributions are defined over parameters. The ability to make such statements makes Bayesian approaches compelling to many scholars. See Berger [1985].

The next section presents the formal concepts of hypothesis testing in abstract terms, and the subsequent sections present specific types of tests that are common in applications.

Suppose you and a friend, with too much spare time, are arguing about whether a U.S. quarter is fair, that is, if the probability of head and tail are both 0.5. Your friend adamantly insists the coin is fair, but you believe it is biased toward heads. After arguing about it in theoretical terms for a while (e.g., you got it at a trick shop for $2, so it must be biased; it looks and feels like any quarter, so it must be fair and the only "trick" was that you paid some huckster $2 for an ordinary quarter), you decide to take it to the data.

You flip the coin 10 times, observe 9 heads, and then the coin rolls down a sewer drain never to be seen again. So much for the coin, but what about the argument? This evidence does not conclusively prove one of you right. It is possible to observe 9 heads in 10 flips if the coin is fair. Although we expect 5 heads in 10 flips from a fair coin, we don't always get what we expect from a stochastic DGP. The fair coin conjecture implies that the only reason to get such samples from a fair coin is due to random variation. In the interest of resolving the dispute, you say to your friend: Let's suppose you're right, that the coin is really fair. Assuming that is true, what is the probability of seeing the sample evidence we did in fact see?

This is a conditional probability and is simple to calculate because on the assumption of the fair coin you observed 10 draws of a Bernoulli distribution with $p = 0.5$ (i.e., a binomial$(10, 0.5)$ distribution). Under this distribution each possible sequence of flips with 9 heads and 1 tail is equally likely; they all have probability $(.5)^9 + (.5)^1 = (.5)^{10} \approx 0.001$. Furthermore, there are 10 possible sequences with 9 H and 1 T: there are 10 possible positions for the T, and the remaining 9 H can occur anywhere in the sample. So the probability of 9 heads in 10 flips is about 0.01. Thus there is about a 1% chance of observing this particular sample, if the coin is really fair.

Not so fast, says your friend. If we had actually observed 10 heads in 10 flips, we'd be counting that against the fair coin conjecture too. It's not fair to the fair coin conjecture to ask it to explain the exact data that happened to occur; we'd certainly consider it a good conjecture if it could explain the observed evidence, or any other possible evidence that is even more extreme relative to what we expect under a fair coin. This seems like a reasonable point, so you grant it, and add the probability of observing 10 heads in 10 flips, about 0.001, to your earlier 0.01, the probability of 9 heads in 10 flips.

You wind up with the following conclusion: if the coin is really fair, the probability of observing the sample you did in fact observe, or something even more extreme than that, is 0.011. Evidence "like" the evidence you actually did see is uncommon if the fair coin conjecture is accurate. This makes it hard to defend the fair coin conjecture, but not impossible. Again, the sample evidence is not strong enough to disprove that conjecture or any other conjecture beyond any doubt whatsoever (except that $p = 0$ or $p = 1$). This is true regardless of the sample size, because any sample sequence is possible for any value of $p \in (0, 1)$.

The only standard that can be met is some sort of "reasonable doubt" about the coin, not absolute certainty. What exactly "reasonable" means is in the eye of the beholder, so suppose you choose your preferred standard of credibility or degree of belief and call it $\alpha\%$. Assuming that the coin is fair, if the probability of the observed data, or more extreme data, is $\alpha\%$ or less, we conclude that the fair coin conjecture is disproved beyond a reasonable doubt. If you and your friend agreed that $\alpha = 0.05$ or 5% is a fair standard of reasonable doubt, then the observed probability 0.011 meets that standard. But if the standard of reasonable doubt is 1%, the observed data do not disprove the fair coin conjecture beyond a reasonable doubt.

This example, although stylized, has the same components and the same logic as standard hypothesis tests used in garden-variety quantitative social science. The conjecture that the coin is fair is the *null hypothesis*, that the coin is biased toward head is the *alternative hypothesis*. The null hypothesis is maintained unless there is relatively strong evidence consistent with the alternative. The sequence of 10 flips is the sample data used to test the hypotheses. The number of heads in the sample is the *test statistic*, and because we know the sample follows a binomial DGP, we know the sampling distribution of the test statistic is binomial. Based on this sampling distribution and assuming the null hypothesis is true, we compute the *p-value*, the probability of observing a test statistic as or more extreme (relative to the null hypothesis) than the one observed in the sample – here, the p-value is 0.011. Finally, we compare the p-value to the "standard of reasonable doubt" α, known formally as the *significance level* of the test.

Where other tests differ from this is in the specification of hypotheses (up to the analyst doing the test), choice of test statistic (up to the analyst in principle but usually prescribed by standard practice), specification of the sampling distribution of the test statistic under the null hypothesis (implied by properties of the test statistic), specification of the significance level (up to the analyst in principle but prescribed by standards in one's field), and computation and interpretation of the p-value (arithmetic and logic, the former but hopefully not the latter usually done by a computer).

8.2 CONCEPTS OF HYPOTHESIS TESTING

There is a tremendous variety of hypothesis testing procedures for different situations, depending on the nature of the hypothesis and how much is assumed about the DGP, but they all have some fundamentals in common. Knowing those fundamentals can help in interpreting hypothesis test results even if the precise details of a test that an analyst performed are unclear. Once the concepts of a null hypothesis, test statistic, and p-value are clear, it is not necessary to endure a disquisition on every type of test for every type of hypothesis for every set of assumptions about a DGP to interpret the test, because they all work basically the same way.

8.2.1 Hypotheses and Parameter Space

Consider a DGP $f(x|\theta)$ with observed data denoted by x and a parameter denoted by θ. This parameter might be the mean of a DGP from which random variables are drawn. Or it might be a slope term in a regression model, such as $E(Y|X) = \alpha + \theta X$. Or it might be the variance of a distribution. It is just a generic name for an unknown parameter. The DGP can be any probability distribution at all (univariate, bivariate, conditional, whatever), and θ can capture any aspect of it (expectation, variance, covariance, whatever).

The parameter θ can take many possible values. The set of possible values for θ is called a *parameter space* and is denoted Θ. In a regression model, the slope θ can in principle be any real number. For a given DGP, the assumption behind classical hypothesis testing is that θ has one specific, fixed value or falls in a definite region of Θ – we just do not have the privilege of knowing it. So although the parameter θ is just a number (or vector) and not a random variable, there is still a range of values for it.

When we observe a dataset, we can suppose that a specific value $\theta \in \Theta$ is determined by some social process, so the DGP is $f(x|\theta)$, and a sequence of N draws of x is made from the DGP. That's our data. What is the value of θ? We don't know; we have to use the data to find out as best we can. That's what makes this a problem of statistics. In probability theory, we know θ.

A *hypothesis* is an assertion that the parameter θ lies in a specific region of the parameter space Θ. If the hypothesis asserts that θ takes one specific value θ_0, it is a simple hypothesis. If it asserts that θ takes a range of values, for example, $\theta < 0$, it is a composite hypothesis.

Of course, because we have observed draws of a random variable (the sample), the draws can take lots of different values for any given value of θ and DGP f. In any real problem, we cannot figure out θ perfectly. A finite dataset will generally never exactly pin down θ. So in a regression model, even if $\theta = 0$ *in the DGP*, it is possible to observe a dataset in which the slope coefficient $\hat{\theta} > 0$ *in the sample*. This is because of random chance in the observations we happen to have observed in the sample; chance separates the sample from the DGP. Thus a hypothesis test can never definitively say whether a hypothesis is in fact true or not. It can only tell us the probability of observing data like that in our sample, given that the hypothesis is true.

In a hypothesis test, there are always two hypotheses: a *null hypothesis*, H_0, and an *alternative hypothesis*, H_1 or H_a. The null says $\theta \in \Theta_0 \subset \Theta$. If that happens to be the case, the null is true; if not, it is false. The alternative says $\theta \in \Theta_1 \subset \Theta$, where $\Theta_0 \cap \Theta_1 = \emptyset$.

It is up to the analyst to specify the null and alternative hypotheses in the test. A typical case in a regression model would specify $H_0 : \theta = 0$ and

$H_1 : \theta \neq 0$. Or, for two groups whose means can be compared, $H_0 : \mu_1 = \mu_2$ and $H_1 : \mu_1 \neq \mu_2$. That is, the null is that the group means are equal and the alternative is that they are different.

Conventionally, the null hypothesis is the one that the analyst argues against. When a researcher advances a novel theory that two variables are related, for instance, the null typically represents the skeptical counterargument that the theory is wrong and they are not related. Tests are setup so that it is fairly hard to find evidence that counts against the null if it is really true. Therefore, when you *do* find evidence against it, that is pretty compelling evidence against the null. Setting up a null in this way, as a hypothesis the researcher believes is wrong and the alternative as a hypothesis the researcher believes is correct, is a way of adopting a high "burden of proof" for the claim the researcher is advancing.

Either or both of H_0 and H_1 can be simple or composite, so $\Theta_0 \cup \Theta_1 = \Theta$ is not necessarily true, but it often is true in common tests. A common set of hypotheses in hypothesis tests is $H_0 : \theta = \theta_0$, $H_1 : \theta \neq \theta_0$, where θ_0 is a single number. This is a point-valued null (a simple hypothesis) against a composite alternative. Because the alternative in this case consists of parameter values on both sides of the null, it specifies a *two-tailed test*. Another common set of hypotheses is $H_0 : \theta \leq \theta_0$, $H_1 : \theta > \theta_0$. This is a *one-tailed test*, and consists of a composite null against a composite alternative.

Whether a test is one- or two-tailed depends on which possible samples are counted against the null hypothesis. For instance, if $H_0 : \theta = \theta_0$, does an observed $\widehat{\theta}$ count against H_0 if it is far above or far below θ_0? If so the test is two-tailed. If an observed $\widehat{\theta}$ far above θ_0 counts against H_0, but far below does not (or vice versa), the test is one-tailed.

Because we don't know θ, we don't know whether a hypothesis is true, and we never will. The test assesses the degree of support for the null in the data at hand. It always assesses the degree of support for the null relative to the specified alternative.

It is important for the integrity of test results that H_0 and H_1 not be chosen based on the data that is observed. If we use the data to choose H_0, some of the available sample evidence is "used up." Hypotheses should be chosen on the basis of conjectures or theories about the DGP, not the data, for hypothesis test results to make sense. If the data is used to establish the hypotheses, it cannot provide an independent test of those hypotheses it generated.

8.2.2 Test Statistics

A *test statistic* in a hypothesis test provides the evidence from the sample about the hypotheses. A test statistic is any quantity that can be computed from the sample data and has a known sampling distribution (at least approximately) under the assumption that H_0 is true. Formally, a test statistic is denoted $T(X)$ where X is a shorthand expression for the entire sample of observations, or

$T(X)$: random variable
prob. dist. = sampling dist.
$T(x)$

242   *Statistical Modeling and Inference for Social Science*

$T(X|\theta)$ to note its dependence on the true parameter θ. Because $T(X)$ is computed from sample data, it is a random variable and its probability distribution is its sampling distribution. As with our earlier conventions, the random variable itself is $T(X)$, and the value observed in any particular sample is $T(x)$.

Because $T(X)$ has a known sampling distribution given H_0, we can assess the probability of observing the $T(x)$ that was in fact observed (or something "like" that $T(x)$) if the null is actually true. If we can determine only $E(T(X|\theta \in \Theta_0))$ and the standard error of $T(X)$, then from Chebyshev's inequality alone (Chapter 5), we can in principle put a bound on $Pr\{|T(X) - E(T(X|\theta \in \Theta_0))| > |T(x) - E(T(X|\theta \in \Theta_0))|\}$ that must hold for any sampling distribution. But as observed in Chapter 5, Chebyshev bounds are conservative. Knowledge of the actual sampling distribution lets us refine these bounds significantly.

Many useful test statistics are based on a sample analogue of the DGP parameter(s) of interest: for example, $\overline{X}$ is useful for testing hypotheses about μ; an ordinary least squares (OLS) regression slope $\widehat{\beta}$ is useful for testing hypotheses about β in the DGP; sample standard deviation S is useful for testing hypotheses about DGP standard deviation σ (the choice of test statistics in specific cases is explained in greater detail later). It is also common for test statistics to be small in expectation when the null is true and grow larger and larger in expectation as the null gets more and more wrong. This makes them useful in testing the null hypothesis: we can compute the test statistic and see how big it is. If it's small, the null has fared fairly well. If it's large, the null is on shaky ground.

8.2.3 Decision Rules and Ex Post Errors

So far we have covered the hypotheses and the test statistic in a test. The third ingredient in a hypothesis test is a *decision rule*. A decision rule is a set of values of the test statistic that lead to rejection of the null H_0 and a set of values of the test statistic that lead to rejection of the alternative H_1. The set of values of $T(X)$ that lead to rejection of H_0 is called the *rejection region* of the test, denoted RR. Formally, $RR = \{T(X)|H_0 \text{ is rejected}\}$. A decision rule in a test is then a specification of the rejection region in the test.[2]

Although the null and alternative hypotheses need not partition the entire parameter space Θ, in any sensible test the decision rule does partition the range of the test statistic. That is, any feasible value of the test statistic must lead to either acceptance of the null or acceptance of the alternative – never both decisions but always one of them. Simply put, H_0 is rejected if and only if $T(X) \in RR$.

---

[2] It is sometimes asserted that the only viable decisions are to reject the null or fail to reject the null, so that no hypothesis is ever accepted, because "acceptance" somehow connotes belief that it is exactly true. This language is a bit fastidious and has no impact on how a test is executed, so we will not follow it strictly.

In practice, decision rules specify that H_0 is rejected when the computed value of the test statistic in the sample is distant from the value one would expect of H_0 were really true. For example, in a regression model with $H_0 : \theta = 0$ and $H_1 : \theta > 0$, a decision rule would specify that the null is rejected is the slope of the least squares regression line computed from the sample exceeds some prespecified cutoff greater than 0. The null would not be rejected if the computed slope were less than this cutoff. As noted in Chapter 9, the slope from least squares regression is an unbiased estimator of the true slope in the DGP. When $H_0 : \theta = 0$ is true in this case, this means that the expected value of the slope in the sample is 0. When the actual slope departs from this expected value by a large enough quantity and in a way consistent with the alternative hypothesis, the null is rejected.

This is an incredibly important concept in hypothesis testing. When H_0 is true, we can figure out what value the test statistic is expected to have from its sampling distribution. We can compare that value to the value it actually does have in the sample at hand. If expected and actual are very different, it casts doubt on the null. If they are not so different, the observed data is consistent with the null.

That is the idea in hypothesis testing. The devil is in the details, and the meaning of "very different" or "distant" must be made precise. That is where the sampling distribution (assuming the null is true) and often the standard error of the test statistic comes into play. This is discussed in the next subsection.

Because the sample data are never fully informative about whether the null is true, either decision about it (to reject the null or not) can result in an error. First, the null can be rejected when it is in fact true. This is a *Type I error*. Second, the null can be accepted when it is false. This is a *Type II error*. For any given decision rule (except trivial ones), each type of error has some probability of occurring for each value $\theta \in \Theta$. The probability of a Type I error is sometimes called the *size* of the test, and 1 minus the probability of Type II error is called the *power*. ~~significance/size of the test: P(Type I error)~~

8.2.4 Significance

~~1 − P(Type II error): power~~

Suppose that $T(X) \in RR$. How much doubt does this case on H_0? It depends on the probability of the event $T(X) \in RR$ assuming that H_0 is true. If $Pr[T(X|\theta \in \Theta_0) \in RR]$ is small, then the event $T(X) \in RR$ is unlikely to occur when the null is true. In this case, $T(X) \in RR$ casts doubt on the null.

The probability $Pr[T(X|\theta \in \Theta_0) \in RR]$ is the *significance level* or *size* of the test, and is denoted by the shorthand $\alpha \in (0, 1)$. Note also that it is the probability of a Type I error: the null is true by assumption in that expression, yet the test statistic is in the rejection region. So the null gets rejected incorrectly. Note that by a straightforward implication of probability as long-run frequency (Chapter 4), if H_0 is literally true and 100 tests of size α are conducted in independent samples, then we expect that in $100 \times \alpha$ of those tests, $T(X)$ will be in the rejection region. So incorrectly rejecting a true null (and failing to reject a false null) are inherently possible in hypothesis testing; for any given test, we don't know whether it's one of the $100 \times \alpha$ incorrect ones.

The size and area of the rejection region determine the significance level α, and in tests that follow this format, the rejection region is chosen precisely so that the test has a desired size α. That is, α and the coverage of RR are directly linked; it is the choice of α by the analyst that pins down RR.

There is, of course, no universally compelling or accepted choice of α because there is no universal standard as to how much degree of doubt in H_0 is too much for H_0 to bear. Smaller values are better, all else constant, but for a given sample size N, lowering α always has a cost: namely, it makes it harder to tell that the null is false when it really is false, raising the probability of Type II error. This is simply a *size–power trade-off* in specifying a test and is discussed in more detail in a subsection on test power.

Conventionally, analysts focus on $\alpha = 0.10, 0.05$, or 0.01. These different values of α imply different rejection regions in the test. The idea is that these are relatively small, so that Type I errors are relatively unlikely; thus when $T(X)$ really is in RR, it casts doubt on H_0.

Putting the ingredients so far together, what happens in a hypothesis test is that an analyst specifies the null and alternative, identifies a test statistic and how it's distributed when H_0 is true, specifies the significance level, which in turn defines the rejection region, computes the value of test statistic in the sample at hand, determines whether the computed test statistic is in the rejection region or not and decides what to do with the hypotheses accordingly. The analyst would report H_0, H_1, $T(X)$, α and/or RR, and the decision to reject H_0 or not.

8.2.5 *p*-Values

The "conventional" result of a hypothesis test is a simple directive – reject H_0 or do not reject H_0. This obscures much available information.

Specifically, reporting only a reject or do not reject decision and the test size α obscures the degree of support for the alternative hypothesis and against the null in the data. All test statistics in the rejection region are treated the same way, whether they are wheezing past the boundary or blow past it. And all test statistics not in the rejection region are treated the same way, whether they are "marginally" significant or not.

To report this extra information about degree of support for the hypotheses, analysts typically use *p-values*. The *p*-value is the probability, assuming H_0 is true, that the random test statistic is at least as extreme (relative to the expected value under H_0) as its observed value. Thus, in a one-tailed test in which H_1 asserts that θ is greater than any value in Θ_0, the *p*-value is

$$p = \Pr[T(X) \geq T(x) : \theta \in \Theta_0]. \tag{8.1}$$

given

(Here ":" denotes "given" in the sense of conditional probability; because of absolute values and conditioning in these expressions, this formulation is clearer.) In a one-tailed test in which H_1 asserts that θ is less than any value in Θ_0, the p-value is

$$p = \Pr[T(X) \le T(x) : \theta \in \Theta_0]. \tag{8.2}$$

In a two-tailed test,[3]

$$p = \Pr[|T(X) - E(T(X))| - |T(x) - E(T(X))| \ge 0 : \theta \in \Theta_0]. \tag{8.3}$$

Note, therefore, that if the sampling distribution of $T(X)$ is symmetric around its expected value under H_0 (true for tests based on the z and t distributions), the p-value in a one-tailed test is half the p-value in a two-tailed test, and in general p-values in one-tailed tests are always smaller than in two-tailed tests. This is one reason that many researchers prefer two-tailed tests unless there is a good reason to prefer one-tailed; choosing a one-tailed test because it leads to a smaller p-value is rather disingenuous.

Thus a p-value is a formalized expression of the *degree of support*, or *weight of the evidence*, in favor of the null. As a conditional probability, a p-value is always between 0 and 1. When the p-value is close to 0, the weight of the evidence in favor of the null is small. P-values convey strictly more information than reject or do not reject H_0 decisions in a test with α significance level. If the p-value is less than α, we know that an α-level test would lead to rejection of the null. It is common to use p-values and sharper judgments of "statistical significance" or insignificance in the same narrative, for example, to report a p-value of 0.02 and also to refer to the test result as statistically significant or to report a p-value of 0.11 and also to refer to the test result as statistically insignificant.

The p-value is not the probability that the null is true. The null is either true or false; it has no probability attached to it in frequentist or classical procedures. The p-value in a two-tailed test is the conditional probability of observing $|T(X) - E(T(X))| \ge |T(x) - E(T(X))|$, *given* that H_0 is true. Note that $T(X)$, a random variable, is on the left side of the inequality; $T(x)$, the observed value of the test statistic in a given sample, is on the right. The absolute value of the differences on each side of the inequality indicates that it does not matter whether the statistic is above or below its expected value under H_0; all we care about is the probability that the test statistic is further away from its expectation than was actually observed.

Certain observable data and certain values of sample quantities have greater or lower probability when the null is true, and the probability of these datasets

---

[3] If H_0 is composite so that Θ_0 contains more than one point, p-values are computed on the assumption that $\theta \in \Theta_0$ is as close as possible to the alternative region Θ_1. This is conservative in the sense that it makes the evidence against H_0 and for H_1 as weak as possible.

and values changes as the parameters of the DGP change. That is where probability enters into the classical hypothesis testing world (and the only place it enters). It makes no sense from a frequentist standpoint to discuss the probability that the null hypothesis is true or false – the parameter of the DGP has a specific value, and it's not a random variable – and classical hypothesis tests do not address this question.[4]

In all computations of p-values, we start by identifying a test statistic, and identifying its observed value. The test statistic is a random variable. We then pin down the parameters of the sampling distribution of $T(X)$ by assuming that H_0 is true. The p-value is then the probability, assuming H_0 is true, that the random test statistic is at least as extreme as its observed value. In most cases computer software automates this process and returns a p-value to be interpreted.

A hypothesis test can then be viewed as a stylized "trial" for the null hypothesis, which is assumed to be true unless it can be shown "beyond a reasonable doubt" that it is false. Standard significance levels (0.10, 0.05, 0.01) supply the standard of "reasonable doubt," and the p-value summarizes the degree to which the evidence in the sample meets that standard.

8.2.6 Test Power

The discussion of test size/significance made two facts apparent: first, tests with smaller significance levels are better, all else constant, than tests with larger significance levels: they make it less likely for $T(X)$ to be in RR when H_0 is really true. Second, test size is up to the analyst in any given problem.

But small significance levels cut two ways. True, it makes it harder for $T(X)$ to wind up in RR when H_0 is actually correct. But they also make it harder for $T(X)$ to wind up in RR when H_0 is actually false. Smaller significance levels make it harder to commit a Type I error, but holding sample size fixed, they also make it easier to commit a Type II error. So there is a cost to shrinking the significance level.

This cost in conventional hypothesis testing is expressed in terms of test power. The *power of a test at parameter θ* is the probability that the test statistic is in the rejection region when the DGP's parameter is θ. More compactly the power at θ is expressed as $\pi(\theta) \equiv \Pr\{T(X|\theta) \in RR\}$.

For a simple null and when $H_0 : \theta = \theta_0$ is true, the only way for $T(X) \in RR$ to occur is by making a Type I error. The probability of that has already been

---

[4] Of course, if we have a prior probability distribution over θ, then the conditional probability in a p-value can be turned around using Bayes's theorem to give the conditional probability that θ lies in any particular region, given the observed data. In Bayesian terms, we use the observed data to update the prior over θ and arrive at a posterior over θ given the data X. This is the realm of Bayesian statistics, which is not covered in this book. See Berger [1985] and Gelman and Hill [2006].

denoted α, the size of the test. So in any test, we know straight away that $\pi(\theta_0) = \alpha$. That's the power of the test at the value of θ such that H_0 is true: it's just the size.

What about the power of the test when the null is not true? In the typical case with a point-valued null $\theta = \theta_0$ and composite alternative $\theta \neq \theta_0$, this question as posed is not specific enough to answer. Notice that the power function $\pi(\theta)$ is defined for a specific value of θ: it maps a specific DGP parameter into a power value. Because there are (in most applications) uncountably many values of θ for which $H_0 : \theta = \theta_0$ is false and $H_1 : \theta \neq \theta_0$ is true, there is no one single "power of the test when the null is not true." There are many power values associated with each of the many values of θ for which the alternative is true.

The exact value of the power function for specific parameters depends on the specific test. What is generally true of tests used in applied quantitative research, however, is that as H_0 becomes "more incorrect," the value of $\pi(\theta)$ grows. More specifically, consider the parameter region Θ_0 in which the null is true. As the true parameter θ gets further and further from this region, it is more and more likely that $T(X|\theta) \in RR$, raising the probability of rejecting the (false, by assumption) null, and raising the power of the test. This is quite sensible: when the null is very wrong, it is easier to determine this from data. It's when the null is only a little wrong – the true parameter is outside Θ_0 but not too far outside – that discriminating null from alternative is difficult.

The "ideal power function," the one an omnipotent analyst or one with an infinite sample size would work under, is easy to establish. It specifies $\pi(\theta) = 0$ for $\theta \in \Theta_0$, and $\pi(\theta) = 1$ for $\theta \notin \Theta_0$. That is, for the ideal power function, the test statistic has no chance of winding up in the rejection region when the null is true and no chance of falling outside the rejection region when the null is false – even false by just a little bit.

Needless to say the ideal power function is unattainable in practice. First of all, as noted earlier, the power at $\theta = \theta_0$ in a test with a point-valued null is simply the size α of the test. And, in any sensible test, the probability of rejecting the null is higher when the null is false than when the null is true. So the power of a test is in fact never 0 in finite samples. Second, the power is also never one in finite samples. For $\theta = \theta_0 + \varepsilon$, the null is false but just barely so; the power is typically just barely greater than α.[5] Only as the true parameter approaches infinite distance from the null parameter θ_0 does the power of the test converge to 1. Otherwise, there is some probability of a test statistics not being in the rejection region even when H_0 is false, of making a Type II error.

It was already noted that when H_0 is true, the power is α, the probability of Type I error. This is obvious from the definition of power (which makes you wonder why this is the third time I've noted it). When H_0 is false, the power is 1 minus the probability of a Type II error, itself known as $\beta(\theta)$. This too is clear from the definition of power. Note that unlike the probability of Type I

---

[5] Which is to say, the power function for most common parametric tests is continuous.

$\beta(\theta):$ ~~Type II error~~ $= 1 - P(\text{Type II error})$ when H_0 is false

error, the probability of Type II error is a function of θ, the true parameter of the DGP.

For a fixed sample size N, test size and test power are generally in conflict. That means we can make the size as small as we want, but only at the cost of decreasing the power. And for given N the test can as powerful as desired but only because of an unreasonable burden on the null hypothesis. By increasing N, an analyst can increase power and decrease test size simultaneously. Otherwise, making one aspect of a test more appealing means making the other less so.

In social science analysis with observational data, analysts often do not pay much attention to test power. Scholars from the biostatistics and epidemiology tradition, and sometimes experimental psychology, typically pay a lot more attention to it because as part of their research design they often choose the number of subjects or observations. So having chosen a test size, sometimes scholars can choose N to achieve a certain level of power in a given test.

With observational data of the kind we often have in social science (or even survey data, chosen to achieve representativeness, in some sense, given survey costs), we typically take the N we can get without grossly violating the assumption of a homogenous DGP (at least conditional on covariates) behind all N observations. Then, given that N, scholars focus on significance α or p-values in a test.

To some extent, this focus is justified because common tests (such as those discussed in the next few sections) can sometimes be shown to be the most powerful tests of any size α test for the hypotheses in question (these are *uniformly most powerful* or UMP tests). This is not a widely applicable justification, but it sometimes works. In any case, we will not dwell on it. Even with an UMP test, however, priority is given to size and the most powerful test *of a given size* is then determined. If Type I and Type II errors have costs, we could explicitly take account of them in choosing a decision rule that implies some probability of making each error. That is the starting point of statistical decision theory, an identical twin of expected utility theory. For better or worse, standard practice in applied statistics does not dwell on these issues.

Sometimes the natural null hypothesis in a test is the principal prediction of a theory a researcher is advancing. For instance, in his seminal work on legislative organization, Krehbiel [1991] argued theoretically that the pivotal members of committees in Congress should be ideologically indistinguishable from the pivotal member of Congress. Given a measure of ideology (see Poole and Rosenthal [2007] for discussion), Krehbiel's theory predicts that the distribution of committee medians in an "ideology space" has the same mean as the the the distribution of congressional chamber medians. Thus the conventional null hypothesis of no difference in distributions is the theory's prediction.

Sometimes in such situations, analysts present *post hoc power calculations* (see Cox and McCubbins [2005] for an example). Post hoc power calculations assume that the null is incorrect, and the actual value of the parameter is exactly the one observed in the sample. They then present the probability the test statistic is in the rejection region for the null, given this parameter value. There is certainly nothing wrong with this practice, but it does not actually present any additional information beyond a p-value. It is simply a different way of presenting the information from the sample about the validity of H_0. The reason is that it cannot add any new information to that issue. In particular, assuming that the unknown parameter is exactly equal to the value observed in the sample does not make it so.

8.2.7 False Positives in Multiple Tests

The concepts and logic of hypothesis testing laid out above take a single hypothesis test in isolation. In reality, it is common for researchers to executive multiple hypothesis tests simultaneously. In particular, the significance level $alpha$, which represents the probability of a "false positive" or Type I error in a single test, needs careful attention. With multiple tests, the probability of at least one false positive or Type I error in the entire group of tests is not the same as the significance level α of a single test.

Think of it like a coin flip: a single test is like one flip of the coin, and α is the chance that the coin comes up "heads" on one flip. This is just our old friend, the Bernoulli distribution. But what is the probability of at least one head in N flips? This falls out of the Bernoulli's close relative, the binomial distribution. If all flips have α probability of a head, the probability of 0 heads (no Type I errors) in N flips is $(1 - \alpha)^N$. Because $\alpha > 0$, this gets smaller as N gets bigger. The more tests are performed, the more likely one of them shows a significant result that is actually in error.

Somewhat more concretely, if 10 hypothesis tests are performed, and H_0 is true in all of them, we'd expect, on average in repeated sampling, one of those 10 tests to show a statistically significant result at the $\alpha = .10$ level. There might be 0 false positives in a given sample, there might be more than one false positive; we don't know in any given sample and we never will. But we expect one mistake out of 10 tests. This is because α, by definition, is the probability of a false positive; in 10 independent tests, the expected number of false positives is αN.

If we want to ensure that the expected number of false positives in N tests is no greater than (for example) α, then we have to adjust the significance level in each individual test. If all N tests are independent and each is conducted at the $\frac{\alpha}{N}$ significance level, then the expected number of false positives in N tests is exactly α. This is called a *Bonferroni correction*. The Bonferroni correction is fairly conservative; it makes finding a significant result in any one test more difficult (or more unusual, if H_0 is true), and in that way controls the probability of finding any significant results in the group of tests as a whole.

Most of the time, researchers do not apply Bonferroni or other multiple-test corrections themselves. For one thing, the incentives are wrong. In most research the null hypothesis is something to argue against, and Bonferroni corrections make it harder to do so, because a true H_0 is less likely to be rejected in any test. But it is not terribly unusual for a critic to respond to picking one or a few significant results out of a long list of tests by pointing out that a multiple test correction to α is necessary before the test result is believable.

8.2.8 Publication Bias and the File-Drawer Problem

Everyone agrees that lower p-values or significance levels are better. In most disciplines and for many specific journals, there is an explicit or implicit requirement that key findings must meet a .05 significance threshold or better to merit publication. This is a necessary or "nearly necessary" condition, not sufficient; plenty of uninteresting findings pass $\alpha = .05$ but shouldn't be published anyway.

But this creates an interesting problem. Even if H_0 is true in a test, by definition 5% of the tests conducted on random samples will pass the $\alpha = .05$ threshold anyway. And even if H_0 is false, with some probability (defined by the power of the test), a test from a random sample gives a relatively high p-value anyway.

If all papers have to pass, say, $\alpha = .05$ to have a real chance of publication, then researchers who obtain "null" findings, p-values below this threshold, might as well keep their papers in their "file drawer" rather than submitting them for publication. This is true even if H_0 is false in that context (which the researcher of course never knows for sure). But researchers who obtain significant findings with p-values below .05 might think they have a credible shot at publication, so they should submit their papers. This is true even for those papers that obtain "false positives," significant results even though H_0 is true.

Given this file-drawer problem, the set of papers published in journals is a truncated sample of all papers written. It is truncated on the basis of an observed test statistic, not the true statistic in the DGP, around which the observed one is distributed with some error. This truncation introduces *publication bias*: a systematic difference between the magnitude of some effect claimed in published research and the actual effect in the DGP. The problem will be especially acute if researchers prefer to make bold, provocative claims that are likely to be false ex ante; even some of these analyses will show significant results, with probability equal to the significance level. When findings are bold as well as statistically significant, they have a good chance of publication.

Note that this bias does not occur because of fraud or dishonesty in analyzing data or reporting results. It is not a result of data fabrication and the like (not to say that such malfeasance never occurs). Nor can it be eliminated by peer review; reviewers, like authors, can only see (at most) reported p-values in the actual data at hand. The bias results from the process by which papers are selected to appear (or not appear) in peer-reviewed journals.

Formal tests for publication bias have been developed (e.g., Gerber et al. [2001]). But the main point here is that, first, a healthy skepticism is warranted about the magnitudes of effects claimed in all published research where statistical significance is a criterion for publication. Publication is necessary for communication of findings, but ironically, for a paper to be published is *bad* news about the validity of the effect sizes claimed in it. Second, the more a literature is infected by publication bias, the less likely published results in that literature are to hold up successfully under future replication by other scholars. Again, this is not because the initial published results are fraudulent or the result of malfeasance, and the ensuing debate should be conducted accordingly.

8.3 TESTS ABOUT MEANS BASED ON NORMAL SAMPLING DISTRIBUTIONS

Classical hypothesis tests all have the structure laid out thus far. To recap, the hypothesis, parameter space, and test statistics are identified, and the sampling distribution of the test statistic is connected in some way to a known (or approximated) probability distribution. Then the probability of observing something "like" the computed test statistic in the sample, or a more extreme value, can be determined, under the assumption that H_0 is true. This is a *p*-value and is a formalized report of the weight of the evidence in the sample in favor of H_0. When the *p*-value is large, the weight of the evidence in favor of the null is heavy. When the *p*-value is small, the weight of the evidence in the sample in favor of the null is light.

Depending on the test statistic $T(X)$ and the probability distribution of it under H_0, there are many specific tests that have this general structure. The question asked of the hypothesis test, in turn, determines the test statistic and the probability distribution.

Presented now are a number of examples of common and useful tests about unknown means of a DGP. The group of tests in this section share a common factor (besides the ingredients reviewed in the previous section): they all involve a test statistic that is normally distributed under H_0. These are z and t tests. In applied settings, these tests do not, except as noted, require any special information about the parametric family or functional form of the DGP for the sample observations themselves. They all rely on the central limit theorem (CLT) to show that a sample statistic is approximately normally distributed *regardless* of the parent DGP of the sample observations. This is comforting insofar as we would rather not base inference own untested assumptions about the parametric family of the DGP giving rise to the sample.

8.3.1 z Test for a Single DGP Mean

As noted in earlier chapters (e.g., Chapters 5 and 6), one of the most basic and important pieces of information about a DGP is the value of its mean. This section develops two widely used and canonical tests that test the value of a mean from a single DGP. The structure of these tests illustrates concretely how testing works, and these exact procedures are used often in testing hypotheses about slope coefficients in regression models or differences in DGP means, as explained further subsequently. This section proceeds through the logic of the test intuitively and then through the procedure of it methodically. It goes slowly and is explicit because this is our first step into formal hypothesis testing in a specific example.

When we access a dataset we don't know the DGP that created it. We can summarize all manner of features of the dataset itself, but the DGP itself is bigger than a dataset. A dataset might have a mean of 6, even though the DGP that created it has a mean of 4. And so forth.

If we happen to have a null hypothesis that the mean of the DGP is 4 and an alternative that the mean is not 4, what information bearing on these conjectures is contained in the fact that the sample mean was 6? That is the question asked by a hypothesis test about the mean of a DGP. Is 6 a big number compared to 4? If yes, the null has not fared well. If no, the null has done okay, even though the sample mean is not exactly the null hypothesized value.

Whether 6 is big compared to 4 cannot be answered without knowing the variability in the DGP. This variability tells us exactly how unusual a sample mean of 6 is, for a given sample size, when the DGP mean is 4. Suppose, for the sake of argument, that we happen to know the variance of the DGP is 16. (How would we know *this* feature of the DGP, but not its mean? This is not especially realistic. We will relax the assumption that we know this feature later in this section.) And suppose we happen to have 100 independent draws from the DGP comprising the sample, which was used to compute the sample mean $\overline{x} = 6$.

Because we are testing a hypothesis about a DGP mean, it seems sensible to use the sample mean in the test statistic $T(X)$. We know that the sample mean is an unbiased estimator. So if the null is really true, then the expected value of the sample mean is $\mu_0 = E(\overline{X}) = 4$. And with 100 iid draws in the sample when the DGP's variance is 16, we know the standard error of this estimator is $\frac{\sigma}{\sqrt{N}} = \frac{4}{10} = 0.4$. That standard error is, by definition, the standard deviation of the sample mean as a random variable.

We have not said anything yet about the DGP that gave us these 100 elements – what kind of shape does it have, or what function governs its behavior? It turns out that, for hypotheses about the sample mean in a sample with a few dozen observations or more, we don't have to say anything at all about functional form of the DGP that produced the sample.

The reason is that, because of the CLT, we know the sample mean $\overline{X}$ is approximately normally distributed, regardless of the parent DGP that generated the sample data. So by the CLT, and assuming the null hypothesis is true, we know (*i*) the expected value of the sample mean, (*ii*) the standard deviation of the sample mean, and (*iii*) the probability distribution that the sample mean follows. This distribution is (as defined in a previous chapter) the sampling distribution; the CLT says it is normal.

If $\overline{X}$ is normal with $\mu = 4$ and $\frac{\sigma}{\sqrt{N}} = 0.4$, then the standardized variable

$$Z \equiv \frac{\overline{X} - \mu}{\sigma/\sqrt{N}} \tag{8.4}$$

follows a standard normal distribution. This is called a *Z score* or *Z statistic*. This means that $\frac{6-4}{0.4} = 5$ is a draw from a standard normal distribution.

As discussed in Chapter 6, a standard normal variable Z measures the number of standard deviations a variable is away from its mean. Here, that mean is the one conjectured by the null hypothesis. The sample mean actually computed is five standard deviations away from its expectation, which is supplied by the null hypothesis. It was also noted that for any normal distribution, 99.7% of the area under the distribution is less than $\pm$ three standard deviations away from the mean. So for a normal random variable to be five standard deviations away from its mean is rare.

Of course, Chebyshev's theorem also tells us that, and it does not even rely on the assumptions behind the CLT. In particular, Chebyshev's theorem implies that the probability of drawing $\overline{X}$ five or more SEs away from μ is at most $\frac{1}{5^2} = 4\%$. Invoking the CLT to argue that the sampling distribution is normal, we can refine this to say that the probability of drawing $\overline{X}$ five or more SEs away from μ is essentially impossible, for all practical purposes in social science. So adding more assumptions and being more specific about the sampling distribution allows much stronger statements about the probability of seeing the data that was observed, if the null hypothesis is correct.

More generally, when a standard normal distribution for Z is appropriate, z scores of 2 or more (in absolute value) indicate that the data cast serious doubt on the null hypothesis when the sampling distribution is normal. Z scores of 1.6 or more (in absolute value) mean things are not looking great for the null but the doubt placed on it by the sample is less crushing. This z score of five makes the null hypothesis hard to defend.

Even disembodied from any social science content, this is interesting insofar as 6 and 4 seem like they are not too far apart. A slightly more sophisticated view of "closeness" looks at the test statistic's standard deviation, 0.4 in this case. In this light, 6 is *extremely* far from 4. In some other problem with a different DGP, it might not be; another DGP and sample would not make it so unusual to observe a sample mean of 6 with a DGP mean of 4.

So to recap: we computed a sample statistic and figured out how common such a value is if the null hypothesis is really true. This sample casts grave doubt on the null hypothesis because we almost never see samples like this, if the null hypothesis is true.

This loosely conveys the ideas of hypothesis testing. It's an intuitively appealing process, and the result makes sense. We look for the weight of the sample evidence against the null.

This test of the null hypothesis is called a *z test* for a population mean. It has this name because the test statistic is a z statistic. The test applies when we have N iid draws from a DGP in a sample with (*i*) a sample statistic is that is normally distributed with a known mean, when H_0 is true, and (*ii*) known variance of the DGP (as sometimes said, the population variance). Combined, these facts mean that a z score can be constructed and has a standard normal distribution under the null hypothesis. When σ from the DGP is known and N is "large enough," the CLT asserts that z scores constructed from the sample mean are standard-normally distributed, so this test applies when using $\overline{X}$ to test hypotheses about μ.

Formally, the test proceeds in several steps:

1. Identify the hypotheses. Here, $H_0 : \mu = 4 \equiv \mu_0$, $H_1 : \mu \neq 4$.
2. Identify the test statistic and compute it in the sample: here, $T(X) = \frac{\overline{x} - \mu_0}{\sigma/\sqrt{N}}$, and $T(x) = \frac{6-4}{4/10} = 5$. In this test, this number is the computed z score. Call it $\hat{z}$.
3. In a standard normal table, determine $\Pr[Z > \hat{z}]$ and $\Pr[Z < \hat{z}]$. Add these two numbers together; the result is the p-value.
4. Report all of this information: the sample size and mean, the population/DGP variance, the hypotheses (null and alternative), the test statistic, and the p-value.

Carrying these steps into other problems, the only component that might change is the exact value of μ_0 and the computed value of $\hat{z}$. The specification of H_0 is problem specific. Typically when this test is relevant a particular value μ_0 is an obvious choice, either by convention or substantive interest. By far the most common application of the z test is in testing the values of slope coefficients in regression models, where the default and benchmark choice for H_0 is that the slope coefficient is zero. We discuss this application of the z test later.

The foregoing procedure was for a two-tailed test. A one-tailed test is identical except for the computation of the p-value. It works as follows:

1. Identify the hypotheses. Here, $H_0 : \mu \leq 4 \equiv \mu_0$, $H_1 : \mu > 4$.
2. Identify the test statistic and compute it in the sample: here, $T(X) = \frac{\overline{x} - \mu_0}{\sigma/\sqrt{N}}$, and $T(x) = \frac{6-4}{4/10} = 5$. In this test, this number is the computed z score. Call it $\hat{z}$.
3. In a standard normal table, determine $\Pr[Z > \hat{z}]$. This is the p-value.
4. Report all of this information: the sample size and mean, the population/DGP variance, the hypotheses (null and alternative), the test statistic, and the p-value.

The only difference is in the computation of the p-value. For a one-tailed test, sample means on only one side of μ_0 count as evidence against the null. For a two-tailed test, sample means far away from μ_0 and on *either* side of it count as evidence against the null.

The one-tailed test just discussed happened to specify a null hypothesis that did not contain the sample mean. It had $H_0 : \mu \leq 4$ and $\overline{x} = 6 > 4$. There is no value in the null parameter region Θ_0 that yields the observed sample mean

$\bar{x} = 6$ as its expected value or the mode of its density. This implies sample evidence that is not rock-solid consistent with the null; the null has some explaining to do in the face of this sample. What if instead we had $H_0 : \mu \geq 4$ and $\bar{x} = 6$? Now a member of the null region Θ_0 yields 6 as the expected value of $\overline{X}$. This does not change anything about the procedure of the one-tailed test just established. It will report in a larger p-value, but that is the only change. This change makes sense: the weight of the sample evidence against this null $H_0 : \mu \geq 4$ is less than the weight of the sample evidence against $H_0 : \mu \leq 4$. So the p-value in the former case is larger.

8.3.2 t Test for a Single DGP Mean

In most applications, the defect in all of the foregoing discussion is that it assumes σ is known. The example z test above illustrates this; the example is so stylized because real-world examples with unrestricted domain and a known DGP variance are hard to come by. In reality, we usually do not know σ but must estimate it, usually with sample standard deviation S. Using S in place of σ to construct standard errors is called bootstrapping (cf. Chapter 7).

This change does not cause any real difficulty for testing practice, but it does change the test statistic used. Instead of using a z statistic $\frac{\overline{X}-\mu_0}{\sigma/\sqrt{N}}$, we can use a t statistic $\frac{\overline{X}-\mu_0}{S/\sqrt{N}}$. As noted in Chapter 7, replacing the DGP standard deviation σ with its estimate, the sample standard deviation S, changes the distribution from a standard normal to Student's t. Once the change in the test statistic is recognized, however, the test procedure is exactly the same. All of the steps and comments about p-values, one- and two-tailed tests, and so on, are the same. One would compute a t statistic in the sample, $\hat{t}$, and refer to a t table or t distribution (in practice, computer output) rather than a standard normal table to determine the p-value.

Using a t statistic rather than a z statistic makes this t *test for a population mean*. It applies when we have an iid sample with N elements, use a statistic from that sample that is approximately normally distributed with a known mean when H_0 is true, and need to estimate the variance of the DGP (and therefore the standard error of our normally distributed sample statistic).

Strictly speaking, the t statistic $\frac{\overline{X}-\mu}{S/\sqrt{N}}$ only follows Student's t distribution when the parent DGP generating the sample is normal (see Chapter 7). However, as noted in that chapter, the t distribution gives a good approximation to the sampling distribution of a t statistic even when the parent population is not normal. The key issue is the correlation between $\overline{X}$ and S; these are independent random variables for a normal DGP, and therefore the denominator of the t statistic adds unconditional noise, uncorrelated with the numerator, to the statistic. In many situations, under the null hypothesis that $\overline{X} = \mu$, the correlation between $\overline{X}$ and S is not overwhelming. The approximation is good enough that applied analysts typically invoke Student's t as the sampling distribution for the t statistic without great concern over the nonnormality of the DGP. If this does turn out to be a concern or if an analyst simply wants to double-check t test findings with a test that does not rely on normality of the DGP, the Wilcoxon rank-sum test (discussed later) is a good nonparametric option, that is, it does not make any assumptions about the DGP (it is, by the same token, less powerful; in statistics it is hard to get information for free).

A simple example is whether Americans, on average, have an accurate sense of the share of foreign-born residents in the U.S. population. The census bureau estimates that as of 2007, about 11% of the U.S. population was foreign born. In a nationally representative survey of 400 U.S. residents, Citrin and Sides [2008] asked respondents to report their belief about the share of foreign born residents in the United States. The mean response was 28% with a standard deviation of 7%. A t test is a natural approach for assessing whether the respondents are right on average or not. Clearly, of course, the mean response in the DGP is way off, and we do not need a statistical test to make that qualitative judgment. The example is still useful to illustrate the mechanics of the test and to quantify exactly how wrong Americans are about this.

If μ_0 represents the mean guess in the population that gave rise to the sample, this suggests the hypotheses $H_0 : \mu_0 = 11$ and $H_1 : \mu_0 \neq 11$. Note, again, that the hypotheses relate to unobservable parameters of the DGP behind the sample. We know for sure that the mean guess in the sample is way off. The question now is whether we can maintain the belief, in light of this sample, that Americans on average do estimate the share of foreign born residents relatively well and that the only reason the sample mean was so far off the mark was random chance in the set of people who happened to be surveyed.

The bootstrapped SE of the sample mean is $\frac{s}{\sqrt{300}} \approx 0.4$. So the test statistic is $t = \frac{28-11}{0.4} \approx 69$. The observed sample mean is about 69 bootstrapped SEs away from the value of the sample mean expected under the null hypothesis. Obviously, that is a lot. Because Student's t distribution with 299 degrees of freedom is essentially identical to a standard normal distribution, we can conclude that the p-value is 0 for all practical purposes. If the population of respondents correctly estimates the share of foreign-born residents on average, there is essentially zero chance of drawing a sample like this. Because we did in fact draw this sample, we can conclude that the population of respondents do not give a correct estimate on average, that is, H_0 is rejected at any conceivable significance level.[6] Alternatively, we could say that the mean estimate is significantly different from the true value of 11%.

Student's t and the standard normal distributions differ when the sample size is a few dozen or less. The difference is that the t distribution has thicker tails. But even if we drew a sample of size 4 with this mean and standard deviation,

---

[6] Americans are not alone in their gross misestimation of the share of foreign-born residents. Citrin and Sides [2008] noted that this sort of misestimation is common in Organisation for Economic Co-operation and Development countries, although American respondents are further off than respondents in most other countries. Respondents from France, the United Kingdom, Belgium, and the Netherlands are just about as bad.

the t statistic of 69 would still lead to rejection of H_0 under any significance level.

Usually, t tests are carried out using computer software that automatically returns a p-value in the test. With a t statistic of 69, any software would return a p-value of 0 to several decimal places. This simply means that the result is highly significant. If the test is carried out by hand, a t table must be consulted to evaluate the result. Unlike a standard normal table, which contains probabilities of drawing zs further out in the tails than any given value of z (i.e., these tables contain p-values directly), t tables contain "critical values" of the t statistic. A critical value for a hypothesis test with significance level α is not a probability but a value of the test statistic. If the test statistic meets or exceeds the critical value, the null hypothesis is rejected at the α significance level. If the test statistic is less than the critical value, the null hypothesis is not rejected at the α significance level. Typically, t tables list critical values of the t statistic for degrees of freedom (df's) ranging from 5 to 30 and at least for common significance levels $\alpha = 0.10$, 0.05, and 0.01. Usually, the critical values assume a two-tailed alternative hypothesis.

It is important to note how the significance level of a z or t test is affected by nonindependence among observations. In the case of a sample mean used in a test statistic, this effect can be seen in the relation $Var(X + Y) = Var(X) + Var(Y) + 2Cov(X, Y)$. When random variables are positively correlated, the variance of their sum exceeds the sum of their variances. Therefore, failing to account for positive correlation among members of a sample, and instead computing the standard error of the sample mean as if they were independent, overstates the precision of the mean as an estimator. It will likewise overstate the significance of findings in hypothesis tests (i.e., p-values will be understated). It makes the evidence against the null in the data appear stronger than it really is and raises the risk of falsely concluding that a theory that requires rejection of the null is useful when that theory really false (i.e., raises the probability of Type I error).

Sometimes the test statistic is so far into the rejection region that this doesn't matter; if $t = 69$ in a t test, a little correlation between sample observations will not make any difference. But in other cases, correlation within the sample well might matter. If there is a convincing story for why observations in the sample are correlated, for example, because the units in the sample interact with each other in some way, it is appropriate to be circumspect when the test statistic is close to the boundary of the rejection region, or the p-value is close to conventional cutoffs for "significance."

8.3.3 z Test for a Population Proportion

We noted in the previous subsection that the z test requires knowledge of σ, which is an unrealistic assumption when the whole point is that we don't know the DGP's properties.

There are some cases, however, when a z test is appropriate even though the DGP's variance is not known in general. Such cases arise when the null hypothesis establishes a value not only for the mean of the DGP but the variance of the DGP as well – so *if the null is true*, the variance is known, even though it is not known if the null is false.

A leading case of this is a sample of N draws from a binomial(N, p) distribution. As noted in Chapter 6, the expected value in such a distribution is Np and the variance is $Np(1 - p)$. The important thing about this is that for a given N, the same parameter p that determines the mean also determines the variance. A hypothesis that establishes the value of p is a hypothesis about the mean of the DGP, and simultaneously the variance as well. The Poisson distribution is another case of this, although invoking that distributional assumption is usually more delicate. If the sample can in principle only consist of 0's and 1's, we need only assume independence across sample observations to arrive at a binomial distribution. So for dichotomous data, it is natural to invoke a z test, not a t test, in tests about the proportion of 1's in the DGP.

The z test is relevant for proportions because they are nothing but sample means in binomial data. A proportion is computed by dividing the number of 1's in the data by N. When N is relatively large, the CLT asserts that this particular sample mean is approximately normally distributed, and under H_0, its standard error is known – it need not be estimated. Therefore the approach for a z test for a single population mean can be applied here as well.

For a concrete example, suppose a poll of 1,000 voters drawn by simple random sampling (iid draws) shows that 43% have a favorable opinion of how the president is handling his job, and the rest do not. If the true support in the population is actually dead even, what is the probability of observing sample support for option 1 *closer* to the population level than 43%?

"True support is dead even" means that we should evaluate the probabilities in question assuming 50% support for each option. This assumption about the unknown parameters allows us to evaluate the probability of observing particular values of statistics in the sample. We are looking for the probability that the sample support is within 0.07 points of 0.5; that probability is the *p*-value in a two-tailed test that the true support in the population of respondents is 50-50.

The conjecture $p = .5$ can be used to calculate the standard error of the sample proportion $\hat{p}$ as $SE_{\hat{p}} = \sqrt{\frac{(.5)(.5)}{1000}} = .0158$. The sample proportion is $z = \frac{.07}{.0158} = 4.43$ SEs away from the conjectured proportion $.5$. Locating $z = 4.43$ in the standard normal table would, if we could find it, give the probability that the actual observed proportion is further out in *one tail* than $.07$. But this probability is zero to several decimal places for such a large value of z. We would double this probability to get the probability of observing sample support more than $.07$ units away from $.50$ in absolute value. But doubling an approximate zero still gives approximately zero.

This means that, assuming the options actually have equal support, the probability of observing sample support closer to $.50$ than $.43$ is about 1.

Because we did not, in fact, observe sample support that close to .50 – and we would basically *have* to if .50 were the true level – this casts extreme doubt on the conjecture that the options each have 50% support. We have simply computed (and found to be roughly 0) the *p*-value in a two-sided hypothesis test of $p = .5$.

8.3.4 Difference in Means *t* Test

Thus far all the tests in this section have addressed whether a parameter of a DGP, estimable by a normally distributed random variable, is equal to a specific number or not. A lot of important questions that social scientists care about can be framed in that way. Yet these questions cover only a small part of hypothesis testing methodology as it is used in social science. Another large set of questions can be addressed by asking whether a specific parameter is equal in two DGPs, or whether the two DGPs have a different parameter. This requires some modification of the tools developed thus far.

Substantively, this is an important set of questions often addressed in social science and policy research. Do democracies have "more generous" welfare states than nondemocracies? Does Congress delegate more policy-making authority to bureaucrats under unified than divided government? Does Congress pass more pieces of "important" legislation under unified than divided government? Do heads of state stay in power longer in nondemocracies than democracies? Does the economy grow faster under Democratic presidents than under Republican presidents? Only substantive expertise can provide a suitable meaning to "more generous," "more important," and the like, but with that meaning established, one useful way to address such questions is with a hypothesis test.

Consider two DGPs 1 and 2, with means μ_1 and μ_2. A natural specification of the null hypothesis for all the foregoing examples – and others in this class – is $H_0 : \mu_1 = \mu_2, H_1 : \mu_1 \neq \mu_2$. This hypothesis does what the null is typically supposed to do: express skepticism about whether some variable or category has an effect on another variable. For example, this null asserts that the behavior of Congress is the same under unified and divided government. If one has a theory claiming this behavior is different, it is important to set up the null this way because it means one must overcome skepticism and show that the relationship is strong enough that it must be recognized.

To test this hypothesis consider a sample of iid observations from the two DGPs 1 and 2. Assume also that observations in sample 1 are independent of those in sample 2. The sample sizes are N_1 and N_2, the means are $\bar{x}_1$ and $\bar{x}_2$, and the standard deviations are s_1 and s_2.

Given the hypotheses, we need a test statistic with a known distribution when H_0 is true. How can we use the information so far to identify one? Each sample mean is approximately normally distributed by the CLT. Furthermore, the difference of two normal random variables is itself normal. The sample means are independent normal random variables, so their sum is also normal (the difference is just a type of sum); and by independence, their variances add to give the variance of their difference. Therefore, the test statistic

$$z_{dif} = \frac{(\bar{x}_1 - \bar{x}_2) - (\mu_1 - \mu_2)}{\sqrt{\frac{\sigma_1^2}{N_1} + \frac{\sigma_2^2}{N_2}}} \tag{8.5}$$

follows a standard normal distribution. If we knew the σs, this z statistic would provide the basis for a two-sample z test for difference in means.

In the case of a single DGP, we had good luck taking the z statistic and replacing σ with s; this gave us a t statistic. We can try the same thing here. Given $H_0 : \mu_1 = \mu_2$, we obtain the t statistic

$$t_{dif} = \frac{(\bar{X}_1 - \bar{X}_2)}{\sqrt{\frac{S_1^2}{N_1} + \frac{S_2^2}{N_2}}}. \tag{8.6}$$

This statistic is the basis for *Welch's two-sample t test*. Theoretically, this statistic actually does not exactly follow Student's t distribution, even if both parent DGPs are exactly normal. This is known as the *Behrens-Fisher problem*; if the two DGPs have different variances, the sampling distribution of t_{dif} is not known exactly. Contrast this with the one-sample case, in which, at least for a normal DGP, $t = \frac{\bar{X}-\mu}{S/\sqrt{N}}$ exactly follows Student's t distribution. Thus the statistic t_{dif} for Welch's t test only approximately follows Student's t. The main complication for applied purposes is in computing the degrees of freedom. In practice, this calculation is automated by computer software; formally, for Welch's t test, $d.f. = \frac{(s_1^2/N_1 + s_2^2/N_2)^2}{(s_1^2/N_1)^2/(N_1-1) + (s_2^2/N_2)^2/(N_2-1)}$. Because the variances in the DGPs are not assumed to be equal in this test, it is sometimes known as a *heteroscedastic t test*.

There is one special case where a t statistic for a difference in means test does exactly follow Student's t distribution. It occurs when both DGPs happen to have the same variance. In the equal variance case, the information in both samples can be pooled to estimate a single common variance. This is the basis of the *homoskedastic, equal variance, or pooled variance t test*. To form this test statistic, first compute the pooled standard deviation as $S_p = \sqrt{\frac{(N_1-1)S_1^2 + (N_2-1)S_2^2}{N_1+N_2-2}}$. This is simply a weighted average of the standard deviation from each sample, where the weights are given by the sample sizes. The pooled variance t statistic is then formed as

$$t_p = \frac{\bar{X}_1 - \bar{X}_2}{S_p\sqrt{1/N_1 + 1/N_2}}, \tag{8.7}$$

which follows Student's t with $N_1 + N_2 - 2$ d.f.'s. Equal variance is often simply assumed or asserted in this test, although this too is a hypothesis that can be tested (in an F test, discussed later).

One way or the other, heteroscedastic or homoscedastic, we now have a test statistic, and at least an approximate sampling distribution for it under the null hypothesis of equal means in the DGPs. It bears repeating that the sampling distribution is valid assuming that the samples are statistically independent. With these ingredients in hand, the test proceeds as in the one-sample t test. We simply calculate (or have a computer calculate) the test statistic in a given dataset, and refer to a t table (or have a computer do it) to determine the p-value. This p-value reflects the probability of observing a test statistic further away from its expected value under the null than the test statistic actually observed in the sample, as always.

A finding of significant difference in a difference in means test is a finding of a type of relationship. The two DGPs being compared may represent two treatments, in the experimental terminology. Divided and unified government are alternative "treatments" of sorts, and all these questions about Congress doing more of something under unified than divided government are interesting because divided government may have a causal effect in a separation of powers system that we can identify statistically and make sense of theoretically. Finding that causal effect is at some level the payoff of empirical research.

But if someone were to find a significant difference in the amount of some activity under these types of government, it would not be a finding that divided government causes the difference. It is a finding of association between divided government and the outcome variable, and as such, is subject to the whole battery of interpretations of association. Causation is only one. When causal effects are in question, the researcher's job is not just to establish a statistical relationship but to argue that other alternative explanations cannot account for the relationship while a plausible theory of the treatment effect can.

8.3.5 Difference in Proportions z Test

Consider a sequence consisting of N_1 iid draws, all 0's or 1's, of one random variable Y_1, and a sequence consisting of N_2 iid draws, again all 0's and 1's, of another variable Y_2. Each random variable i has a probability π_i of coming out as 1 in any independent draw and $1 - \pi_i$ of coming out 0. This probability π_i is also the expected value of the random variable in any given observation, and $\pi_i(1 - \pi_i)$ is the variance of the random variable in any given observation.

Each sequence of draws is a random sample from a DGP defined by π_i. Each sample has a proportion of 1's denoted p_i; this is the tally of 1's in the sample divided by N_i. It is also the sample mean $\overline{X}$. As such, the CLT ensures that the sample proportion for each sample is approximately normally distributed.

An important substantive question in many cases is whether $\pi_1 = \pi_2$. That is, do the DGPs underlying each random sample have the same expected value? Examples are easy to construct: in the United States, is the president more likely to veto a bill under divided than unified government? Or more likely to veto a piece of "major legislation" than ordinary legislation? Are pairs of contiguous democratic states less likely to experience militarized conflict than pairs of contiguous states in which at least one member is not a democracy? In parliamentary democracies, are minority coalitions more likely to dissolve under a no-confidence vote than majority party governments? Is democracy more likely to take root in a state with low income inequality than with high income inequality?

All of these questions involve the phrase "more likely." They are comparisons of the chance of an event under two sets of conditions (or more if desired). There are a variety of other statistical approaches to answering some of these questions that have been pursued in the respective literatures, but all of them are (*i*) interesting and (*ii*) comparisons of chances in DGPs.

Most often, an analyst would approach these questions with a theory asserting that the conditions do indeed make a difference for the chance of the event in question, for example, that divided government does indeed raise the likelihood of a president vetoing legislation in the U.S. Therefore, the claim is convincing when it can overcome skepticism about the claim. When the claim is "these conditions have an effect," the skeptical response is "no they don't."

That skepticism is expressed in the null hypothesis $H_0 : \pi_1 = \pi_2$. The alternative will typically be two-sided, $H_1 : \pi_1 \neq \pi_2$, for reasons discussed above for the z test for a population mean, but the most important thing is to state clearly what the alternative is when reporting a p-value.

Assuming H_0 is true, we know the variances of the DGPs for each single observation are equal. So we can pool all observations to estimate the standard error of each sample proportion.

8.3.6 Matched Pairs t Test

In some research designs, an analyst observes a unit with a treatment and without it. This occurs if a collection of units is each observed, and its behavior on some outcome variable recorded, before treatment and again after treatment. The before-treatment observations then serve as a kind of control against which the after-treatment observations can be assessed.

Consider a group of states that signs a treaty: their behavior on the treaty-controlled policy measure can be observed both before and after the treatment. The *matched pairs* approach is a way of using each unit as its own control, holding constant for purposes of treatment evaluation any idiosyncratic individual-level effects on the outcome variable. This is a *within-subjects* comparison.[7] If the first observation for a given unit provides some information about its second observation (i.e., observations are positively correlated within unit) – say, a state with above average pretreaty nuclear capability is likely to have above average posttreaty capability – then a matched pairs test has

---

[7] In contrast, *between-subjects* comparisons attempt to use different subjects as controls for each other.

greater power than a two-sample test using the same data (taking pretreatment observations as the first sample and posttreatment observations as the second). This is its principal advantage.

A matched pairs t test is as simple to perform as any t test. For each unit i observed, compute the difference d_i in the pre- and posttreatment outcome measures. Then take this set of differences, one for each unit, as a sequence of observations in a garden-variety t test for a single population mean: compute the mean $\bar{d}$ of the difference variable and the standard deviation s_d of the difference variable. Use these and the number of units N (i.e., sample size) to construct a t statistic. A test of the null hypothesis that this statistic is zero against a one- or two-sided alternative is a matched pairs t test that the intervention or treatment has no effect.

This language about treatment effects can be deceptive. A finding of significant differences in the treated and untreated groups is, once again, a finding of an association. Such a finding cannot explain the association in causal terms by itself. Simply performing a matched pairs t test does not do anything to establish exogeneity of the treatment or rule out intervening variables. The hypothesis test takes the research design as given; it does not correct the flaws in a weak design. A significant result in a matched pairs t test does not by itself justify causal claims.

The case of treaty signatories is again a good example. The behavior of the signatories may be different after signing than before it. Does that mean signing the treaty caused the change? The relationship itself does not demonstrate this (see Simmons and Hopkins [2005], Von Stein [2005]). It is also possible that the signatories expected a change in the variable the treaty is designed to control – and signed it with knowledge of this – in hopes that they might gain some credibility or good faith with other states, while avoiding serious economic hardship. The Montreal Protocol on chlorofluorocarbons (CFCs) is a case in point: the United States signed the treaty with full knowledge that aerosol makers were capable of developing alternative propellants for spray cans without much hardship. By signing the treaty, was it binding its future self, or was it taking advantage of an autonomous, unrelated development to gain some credit in international environmental politics? Maybe an international relations expert on treaties knows the answer to this, and maybe it is absurd. The point is that such absurdity (if in fact it is) is not demonstrated by a significant difference in the CFC emissions of a nation-state before and after signing the treaty. It could be expectation of a change in emission that made signing the treaty benign.

8.4 TESTS BASED ON A NORMAL DGP

Whereas the previous section dealt with tests in which $T(X)$ is approximately normally distributed (invoking the CLT to justify this), in this section we cover tests that, strictly speaking, assume that *the DGP itself* is normally distributed.

These are tests about the variance of the DGP. These variance tests invoke the χ^2 or F distributions for their test statistics, and, as discussed in Chapter 7, this actually does require the parent DGP to be normal or reasonably close to it. These tests can handle some departures from exact normality in the DGP, but the approximation breaks down unless the DGPs exhibit sufficient symmetry (Casella and Berger [2002]).

8.4.1 Single Variance χ^2 Test

Central tendency, the focus of all formal tests developed so far, is only one of many features of a distribution. It is an important one, especially when dealing with systematic part of random variables, but it is still only one feature. Sometimes a researcher's real interest is in the variability of a random variable.

Suppose that the sample observations are iid draws from a normal distribution, that is, $X_i \sim N(\mu, \sigma)$, $X_i \perp X_j, \forall i, j$. We saw in Chapter 7 that in such a case the sample variance is part of a statistic, specifically $\frac{(n-1)s^2}{\sigma^2}$, that follows a χ^2 distribution. That this statistic involves *both* the population variance σ^2 and has a known probability distribution (to wit, a χ^2) makes it valuable for making inferences about σ^2 using s^2, the same way we make inferences about the population mean μ using $\bar{x}$.

In particular, with a guess about the true value of σ^2, we expect $\frac{(n-1)s^2}{\sigma^2}$ to be small if that guess is correct. We can explicitly characterize which values of this quantity are "small" because we know the distribution from which $\frac{(n-1)s^2}{\sigma^2}$ comes. So if we assume some specific value of σ^2 and, based on a sample, compute a value of $\frac{(n-1)s^2}{\sigma^2}$ so large that the probability of observing that value (or larger) under the χ^2 is too small for our taste, say less than .01, we might want to reject our initial guess about σ^2 as inconsistent with the data. That's a bit of a mouthful, but it is exactly what classical/frequentist hypothesis testing is all about.

To be more formal, for the iid $N(\mu, \sigma)$ draws, consider $H_0 : \sigma \leq \sigma_0$, $H_1 : \sigma > \sigma_0$. Then if H_0 is true the test statistic $T(X) = \frac{(N-1)S^2}{\sigma_0^2}$ has a χ^2 distribution. In a specific case, one computes s and $T(x)$, and refers to a χ^2 table to determine $\Pr[T(X) > T(x)|\sigma = \sigma_0]$. This is the probability of observing a test statistic more extreme than the one actually observed, if H_0 is actually true – otherwise known as a p-value.

8.4.2 Difference in Variance F Test

An F distribution is natural for comparing two variances. For example, because the t statistic for a difference-in-means inference (as described in the previous section) depends on whether the two groups have the same variance, it can be useful to perform an F test to see. The initial conjecture is that the two samples are from populations with the same variance; then, all else constant, a large value of the computed F statistic – based on the respective sample sizes and sample variances s^2 – casts doubt on that assumption, but a small value does not. In this context, an F test, like a χ^2, is relatively sensitive to departures from normality in the underlying population distribution.

Consider, for example, the proportion of the vote for the Democratic presidential candidate in U.S. states. Taking each state as a single observation and pooling all (presidential election) years from 1900 to 2004 inclusive, Democratic presidential vote share turns out to be approximately normally distributed. Its mean is 46.97% and its standard deviation is 14.11%. There are 1,300 state-year observations in this sample.

What is it a sample from? Clearly there is only one United States over this period and it had a fixed collection of states. It is not as if there is a larger set of results out there and we have accessed a small part of it. This is the entirety of the one and only realization of history as far as state Democratic presidential vote share is concerned. Yet it would be outlandish in the extreme to assert that we have a complete theory of Democratic presidential vote share at the state level over this time period. Conditional on any set of explanatory factors, we remain uncertain as to what caused state-to-state variation in vote shares. In one sense, this is literally the definition of random, making the state-level vote share a random variable. We have some realizations of it, and we can measure the central tendency and variability of those realizations. They appear to follow a normal distribution, and a test that they do cannot reject the null hypothesis of normality.

The variability of state Democratic presidential vote share is interesting because it says something about local variation in political party strength and political leanings. Was the variance of state Democratic presidential vote share different in the early part of the century than the later part? The most important consequence of randomness explained in the previous paragraph is that the sample variances might be different even if the variances in the DGPs for the early and late periods were identical. In other words, looking only at the trajectory of history as it unfolded and comparing the numbers measuring variability in the early part of the century and variability in the late part without accounting for randomness behind the data, we can easily fool ourselves. The standard deviations are going to be different, at least a little, and with no accounting for uncertainty, that would be the end of things. We would conclude there is a difference, even if there is not.

Given normally distributed data, an F test is a natural way to explore this while accounting for randomness behind the observed data. Lacking a theory to explain the difference, we have no reason to expect the variance to have increased or decreased. A natural test is $H_0 : S^2_{early} = S^2_{late}$ versus $S^2_{early} \neq S^2_{late}$, where "early" includes years 1900–1944 and late includes 1948–2004. There are 556 early observations, with a mean Democratic presidential vote share of 50.31% and standard deviation $S = 17.89\%$. There are 744 late observations, with a mean Democratic presidential vote share of 44.47% and standard deviation $S = 9.72\%$. The ratio $\frac{S^2_{early}}{S^2_{late}}$ follows an F distribution with $(555, 743)$

degrees of freedom, if the null hypothesis of equal variance is true. The observed value of the test statistic in this sample is $\frac{320}{94.5} = 3.39$. The p-value is absurdly small. Thus, the variance in state-level Democratic presidential vote share has been significantly smaller since World War II than during and before it. How to account for this change is obviously not our point here (although the fall of the Solid South is probably a good place to start), but it is an interesting case of apparent homogenization of presidential politics across geographic units that used to be much more disparate.

8.5 TESTS ABOUT REGRESSION COEFFICIENTS

Our development of the core methods of hypothesis testing has thus far focused on tests about a single parameter of an unconditional DGP (i.e., μ or σ^2) or comparisons of those parameters from two DGPs (differences in μs or ratios of σ^2s). This is useful to understand the methods and sometimes interesting in actual research (especially the tests for comparing parameters).

However, in applied research using statistical models, by far the most common application of hypothesis testing deals with slope (sometimes intercept) parameters in regression models. So in this section, we extend the hypothesis testing methodology to deal with this. As we will see, the extensions are not so onerous because common estimation approaches for regression such as OLS imply that estimated slopes $\hat{\beta}$ are approximately normally distributed. So the z and t test methodology laid out earlier, as well as the F test, is the coin of the realm in tests about regression slopes as well.

8.5.1 z and t Tests for Regression Coefficients

One of the pitfalls of using regression coefficients computed from a sample to explore relationships between Y and X in the DGP is that $\hat{\beta} \neq 0$ is possible even if $\beta = 0$. Thus a sample may, by random chance, indicate that X and Y appear correlated in the data even if they are uncorrelated in the DGP. If an analyst has a theory asserting that X and Y are correlated, and this type of false support for that theory is obtained, it raises the possibility of Type I error, of concluding that a theory has some explanatory power when in fact it does not. Hypothesis testing in regression models is designed to account for this problem.

The hypothesis testing methodology developed so far in this section allows for tests that a normally distributed random variable is equal to a specific, fixed number. Perhaps the most common application of this methodology in quantitative social science is in testing for an effect of an explanatory variable on a dependent variable in a regression model. This is simply a test that the slope coefficient for that covariate is nonzero.

Recall that regression models allow a link between the systematic part of a random variable Y and a set of explanatory variables. That is, they specify the conditional mean of Y as a function of given covariates. Is a change in a covariate associated with an increase, decrease, or no change in the expected value of Y? If there is a change in $E(Y|X)$, how big is it? These are some of the questions that regression models are useful for answering.

Because the OLS regression coefficient $\widehat{\beta}$ is a weighted sum of the dependent variable (Chapter 7), by the CLT, it has an approximately normal sampling distribution. This does not result from the DGP of $Y|X$; it results to the extent that $\widehat{\beta}$ is a weighted sum of not-too-highly-correlated draws of Y_i. This fact makes it simple to test hypotheses about individual slope coefficients in the regression model.

To know when tests resulting from this approach are believable, it is important to know the theory behind the sampling distribution. This tells us what assumptions we need to swallow to believe the results. The assumption of normal Ys is not necessary to get an approximately normal distribution of $\widehat{\beta}$ as long as the sample size is relatively large (several dozen) and the observations of Y_i are reasonably close to independent. These are the conditions for the approximation by normality under the CLT credible. To make sure the sampling distribution is centered in the right place, the actual value of β from the DGP, we need to assume that a linear function of $E(Y|X)$ in the DGP is about right and that all covariates are exogenous. Without these assumptions, the close approximation of the sampling distribution to normal is really irrelevant; it is a fast train to the wrong station.

The starting point for many investigations of regression models is whether one covariate has a significant effect on the dependent variable, holding other covariates constant. When a theory asserts a relationship between two variables, such a significant effect is an important result to demonstrate. A hypothesis test about whether a regression coefficient is zero helps to establish that the relationship between dependent variable and covariate is not simply picking up the effect of chance variation in Y.

For this reason, the conventional (and default, in most computer programs) null hypothesis is $H_0 : \beta = 0$. The point of tests for regression coefficients is to evaluate how credible this hypothesis is, in light of the observed $\widehat{\beta}$. If $\widehat{\beta}$ is more than a couple SEs away from 0, this null hypothesis is not credible; the data casts doubt on it.

Because $\widehat{\beta}$ is approximately normal, assuming that the model's error variance is known, common across all observations, and equal to σ^2, the z statistic for a regression slope is simply

$$Z_{\widehat{\beta}} = \frac{\widehat{\beta} - \beta_0}{\frac{\sigma}{\sqrt{N-1}s_x}}, \tag{8.8}$$

where β_0 is supplied by H_0. The denominator is the OLS regression standard error, as in Equation 7.12. This z score follows a standard normal distribution. It can be used in hypothesis testing exactly as the z statistic was used for the mean.

As always, the z statistic assumes that σ in the DGP is known. When the Ys all have the same variance conditional on covariates (i.e., homoskedasticity holds), but it must be estimated from the resdiuals, we enter t statistic land. For OLS slopes,

$$T_{\widehat{\beta}} = \frac{\widehat{\beta} - \beta_0}{\frac{s_e}{\sqrt{N-1}s_x}}. \tag{8.9}$$

The approach to hypothesis testing is again the same as with the t statistic for means, except in the regression model, the t statistic has $N - k$ degrees of freedom, where N is the sample size and k is the number of slopes plus one (for the intercept), that is, the total number of parameters estimated.

As noted, the "ordinary" t statistic for regression slopes assumes homoskedasticity. Under heteroskedasticity, we can use the Huber-White or heteroskedasticity consistent standard errors defined in Equation 7.18 to construct the *heteroskedasticity consistent t statistic*,

$$T_{\widehat{\beta}}^{HC} = \frac{\widehat{\beta} - \beta_0}{\sqrt{\frac{\sum((x_i-\bar{x})e_i)^2}{(N-1)s_x^2}}}. \tag{8.10}$$

This is still a t statistic, so the testing methodology and interpretation of results is the same as for any other t statistic. Heteroskedasticity only changes the standard errors we use to get to a t statistic in the first place. Likewise for other OLS standard errors that are robust to failures of iid (e.g., Newey-West standard errors for serial correlation or panel corrected standard errors for iid failures in panel data; see Chapter 7), the standard error used to compute a t statistic changes, but everything else about hypothesis testing stays the same.

These z and t statistics apply to the case of a bivariate regression model. In a multiple regression model, every covariate j has its attendant $\widehat{\beta}_j$ and a standard error for that specific $\widehat{\beta}_j$. Thus each parameter β_j can be subject to its own hypothesis test about its value, with t statistics computed the same as shown previously (except the standard errors change again because they are more complicated than these in multivariate models).

Typically, computer packages report several pieces of information for each covariate j: its estimated slope $\widehat{\beta}_j$, its estimated standard error (according to whatever assumptions about heteroskedasticity the researcher has invoked in computer commands), the t statistic, and the p-value in a hypothesis test with $H_0 : \beta_j = 0$.

For linear models of $E(Y|X)$, the variance of Y (or ε) given X has to be estimated,[8] so linear regression models almost always work with t statistics. On the other hand, for some DGPs in generalized linear models, knowing $E(Y)$ also implies that $Var(Y)$ is also known. In these cases, when H_0 pins

---

[8] The issue is not the functional form per se, but rather that the restriction on the conditional DGP mean in H_0 are not also restrictions on the conditional DGP variance in these models.

down $E(Y|X) = E(Y)$ for each X, $Var(Y)$ is also pinned down by H_0 for free; it need not be estimated under H_0. So in models with this characteristic, researchers use (and computers report) z statistics, not t statistics. In Chapter 6, we saw that this property holds for, among others, the Bernoulli, Poisson, and exponential distributions. So in logit, Poisson, and exponential hazard models, hypothesis tests for each β_j are based on z statistics.

For instance, take a Poisson model, where $E(Y) = Var(Y) = \lambda$ and $\ln(E(Y|X)) = \alpha + \beta_X X$. The conventional null hypothesis says $H_0 : \beta_X = 0$. If H_0 is true, then $E(Y|x) = e^{\alpha}$, $\forall x$, which means $E(Y|X)$ is not a function of X, so $E(Y) = e^{\alpha}$. Then $Var(Y) = e^{\alpha}$ too. In this way, H_0 in this model implies that $Var(Y)$ need not be separately estimated.

There's something a little bit strange here. We have studied the sampling distribution of $\widehat{\beta}$ for OLS in some depth but have not yet studied the sampling distribution from generalized linear models at all. So it's strange that we're addressing the standard error of a test statistic before addressing any other aspects of the sampling distribution. We cover this in more detail in Chapter 9, under maximum likelihood estimation. But while we're on the topic of the need to estimate error variances in linear regression models, it is worth noting that this is not true for other kinds of regression models.

A Note on Reporting Model Results

When reporting results from regression models, researchers often cull some of information from computer output for presentation. Many researchers report just two numbers for each explanatory variable j: the value $\widehat{\beta}_j$, and the (estimated) standard error of that slope coefficient. These two numbers are sufficient for testing the null hypothesis that the slope coefficient in the DGP is equal to any particular number. For example, if the null hypothesis is $H_0 : \beta = 0$, simply divide the sample regression coefficient $\hat{\beta}$ by the estimated standard error to obtain the t statistic for that covariate. A simple rule of thumb is that if the coefficient is twice as large in absolute value as the estimated standard error, the slope coefficient is significantly different from zero. Most analysts simply say that such a coefficient "is significant."

It is handy for readers to have a table with results from one or more models, especially if they have the same covariates or the same dependent variable. To actually communicate the relevant information to the reader, the table must contain, at minimum, the sample size N used for each model, and $\widehat{\beta}_j$ and $\widehat{SE}(\widehat{\beta}_j)$ for each variable j as well as the intercept. This is true for results from any model, whether linear regression, logit, Poisson, exponential hazards, or otherwise. For OLS results, the table should also include the R^2; for other models, it should include some other measure of goodness of fit if a sensible one is available (I say a bit more about some of these in Chapter 9).

All of this should be considered nonnegotiable. Other results such as t/z statistics, p-values, confidence intervals (see Chapter 9), and little stars or asterisks on the coefficients to indicate significance may be helpful too and should be included as space allows and their informativeness to the reader dictates. Then, in the words surrounding this table, the results should be inter-preted narratively – in terms of the substantive impact each variable has on the dependent variable, of statistical signficance, and of the overall takeaway for whatever theory motivated the use of this model in the first place.

8.5.2 Comparing Regression Slopes

Theories do not have to end with claims about the list of explanatory factors that affect $E(Y|X)$ or some other attribute of the DGP. They may imply that one variable has a bigger effect on $E(Y|X)$ (etc.) than another one. A theory of intergenerational transmission of economic opportunity might imply that an individual's socioeconomic class is affected more by his or her parents' socioeconomic class than by his or her own educational attainment. Or a theory of voter mobilization may imply that appeals to vote by a candidate matter less for influencing the decision to vote than appeals by a voter's friends. If X represents the number of appeals by a candidate and Z the number of appeals by friends, this is not only an assertion that $E(Y|X) = \alpha + \beta_X X + \beta_Z Z$. It is also an assertion that $\beta_Z > \beta_X$.

Because $\widehat{\beta}_X$ and $\widehat{\beta}_Z$ are both draws of random variables, it is clearly not sufficient to claim support for this theory by pointing out that the latter is larger than the former in a list of OLS regression coefficients computed from a sample. It is possible to obtain this result by chance, even if the theory is wrong. The comparison also cannot be made by pooling the standard errors of the two $\widehat{\beta}$s, because this ignores that they may be correlated with each other.

The hypothesis is about the quantity $\beta_X - \beta_Z$. The natural null hypothesis is that $\beta_X - \beta_Z = 0$, so the numerator of a t statistic to test this null hypothesis is simply $\widehat{\beta}_X - \widehat{\beta}_Z$. This is just like the situation for testing a difference in means. What is needed is a standard error of the difference in the two $\widehat{\beta}$s.

We have noted a couple times that for random variables X and Y, $Var(X + Y) = Var(X) + Var(Y) + 2Cov(X, Y)$. The same result applies here. If X and Z are correlated, $Cov(\widehat{\beta}_X, \widehat{\beta}_Z) \neq 0$. So we can't just pool the standard error of each $\widehat{\beta}$ somehow to get the standard error of their difference.

Information about this covariance is captured in the *variance–covariance matrix* for OLS coefficients. If there are two slopes and one intercept in the model, this is a 3×3 matrix. Moving diagonally from the upper left to the lower right of this matrix, the components capture the variance of $\widehat{\alpha}$, $\widehat{\beta}_X$, and $\widehat{\beta}_Z$. Off this diagonal, the components capture each pair of covariances between these estimators. The covariance of $\widehat{\beta}_X$ and $\widehat{\beta}_Z$ can be obtained from this matrix to pin down $Var(\widehat{\beta}_X - \widehat{\beta}_Z)$, and the square root of this is the standard error we need for the t test comparing β_X and β_Z.

Beyond that, at this point, we can leave the details for the computer to figure out. Computer software packages automatically compute the variance–covariance matrix of the $\widehat{\beta}$'s to determine their standard errors. Any good dedicated statistics software package will have a way to test $H_0 : \beta_X = \beta_Z$.

Even with a "bad" statistics package by this standard, all is not lost. Let $\delta \equiv \beta_X - \beta_Z$; then it is also true that $\beta_X = \delta + \beta_Z$. We can use this to replace β_X in the postulated model and obtain $E(Y \mid X, Z) = \alpha + (\delta + \beta_Z)X + \beta_Z Z$, or $E(Y \mid X, Z) = \alpha + \delta X + \beta_Z(X + Z)$. The null hypothesis is $\delta = 0$, and if $\beta_Z > \beta_X$, then $\delta < 0$.

This model can be directly estimated by OLS, where the researcher uses observed values of X and observed values of $(X + Z)$ as covariates. This model gives an estimate of δ and its standard error, and these in turn determine the p-value in its t test. The null hypothesis $\delta = 0$ is exactly what we wanted to test in the first place. So we could have avoided the heartache about the variance–covariance matrix of $\widehat{\beta}$ by expressing the model differently, but this is a good place to introduce the concept anyway. Either way, a comparison of β_Z and β_X cannot reasonably be made simply by eyeballing their respective OLS estimates.

But why stop at comparing two slopes within the same model? In some cases, we have reason to compare slope coefficients from two models estimated from two datasets. For example, one might compare the effect of parents' socioeconomic (SES) class on their childrens' socioeconomic class in the United States, in, say, 1960 versus 2010. If child's SES (as an adult) is the dependent variable, and parents' SES (in the previous generation) the covariate, data from 1960 allows estimation of an effect of parent on child for that year, and likewise for 2010. Then given these estimates, we could compare $\widehat{\beta}^{1960}$ and $\widehat{\beta}^{2010}$. A hypothesis test is required because the estimated parameter from both years is a draw from the respective sampling distributions of those parameters. The question is substantively interesting because it says something about the change in intergenerational transmission of social class and economic opportunity over time in the Land of Opportunity.

As another example Gailmard and Jenkins [2007] showed that the success rate of the majority party on bills in the U.S. Senate is affected by ideological disagreements with the minority party in about the same way as the success rate of the majority party in the U.S. House of Representatives. This is interesting because it runs counter to the conventional wisdom in political science that the House majority party is, for a variety of institutional reasons, better able to foist its will on the whole chamber than the Senate majority party.

The comparison begins with two models, one for each chamber. We estimated a model of the majority party success rate on bills in the Senate, as a function of ideological disagreement with the minority party as well as other covariates.[9] Call the estimated slope term on ideological disagreement with the minority in this Senate model $\widehat{\beta}^S$. Then we estimated an analogous model

---

[9] Actually the comparison began with measurement of several amorphous concepts, including "majority party success on chamber bills" and "ideological disagreement with the minority party." Both of these concepts had reasonably accepted operationalizations from prior work in the literature. But those are substantive issues in the American politics literature so they are best set aside here.

for the House of Representatives and obtained the analogous slope $\widehat{\beta}^H$ in that model.

The substantive question is this: in the respective DGPs for the House and Senate data, is $\beta^S = \beta^H$? The variance–covariance matrices for the respective OLS models for the House and Senate do not contain information necessary to establish $Cov(\widehat{\beta}^S, \widehat{\beta}^H)$. We proceeded with something called a *Wald test*. The details, although not exceedingly complicated in their basics, are beyond our scope at this point, except to note that this type of test is useful for making comparisons of parameters across models.

Another approach using the testing methodology developed above would also be possible. We could have combined all the data from the House and the Senate into one "grand sample." In this dataset, we could have defined a "Senate dummy" that equals 1 for observations drawn from the Senate, and 0 for observations drawn from the House. Let X denote the relevant covariate on majority–minority party disagreement, and S the Senate dummy. Note that $1 - S$ is, in effect, a "House dummy."

Then we could have included an interaction term for XS and $X(1 - S)$, as well as the dummies S and $1 - S$ themselves, and estimated the single model with four covariates: $E(Y \mid X) = \alpha_H(1 - S) + \alpha_S S + \beta_X^H X(1 - S) + \beta_X^S XS$. (This model ignores all other covariates we used to make the exposition simpler.) This model uses only Senate observations to estimate β_X^S, because $S = 1$ is required for that term to actually enter the equation. And it uses only House observations to estimate β_X^H. The term α_H is a House-specific intercept and α_S is a Senate-specific intercept. There is no overall intercept because it is redundant with the two chamber-specific intercepts.

With this model the hypothesis test on $\beta_X^S - \beta_X^H$ could have been executed on the basis of the method developed earlier for comparing parameters within a model. In small samples, this would generally yield different p-values than the Wald test. Note that the size of the grand sample of House and Senate observations would be used for N in computing standard errors, so that estimates have a sort of "undeserved" precision in this approach. But it is relatively straightforward to implement.

This subsection illustrates two points. First, when comparing slope terms in a model, a hypothesis test is required because all we can observe about those terms are draws of random variables, and we must account for the possibility that these may differ by chance alone. Second, to actually implement these tests, usually several approaches are possible, and it may be possible to fit them into the "standard" methodology for tests in regression models by redefining the model a bit.

8.5.3 *F* Tests in Regression

The tests for regression we've encountered thus far capture a wide array of possible arguments about DGPs. They can be boiled down to two forms:

testing whether slope terms are each equal to a particular number ($\beta_X = 0$ for the typical H_0 we've seen), and testing whether slope terms are equal to each other. Perhaps surprisingly, these tests do not cover the case of whether a group of parameters are simultaneously equal to each other and to a particular number. A hypothesis like this entails a joint restriction on several parameters at the same time.

The F test handles this task well. In brief, the idea is to estimate a model that ignores the hypothesis and determine its explanatory power for Y. Then estimate a model that is identical except that the restriction in the hypothesis is imposed and determine its explanatory power for Y. The point is that if the hypothesis is correct, the explanatory power of the model with the hypothesis imposed on it should not be much smaller than the explanatory power of the model without the hypothesis imposed.

The default example of an F test in OLS regression is that in the model $E(Y|X, Z) = \alpha + \beta_X X + \beta_Z Z$, $H_0 : \beta_X = \beta_Z = 0$. If the null is correct, the actual model is $E(Y|X) = \alpha$. The null says that the whole set of covariates, as a group, has no explanatory power for Y. If that is true, then R^2 from the "smaller" model should not be much lower than R^2 from the "larger" model.

Now, the F test is about comparing variances, as we saw earlier. Here's where that comparison comes in: for a given set of observations of Y, comparing the R^2's from the models is just another way to compare the error variances. The R^2s of the smaller and larger models have the same denominator (variance of ys). They might differ but only in their numerators – the variance of the residuals. The variance of the residuals, of course, is just a sample estimate of the variance of the errors in the DGP. So the F test is a way to compare the variances of the errors in the smaller and larger models.

This $H_0 : \beta_X = \beta_Z = 0$ is different from either the pair of hypotheses $H_0^X : \beta_X = 0$ and $H_0^Z : \beta_Z = 0$, or the hypothesis that $\beta_X = \beta_Z$. The former ignores the simultaneity of the H_0 we're looking at now, and the latter ignores that we are asking whether the parameters are both 0.

The null hypothesis imposes a set of *linear restrictions* on the model. A linear restriction is a system of equations, where each one of them says that a linear combination of some parameters is 0. The "smaller" model is called the *restricted model* and the "larger" one is the *unrestricted model*. Imposing linear restrictions is what creates a nested model. The restricted model is sometimes said to be *nested* in the unrestricted one. Of course, it is impossible for the restricted model to have a larger R^2 than the unrestricted one. If H_0 is correct, they will have the same R^2. But neither X nor Z nor their pair can actively remove information about Y; they cannot (individually or as a pair) have negative explanatory power.

Formally, consider a sample of size N, an unrestricted model with k parameters including the intercept and a null hypothesis that restricts the value of r parameters. Let R_0^2 denote the R^2 from the model with the restrictions in H_0

imposed, and R_1^2 the unrestricted model. Then the mathematical form of this F statistic is

$$F = \frac{(R_1^2 - R_0^2)/r}{(1 - R_1^2)/(N - k)},$$ (8.11)

where r are the numerator degrees of freedom and $N - k$ are the denominator degrees of freedom. The numerator captures the amount of fit gained by dropping the restrictions in H_0. The null hypothesis implies that this should be about 0. The denominator captures the degree to which Y's variance is not explained even by the unrestricted model. It gives a way to norm the gain in explanatory power under the unrestricted model. If even the unrestricted model has low explanatory power, then its gains relative to the unrestricted model are still relatively unimportant for explaining Y's variance.

The default F statistic in OLS regression is from the test that all slopes are simultaneously 0. But all manner of linear restrictions can be fit into the F test framework. An example, in fact, is another way to test the null hypothesis that $\beta_X = \beta_Z$. Imposing this restriction gives the model $E(Y|X) = \alpha + \beta(X + Z)$. So a researcher could estimate the unrestricted model $E(Y|X) = \alpha + \beta_X X + \beta_Z Z$, then define the new variable $x + z$ in the dataset and estimate the restricted model. If this null is correct, the loss of fit should be small. However, a large loss of fit alone does not provide information about which slope is larger, whereas a t statistic does this automatically (through its sign).

8.6 EXAMPLE: PUBLIC DEBT AND GROSS DOMESTIC PRODUCT GROWTH

In this section, we explore the application of the hypothesis testing methods developed earlier in a linear regression model. We will see how researchers execute and interpret hypothesis tests for individual regression coefficients, how substantive theories are sometimes translated into comparisons of regression coefficients, and how those comparisons can be done statistically in a hypothesis test.

The application concerns the effect of the public debt a country carries on its economic growth. Reinhart and Rogoff [2010] wrote an influential paper arguing that when a country's public debt grows relative to its gross domestic product, its economic growth suffers. They also argued more specifically that when the ratio of public debt to GDP exceeds 90%, the GDP growth rate in that country is significantly lower (essentially 0 or slightly negative) than for countries that carry lower debt to GDP ratios.

This is immensely important for ongoing debates about the benefits and costs of retrenchment in public spending in the wake of the economic crisis that began in 2008. Of course, for policy purposes, the ultimate importance of Reinhart and Rogoff's argument is about causation. What we need to know is, if a country lowers its debt/GDP ratio, will that cause an improvement in its economic performance or not? A strenuous theoretical debate took off in the economics literature on this point. Reinhart and Rogoff purported to show that the observable evidence squares with the theory that high debt does indeed lower economic growth. Their research design consists of cross-national regressions; the unit of analysis is a country-year. This is not a strong design from the standpoint of demonstrating causation itself (see Chapter 10), but because the prevailing theories seem to point in opposite directions about the effect of debt/GDP on economic growth, the correlational evidence alone is still important for adjudicating which theory better explains empirical observation.

Herndon et al. [2013] replicated the analysis of Reinhart and Rogoff [2010] and offered a strong critique of their findings and conclusions. Their dataset consists of annual observations of public debt and GDP from 1946 to 2009 (when available; some country-years were missing) for 20 "advanced economies." All these country-year observations were pooled and given equal weight.[10] The dependent variable is the GDP growth rate. The explanatory variables are a sequence of dummy variables indicating whether the debt to GDP ratio in a country year falls in the range of 30–60%, 60–90%, 90–120%, and above 120%. The excluded category is a debt to GDP ratio of 0–30%; therefore, all parameter estimates reflect the effect of moving *from* a debt to GDP ratio below 30% *to* a debt to GDP ratio specified by one of the dummy variables.

Herndon et al. estimated this model by ordinary least squares. The standard errors are the "default" standard errors, assuming that observations are independent and homoscedastic. By pooling all observations, Herndon et al. assumed the DGP is homogeneous in all years and countries covered in the sample; the only possible differences between observations of the dependent variable are due to the covariates and to draws of a random variable from the same distribution for all country-years. In addition, the missing data (from country-years not available) is assumed to follow the same distribution as the available data, so that the parameter estimates apply equally well to country-years missing from the dataset as those present. These assumptions make the statistical model (and the problem of inference based on it) relatively simple; all of them are subject to critique and further exploration.

The parameter estimates and standard errors from this model are displayed in Table 8.1.[11]

---

[10] This is an important difference between Herndon, Ash, and Pollin and Reinhart and Rogoff. Reinhart and Rogoff treated a country with 20 years of data as equivalent to a country with 5 years of data. There might be reasons to do this, but Herndon, Ash, and Pollin point out that Reinhart and Rogoff did not explain this choice in any detail.

[11] There is no intercept in this table, or in this model, so that the coefficients can be interpreted as effects of the debt/GDP level relative to the excluded category.

TABLE 8.1. *Effect of Debt/GDP Ratios on GDP Growth Rates*

Variable	$\widehat{\beta}$	$\widehat{SE}$
30–60%	−1.08	0.20
60–90%	−0.99	0.25
90–120%	−1.77	0.36
120+%	−2.61	0.54
$\overline{R}^2 = 0.04$		

They show that compared with a public debt/GDP ratio below 30%, a debt/GDP ratio of 30–60% is associated with a reduction in GDP growth of 1.08 percentage points in this dataset, on average. Compared with a public debt/GDP ratio below 30%, a debt/GDP ratio of 60–90% is associated with a reduction in GDP growth of 0.99 percentage points, and so forth.[12] All coefficients in this model are interpreted relative to the same baseline category, public debt/GDP ratio below 30%.

Taken by itself, each parameter estimate is negative and statistically significantly different from 0, based on the standard errors used in this analysis. The *t* statistic in each of these cases, $\frac{\hat{\beta}}{SE(\hat{\beta})}$, is well above 2 in absolute value. This means that when debt/GDP is in any one of these categories, the GDP growth rate is significantly lower than it is when debt/GDP is below 30%.

As an aside, it is probably optimistic to assume that the observations are iid, so that these standard errors are valid. It seems reasonable that, based on economic cycles, a given country's GDP might be positively correlated over time – good years might tend to be followed by good years, and bad followed by bad. This suggests that serial correlation is worth investigating. In addition, it seems reasonable that some countries tend to have larger year to year economic fluctuations than others. For example, some might have discovered significant resource wealth; others might have been unusually susceptible to oil shocks. This suggests that the year to year variance in GDP growth may not be the same for all countries. Moreover, variance in GDP growth across countries in a given year need not be the same at every point in time. As national economies become more tightly linked, national business cycles might harmonize, so that in a given year there are fewer wide disparities in GDP growth across these countries. In short, for several reasons, heteroscedasticity is also likely an issue.

[12] Much of the media reaction to the Herdon et al. critique focused on the fact that their estimates of average GDP growth for very high debt/GDP countries were much greater than these estimates in Reinhart and Rogoff. Substantively, that is, of course, important. But this discussion is about how theories translate into hypotheses and how those can be tested in regression models, so the magnitudes of GDP growth are not as relevant for us right now.

Whether any of these points is valid has to do with the substance of economics, but if any of them hold up, the standard errors in Table 8.1 are not right. There are innumerable ways to specify standard errors in regression models (see Chapter 7 for small introduction to this large issue); from a pragmatic standpoint, it is often useful to ensure that key significance results hold up under a variety of them.

In any case, the Reinhart-Rogoff argument is not just that these parameter estimates are all negative and significant. Rather, if increasing debt/GDP implies reduced economic growth, then the parameter estimates should be *increasing in absolute value* for greater debt/GDP categories. That is, debt/GDP = 70% is not just as bad for GDP growth as debt/GDP = 40%, on their argument; it is worse. And if debt/GDP > 90% is particularly bad for GDP growth, then the coefficients for those debt/GDP levels should be significantly greater in absolute value than the coefficients for lower debt/GDP ratios. In other words, the key hypotheses from the Reinhart-Rogoff argument are not about comparisons of a given coefficient to 0 (or any other specific number) but about comparisons of some coefficients to other coefficients.

From a naive, naked-eye comparison we can see that, indeed, −1.77 is larger in absolute value than −1.08. But we now also know that these numbers are realizations of random variables, and they cannot be adequately compared in this fashion. The difference between −1.77 and −1.08 could arise because the Reinhart-Rogoff argument is correct – debt/GDP above 90% is especially detrimental for GDP growth – or they could arise by chance error. Sorting this out is the job of a hypothesis test comparing model coefficients.

Herndon et al. explored this. Specifically, they tested the hypothesis $H_0 : \beta_{30-60} = \beta_{60-90} = \beta_{90-120}$. This null hypothesis says that all debt/GDP categories from 30% up to 120% are equally detrimental, relative to the 0–30% range. The Reinhart-Rogoff argument implies that this null hypothesis is false, and these parameters are not all equal to each other.[13]

Because H_0 is a restriction on the value of multiple parameters in the model, and because this is a least squares regression model, an F test is suitable to test H_0. To actually implement the F test in computer software, one estimates the regression model in Table 8.1, then specifies an F test is to be executed for H_0. The computer software automatically takes care of the rest. What happens is that the computer estimates the model *assuming* that H_0 is true, that the first three parameters in the model are in fact the same. Then it compares the R^2 from this restricted model to the R^2 from the model in Table 8.1, 0.04. These R^2 values have the same denominator (total variance of Y); the numerator is the variance of Y "explained by" each of these regressions. If the explained variance is significantly greater without H_0 imposed than with it, then H_0 does a poor job of explaining the observed results. In this way, an F test in regression

---

[13] Again, it implies more than this, but it does imply this.

models is simply a comparison of two variances, which is what F tests are always about.[14]

Herndon et al. found that the p-value in this test is 0.11 and observed that H_0 is not rejected at conventional significance levels. On a strict interpretation, the Reinhart-Rogoff argument that 90% is an important threshold does not hold up at the level we usually require in social science. On the other hand, the largest p-value at which one could "conventionally" claim that H_0 rejected is 0.10, which is pretty close. It seems odd at some level to define the state of scientific knowledge, not to mention macroeconomic policy that affects the lives of hundreds of millions of people, based on a substantively trifling difference between 0.11 and an arbitrary cutoff of 0.10. It seems judicious, but frustratingly ambiguous, to conclude that the 90% threshold is not of overwhelming significance compared with other debt/GDP levels, but it is still reasonably difficult to explain the observed data as if it's irrelevant. But the drive to publish and claim scientific status does not respond well to judicious claims of ambiguity.

From a statistical modeling standpoint, there is no reason why the explanatory variable, debt/GDP ratio, must be entered in terms of these categories. It would also be perfectly possible to estimate the model $E(Y|X) = \alpha + \beta X$, where Y is the GDP growth rate and X is the debt/GDP ratio. Then β would capture the effect of a 1 percentage point increase in the debt/GDP ratio on the GDP growth rate. If one were interested in the 90% debt/GDP threshold specifically, one could estimate $E(Y|X) = \alpha + \beta_1 X + \beta_2 Z$, where $Z = 1$ if $X > 0.9$ and $Z = 0$ otherwise. Then the hypothesis $H_0 : \beta_2 = 0$ allows a simple t test of whether crossing the 90% threshold imposes an additional penalty on GDP growth, as part of the standard model output. These specifications do not lend themselves as well to thinking of broad debt/GDP categories as the model in Table 8.1, so if there is something important about that in the macroeconomic substance of the question, they are presumably less suitable.

8.7 NONPARAMETRIC TESTS

The hypothesis tests we have reviewed here all have something in common: they assume that the DGP has a particular form (normal, Poisson, etc.) and derive the properties of the test statistic (particularly its sampling distribution) based on that fact. And if the DGP can reasonably be asserted, or it is not possible to make much headway without assuming one, those tests are the way to go.

---

[14] So even though H_0 is about a comparison of parameters, the estimates of those parameters from Table 8.1 are not actually compared with each other in an F test. If H_0 is a comparison of two coefficients from OLS regression, it can be executed in either an F test similar to this one, or t test comparing those coefficients from the model output without implicitly estimating a "null" model.

TABLE 8.2. *Attempts to Influence Others' Votes, by Frequency of Church Attendance*

Church Attendance	Attempts to Influence Others' Votes				N
	Often	Sometimes	Rarely	Never	
Never	15	31	23	127	196
Several times/year	20	61	48	141	270
Once/month	22	37	16	78	153
Once/week	35	93	46	195	369
>Once/week	16	33	15	82	146
N	108	255	148	623	1,134

However, any conclusions based on assumed forms of the DGP are dependent in some part on those assumptions. When possible, it is preferable to avoid drawing conclusions that are model-dependent, that is, dependent on a specific model of the DGP. This is the point of *nonparametric* statistics, which is a large field with a long history that social scientists probably don't pay enough attention to (see Siegel and John N. Castellan [1988] and Pagan and Ullah [1999] for references). There are a few basic nonparametric tests that do things social scientists often want to do in quantitative work, and they are described in this section.

8.7.1 Contingency Tables: χ^2 Test of Association

Thus far we have encountered the χ^2 distribution as the sampling distribution of the sample variance when a sample is iid normal. But the χ^2 is the approximate sampling distribution for test statistics in many other tests, especially nonparametric tests. One of these, and one of the earliest formal tests developed in statistics, is the χ^2 test of independence or nonassociation of two categorical variables. This test addresses a natural hypothesis – whether two variables are stochastically related or not – in an important class of data – when the variables take a small number of distinct, possibly nonordered values.

Data in these cases are often arranged in a table in which cells that show how many observations out of a total of N fall into a combination of each variable's value. This is simply the same sort of crosstab or contingency table introduced in Chapter 2. The following crosstab (Table 8.2) is the same as the one introduced in that chapter, based on General Social Survey data on church attendance and attempts to influence the political beliefs of others. We can now explore this crosstab terms of statistical inference about the underlying relationshships.

A natural question in a contingency table is whether the variables displayed are related in some way. Do more religious people (in the sense of church attendance) attempt to influence the votes of others more than less religious people? Perhaps yes, if religious people are more interested in inducing others to share their opinions in general (which may be both a cause and a result of their religious behavior) or if they simply have richer social networks and more opportunities to influence others than nonreligious people. This is another version of a question we have asked many times – namely, are these variables independent?

The χ^2 of independence is designed to handle this exact type of situation. The key idea is that, taking the total number of observations in each row and each column as given, independence pins down how many observations should be in each cell. Fixing the number of observations in the column, independence implies that those observations are split among the rows in proportion to the number of observations in that row, and this is true for all columns. If a disproportionately large percentage of observations was in a given row for one column but not another, the row and column variables could not be independent – they would be related in the sense that we get a proportionately larger frequency of one variable as the other one changes in some way.

Thus, suppose that N_c observations are in column c out of N observations total, so $\frac{N_c}{N}$ is the *percentage* of all observations in column c. Independence means that the *number* of these observations in each row for column c is proportional to N_r, the number of observations in a given row. Then we would expect $\frac{(N_r) \times (N_c)}{N}$ of column c's observations to be in row r if the row and column variables are independent. This satisfies the proportionality notion for independence in contingency tables just laid out and also results in the correct total number of observations in the table (N).

Given all that, the logic of the χ^2 test of independence is simple. This expected tally $\frac{N_c N_r}{N}$ can be computed for each column c and row r, resulting in one expected tally for every cell of the table. And this expected tally from each cell can be compared with the actual tally from each cell. Because of random noise in the data, of course we do not expect the actual tally always to exactly equal the expected tally in every cell of the table. But if, in aggregate, the actual number of observations in each cell is far from the number expected under independence, the data casts doubt on the assumption of independence. If, on the other hand, the actual tally in each cell is not far from the tally expected under independence, then the data does not cast doubt on the assumption of independence. The details involve identifying the test statistic and showing that the test statistic does indeed converge in distribution to a χ^2 as $N \to \infty$. The limiting χ^2 distribution then provides a metric of "close to" and "far from" to evaluate the null hypothesis of independence.

Formally, let $O_{i,j}$ denote the number of observations in row i, column j. Let $E_{i,j}$ denote $\frac{N_i N_j}{N}$, the expected number of observations in row i, column j if the row and column variables are independent. Let R denote the number of rows and C the number of columns. Then the test statistic is

$$\chi^2 = \sum_{i=1}^{R} \sum_{j=1}^{C} \frac{(O_{i,j} - E_{i,j})^2}{E_{i,j}}. \tag{8.12}$$

If the null hypothesis of independence is true and the sample consists of iid draws from a given DGP, this statistic converges in distribution to a χ^2 with $(R - 1)(C - 1)$ degrees of freedom. Note therefore that the test statistic is only approximately χ^2 distributed in finite samples. This test is nonparametric in the sense that no assumptions about the DGP need to be made for these properties to hold.

As with any test statistic, it is useful to think about situations that would lead to a large value of χ^2 or a small value. Note that the numerator of the test statistic contains a square – the squared difference between the observed tally in a cell and the tally expected under independence. So if the observed tally is far above expected, or far below, the contribution to the test statistic is a large positive number. If the observed tally is close to the expected tally – above or below – the contribution to the test statistic is a small number. So if the test statistic is relatively large, the null hypothesis of independence is doubtful. If the test statistic is relatively small, the null hypothesis of independence is credible. This χ^2 test is therefore inherently one-tailed. The p-value is the probability of observing a χ^2 statistic further out in the right tail than the value that was actually observed. As always, this formalizes the degree of support the sample offers the null hypothesis or alternatively how much doubt the sample casts on the alternative hypothesis.

Concretely, examine the first row of the table on church attendance and attempts to influence other voters: respondents who never attend church. There are 196 of them out of 1,134, about 17%. If church attendance and attempts to influence other voters are independent, then about 17% of the people who often attempt to influence others' votes should attend church: that's 17% of 108, or 18.36 people. In fact, we observed 15 people in this cell, which seems not too far from what was expected in this case based on the assumption of independence. To execute a χ^2 test of independence, we find the expected entry in each cell of the cross tab, and the difference between the observed entry and the expected entry. This difference between observed and expected is then squared, and divided by expected. These operations are repeated for every other cell, and the resulting number for each cell is summed to obtain the test statistic.

In this case the result is a χ^2 value of 22.61. From a distribution with $4 \times 3 = 12$ df's, the p-value of this statistic is about 0.03. So this data is fairly unusual if, in fact, frequency of church attendance is independent of frequency of attempts to influence other voters.

All this p-value tells us is that the data is unusual if the null is correct. It does not tell us what particular form the association between the row and column variables might take. The alternative hypothesis is simply that the row and column variables are not independent; the nature of the relationship is not specified. So as far as we can tell from the p-value, there might be a linear increase in attempts to influence others as church attendance increases, or a linear decrease in attempts to influence others, or any number of nonlinear relationships (e.g., attempts to influence others peak for moderate church attendance and decrease for very frequent or infrequent church attendance).

In this particular case, it appears that the infrequent churchgoers are also less likely to try to influence other voters. The larger values of $\frac{(O_{i,j}-E_{i,j})^2}{E_{i,j}}$ tend to be concentrated in these upper-right cells of the table. And there are a variety of reasons why this is not surprising; churchgoers may be more likely to vote in the first place, thus better placed to influence the votes of others; some frequent churchgoers consciously try to draw others to their spiritual beliefs as a matter of religious creed and may find it natural to do so in politics as well, for example.

However, we cannot interpret a low p-value as an endorsement of this relationship identified after observing the data. If we use the data to inform a conjecture about the nature of the relationship between the column and row variables, we cannot treat the same data as a test of the relationship in the same sense that a new dataset would be. If the data leads to the conjecture in the first place, it obviously does not provide an independent test of the conjecture. This sort of "data mining" overstates the statistical power of the test results that emerge from it.

8.7.2 Mann-Whitney-Wilcoxon U Test

Our primary tools for comparing whether the central tendency of one group exceeds that of another is a difference in means test. These tests do not make a lot of assumptions on the DGP, but we at least need a "large enough" N for each sample to feel comfortable about using the standard normal as the approximate sampling distribution. In addition, in the realistic situation where σ^2 for each group is unknown, the t tests we've encountered either require assumptions about equal variances or have somewhat less rigorous justifications for using the t as the sampling distribution. Finally, because z and t tests are based on sample means, the results are sensitive to outliers in the data, that is, a small number of observations very different from any others, and possibly generated by a different process entirely.

An alternative, fully nonparametric test dispenses even with these assumptions or any others about the DGPs and still allows for comparisons of central tendency between groups. This is alternately known in various contexts as the *Wilcoxon rank-sum test*, *Mann-Whitney test*, or *U test*. It assumes that observations are independent within samples and across samples. It also assumes that observations are at least ordinal; cardinal observations are also fine.

Specifically, consider N_1 independent draws from DGP 1, and N_2 independent draws from DGP 2. The null hypothesis is that DGP 1 and DGP 2 are the same; the alternative is that they are different (however, one-tailed versions are available).

To implement the test, combine all the observations into one pool of size $N = N_1 + N_2$. Again, all observations within N are assumed to be mutually independent. Then order all the observations from smallest to largest. Then rank each observation in this ordered list, 1 for the lowest, on up to N for the greatest (ties are assigned their average rank). Each observation's rank in this list is denoted R_i.

Then pick one of the two groups, either the draws from DGP 1 or from DGP 2; it does not matter which (the smaller group is easier for computation by hand). Add up the ranks R_i for each observation in this sample.[15]

The idea in the test is that, if H_0 is true, each possible list of rankings for group 1 should be equally likely. This in turn allows exact computation of the probability of each possible rank sum for each group under H_0. If the probability of the observed rank sum, or one more extreme than that, is small, it casts doubt on H_0. In small samples (less than a couple dozen), computers typically use the exact distribution of rank sums under H_0. In large samples, the sampling distribution of the test statistic converges to normal, so computers use a normal approximation instead.

For instance, suppose two men and two women place themselves on a 7-point scale representing their own ideology on social issues, with 1 being the most liberal and 7 being the most conservative. Suppose the men give self-placements of 2 and 5, and the women give self-placements of 3 and 6. Combining these four observations into one ordered list gives $(1, 2, 5, 6)$, with attendant ranks 1, 2, 3, and 4. The sum of the ranks for women is $2 + 4 = 6$.

Now, in a repeated sample, the women might have come out with ranks of $(1, 2)$, $(1, 3)$, $(1, 4)$, $(2, 3)$, $(2, 4)$, or $(3, 4)$. If H_0 is true and the DGPs of men's and women's self placements are equal, these ranking pairs are all equally likely, with probability $\frac{1}{6}$ each. Furthermore, the possible rank sums are 3, 4, 5, 6, and 7. The rank sum of 5 can occur in two ways (ranks $(1, 4)$ or $(2, 3)$), so it has probability $\frac{1}{3}$ under H_0. All other rank pairs can only occur in one way so have probability $\frac{1}{6}$ under H_0. So we have the exact sampling distribution of the rank sum under H_0. It is symmetric around its mode, which is 5.

Clearly, the probability of a rank sum of 6 or greater is $\frac{1}{3}$. This is the p-value in a one-tailed version of the test. The probability of a rank sum that differs from the mode by 1 or more is $\frac{2}{3}$; this is the p-value in a two-tailed test.

This N is so small that no observation would be give a p-value below $\frac{1}{6}$, and even that is only attainable in a one-tailed test. But it does illustrate the idea and mechanics implemented by a computer. A larger sample size is more complicated in that there are more possible combinations of ranks for the N_k observations in sample k, and more possible rank sums, so the arithmetic used to construct the sampling distribution of the rank sum is more involved. But the idea is not different.

---

[15] Because the number of possible rankings of the N observations is known, the rank sum for group 2 is known once the rank sum for group 1 is computed. That is why it doesn't matter which group is used to compute the rank sum.

8.7.3 Kolmogorov-Smirnov Test for Difference in Distribution

All the tests covered in this chapter thus far relate to the central tendency, spread, or association in a distribution or pair of distributions. For several reasons, it is sometimes also interesting to test hypotheses about whether two random variables have different distributions – not in their mean or spread, but in general or anywhere. One of the more common tests to answer such questions is the Kolmogorov-Smirnov test, a nonparametric test for difference in distributions.

There are two variants of the Kolmogorov-Smirnov or KS test, a one-sample and two-sample version. They both require construction of an *empirical cumulative distribution function (CDF)* based on the sample(s) of observed data. This is an empirical/sample analogue to the cumulative distribution function introduced in Chapter 4. Details are covered subsequently, but the idea is to tabulate the percentage of sample observations that fall at or below any given value. Thus at least $\frac{1}{N}$ of the observations always fall at or below the minimum value of the variable in the sample, and 100% of the observations fall at or below the maximum value in the sample.

The one-sample KS test asks whether the sample CDF is significantly different from the CDF that would be expected in the sample if the DGP were a particular distribution that the analyst specifies, called a *reference distribution* in this test. Thus, it is a test of whether the DGP behind the sample is the same as the reference DGP or not. The null hypothesis is that the reference distribution generated the sample data.

A useful application of this test arises when an analyst is interested in the functional form of a DGP to develop a particular parametric model or execute a specific parametric test. For instance, before carrying out a χ^2 variance test, which is strictly valid only for a normal DGP, an analyst might use a one-sample KS test to check whether it is reasonable to assume a normal DGP. Note that in this case, unlike other hypothesis tests encountered earlier, the null hypothesis is not usually one the analyst argues against.

The two-sample KS test asks whether two samples were generated by the same DGP. This is accomplished by comparing the empirical CDFs from the two samples; if they have the same DGP, these empirical CDFs should never be all that different from each other. The null hypothesis is that the two samples have the same DGP. The two-sample KS test therefore is similar in spirit to the tests for difference in means, medians, and variances that we covered above but is more general. The KS test asks whether two distributions are different in any way, not just in their central tendency or spread. By the same token, it is less powerful than tests for difference in means or variance, that is, it is not as good at rejecting the null hypothesis when it is "a little bit false." This is the cost of some of the attractive features of the KS test; that it is not focused only on one particular type of difference and it does not impose any parametric structure on the DGPs.

One-Sample Test

KS tests require construction of an empirical CDF, $\widetilde{F}(x)$. This function captures the share of the sample observations at or below the value x. Computer software such as Stata or **R** automates this, but if it is done manually, it is easiest to order the sample observations from lowest to highest, and construct $\widetilde{F}(x)$ iteratively. If x_m is the minimum value in the sample, $\widetilde{F}(x) = 0$ for any $x < x_m$. By definition, there aren't any observations below the minimum value, so the share of sample observations below x_m is 0. If there are k_m observations for which $x_i = x_m$, then $\widetilde{F}(x_m) = \frac{k_m}{N}$. Then if x_{m+1} is the next lowest value observed in the sample, $\widetilde{F}(x) = \frac{k_m}{N}$ for any $x \in (x_m, x_{m+1})$. These brackets are rounded to denote an interval that does not include its end points; the observations at x_m have already been accounted for, and those at x_{m+1} will be accounted for in the next step. If there are k_{m+1} observations for which $x_i = x_{m+1}$, then $\widetilde{F}(x_{m+1}) = \widetilde{F}_m(x) + \frac{k_{m+1}}{N}$. This procedure can be iterated to construct $\widetilde{F}(x)$ for any value of x up to the maximum value observed in the sample, where $\widetilde{F}(x) = 1$ will result. For any x above the maximum value, $\widetilde{F}(x) = 1$ as well; 100% of the sample observations are at or below the maximum value.

The one-sample KS test compares the empirical CDF to a reference CDF, $F(x)$. This is a known distribution such as the normal, exponential, or any other distribution to which the analyst is interested in comparing the DGP of the sample. The next step of the one-sample KS test is to identify $F(x)$ for each of the value of x in its domain.

The test statistic in the one-sample KS test is conceptually simple. For each value of x in the domain of of the reference distribution, identify $|\widetilde{F}(x) - F(x)|$, the absolute value of the difference between the empirical and reference CDFs at that x. In principle this produces one difference for every possible value of x. The KS test statistic is the maximum value of these absolute value differences. Formally, with a sample of size N, the test statistic is

$$D_N = \sup_x |\widetilde{F}(x) - F(x)|. \tag{8.13}$$

Here "sup" refers to the supremum – equivalent to the maximum value in the set of differences, if one exists, or the least upper bound of the set of differences, if no maximum exists.

The idea behind this test statistic is that if $\widetilde{F}(x)$ really is obtained from a sample generated by $F(x)$, as the null hypothesis maintains, then $\widetilde{F}(x)$ and $F(x)$ should never be far apart. To test that, we need only look at their maximum difference; that is essentially the test statistic. If we want to know if the distributions are different at at least one point, it is sufficient to inspect their largest difference at any point. Formally, if $F(x)$ is the DGP for the sample, then as $N \to \infty$, $D_N \to 0$ with probability 1. The sampling distribution of the KS statistic is based on the rate at which D_N converges to 0 under the null hypothesis.

Deriving the exact sampling distribution of the statistic D_N is mathematically beyond the scope of this presentation; although its functional form does not involve any deeply fancy mathematics, it is not particularly revealing. The most important point is that it does not depend on $F(x)$, the reference distribution. In practice, KS tests are usually executed using computer software that reports a p-value. If done manually, a variety of sources contain critical values of D_α such that if D_N is larger than the critical value, $F(x)$ and $\widetilde{F}(x)$ are significantly different at the α significance level.

Two-Sample Test

The two-sample KS test is similar to the one-sample test, except that there is no reference distribution and empirical CDFs are constructed for each of two samples. The null hypothesis is that the samples are drawn from the same DGP, although that DGP is not specified. If $\widetilde{F}_1(x)$ and $\widetilde{F}_2(x)$ are the empirical CDFs from the two samples, respectively, and their sizes are N_1 and N_2, the two-sample KS statistic is

$$D_{N_1, N_2} = |\widetilde{F}_1(x) - \widetilde{F}_2(x)|. \tag{8.14}$$

The idea behind the test statistic is similar to the one-sample test: if the sample DGPs are really identical, their empirical CDFs should never be far apart. If we are interested in whether they are different *anywhere*, we can focus on their largest observed difference. As the sample sizes increase, the test statistic converges to 0 with probability 1; in finite samples the empirical CDFs may differ due to chance. As with the one-sample KS test, the derivation of the exact sampling distribution is beyond our scope. In practice the test is either carried out on a computer, or if done manually, the computed value of the test statistic can be compared to known critical values.

The two-sample KS test can be used to compare the DGPs behind two samples in more general terms than the tests described earlier. If two samples have different means, they certainly have different distributions, but the converse is not true: there are many ways for DGPs to differ other than their means. Often our interest centers not just on differences but on whether two distributions can be ordered or one is greater than the other in some sense, for example, voters who vote in primary elections are ideologically more extreme than voters who vote in general elections only, or elected judges give harsher criminal sentences than appointed judges. Evaluating these questions in terms of means of two distributions or a change in a conditional mean is only one way to address them. First-order *stochastic dominance* (FOSD) is a strong sense in which one distribution can be said to be greater than another. Distribution A first-order stochastically dominates distribution B if $F_A(x) \leq F_B(x)$ for every value of x, and $F_A(x) < F_B(x)$ for at least one x. FOSD means that the CDF of the dominated distribution is always above the CDF of the dominant distribution, that is, for any value of x, the dominant distribution places greater weight on larger values than the dominated distribution does. If the KS test shows significant differences in distribution and one empirical CDF is always below the other, it is reasonable to conclude that the distributions can be ordered in the sense of FOSD.[16]

Another useful application of the two-sample KS test arises in matching, a technique for establishing causal statements in observational data (cf. Chapter 10). Loosely speaking, matching is concerned with the causal effect of a "treatment" on an outcome. To identify this effect, matching ideally constructs two subsamples, one with and one without the treatment, that have identical distributions of all other observable covariates that might affect the outcome. The idea is that these subsamples are identical in all respects that might be relevant for the outcome besides the treatment, and so any differences in outcomes across subsamples must be due to the treatment itself. A crucial step, therefore, is to establish that the matched subsamples have identical distributions of all covariates other than the treatment. The two-sample KS test is a common and useful test to investigate this.

8.8 CONCLUSION

Hypothesis testing is one of the most common inference procedures used in quantitative social science and policy research. Hypothesis testing starts with a conjecture about some unknown parameters of a DGP and then determines the probability of observing a sample "like" the one that was actually observed, assuming the conjecture is true. If that probability falls below some relatively small cutoff, the DGP parameters are deemed significantly different from the values specified in the conjecture.

This chapter has presented some of the most common tests encountered in applied research and the general concepts behind all classical hypothesis testing. There are practically innumerable other tests available to address specific inference problems beyond those addressed here. Given a substantive inference problem, implementation is generally a matter of identifying the test statistic and its sampling distribution. Given a p-value or significance level, all classical tests can be interpreted in the same way, despite differences in their implementation and substantive motivation.

The most important moral of the story in hypothesis testing is not the procedure of any particular test. It is that a realization of a random variable should never be compared to any benchmark or any realization of any other random variable without a hypothesis test to give context for the difference. Because anything computed from a sample drawn from a DGP is a realization of a random variable – means, variances, medians, regression coefficients, for

---

[16] The KS test is not well suited to second-order stochastic dominance (Chapter 6) because this refers to only one type of difference in distributions (a mean preserving spread), whereas the KS test is not that specific.

example – this has far-reaching consequences for how we interpret quantities in social science research.

Hypothesis testing starts with a specific conjecture about a DGP, usually identified by some theory about the social process modeled in the DGP and asks whether that conjecture is reasonable in light of observed data. A complementary approach to inference simply asks, for a given sample of observed data, what statements about (specific parameters of) the DGP are reasonable? And what methods can we use to parse sample data so as to arrive at such statements? This is the point of the theory of estimation, which is considered in the next chapter. One branch of the theory of estimation attempts to identify a range of parameter values in the DGP that are reasonable in light of the sample data. This is rather literally a complement to a hypothesis test, and the resulting range is called a *confidence interval*. Another branch of estimation theory deals with methods to parse sample data that lead to a single "best" (in some sense, to be discussed further) estimate of a parameter. These estimates are *point estimates*. We review methods of estimation that are commonly used for statistical models developed earlier in this book (Chapter 6), and attempt to better understand why they are so common.

PROBLEMS

1. In the 2008 presidential election, in the 29 states won by Barack Obama, average annual per capita income was $44,500, with a standard deviation of about $5,400. In the 21 states won by John McCain, average annual per capita income was $38,500, with a standard deviation of about $4,600.[17]

   (a) Test the hypothesis that average annual per capita income is the same in Obama and McCain states. State the type of hypothesis test you perform. Obtain the z-score and compare the p-value to conventional significance benchmarks.

   (b) It is often supposed that the higher a person's income, the more likely they are to vote Republican. Does the result of the hypothesis test above necessarily contradict this supposition? If so explain why; if not explain how they might be consistent with each other.

2. A coin is flipped 14 times and 5 heads are observed. Test the hypothesis that the coin is fair, with a test statistic based on (*i*) the share of heads in the sample, assuming this share is normally distributed by the central limit theorem, and (*ii*) the number of heads in the sample, and its exact distribution.

3. Complete the computation of the test statistic and verify the p-value for the χ^2 test in Table 8.2, on whether attempts to influence how others vote is independent of church attendance.

---

[17] This data is very slightly massaged to ease computation.

4. Consider a single observation taken from a Poisson distribution. The observation is 5. Identify a test statistic and a p-value for a one-tailed test of $H_0 : \lambda = 3$ versus $H_1 : \lambda > 3$.

5. Draw 40 observations from a Poisson distribution with $\lambda = 5$.
   (a) Execute a t-test of whether the mean of the DGP is 5 or not.
   (b) Execute a t-test of whether the mean of the DGP is 8 or not.

6. Now draw 33 observations from an exponential distribution with $\theta = 5$. Use a heteroskedastic difference-in-means t test to determine whether these 33 observations come from a DGP with the same mean as your 40 draws from the Poisson.

7. Execute a Kolmogorov-Smirnov test of whether your 40 [33] exponential draws come from the same distribution as your 33 [40] Poisson draws.

8. Consider the linear regression model $E(Y|X_1, X_2) = \alpha + \beta_1 X_1 + \beta_2 X_2 + \beta_3 X_1 X_2$, estimated by ordinary least squares.
   (a) What null and alternative hypotheses and what test statistic would you use to investigate whether X_2 adds any explanatory power to the model?
   (b) What null and alternative hypotheses and what test statistic would you use to investigate whether X_2 effects the effect of X_1 on $E(Y|X)$?
   (c) In the regression model as written, what is the standard error of the total effect of X_1 on $E(Y|X)$? Express it in general terms that can be obtained from the variance-covariance matrix.

9

Estimation: Recovering Properties of the Data-Generating Process

In hypothesis testing, we make conjectures about the data-generating process (DGP) and assess the weight of evidence that the sample offers in support of them. The conjectures about the DGP that are subject to testing should have some theoretically interesting foundation, but they are made before any evaluation or analysis of the observed sample data. Hypothesis testing does not address where the conjectures come from; they are taken as given, supplied by theory, and are tested against data.

Statistical *estimation*, by contrast, does not take as given conjectures to be evaluated. Instead it uses the observed data to make conjectures about the unobserved DGP that are in some sense good or reasonable. There are two general types of estimation, *interval estimation* and *point estimation*. These types of estimation are treated in this chapter.

Interval estimates specify a range of values that are all "reasonable" guesses about an unknown parameter of a DGP. Typically the interval estimate contains the parameter of a DGP in a user-specified probability of random samples. Interval estimates are useful because they combine a sense of the "best guess" of a parameter's value and some uncertainty about that best guess into one statement. Another name for an interval estimate in classical statistics is a confidence interval. Although a hypothesis test asks whether a particular conjecture about the DGP is reasonable in light of the data, a confidence interval can be thought of as a range of reasonable conjectures about the DGP.

Point estimation builds on a key result of random sampling – namely, a sampling distribution. The discussion of sampling in Chapter 7 showed that in important cases, the sampling distribution of a statistic is related to a DGP parameter in a specific way. By the same token, such a statistic can be used to estimate the unknown DGP parameter; by way of its sampling distribution, such a statistic provides information about the parameter that can be precisely expressed. Not surprisingly, for example, the results in Chapter 7 on the unbiasedness, efficiency, and sampling distribution of the sample mean suggest that $\overline{X}$ is a good estimator of the expected value of a DGP (i.e., the population mean).

For both point and interval estimation, there is an important terminological point that parallels a distinction we have already gotten used to: that between a random variable (a function of the sample space of an experiment) and a realized value of the random variable (a number observed in a specific experiment). In estimation, this shows up as the distinction between an *estimator*, a function of the sample data, and an *estimate*, a value of the function in a particular sample. An estimator is a random variable, whereas an estimate is a realized value of the estimator. As X and x denote a random variable and a realized value of it, respectively, so $T(X)$ and $T(x)$ denote an estimator and an estimate. We have already seen a few examples of this; $\overline{X}$ is an estimator – a function telling us how to determine the sample mean for any given sample – while $\overline{x}$ is an estimate.

9.1 INTERVAL ESTIMATION

An interval estimate or *confidence interval* specifies a range of values for an unknown parameter of a DGP, that are "reasonable" in light of observed sample data at hand. It is, in a sense, the inverse of a hypothesis test, which starts with a specific conjecture about the DGP and examines whether it is reasonable in light of the observed data. This "inversion" is more than a heuristic interpretation of the relationship between tests and interval estimators, as we will see.

The standard of "reasonable" is similar to the significance level in a hypothesis test. Consider the mean of a binomial DGP with N iid draws as a concrete case – it is an unknown parameter we would like to learn something about, based on an observed sample. From the sample, we compute the mean $\overline{x}$. For instance, suppose we are interested in the percentage of registered voters who approve of how the U.S. president is handling his or her job on a particular date. This unknown percentage is ρ. To learn something about this, we obtain a sample of 900 registered voters, drawn independently from the population of all registered voters, and record that 53% of the 900 respondents approve. This 53% or .53 is the proportion of 1's in the sample, p. Because p is just a sample mean, we know from Chapter 7 that $E(p) = \rho$, so that $p = .53$ is the best guess about ρ in the sense of unbiasedness and mean squared error. So if we had to make one single guess about ρ, in this sense the observed sample mean .53 is our best bet. Whatever is a set of reasonable guesses about ρ in light of the sample, 53% must be in it.

But this is just the best guess, not the only good guess. What about a guess that $\rho = 52.9$? That would also be a pretty good guess, in the sense that we are not much more likely to see a sample of $N = 900$ with a mean around .53 if $\rho = .53$ than if $\rho = .529$.

Now, a particular value of the DGP mean μ induces a probability distribution over all possible values of $\bar{x}$. What this means is that when μ is fixed, some values of $\overline{X}$ are more likely than others. We know, after all (by the central limit theory, or CLT) that at least if N is relatively large, $\overline{X}$ is normally distributed with mean μ and standard deviation $\frac{\sigma}{\sqrt{N}}$.

But we are not dealing with the case in which μ is known and $\overline{X}$ is uncertain; we are dealing with the case where $\bar{x}$ is observed and μ is unknown. Nevertheless the probability distribution over $\overline{X}$ generated by a specific value of μ means that a guess about μ is unreasonable if it is too far away from $\bar{x}$. We observed the sample mean for sure, and it is not reasonable to claim that a wildly unusual event has happened – which is what we are in effect claiming if we conjecture that μ is far away from $\bar{x}$. What needs to be made precise here is the notion of "far away." The standard error of $\overline{X}$ accomplishes that.

To sum up: a confidence interval is a set of guesses about μ that are close enough to the observed $\bar{x}$, in terms of its standard error, to be "reasonable." An unreasonable guess is one that is far away from $\bar{x}$ in SE terms. If an unreasonable guess is actually accurate, it means that an extremely unusual sample occurred. Extremely unusual things do happen, but not usually, so it's better to guess that the DGP is such that what did in fact happen was not extremely unusual.

None of this reasoning would change if, instead of the DGP mean μ and observed sample mean $\bar{x}$, we had been talking about any DGP parameter θ and any sample estimator $\widehat{\theta}(\mathbf{x})$. The bold font $\mathbf{x}$ just indicates that $\widehat{\theta}$ is computed from a list or vector of observations in the sample, not a single number. As long as we know the sampling distribution of $\widehat{\theta}$ or at least its standard error, we can determine a range of θ values that are reasonable guesses, by some definite standard, given the sample information. In other words, confidence intervals can be constructed for any parameter from any distribution.

In light of this, an *interval estimator* is a rule that, when applied to various random samples from a DGP, generates an interval containing the true parameter of interest with some probability specified by the analyst. This probability is sometimes called a *coverage probability* because it is the probability that an interval generated according to a certain procedure actually covers the DGP's true parameter. Note carefully what is fixed and what is variable: the interval itself is the random quantity, and it varies from sample to sample. The parameter of the DGP just sits there, a fixed quantity, and is the same in all samples repeated from the same DGP.

Coverage probability is where we get specific about the amorphous idea of "reasonable" that we've used to develop the logic. The most common coverage probabilities that researchers invoke are 90%, 95%, and 99%. The coverage probability is denoted $(1 - \alpha)$, and is known as the *confidence level* of an interval estimator.

It is up to a researcher to decide on a choice of coverage probability (i.e., confidence level) and in this way determine how far away from θ the observed $\widehat{\theta}$ can be and still count as reasonable. Just as "reasonable" is a judgment call, there is no prescription about the right coverage probability to use. Some disciplines or journals insist on 95% or whatever, but this is a disciplinary convention.

9.1.1 Confidence Intervals for Normal Sampling Distributions

A simple case of interval estimation is a confidence interval for the mean of a normal distribution. It is helpful to make some of this concrete. Specifically, consider N iid draws from a $N(\mu, \sigma^2)$ population or DGP, where σ^2 is known but μ is not. Then the sample mean $\overline{X}$ follows a normal distribution exactly.[1] Furthermore, the expected value of $\overline{X}$ is just μ, and the standard deviation of $\overline{X}$ is $\frac{\sigma}{\sqrt{N}}$, the standard error of the sample mean. It follows that there is probability 0.95 of drawing a value from the distribution of $\overline{X}$ in the interval from $\mu - 1.96 \times \frac{\sigma}{\sqrt{N}}$ to $\mu + 1.96 \times \frac{\sigma}{\sqrt{N}}$. The 1.96 and .95 go together by the 1-2-3 rule for normal distributions (see Chapter 6). More compactly,

$$\Pr(\mu - 1.96 \times \frac{\sigma}{\sqrt{N}} \leq \overline{X} \leq \mu + 1.96 \times \frac{\sigma}{\sqrt{N}}) = 0.95. \qquad (9.1)$$

Of course, part of the reason we draw samples is to learn about DGPs, meaning that in real problems it is usually true that μ is unknown. But Equation 9.1 can be easily reformulated by rearranging the part inside $\Pr(\cdot)$. Specifically, this can be expressed equivalently by (*i*) adding $1.96 \times \frac{\sigma}{\sqrt{N}}$ on both sides of the first inequality, and (*ii*) subtracting $1.96 \times \frac{\sigma}{\sqrt{N}}$ on both sides of the second inequality. Each inequality can be taken as a statement by itself, and the same operation on each side of it will preserve the truth of it. This simple algebra then yields

$$\Pr(\overline{X} - 1.96 \times \frac{\sigma}{\sqrt{N}} \leq \mu \leq \overline{X} + 1.96 \times \frac{\sigma}{\sqrt{N}}) = 0.95. \qquad (9.2)$$

The inequalities inside $\Pr(\cdot)$ in Equation 9.2 define the formula for the 95% confidence interval for μ, when N iid draws are taken from a normal DGP with known variance.

The only random variable in Equation 9.2 that could vary from sample to sample is the sample mean $\overline{X}$. Probability statements can be made about the confidence interval only because of this random variable. In any one sample, the confidence interval either does or does not cover the true parameter. If we took many samples from the same DGP with the same parameter value(s) in each one, the confidence interval computed according to Equation 9.2 would cover the true parameter in $(1 - \alpha)\%$ of them. The sample, and hence the location of the confidence interval, is the random quantity. Coverage of θ is

---

[1] Not approximately; the CLT is not invoked here because the parent DGP itself is normal, and the sum of independent normal random variables is itself normal.

an uncertain event because the location of the interval bounces around from one sample to the next, not because θ changes from one sample to the next. It should go without saying, but is too often overlooked, that the coverage probability for an interval will only be what the researcher believes it is, if the underlying model of the DGP is correct. Everything else in the equation is a fixed quantity across samples from the parent DGP. It is important never to ascribe probabilistic behavior to μ because it is not varying across samples.

The confidence interval in Equation 9.2 is the smallest (narrowest) interval with the property that an interval computed based on this formula will contain the DGP mean μ somewhere in its boundaries in 95% of samples. This is because the interval is centered at $\overline{X}$, and because $E(\overline{X}) = \mu$, the relatively high-density portion of the normal curve (the thick middle section) is where we draw most of these values. We don't spend much time out in the thin tails when an interval is constructed this way, where it would take much more real estate on the x-axis to cover 95% of the area under the curve.

How can the coverage probability of the interval be changed? In Equation 9.2, it is determined by 1.96. To construct a 99% confidence interval, 1.96 can be replaced by 2.575. Just as 95% of the observations under a normal curve lie ± 1.96 standard deviations away from the mean, so 99% lie ± 2.575 standard deviations away from the mean. And for a 90% confidence interval, 1.96 can be replaced by 1.645. For a normal distribution, this multiplier represents the number of standard deviations away from the mean a variable can be. With one of these alternative confidence levels $(1 - \alpha)$, the derivation of the $(1 - \alpha)$ level confidence interval is the same as above.

This also highlights the effect of increasing the confidence level on the width of the interval, for a given DGP. Specifically, greater confidence requires a wider interval. This is pretty intuitive because no new information has been added to the problem just by changing the desired confidence level. So to be more confident that the interval covers the mean, the only option is to increase the width of the interval. Of course, as the sample size goes up and everything else including the confidence level stays fixed, the width of the confidence interval goes down. This too is intuitive: more observations do add more information, and because the desired confidence level has not changed, no extra demands have been placed on this information. So it can be used to shrink the interval.

While the confidence interval in Equation 9.2 is presented as a confidence interval for μ, exactly the same logic would work for any parameter whose DGP is normal with known variance. Thus confidence intervals for β, when the sampling distribution of $\widehat{\beta}$ is normal, have the same structure.

And although this confidence interval is an exact one for an exact normal distribution, it also works well as an approximate confidence interval for approximate normal distributions. Recall that no matter what DGP governs the variables in a sample, sample means are approximately normal by the CLT as long as sample observations are not excessively correlated. So for any DGP, an approximately $(1 - \alpha)\%$ confidence interval can be constructed for μ can be constructed using this formula. Coverage probability is approximate rather than exact, because the sampling distribution of $\overline{X}$ in these cases is not exactly normal.

9.1.2 Confidence Intervals with Estimated Standard Errors

Needless to say, assuming iid draws from a DGP with known variance does not give an overwhelming feeling of verisimilitude. The picture improves slightly if we allow for the fact that the standard deviation of the parent (and so the standard error of the mean) must be estimated with the sample standard deviation S. As noted in Chapter 7, this estimation takes us away from a normally distributed sample mean; instead $(\overline{X} - \mu)/(S/\sqrt{N})$ follows Student's t distribution with $N - 1$ degrees of freedom.

However, this change does not complicate or change the idea of a confidence interval at all. It simply changes the sampling distribution of $\overline{X}$, or the distribution with respect to which probability statements must be made. The only real consequence in actually constructing confidence intervals is that it changes the multiplier one must use to achieve a coverage probability of $(1 - \alpha)$.

For example, with 20 degrees of freedom ($N = 21$), the required multiplier for a 95% confidence interval is approximately 2.086, as determined in a distribution table for Student's t. This means that

$$\Pr(\overline{X} - 2.086 \times \frac{S}{\sqrt{N}} \leq \mu \leq \overline{X} + 2.086 \times \frac{S}{\sqrt{N}}) = 0.95. \qquad (9.3)$$

Compare Equations 9.2 and 9.3. The latter includes S instead of σ and has a larger multiplier to achieve the same level of confidence 0.95. The t distribution has thicker tails than the normal, which in turn arise loosely speaking because two quantities are being estimated (mean and variance) rather than one. These tails in turn imply that a given interval around the mean contains less of the density of the distribution for the t than for the normal. In turn, for the t distribution the interval must be widened to ensure that the same amount of the density is covered. Other than these changes, however, the confidence intervals for the normal and t cases are basically the same. Confidence intervals generally have this structure.

All else constant, narrower confidence intervals are better because they mean that a more precise statement about the location of μ can be made without sacrificing the confidence level. With that in mind, it is helpful for the statistic on which confidence intervals are based to have a small standard error. Later in the chapter, we will come to see this as the issue of *efficiency* of the point estimator on which the confidence interval is based.

Confidence intervals are most commonly based on a random variable with a known or approximate sampling distribution. The sampling distribution is what allows for desired coverage probabilities to be boiled down to a multiplier to include in a confidence interval. These examples work for a normal, approximately normal, or Student's t sampling distribution. Statistics packages can give a confidence interval for most any sample quantity with a sampling distribution. The form will differ depending on the distribution, but they all have the same interpretation as these confidence intervals.

Given this, the exact form of a whole variety of them is not that important. It is important to understand how assumptions about the DGP and sampling process affect the sampling distribution, and the idea of a confidence interval.

However, if at least the standard error of a statistic could be estimated but no assumptions were made about its sampling distribution, we could still use Chebyshev's theorem (Chapter 5) to formulate a (conservative) confidence interval. This is not common in real settings, but it illustrates that the concept of a confidence interval is compatible with a fair degree of skepticism about the sampling distribution.

9.1.3 Confidence Intervals and Hypothesis Tests

Given that significance levels in hypothesis tests are denoted α, it may seem conspicuous that confidence levels in interval estimation are denoted $(1 - \alpha)$. Rather than reflecting a breathtaking lack of imagination about letters to draw from the Greek alphabet, this notation reflects the fundamental similarity of hypothesis tests and confidence intervals.

The most important point is that a confidence interval is the set of null hypotheses not rejected by a hypothesis test. A test with significance level α always has a set of hypotheses it would not reject in a given sample; these hypotheses are exactly the members of the $(1 - \alpha)$ confidence interval. Therefore, tests and intervals are two ways to report very similar information.

To see the equivalence of confidence intervals and hypothesis tests, it is helpful to compare the rejection region of standard tests with the confidence interval computed from the same data and statistic. Let $X_1, \ldots, X_n$ be iid draws from $f(x|\mu, \sigma^2)$, where μ is the population mean and σ^2 the population variance. Assume that n is "large enough." Consider the test $H_0 : \mu = \mu_0$ versus $H_1 : \mu \neq \mu_0$

The test statistic is $\frac{\bar{x} - \mu_0}{\sigma/\sqrt{n}}$. The rejection regions for the $\alpha = 0.01$ and 0.05 level tests are $RR_{.01} = \{z : |z| \geq 2.575\}$ and $RR_{.05} = \{z : |z| \geq 1.96\}$, respectively. The rejection region consists of a set of z values that, if obtained in a sample, will cause rejection of H_0. The numerical component (2.575 or 1.96) is a critical value from the standard normal table. When H_0 is true, the chance that a computed z is more than the critical value of standard errors (SEs) away from the null hypothesized value is α, the significance level. Using this rejection region means, therefore, that a true null will be rejected with probability α. Because these are small, when the null does get rejected, we can be reasonably sure that it's really false.

Meanwhile, the confidence intervals are $CI_{.99} = \{z : z \in (-2.575, 2.575)\}$ and $CI_{.95} = \{z : z \in (-1.96, 1.96)\}$. Clearly, and not coincidentally, the $1 - \alpha$ CI is the complement of the rejection region in the α level significance test.

The equivalence holds for a one-tailed test as well and also illustrates computation of a one-sided confidence interval. Consider $H_0 : \mu \geq \mu_0$ versus $H_1 : \mu < \mu_0$ based on the same model and sample as the example above.

Here the tests only count test statistics below the null hypothesized value against the null. We want a region of zs below 0 that has probability .01 or .05 of occurring. These give rejection regions $RR_{.01} = \{z : z < -2.33\}$, $RR_{.05} = \{z : z < -1.645\}$. We no longer have the absolute value bars around z. Similarly, the confidence intervals are the complements of these regions: $CI_{.99} = \{z : z \geq -2.33\}$, $CI_{.95} = \{z : z \geq -1.96\}$.

Looking back at Equations 9.1 and 9.2, we can see at a fundamental level the reason for the equivalence of confidence intervals and hypothesis tests. Given N iid draws from a normal parent with known variance σ and unknown mean μ, the 0.05-level hypothesis requires the test statistic $-1.96 \leq \frac{\mu - \overline{X}}{\sigma/\sqrt{N}} \leq 1.96$ for the null hypothesis to survive. A sequence of algebra steps called "inverting the test statistic" takes us from this test to the 0.95 level confidence interval $\overline{X} - 1.96 \frac{\sigma}{\sqrt{N}} \leq \mu \leq \overline{X} + 1.96 \frac{\sigma}{\sqrt{N}}$. Generally speaking, inverting a test statistic in this fashion is a useful way to derive confidence intervals. Because the test and the confidence interval are then based on the same sampling distribution of the same statistic, it is no wonder that they are complementary ways of conveying the same information.

Many researchers and statisticians consider confidence intervals somewhat more interesting than hypothesis tests. The reason is that the specific parameter value tested in H_0 is usually not a credible candidate for the actual value of the parameter. If we test $H_0 : \beta = 0$ in a regression model, what is the point? No one seriously believes the parameter is exactly 0, even the idealized skeptic we used to motivate the general logic of hypothesis testing in Chapter 8. Confidence intervals avoid this artificiality by presenting all the credible guesses about the unknown parameter, in the sense of those that would "pass" a hypothesis test at a given significance level. This information could obviously (in principle) be approximated by testing many hypotheses over and over and reporting the results, but given that confidence intervals do this automatically, that is even less sensible than testing that a specific parameter is exactly 0.

9.1.4 Confidence Intervals and Opinion Polls

Confidence intervals have the following structure: "parameter equals statistic plus or minus margin of error." The margin of error in turn is composed of the standard error of the statistic times a multiplier to determine the coverage probability of the confidence interval. The multiplier is chosen based on the sampling distribution of the statistic to determine the coverage probability.

Public opinion polls as conducted by survey organizations (e.g., Gallup, Roper, YouGov/ Polimetrix) have the structure: "unknown population quantity equals sample estimate plus or minus margin of error." The unknown population quantity, the probability of drawing a respondent who answers a certain way on a certain poll question, is a parameter of a DGP. The sample estimate is a statistic, a quantity computed from the observations in a random sample. In other words, an opinion poll is a confidence interval.

Typically an opinion poll margin of error defines a 95% confidence interval. The margin of error is determined by (*i*) 1.96, the multiplier for the standard error of the sample estimate, given that the sample estimate is almost always a type of mean (more specifically, sample proportion) and as such normally distributed, (*ii*) the sample size N, and (*iii*) the sampling process used by the polling or survey organization, details of which may or may not be public.

Parts (*ii*) and (*iii*) jointly determine the standard error of the sample estimate, which is then multiplied by 1.96 to give the margin of error. The standard error may be computed assuming that the "true" population support is 50%. This is a type of conservatism because the standard deviation of a binomial random variable is maximized when $p = 0.5$.

Generally speaking, the standard error in an opinion poll or survey is larger than $\sqrt{\frac{p(1-p)}{n}}$, or the standard error of the sample mean in dataset drawn from a binomial distribution in iid sampling. The reason is that polling organizations do not implement true iid sampling; it is too costly. Instead they typically implement a sampling procedure that gives more variable, less precise estimates because true independence of sample observations is not achieved but is less costly to implement. Note that this does not affect the expected value of the sample mean.

So when a poll finds that "the percentage of likely voters that approve of the president's job performance is 6.2% with a margin of error of ±3%" or some such thing, it is reporting a 95% confidence interval for a population proportion of $[3.2, 9.2]$. This interval also captures the set of null hypotheses about that population proportion that would survive a 0.05 level hypothesis test against a two-sided alternative.

9.2 POINT ESTIMATION AND CRITERIA FOR EVALUATING POINT ESTIMATORS

An *estimator* is any function of a sample space in an experiment. Note that this is exactly the same definition given in Chapter 4 for a random variable. Therefore, an estimator is, foremost, a random variable. As such, it has a probability distribution. The reason is simple: if an experiment is repeated and the DGP is stochastic, in general a different member of the sample space can result in a random fashion. Therefore, the domain value on which the estimator operates also changes randomly, and (unless the estimator is a constant over this range of domain values) the value of the estimator does as well. In other words, an estimator takes on different values as the random draw from the sample space of an experiment changes.

An estimator is also a function. A particular value that it takes (i.e., a value in its range for a given draw from the sample space) is an *estimate*. Finally, an estimator is also a statistic, in the formal sense of a quantity computable from sample observations.

So far this discussion does not demand that estimators actually estimate anything in particular. But of course, the purpose of estimation and estimators is to learn about some parameter of a DGP on the basis of observable data. If the quantity being estimated is some unknown parameter θ, the estimator is denoted $\widehat{\theta}(\mathbf{X})$, where $\mathbf{X} = X_1, \ldots, X_n$ is a list of draws of a random variable, the DGP of which we are trying to learn about. In this notation, the domain of the estimator is the sample data itself. This makes sense: the estimator is computed on the basis of what can be observed. It's not useful if some other information that can't be observed is required to compute it. The sample is denoted with bold font $\mathbf{X}$ to remind us that it is a list of observations. Sometimes it's simpler just to write $\widehat{\theta}$, but the $\mathbf{X}$ is implicitly in there too. No data, no estimator.

On the basis of what is observed, we hope the computed estimate $\widehat{\theta}$ conveys some information about θ. This is all abstract and general, but several estimators are already familiar. The sample mean, median, variance, covariance/correlation, and regression coefficients are some of the most common estimators used in applied quantitative research.

We of course want to rely on estimators that do a "good job" of helping us learn about the DGP. What "good" means is not unambiguous. There are several aspects of "good" in this sense, and there may be trade-offs among them – an estimator that is "good" in one sense may not be in another. Understanding something about how estimators are evaluated, and how "good" estimators for new classes of DGPs are derived, is therefore essential for making good choices among the variety of estimators available for a given dataset in applied quantitative work. The discussion here is just a brief introduction to the issues in evaluating estimators – of what it means for an estimator to do a "good job" of helping us learn about the DGP.

A canonical analogy for evaluating estimators is to think of a parameter as the bull's eye on a target. An estimator is like a dart thrower aiming at the target, and estimates are like specific throws of a dart. The darts can hit many locations on the target, and each thrower has some random variation in the placement of his or her darts.

Of course, when picking teammates for a game of darts, there are several aspects of each thrower to evaluate. Some people throw darts spread all over the board, but spread evenly over all parts of it. Their average throw is right about at the bull's eye, but their throws can wind up anywhere. Other people throw darts precisely but can't ever seem to correct for their own height relative to the dart board, so they may consistently have concentrated throws a little above the bull's eye. Their average throw is not at the bull's eye, but most of the time it's pretty close.

Which thrower would make the better teammate is not obvious. The reason is that the quality of a teammate is a multifaceted concept. A player who is precise and close to the bull's eye on average is clearly better than one who is imprecise and far from the bull's eye on average. But how to trade these aspects of quality against each other is a judgment call.

Evaluating estimators is basically the same as this in many respects. (That's why it's a canonical analogy: it's pretty much correct on the basics.) As random variables, they have expectations and they have variances and many other properties as well. All are important in evaluating estimators, and doing better on one aspect may necessitate doing worse on another.

9.2.1 Bias

The *bias* of an estimator is the expected value of the difference between it and the parameter it is estimating. Formally, bias is

$$B(\widehat{\theta}(\mathbf{X})) = E_X[\widehat{\theta}(\mathbf{X}) - \theta]. \tag{9.4}$$

The subscript X in E_X reminds us that X is the only random quantity here, and it is all that the expectation can be taken with respect to.

An estimator is *unbiased* if for any N, $B(\widehat{\theta}) = 0$. This only means that in expectation the estimator is equal to the parameter; it does not mean that in general, or often, or even with positive probability that the estimator is equal to the true parameter. Indeed, for a continuous random variable, the probability that the estimator is *exactly* equal to the true parameter is 0. This is simply because the probability that a continuous random variable is equal to any specific number is 0.

The sample mean $\overline{X}$ is the most familiar example of an unbiased estimator. We saw this in Chapter 7: $E(\overline{X}) = \mu$. Note that this equality holds for all sample sizes; we never used N to prove it, so N does not affect it. It is true that the sample mean as an estimator gets more *precise* as N grows, that is, the standard error of the sample mean declines with N, so that the sample mean is more and more concentrated around its expectation. But for a fixed sample size, no estimator of μ can improve on the sample mean in terms of bias (and some other terms as well; see below). In other words, there is no "large N" requirement in the justification for the sample mean as an estimator.

The same is true for OLS regression coefficients. To establish unbiasedness (as in Chapter 7), we never used the sample size N. We made heavy use of the assumption that $E(Y|X)$ is linear in covariates, and $Cov(X, \varepsilon) = 0$ or exogeneity of covariates. These are the core assumptions to make OLS regression unbiased. Sample size has nothing to do with it.

Nor, for that matter, does the parametric family of the DGP: nothing about the proof of unbiasedness is per se inconsistent with a Bernoulli or Poisson. DGP for example. To be sure, the links of the means (etc.) of these DGPs to explanatory variables cannot be linear over an unbounded range of X values, because then $E(Y|X)$ would sometimes be outside the feasible set of parameter values for these DGPs (this is the range matching problem mentioned in Chapter 6). But these links may be well approximated by a linear function in some smaller, bounded range of Xs, especially around the mean of X. Because the marginal effects of covariates are often evaluated under the assumption that each covariate takes its mean value, linear regression models may be less problematic than meets the eye.

In any case, the (lack of any) role for the parametric family in establishing unbiasedness of OLS should make readers suspicious about any claim that OLS is "inappropriate" for a particular application because the dependent variable is assumed to follow a distribution other than normal.

Unbiasedness is a nice property, but it is often not possible to find a useful unbiased estimator for nonlinear models, and in any case, favoring unbiasedness even if it leads to a noisy, imprecise estimator is probably unwise.

9.2.2 Mean Squared Error

Bias is nice to avoid, but it is not the only property that matters. It's also nice to have an estimator that varies only a little from sample to sample around a reasonably "good" guess. Would it be acceptable to take a small amount of bias to achieve a 95% reduction in the variance of an estimator? 99%? Whatever – for some percentage reduction in variance and for a small enough amount of bias as the "price" of this reduction, the answer is surely yes. That reflects that we are willing to trade bias and efficiency off against each other, and a lexicographic ranking of them does not allow that.

The criterion of *mean squared error* (MSE) is one way to formalize a trade-off between bias and efficiency when evaluating estimators. For an estimator $\widehat{\theta}(\mathbf{X})$, the estimator's MSE is $E_X[(\widehat{\theta}(\mathbf{X}) - \theta)^2]$. This is equivalent to, and more handily summarized as,

$$MSE(\widehat{\theta}(\mathbf{X})) = Var(\widehat{\theta}(\mathbf{X})) + (B(\widehat{\theta}(\mathbf{X})))^2 \qquad (9.5)$$

where $B(\widehat{\theta}(\mathbf{X}))$ is the bias as defined earlier. The estimator's *root MSE* or *RMSE* is simply the square root of the MSE. On this criterion, a "good" estimator is one with minimum MSE, that is, the value of $\widehat{\theta}(\mathbf{X})$ that minimizes 9.5.

Thus, MSE stays constant with an increase in bias, if a relatively larger decrease in variance is thereby achieved. Because bias is squared, a decrease in bias helps MSE exactly the same as an equivalent decrease in the standard error of the estimator. The estimator's variance is its SE squared, and variance has the same "penalty" for MSE as the square of the bias.

MSE is an important criterion for justifying estimators, but many researchers never quite warm up to the idea of introducing bias on purpose. Thus when minimum MSE conflicts with unbiasedness, people have tended to prefer unbiasedness.

9.2.3 Variance, Precision, and Efficiency

As the MSE criterion suggests, another aspect of a good estimator is that it has low variance. Whatever the expected value of an estimator, low variance is better than high. Low variance means the estimator provides a precise guess about the value of the parameter it is estimating. The variance of an estimator is $Var(\widehat{\theta}(\mathbf{X}) = E_X(\widehat{\theta}(\mathbf{X})^2) - E_X(\widehat{\theta}(\mathbf{X}))^2$, and the *precision* of an estimator is the inverse of its variance.

A closely related criterion is the *relative efficiency* of an estimator relative to another. For two estimators with the same bias (i.e., the same expected value and estimating the same parameter), the relative efficiency is simply the ratio of their variances. An estimator is *efficient* in a class of estimators if it has the minimum variance of all estimators in that class. Such an estimator is also sometimes called the "best" estimator in the class. A special case of this is an efficient estimator among all unbiased estimators for some parameter. Such a thing is called a *uniform minimum variance unbiased estimator* or *UMVUE*. Although not a catchy name or acronym, it does have the virtue of being exactly self-descriptive.

Efficiency of estimators is most meaningfully judged within a class of estimators that share some other desirable property, such as unbiasedness, rather than simply in terms of an estimator's variance by itself. The reason is that it is always possible to find an estimator with 0 variance. For any parameter θ from any DGP and for any sample, let $\widehat{\theta}(\mathbf{X}) = 64$. This estimator has 0 variance, but it is not otherwise especially compelling.

It is not necessary that a collection of estimators of given bias has any member that is efficient, that is, one of these estimators has the lowest variance in the class for any sample size. But when there is one, and the class to which it belongs is an otherwise compelling one (e.g., all unbiased estimators), an efficient estimator is a powerful one.

Unbiasedness and Efficiency of $\widehat{\beta}$: The Gauss-Markov Theorem

Probably the best-known result on efficiency in statistical modeling relates to the OLS estimator of β in a model of linear regression. The *Gauss-Markov theorem* asserts that the OLS estimator has the smallest variance of any unbiased estimator that is a linear combination of observed y_is, under particular conditions. That is, OLS is efficient or "best" in the class of linear unbiased estimators. This provides a powerful rationale for using the OLS estimator, in contexts in which the conditions of the theorem are credibly approximated.

It is hard to think of a better way to go about making inferϵ unknown β.

Now, it might seem that we have already fully justified OL$\!$ this purpose. We saw in Chapter 2 that the OLS regression coefficient gives a smaller MSE than any other guess about y that is a linear function of x. This provides some justification for OLS as a tool for describing relationships that happen to occur in a sample. There is no other way to use the sample information in a straight-line function to make a guess about y that gives a smaller MSE. At the level of the DGP, essentially the same result makes the regression $E(Y|X)$ an interesting object to analyze; if we want to describe Y's general tendency as a function of X, nothing beats the regression in terms of MSE. We saw this in Chapter 5.

But neither the sample nor the DGP version of this result that the regression minimizes MSE tells us that ordinary least squares (OLS) computed *from a sample* is an especially good way to learn about the regression *in the DGP*. The MSE results we saw before are not about inference from sample to DGP. In other words, the MSE results tell us that one piece of information in the sample is the best way to make a guess about a value of y drawn out of the sample; or one piece of information in the DGP is the best way to make make a guess about the value of Y that results from the DGP.

But why do we use this piece of information $\widehat{\beta}$ from the sample to learn about another piece of information β in the DGP? That is a different matter. Even if we want a linear estimator from the sample, why not use one of the innumerable other ones to learn about the regression in the DGP?

The Gauss-Markov theorem provides a good reason, at least within the domain where its assumptions are credible. To be clear, the Gauss-Markov theorem asserts that under certain conditions, for any other linear estimator besides OLS, such that the expected value of the estimator is β, the standard error of this alternative linear estimator is at least as large as the standard error of the OLS coefficient (see, e.g., Wooldridge [2009] for a formal proof). Thus of all linear estimators that are "correct" on average (unbiased), OLS gives the most accurate assessment of β in the DGP in the sense of minimum variance. OLS is therefore sometimes referred to as the *best linear unbiased estimator (BLUE)* of β. This is the takeaway of the Gauss-Markov theorem.

Now as to those "certain conditions." Like the derivation of $E(\widehat{\beta})$ and $SE(\widehat{\beta})$ in Chapter 7, the Gauss-Markov theorem assumes that in the DGP, Y is a linear function of the covariates X, plus a disturbance ε. Also, the theorem assumes[2] $E(\varepsilon) = 0$; that the (finite) variance of ε is σ^2, the same for all observations of Y_i; and that the disturbances are uncorrelated

---

[2] Mean zero is "free" as long as the model contains an intercept because $E(\varepsilon)$ could just be folded into that.

cross observations, so $Cov(\varepsilon_i, \varepsilon_j) = 0, \forall i, j$. Like the earlier derivations, the Gauss-Markov theorem does not make any assumptions about the parametric family generating Y per se. As long as it meets the other assumptions, any DGP such as normal, Poisson, or exponential is fine.

The Gauss-Markov theorem adds the extra assumption that the covariates are fixed values. Suppose that before the sampling of Y_is from the DGP takes place, a value of each covariate is fixed at X_i for each observation i. We can still imagine a new draw of Y_is, but each new draw of Y_i is taken with the same given X_i value in Gauss-Markov land. This is the assumption of *fixed regressors in repeated sampling*. The Y_is in a new sample would still be random given those regressors, so the OLS slope $\widehat{\beta}$ is still a random variable. This assumption gives exogeneity of X "for free." Because the Xs were fixed without reference to the εs in the first place, and Xs do not vary from sample to sample, they cannot be correlated with the disturbances ε.

Altogether, the Gauss-Markov theorem assumes linearity in the DGP, mean zero disturbances, homoskedasticity and independence of observations, and an even stronger condition than exogeneity of regressors. In return for this battery of assumptions, it gives us a BLUE estimator in OLS.

The proof of the Gauss-Markov theorem shows that $\widehat{\beta}$ minimizes the mean squared error of any guess about β that is a linear function of the observed Y_is. This makes it the best possible (linear) guess in an MSE sense about the value of β.

So we have encountered three MSE results about regression. The first is for a sample: the OLS regression is the best (linear) guess about a value of y drawn out of a dataset at random. The second is for a DGP: the conditional mean $E(Y|X)$ is the best guess about Y that can be conditioned on X. The third is for the connection between the sample and the DGP: the OLS slope from the sample is the best (linear) guess about the slope of the regression in the DGP, when the DGP regression is a linear function of X. The Guass-Markov theorem has the most elaborate set of assumptions of these three results because we have to say something about the process of drawing a sample in order to establish what the sample says about the DGP.

9.2.4 Consistency

An estimator is *consistent* if, as the sample size approaches ∞, the probability that the estimator differs from the parameter it estimates by more than some amount approaches zero. The "small amount" can be as small as anyone wants, like one millionth of the size of the very small number you are thinking of right now. Refer to this number as ϵ.

Formally, an estimator is consistent if there is some finite sample size N^* such that, for any $N > N^*$, the probability that $|\widehat{\theta}(\mathbf{X}) - \theta|$ exceeds this ϵ is less than δ, where δ is some other prespecified positive number not larger than 1 (δ, too, can be a nano-sized number). The cutoff value N^* may be very large indeed, and it gets larger as ϵ and δ get smaller. But it exists. Intuitively, this means that in an infinitely large sample, we are completely certain about the location of a parameter in the DGP that generated the sample.

Consistency is defined in terms of a *probability limit*. This is simply the value of a specific probability, in an (imaginary) infinitely large sample. A consistent estimator is one such that

$$\lim_{N\to\infty} \Pr(|\widehat{\theta}(\mathbf{X}) - \theta| < \epsilon) = 1. \tag{9.6}$$

The "lim" part means we're thinking about the upper imaginable limit of the sample size, which is ∞. The expression says that as N approaches this limit, the probability of a specific event approaches 1. That event is $|\widehat{\theta}(\mathbf{X}) - \theta| < \epsilon$, which means that the distance between the estimator and the true parameter is smaller than our very small number ϵ. Consistency says this gets certain in an infinitely large sample.

As $N \to \infty$, a consistent estimator concentrates more and more of its density around the true parameter value, until it finally becomes a spike at the true parameter in an infinitely large sample. Although this seems to pin down the expected value of the estimator when $N = \infty$ at least, consistency is different from an $N = \infty$ version of unbiasedness. But in a sense consistency is more important. If the entire sampling distribution converges to a spike around the true parameter value, it will be close to a correct guess in an infinite sample, so its expected value is somewhat secondary.

A biased estimator may be consistent. Consider $\widehat{\sigma}^2 = \frac{\sum(X-\overline{X})^2}{N}$. Its bias in estimating σ^2 becomes negligible when N is very large. Compare $\widehat{\sigma}^2$ to S^2, which can be written $\frac{N}{N-1}\widehat{\sigma}^2$ but is unbiased (see Chapter 7). The term $\frac{N}{N-1}$ gets closer and closer to 1 as N increases, so $\widehat{\sigma}^2$ and S^2 converge to the same quantity as $N \to \infty$, namely σ^2.

On the other hand, an unbiased estimator may be inconsistent. A classic example involves N draws $Y_1, Y_2, \ldots, Y_N$ from a normal (μ, σ^2) distribution. Clearly, $E(Y_1) = \mu$, so Y_1 is unbiased. But $Var(Y_1) = \sigma^2$ no matter how many other observations are in the sample. So its sampling distribution (which is just the original DGP) does not converge to a spike as $N \to \infty$. So it cannot be consistent.

There is a strong ethos in quantitative methods of treating inconsistency as a deal-breaker for an estimator and treating consistency as at least part of a solid justification for use in applied research. The idea is that if an estimator is not even consistent, there is not much hope for learning about DGP parameters from it. If its sampling distribution doesn't converge to a spike at the true parameter value for infinitely large samples, it is unlikely to perform well in smaller, realistically sized samples. In addition, consistency is a useful basis for justification because, theoretically, it is far easier to establish general properties of estimators in very large samples than in small ones (most sensible estimators have a lot less random noise due to idiosyncratic samples to deal with as $N \to \infty$).

The idea is not that any particular sample size is "close enough" to ∞ to invoke behavior under $N = \infty$ in a finite sample. Rather, it is that if the relative performance of two estimators can be established in a large sample, something strange would have to happen for that performance to be reversed in small ones, so the large sample results provide a window into reasonable small sample performance.

Some estimators commonly encountered in everyday, applied statistical research can be justified partly based on consistency, but not unbiasedness (because this cannot be shown analytically in any sample size). For instance, the conventional estimator of β in logit, probit, Poisson, hazard models, and the like, is consistent. (The method for deriving the estimators in these models is discussed in Section 9.3.) In OLS regression, the Huber-White heteroskedasticity consistent SE (and related SEs such as Newey-West and panel-corrected standard errors) is considered safe and effective for daily use because it is a consistent estimator of the actual but unknown OLS SEs under heteroskedasticity (etc.).

The Law of Large Numbers: Consistency of $\overline{X}$

Now we can add one more property of $\overline{X}$: The sample mean is also a consistent estimator of μ. This is an important result in the theory and history of statistics known as the *weak law of large numbers*.[3]

A more compact expression for consistency is plim $\widehat{\theta}(\mathbf{X}) = \theta$, where "plim" stands for *probability limit*. When a random variable X has a probability limit of Ξ, people sometimes say that "X *converges in probability* to Ξ."

The other time we encountered this idea of "convergence," or the behavior of a random variable as $N \to \infty$, was about the CLT. In that context, we investigated the entire sampling distribution of a random variable as $N \to \infty$, not just the location of a single point where that distribution concentrates all of its weight (which is what the probability limit or consistency is about). The notion of convergence in the CLT is called *convergence in distribution*.[4]

These types of convergence deal with the *limiting* or *asymptotic* behavior of a random variable. An asymptote of a function $f(x)$ is a value y to which $f(x)$ gets closer and closer, as x gets closer to (without reaching) some limit. So in this case, we're looking at the asymptote something that is a function of N, as N approaches (without reaching) its conceivable limit of ∞. The formal analysis of the asymptotic behavior of estimators for $N = \infty$ is sometimes called *asymptotics* or *large sample* theory.

---

[3] The *strong law of large numbers* asserts $Pr(\lim_{N \to \infty} \overline{X} = \mu) = 1$. This is a stronger, more restrictive and difficult to satisfy, notion of convergence than consistency.

[4] The type of convergence considered in the strong law of large numbers is *almost sure* convergence.

9.2.5 The Cramér-Rao Theorem

For an estimator to be consistent requires that it has a certain degree of responsiveness to the observations in the sample. In classical statistics, the sample is the only window into the parameters of the DGP. The law of large numbers and other consistency results rest on the idea that in a very large sample, the data will trace out the entirety of the DGP (a histogram of the sample data will look just like the PMF or PDF that generated it). So consistent estimation has to use that data to learn as much as possible about the parameters of the DGP.

The exact same responsiveness to sample information means that a consistent estimator has to have a certain amount of noise in it. An estimator cannot be both responsive enough to sample information to be consistent and yet sure to bounce around very little from one sample to the next. The reason is that the sample observations themselves are stochastic, and if they bounce around a lot from one sample to the next, then a consistent estimator has to bounce around with them. That is what it means for an estimator to be responsive to the data.

This intuition suggests that there is a lower bound on the variance for consistent estimators. To push variance below this lower bound, an estimator has to compromise responsiveness to the data to such an extent that it is no longer consistent. In fact, this blithe intuition is formalized in a deep result from statistics called the *Cramér-Rao theorem*.

The Cramér-Rao theorem establishes the lower bound of variance for a consistent estimator in terms of the properties of the DGP. This quantity is the *Cramér-Rao lower bound* (CRLB).

To be specific, consider a consistent estimator $\widehat{\theta}(\mathbf{X})$ of the parameter θ of a DGP $f(\mathbf{x}|\theta)$. Assume the DGP can be differentiated in θ twice, and its second derivative is continuous. The Cramér-Rao theorem asserts

$$Var(\widehat{\theta}(\mathbf{X})) \geq \frac{1}{\mathcal{I}(\theta)}, \tag{9.7}$$

where $\mathcal{I}(\theta)$ is the *Fisher information* of the DGP at θ,

$$\mathcal{I}(\theta) = E\left[\left(\frac{\partial \ln f(\mathbf{x}|\theta)}{\partial \theta}\right)^2\right] = -E\left[\frac{\partial^2 \ln f(\mathbf{x}|\theta)}{\partial \theta^2}\right]. \tag{9.8}$$

So the key to the CRLB is the Fisher information. It seems imposing, but it is also important, so we should take a look at it. The middle expression gives us a foothold. Inside of the $E(\cdot)^2$, it contains the derivative of the natural log of the density. The natural log is an increasing, concave function. It tends to have a smoothing effect on densities that are peaked around 0, such as the normal.

Now, the PDF is differentiated with respect to θ. This means, hold the sample data ($\mathbf{x}$) fixed, and look at what happens to the probability of that sample as

TABLE 9.1. *Computing Fisher Information for Two Distributions*

x	$f(x\mid p = .5)$	$f(x\mid p = 1)$	$\Delta(f(x))$	Δ^2
(H, H)	$\frac{1}{4}$	1	$-\frac{3}{4}$	$\frac{9}{16}$
(H, T)	$\frac{1}{4}$	0	$\frac{1}{4}$	$\frac{1}{16}$
(T, H)	$\frac{1}{4}$	0	$\frac{1}{4}$	$\frac{1}{16}$
(T, T)	$\frac{1}{4}$	0	$\frac{1}{4}$	$\frac{1}{16}$

the DGP's parameter θ changes. For an analogy from a case with discrete θ, suppose a coin is flipped twice. The coin is either fair $(p(H) = .5)$ or double-headed $(p(H) = 1)$. The possible samples are $(H, H), (H, T), (T, H), (T, T)$. Because there are only two parameter values, we can't differentiate the mass function. But the derivative of the parameter p is analogous to the difference in the probability of a given sample under the two parameter values. Table 9.1 lists these differences as Δ.

The first column lists the possible samples. The second column lists the probability of each sample for the first possible parameter value (fair coin), and the third column repeats this for the second possible parameter value (double headed coin). The fourth column is the difference in the probability of a given sample across the two possible parameters, which is analogous to the derivative for a discrete parameter space.[5] The fifth column contains the square of each probability difference from the fourth column.

Now the Fisher information instructs us to evaluate the expected value of the quantity in the last column: $\mathcal{I}(p) = E(\Delta^2)$. This expectation is with reference to the PMF $f(x\mid p)$, that is, the probabilities supplied in either the second or the third column, depending on p. This is the only possibility because it's the only probability distribution in the problem. The parameter p is not a random variable in classical statistics and has no distribution.

So we have to compute two expectations, one for each p. That is why $\mathcal{I}(p)$ is a function of p. The first is $E(\Delta^2\mid p = .5) = .1875$. The second is $E(\Delta^2\mid p = 1) = .5625$. These are the analogues to $\mathcal{I}(\theta)$ in this problem.[6]

Although simple, this example reveals a couple of key points that generalize. First, the minimum possible variance depends on the true parameter θ. In

[5] The definition of $\mathcal{I}(\theta)$ contains the derivative (difference) of the natural log of the probabilities, not of the probabilities themselves. This is a minor complication for this exposition, and so we ignore it.

[6] Consistent estimation is a little trickier than usual in this strange parameter space. A consistent estimator is $\widehat{\theta}(H, H) = 1$, and $\widehat{\theta}(x) = .5$ for any other sample. In other words, if the sample (H, H) occurs, the best guess about the parameter is $p = 1$, but if any other sample occurs, the best guess is $p = .5$. The first part is true because $p = 1$ makes the sample (H, H) more likely than the other parameter value makes it; the second occurs because $p = .5$ makes every other sample more likely than the other parameter value makes it. But these ideas foreshadow the theory of maximum likelihood, not introduced until Section 9.3, so we set them aside here.

particular, the minimum possible variance of a consistent estimator of p is smaller when $p = 1$ than when $p = .5$. If $p = 1$ actually holds, our estimator will have smaller variance than if $p = .5$ actually holds. In other words, the consistent estimator changes less from sample to sample when $p = 1$ than when $p = .5$.[7]

Second, the reason the CRLBs compare in that way is that the sample comes down to two factors. First, for a given sample, how much does its probability change from one parameter value to the next; second, for a given parameter value, how widely does the probability distribution disperse its weight over the possible samples? These are the two factors that go into the expected value in the Fisher information.

The first factor has to do with how discriminating the sample is about possible values of θ. If a given sample is likely under one parameter value, say θ^*, but unlikely under all others, then $\frac{\partial \ln f(\mathbf{x}|\theta)}{\partial \theta}$ will be very large around θ^* and very small for all other values of θ. This is analogous to the sample (H, H) in our little table: the value of Δ is relatively large here. This kind of situation contributes a lot to the Fisher information for θ^*. Very discriminating DGPs give relatively high Fisher information.

The second factor has to do with the variance of the DGP itself. If the DGP for θ^* spreads its weight widely over the possible samples, then even a discriminating sample (in the sense of the previous paragraph) doesn't get much weight in determining the expected value of $(\frac{\partial \ln f(\mathbf{x}|\theta)}{\partial \theta})^2$. So the Fisher information could still be low. But if, assuming θ^* is the true parameter value, the DGP concentrates its weight on samples that are very discriminating for θ^*, then the DGP has relatively small variance. So the discriminating samples get a lot of weight in determining $(\frac{\partial \ln f(\mathbf{x}|\theta)}{\partial \theta})^2$. This will contribute to relatively high Fisher information.

So the Fisher information packs a lot of information into a compact expression. The key point is that the CRLB depends on both how discriminating the DGP is about the value of θ (because the derivative of the DGP appears here) and on how widely the DGP disperses its probability weight over possible samples (i.e., its variance). Based on these factors, the Cramér-Rao theorem establishes a "price" of consistency: one must maintain some minimum degree of uncertainty about the actual location of the parameter in exchange for it.

One thing that does not appear in it explicitly is the formula for the consistent estimator $\widehat{\theta}$ itself. The Fisher information, and the CRLB, are about the variance of any possible consistent estimator for the parameter of a given DGP, not just the particular estimator we happen to be working with in a particular case. All

---

[7] In fact, if $p = 1$, only one sample is possible, so the consistent estimator will not change at all from sample to sample. Do not be alarmed. This 0 variance result is not lower than the real CRLB because our simple calculations are not the real Fisher information; they are only illustrative of similar ideas.

the information an estimator can use is in the DGP anyway, which is already in the Fisher information.

9.3 MAXIMUM LIKELIHOOD ESTIMATION

The *method of maximum likelihood* is a widely used technique for deriving estimators in classical, parametric statistics. It depends crucially on specifying the functional form of the DGP correctly, but with that specification, the method is flexible and produces estimators with desirable statistical properties. An estimator obtained from maximum likelihood methods is a *maximum likelihood estimator*, and the approach is referred to as *maximum likelihood estimation*. The acronym *MLE* is used as shorthand for both.

All of the generalized linear models encountered in Chapter 6 (e.g., the logit, probit, Poisson, exponential, Weibull) are typically estimated by maximum likelihood. This may be invisible to the user of statistics software, who simply asks for a Poisson model (etc.) and awaits the output. The computer is programmed to use MLE in these cases because it does a good job, assuming the model is specified correctly (that is something a computer can't figure out for you). A linear regression model can also be estimated by maximum likelihood instead of ordinary least squares, although if Y is normally distributed, it turns out the estimators are equivalent.

It is important for researchers to know, at minimum, *why* their software packages use MLEs. Beyond this, theoreticians of statistical modeling often use MLE to derive estimators for new problems that applied researchers might encounter but for which previous theoreticians have not provided much guidance. Knowing some basic theory of MLE helps a researcher understand the implicit argument methodologists are making when they recommend the use of an estimator obtained by maximum likelihood methods.[8]

The concept of maximum likelihood is simple to explain and illustrate. It is made difficult in practice by analytic and/or computational aspects of finding maximizers of complicated, nonlinear functions. In some simple (but still real-life relevant) problems, an MLE can be found by analytic, calculus-based maximization techniques. But as the requisite maximization problem becomes more complicated, the value of calculus-based techniques degrades rapidly compared with computational search algorithms designed to find maximizers. There are many important features of these algorithms and search procedures that are relevant in an advanced discussion of estimators obtained using them; for example, the search algorithm may affect the "stability" of the estimator or whether it is highly sensitive to slight changes in the estimation problem or

---

[8] Any standard mathematical statistics text will have a more in depth discussion of MLE; see Casella and Berger [2002]. For a compelling argument about the power of the likelihood approach and numerous applications in social science, see King [1998].

TABLE 9.2. *PMFs (columns) and Likelihood Functions (rows)*

x	$f(x\|1)$	$f(x\|2)$	$f(x\|3)$
0	$\frac{1}{3}$	$\frac{1}{4}$	0
1	$\frac{1}{3}$	$\frac{1}{4}$	0
2	0	$\frac{1}{6}$	$\frac{1}{4}$
3	$\frac{1}{6}$	$\frac{1}{3}$	$\frac{1}{2}$
4	$\frac{1}{6}$	0	$\frac{1}{4}$

underlying DGP. But the analysis of numerical or simulation based maximization methods for complicated objective functions is beyond our scope here, where we really need to establish the core idea.

In a nutshell, the MLE of a parameter is the parameter value that makes the data that was actually observed as likely as it could possibly have been. An MLE is the result of searching over all possible parameter values[9] and selecting the one that, given the other features of the DGP (to wit, its functional form), makes the actual data that was observed is as likely as it can be. This is a process of maximizing the likelihood function generated by a probability distribution.

The information about the likelihood of the observed sample data comes from an assumption about the DGP. If we know the DGP is Bernoulli and sample observations are independent, the DGP's parameter p determines the probability of observing any particular sample that might be drawn. If we observe a sample of four iid draws from a Bernoulli distribution, then $p = 1$ implies that the probability of observing the sample $\{1, 0, 1, 1\}$ is 0. More generally, using the binomial coefficients from Chapter 4, we can identify the probability of observing this particular sample for any value of p, assuming this is really the DGP. Given that we do observe this sample, what's the best guess about p? The idea in MLE is that it's the one that makes the probability[10] of the observed sample as large as possible.

That's the idea. The formal concept of a likelihood function takes some getting used to. Here is a simple example. One observation is taken on a discrete random variable X with PMF $f(x|\theta)$, $\theta \in \{1, 2, 3\}$, as in Table 9.2.[11]

---

[9] This phrasing reveals why the computational approach to finding MLE's is subtle. Typically, there is an uncountable infinity of possible parameter values, because the parameter lies somewhere in an interval. But a computer, as a finite state machine, cannot possibly evaluate an uncountable infinity of possible points. Therefore, it must base its answer about the MLE on a search of finitely many points, and so the way in which it chooses points can be very important for ensuring that an even *greater* likelihood of observing the data would have been obtained at some possible parameter value that the computer happened not to evaluate.

[10] Or density, for continuous distributions.

[11] This example is inspired by Casella and Berger [2002].

The idea is that "nature" picks a value of θ and keeps it a secret, but "nature" does let us see one draw from the distribution $f(x|\theta)$. We want to guess the value of θ that nature picked, given the value of X that was observed.

The table presents all the possible probability distributions for X. They are in the columns, specified by each value of θ. Note that for each value of θ, this table does indeed give a PMF. Fixing a column and adding down through the rows produces a sum of 1. Moreover, each entry is nonnegative. Because this gives the probability of each possible X, it must be a distribution.

The table also presents all the *likelihood functions* that can be constructed from the observed sample (again, the sample is just a single draw from one of these DGPs). There is one likelihood function for each value of x that might be observed. The likelihood for a given x gives the probability of having observed that x for each value of θ. The rows of the table contain the likelihood function for each possible sample. The likelihood function is denoted $L(\theta|x)$.

Whereas the PMF gives the probability of each x for a given θ, the likelihood gives the probability of a given x for each θ. Thus the collection of distributions and the collection of likelihood functions in this probability model present the same information in different packaging. There is one PMF for each value of θ, and it returns the probability of each sample given that θ. And there is one likelihood function for each possible observed sample x; it returns the probability of observing that given x for each possible value of θ.

So once we know the general PMF and the set of possible parameter values, we also automatically know the likelihood function. This PMF and its parameter θ specify the DGP of the sample. This illustrates why MLE, which is based on the likelihood function, requires a parametric specification of the DGP. That specification is where the likelihood function comes from.

The maximum likelihood estimator for θ in this probability model specifies the value of the θ that maximizes the likelihood function for each possible realization of X. The MLE in this case, denoted $\widehat{\theta}(x)$, is 1 for $x = 0$ or 1, and is 3 for $x = 2, 3$, or 4. The MLE, like any estimator, is a function of the sample observed, and gives the parameter value that makes the observed data more likely than any other parameter value makes it. That is clearly the case here: in each row of the table, the MLE is the header of the column in which the largest probability lies. So if you observe a draw of $x = 3$, the idea of maximum likelihood says that the "best guess" about the value of θ is 3. The reason is that this value of θ maximizes the chance of seeing what was actually observed. As always in classical statistics, it is the sample that is a random variable.

The specifics are more complicated in case the parameter space is continuous and/or multidimensional, and the sample has many observations of a continuous random variable, but the basic idea in this simple table carries through to those cases and it's helpful to remember it.

Note that the likelihood function may or may not be a PMF. In the earlier example, consider the likelihood for $x = 3$, $L(\theta|3)$. Its entries are $\frac{1}{6}, \frac{1}{3}, \frac{1}{2}$, the probability of observing 3 as the x-value under each possible parameter value.

As it happens, this is a PMF: each entry is nonnegative and their sum is 1. But this is a coincidence: consider $L(\theta|4)$. This is not a PMF. Its entries, although nonnegative, do not sum to 1. The point here is simply that a likelihood is not guaranteed to be a probability distribution in the formal sense. It's not guaranteed *not* to be one either.

More formally, let $f(\mathbf{x}|\theta)$ denote the PMF of a sample of N observations of the random variable X. Given this PMF, the likelihood function is

$$L(\theta|\mathbf{x}) = f(\mathbf{x}|\theta), \tag{9.9}$$

and the maximum likelihood estimator is

$$\widehat{\theta}(\mathbf{x}) = \mathrm{argmax}_\theta\, L(\theta|\mathbf{x}). \tag{9.10}$$

The notation "argmax " refers to the *arg*ument that *max*imizes the function on the right hand side. That is, it is the value of θ at which the maximum of $L(\theta|\mathbf{x})$) occurs.

If the sample observations are iid, the sample PMF used in Equation 9.9 is the N-fold product of the PMF from which every observation is drawn, or $f(\mathbf{x}|\theta) = \prod_i f(x_i|\theta)$. So then the likelihood function is an N-fold product too. Products can be a bit difficult to maximize.[12]

For this reason, it is more common to encounter the natural log of the likelihood function, called the *log likelihood*, rather than the likelihood function itself. Assuming an iid sample, the log likelihood function is

$$\ln L(\theta|\mathbf{x}) \equiv \mathcal{L}(\theta|\mathbf{x}) = \sum_i \ln f(x_i|\theta). \tag{9.11}$$

Again, the summation is only valid because the sample PMF is a product of individual PMFs, and that is only true because of independence.

This log transformation works because one of the basic properties of the natural log is $\ln(ab) = \ln a + \ln b$. So products are additive in natural logs. An additive function is usually easier to maximize than a multiplicative one.[13] And because the natural log is an increasing function, $\mathcal{L}(\theta|\mathbf{x})$ is maximized at the same point as $L(\theta|\mathbf{x})$. Of course, the *magnitude* of the function at this maximizing point is different,[14] but that doesn't really matter. MLE is about finding the value of $\widehat{\theta}$ that maximizes the likelihood function, and the same value of $\widehat{\theta}$ maximizes the log likelihood function as well.

Clearly, given the way a likelihood function is defined, maximum likelihood estimation is impossible without a specific assumption about the distribution

---

[12] For instance, the first derivative of a product is not the product of the first derivatives; it involves a lot more algebra.

[13] For instance, the derivative of the sum with respect to θ is a sum of individual derivatives.

[14] In practice, log likelihoods are negative numbers and often in the hundreds or thousands in absolute value. The likelihood is a turned-around probability, so $L(\theta|x)$ is always between 0 and 1. Because $\ln 1 = 0$ and the natural log decreases quickly below $x = 1$, it is always going to be negative and sometimes startlingly so.

over the members of the sample. Without a PDF/PMF for sample elements, there is no likelihood, and nothing to maximize. This is not true for estimation procedures such as least squares or the method of moments, although placing error bounds on estimators obtained from those procedures, or making inferences, usually does require an assumption about the population distribution. In any case, MLE is powerful and appealing (see below) if an analyst is comfortable with a specific distributional model for his or her data. But it is a highly parametric method and inherits skepticism about parametric assumptions.

9.3.1 Maximum Likelihood Estimation of Regression Models

All the foregoing works out the idea of MLE for estimating a parameter of an unconditional DGP. In social science research, MLE is most often used to estimate the parameters of linear regression and generalized linear models ($g(E(Y|X)) = \alpha + \beta X$ where g is an invertible function), such as the logit, Poisson, and negative binomial models.

The idea of this is a pretty natural extension of the general ideas above. Take the bivariate normal linear regression model as an example: $f(y|x, \mu, \sigma^2)$ is the normal density with mean $\mu(x)$ and variance σ^2 (note that this assumes constant variance or homoskedasticity). This is the DGP of Y. This model also asserts $\mu(X) = E(Y|X) = \alpha + \beta X$. Given a value of X, knowing $\mu(X)$ requires knowing α and β.

So the formula for the conditional density[15] of y is $\frac{1}{\sigma\sqrt{2\pi}} e^{-\frac{1}{2\sigma^2}(y-\alpha-\beta x)^2}$. The important point about this is how the model $\alpha + \beta X$ appears. It is used to replace $\mu(X)$ in the normal density, in the exponent of e. Written this way, the density expresses both the assumption about Y's DGP and the link of its parameter μ to the explanatory variable X. Mathematically, we need this because we need α and β to appear in the likelihood function. Those are the parameters (along with σ^2) with which we need to maximize the likelihood function, so obviously we need to express how the likelihood function depends on them.

Assuming N independent draws of Y in the sample, the likelihood function for the bivariate normal model is

$$L(\alpha, \beta, \sigma^2|\mathbf{y}) = \prod_{i=1}^{N} \frac{1}{\sigma\sqrt{2\pi}} e^{-\frac{1}{2\sigma^2}(y_i-\alpha-\beta x_i)^2}$$

$$= \frac{1}{(\sigma^2 2\pi)^{N/2}} e^{-\frac{1}{2\sigma^2}\sum_{i=1}^{N}(y_i-\alpha-\beta x_i)^2}$$

$$= \frac{K}{(\sigma^2)^{N/2}} e^{-\frac{1}{2\sigma^2}\sum_{i=1}^{N}(y_i-\alpha-\beta x_i)^2}. \tag{9.12}$$

---

[15] See Chapter 6 for an extended discussion of this formula and how to parse each of its terms.

To get from the first line to the second, we leaned on the fact that $e^a e^b = e^{a+b}$. That is why there is already a sum over N terms in here even though we haven't gone to the log likelihood yet. To go from the second to the third line, we just rewrote the part before e as a constant K to reduce clutter. None of the components of K are functions of the parameters. So this shows as clearly as possible how the likelihood depends on the three parameters α, β and σ^2. Now the log likelihood:

$$\mathcal{L}(\alpha, \beta, \sigma^2 | y) = \ln K - \frac{N}{2} \ln \sigma^2 - \frac{1}{2\sigma^2} \sum_{i=1}^{N} (y_i - \alpha - \beta x_i)^2. \qquad (9.13)$$

We get to this $\mathcal{L}$ from L because, first, the natural log of a ratio is a difference (just as the natural log of a product is a sum); second, ln is the inverse of e to $\ln(e^x) = x$.

Now, because we want to maximize $\mathcal{L}$, we could just plunge ahead with some calculus – differentiate $\mathcal{L}$ with respect to all three parameters, obtain first order conditions, and solve them for α, β, and σ^2. We'd be on sure footing to do so because $\mathcal{L}$ is clearly differentiable and concave as a function of each parameter (and a second-order condition would verify this anyway). Mathematically, these derivatives are not that difficult to obtain.

But before doing this, look a bit at $\mathcal{L}$. The only part of it that includes α and β, and so the only part that can matter for determining the MLEs of these parameters is $\sum_{i=1}^{N} (y_i - \alpha - \beta x_i)^2$. We have seen this before, in the Appendix to Chapter 2: it is the sum of squared residuals in the sample. Note also that in $\mathcal{L}$, this sum of squared residuals has a negative sign in front of it. In OLS, we minimize this sum of squares. In MLE, we maximize -1 times the sum of squared residuals.

These are the same problem, so they have the same solution. For the normal linear model, $\widehat{\beta}^{OLS} = \widehat{\beta}^{MLE}$. It might seem pointless to construct this whole MLE apparatus for estimation when it just gives the same answer as OLS. But these approaches do not always coincide for models besides the normal linear one, and there are reasons (laid out subsequently) to trust MLEs when they are available and we have a lot of confidence in the underlying model of the DGP.

More important, MLE is a widely applicable approach that makes sense in estimation problems whenever a DGP can be postulated, whereas OLS might not. Viewed in this light, the correspondence of MLE and OLS for the normal linear model should give us some confidence in MLE. From the Gauss-Markov theorem (Chapter 7), we already know that, if the statistical model is correct, OLS gives the best linear unbiased estimator (BLUE). The MLE coincides with this solution in a problem where both OLS and MLE are applicable, which should give us some confidence that MLE does something sensible in problems where it but not OLS is a natural estimation approach.

It turns out, however, that there is one difference between the MLE and OLS results for the normal linear model. It pertains to the estimate of σ^2. In

OLS, σ^2 is estimated as $\frac{\sum(y_i - \widehat{\alpha} - \widehat{\beta}x_i)^2}{N-1}$. This is the "conventional" estimator of sample residual variance introduced in Chapter 2 and shown to be unbiased in Chapter 7. But working through the first-order condition for σ^2 from $\mathcal{L}$ shows that the MLE for σ^2 is $\frac{\sum(y_i - \widehat{\alpha} - \widehat{\beta}x_i)^2}{N}$. The difference is in the denominator. So the MLE for σ^2, called $\widehat{\sigma}^2$, is not unbiased. Computer software packages commonly give the OLS estimator of σ^2 by default but can give the MLE if asked for it.

This illustrates an important point about MLEs. Even if an unbiased estimator is available, the MLE may not coincide with it. The reason is that MLE considers not just the bias of an estimator but also its variance. And $\widehat{\sigma}^2$ has smaller variance than the OLS estimator of σ^2. Even though bias should be avoided if possible, it is not the only consideration for an estimator. The MLE balances bias against variance. We return to this in Section 9.3.3.

This exposition has considered the normal linear model, but MLE for model parameters works the same way conceptually for other models where a full DGP is specified. For instance, estimators for all the generalized linear models laid out in Chapter 6 can be obtained similarly. The function for the PMF/PDF of the sample ys will be different, of course, and the link from the DGPs parameters to the covariates will be different too. These differences change the algebra but not the sequence of steps in obtaining estimators or the general theory behind these steps.

In general, whatever model is used, this approach illustrates the great power of models for making inferences about DGPs. With a full statistical model specified, all information in the data is funneled into estimating a small number of parameters. The model does tremendous work to structure the estimation problem facing the researcher. When a model is not specified and the data has to "speak for itself" entirely, the use of sample information is not so concentrated. As a result, estimation and inference with a full model specification is typically much more efficient and more statistically powerful – model-based estimation is better able to distinguish alternative parameter values for a given sample size, which leads to sharper substantive conclusions.

The pitfall, of course, is that the model may not so much an artful simplification as a caricature or simply absurd. In that case, assuming a model still does just as much to structure the estimation and inference problem – it just does so in the wrong way. Assuming a parametric DGP or a specific functional form to link parameters and covariates (linear or otherwise) does a lot of work, but if they are not in reasonable correspondence with the actual DGP, all that structure can obscure more about the relationships in the data and underlying processes as it reveals.

Statistics cannot tell a substantive researcher whether a particular model is "right" or "wrong" for a particular application. Statistics works well as a complement to researchers who figure that out for themselves based on their knowledge of what they are studying; statistics then offers a way to learn as much as possible about the DGP and to estimate the uncertainty about what was actually learned.

A Note on Reporting Model Results

In software packages, results of estimation by MLE typically include the estimated $\widehat{\beta}$s, estimated standard errors for these, t or z statistics from the test that each individual parameter is really 0, p values for those tests, and confidence intervals.

Similar to the point in Chapter 8, researchers should report model results in a table that contains, at a minimum, the MLE for each β and α in the model, their respective estimated standard errors, and the overall sample size used for estimation. It is also a good idea to indicate what the dependent variable is at some point in the table. The reported estimates of β and its SE do not have to include every decimal place that the computer output gives. A good rule of thumb is that one need not report more decimal points for a coefficient than the standard error allows one to tell apart confidently.

It is optional and sometimes helpful to include in the table p-values, t/z statistics, confidence intervals, and little stars or asterisks on coefficients to indicate whether it passes conventional thresholds of statistical significance. Then in a narrative around the model, the substantive implications of each β estimate and various hypothesis tests should be discussed.

As we saw in Chapter 6, the estimated βs from nonlinear regression models (e.g., Poisson, logit, probit, exponential hazard) do not themselves indicate the marginal effects of the respective covariates on $E(Y|X)$. Of course, as also seen in Chapter 6, the sign of β for a covariate usually determines the sign of its marginal effect, and in social science theory, showing that the sign of a marginal effect accords with some theory is often the end of the game. Theory often deals with "bigger" or "smaller" or "more" or "less," whereas the exact magnitude of an effect is often (not always) unspecified or impossible to specify without absurd assumptions. A theory that contends that a child's socioeconomic status as an adult increases with their parents' socioeconomic status does not usually specify how big this effect is expected to be, it only asserts that it is positive.

Nevertheless, marginal effects are almost always more substantively interesting than (and always at least as interesting as) the estimated coefficients themselves. So either in the narrative around the model or in the table of results in lieu of reporting the MLE for each β, some discussion of marginal effects is useful to readers.

Many statistics software packages have simple commands to obtain marginal effects in these sorts of models after the estimation is performed. Note, however, that to establish a specific value of the marginal effect, a specific value of x must be inserted. For instance, in a bivariate Poisson model, the marginal effect of X on $E(Y|X)$ is $\beta e^{\alpha+\beta X}$. The computer will use the MLEs (or output of whatever estimator is used) for the parameters, but until a value of $X = x$ is specified, this is a function and not a number.

The easy way to handle this is to compute the marginal effect when each covariate is equal to its mean. A perhaps more satisfying piece of information is the expected value of the marginal effect, because that weights all the possible

TABLE 9.3. *PMFs (columns) and Likelihood Functions (rows)*

x	$f(x|1)$	$f(x|2)$	$f(x|3)$
0	$\frac{1}{3}$	$\frac{1}{4}$	0
1	$\frac{1}{3}$	$\frac{1}{4}$	0
2	0	$\frac{1}{6}$	$\frac{1}{4}$
3	$\frac{1}{6}$	$\frac{1}{3}$	$\frac{1}{2}$
4	$\frac{1}{6}$	0	$\frac{1}{4}$

marginal effects at each $X = x$ according to their probability. In any case, even marginal effects at the mean of the Xs are a step in the right direction.

Computer output also typically includes the computed log likelihood of the data, assuming the MLEs are correct estimates of the unknown parameters. As noted earlier, these log likelihoods are often negative numbers with absolute magnitude in the hundreds or thousands. Sometimes researchers report the log likelihood as some measure of the model fit (because R^2 is not meaningful in most ML models, e.g., generalized linear models). This is fine but usually not informative to readers, for whom this particular number usually lacks any context.

9.3.2 Likelihood Ratio Tests

Likelihood functions are the basis of a powerful approach to hypothesis testing, especially in regression modeling and generalized linear models, called *likelihood ratio testing*. Likelihood ratio tests or LRTs are based, naturally enough, on a quantity called the likelihood ratio.

When applied to models, the general idea is not unlike the F test for regression introduced in Chapter 8. The null hypothesis restricts the model parameters in some way, so estimate the model assuming that restriction is true and obtain the likelihood. Then estimate the model ignoring the restriction in H_0 (the unrestricted or unconstrained model), and obtain that likelihood. If the likelihoods are very different, it casts doubt on H_0, but if they are similar, it lends credence to H_0.

To see the mechanics in a simple case, go back to the PMF/likelihood in the table at the start of this section (printed again as Table 9.3):

Consider the hypothesis $H_0 : \theta = 1$. In the probability model from the table, $\lambda(x) = \frac{L(1|x)}{\max_\theta L(\theta|x)}$ is the likelihood ratio for $\theta = 1$. The numerator of $\lambda(x)$ is the probability of the observed sample x, assuming H_0 is true. The denominator of $\lambda(x)$ is the probability of the observed sample, assuming the MLE is the true parameter value.

So $\lambda(x)$ gives the probability of the sample assuming $\theta = 1$, relative to the probability of the sample assuming θ is the MLE. By definition, the denominator is as large as the likelihood can get for the given sample. So the denominator is never smaller than the numerator, and they are both always nonnegative by the definition of a PMF. So $0 < \lambda(x) < 1$.

Thus $\lambda(x)$ is the degree or weight of the sample evidence in favor of $\theta = 1$ as the true parameter value: if $\lambda(x)$ is close to 1, then assuming $\theta = 1$ is not a bad guess about the parameter value. But if $\lambda(x)$ is far from 1, it means that assuming $\theta = 1$ makes the observed sample a lot less likely than it is under the MLE.

The idea behind a likelihood ratio test is that if a hypothesis about a parameter value is really true, then imposing it as a restriction on the parameter shouldn't cause much reduction in the explanatory power of a model (i.e., its ability to make what we saw as likely as possible). In that case, the likelihood ratio will be close to 1.

In applications an LRT actually doesn't involve a ratio at all. Instead, the test statistic is $-2[\mathcal{L}(\theta_0|\mathbf{x})) - \mathcal{L}(\theta_{MLE}|\mathbf{x}))]$. This $\mathcal{L}$ is just the log likelihood we've been dealing with already. It can be shown that if $H_0 : \theta = \theta_0$ is true, the LR test statistic follows a χ^2 distribution. Note that the term in brackets can never be a positive number, by the definition of a maximum, so the whole quantity can never be negative. A large value casts doubt on the hypothesis that θ_0 is true because it means that *assuming* it's true greatly reduces the probability of seeing what we actually saw.

9.3.3 Properties of MLEs

The idea behind maximum likelihood estimation – identify the parameter values that make the observed data as likely as possible – makes a certain degree of intuitive sense. For that reason alone, MLE theory is a compelling approach to estimation for many scholars. However, we users of statistical models should not be excessively fixated on the theoretical niceties of a theory of inference. Our specialization puts us in a bad position to adjudicate debates about theoreticians of estimation. Plenty of theories with compelling foundations have strange results.

In this respect, another necessary justification for applications of MLE or any other theory of estimation is the properties that inhere in estimators derived from that theory. MLE has garnered such a wide following among applied researchers who use statistical models because MLEs have attractive properties under certain conditions, at least in terms of large sample theory.

In particular, given a correct specification of a statistical model (DGP and, if relevant, links of parameters to covariates), MLEs are

1. consistent,
2. asymptotically efficient, and
3. asymptotically normally distributed.

Thus given a correctly specified model, an MLE of its unknown parameters provides a better and better approximation of the true parameter as sample size N grows. Furthermore, among all consistent estimators, an MLE has the lowest variance as sample size increases without limit. It might seem surprising that this fact is even knowable – who can say what the lowest possible variance is for a consistent estimator? Finally, an MLE is arbitrarily well approximated by a known and convenient sampling distribution as N grows arbitrarily large.

Asymptotic efficiency is established by showing that the asymptotic variance of an MLE is the CRLB. So an MLE is as precise as possible given that it is consistent. A clue about the link between the asymptotic variance of the MLE and the CRLB comes from inspecting the latter and noting that it depends crucially on the derivative of the log likelihood function (see the Fisher information in Equation 9.8), which is also what is used to establish the MLE.

Proof of these properties requires some formal conditions as well as results from mathematical statistics that are beyond the scope of this book. On the conditions, briefly, they hold that the DGP $f(\mathbf{x}|\theta)$ is twice differentiable in θ (it is a lot harder to maximize things that can't be differentiated), that each of the parameters lies in a *closed* and *bounded* region of the real numbers $\mathbb{R}$ (closed means that the parameter region includes the end points of its interval, and bounded means that the end points are not infinite. This is helpful for ensuring that a maximum always exists because MLE is never trying to find the largest number smaller than some end point) and that the parameter lies in the *interior* of the parameter space (so MLE is not trying to find a maximum that exists on a boundary, which is hard for optimization methods to do). These conditions are sufficient but not necessary for the three key properties of MLEs to hold, meaning that they are useful for doing proofs, and they match up reasonably well to applied settings.

It should be stressed that these properties inhere in MLEs only if the likelihood function is correctly specified, which means that the analyst is correct about the DGP from which the sample observations are drawn. This includes not only its functional form but also iid or any particular departures from it.

In addition, all of these properties typically used to justify MLE's are "large sample" or asymptotic properties. In some applications, those are credible. In others, they are not. Consistency of an estimator is often taken as the most important requirement, but a good case can be made that an estimator's mean squared error in common sample sizes is a more important property. Typically, however, much less is known about MSEs than asymptotics of estimators, and an MLE with attractive asymptotics is a safe choice in terms of being defensible.

Another nice property of MLE is that if a parameter for a given DGP has an UMVUE, the MLE is it (Casella and Berger [2002]). On the other hand, MLEs need not be unbiased. A classic example, related to what we saw for the MLE of the normal linear model, is the MLE of σ^2 for a normal (μ, σ^2) DGP with iid draws. That MLE is simply $\widehat{\sigma}^2 = \frac{\sum_{i=1}^n (x_i - \bar{x})^2}{n}$, which we already know is biased (Chapter 7).

The right skew of the χ^2 distribution illustrates why the MLE $\hat{\sigma}^2$ is a biased estimator of σ^2 for a normal DGP. This skew implies that the expected value of the distribution lies to the right of the "hump," the point at which the distribution has the greatest density (otherwise known as the mode). But MLEs are designed to find that mode and pick as the estimator the point on the horizontal axis at which the peak of the sampling distribution occurs. Loosely speaking this means an estimator with a mean that is the true mean of the χ^2 has to give bigger estimates, in any given sample, than one chosen to find the hump of the likelihood function. But it is also clear that the difference between $\hat{\sigma}^2$ and S^2 gets smaller and smaller as n grows. The denominator of each converges to ∞ as the sample size grows, so that any given difference in their numerators is swamped.

On the downside, in addition to the fact that these justifications are asymptotic and may be of great use for finite samples, MLEs are not necessarily robust to model *misspecification*. It is one thing to have to assert a parametric DGP and model to get an MLE; it is another (and worse) that MLEs may perform poorly when the actual model departs, even slightly, from the one assumed. *Robustness* concerns the performance of estimators (e.g., consistency, efficiency) under model misspecification. Simply put, MLEs in some cases can give serious misestimates if the actual DGP does not conform to the model.

For a simple example, consider estimating the mean of a normal DGP if there is a small probability that some observations are *outliers*, drawn from a different DGP with a very different mean or variance. The sensitivity of $\overline{X}$ and $\hat{\sigma}^2$ to the data that give them nice properties as MLEs make their values highly susceptible to a few small number of outliers, making it difficult to use them to estimate the "core" (nonoutlier) DGP.

Obviously, nonparametric approaches as briefly introduced in Chapter 8 are robust to model misspecification since they don't specify one. There are other, intermediate approaches in statistics as well. If the model is accurate, robustness comes at the cost of statistical power and efficiency in estimation. The less information about the DGP is used to structure estimation, the less precise those estimates will be. A statistical model does a great deal to structure the problem of estimation and inference, focusing all the sample information on estimating just a couple of parameters. But if the model is inaccurate, all the statistical power in the world that results from assuming it is does not help much.

There is, of course, a large literature in statistics on robust estimation. It is beyond the scope of a basic textbook, but see Greene [2011] or Cameron and Trivedi [2005] for some coverage.

9.4 BAYESIAN ESTIMATION

This book has dealt throughout with classical or frequentist statistics. The DGP has fixed parameters that we do not happen to know. A sample drawn from a DGP with those fixed properties helps us to learn about them, which is what the theory of statistics is all about. We can never learn the fixed DGP properties perfectly in finite samples because part of what we see is the consequence of random chance. In the classical statistics world, parameters are fixed numbers, and it makes no sense to speak of them in probabilistic terms. We may not know them but they are fixed and not random. Sample observations are random, and all statements of probability and randomness in classical statistics apply to sample data.

A rather different approach known as Bayesian statistics has been gaining in popularity for a couple decades. Bayesian statistics has some philosophically appealing aspects, but in real applications it tends to be computationally intensive. As computer power has grown, it has become possible for closeted Bayesians to peddle their wares in real empirical settings. In recent years, some areas of research have seen dramatic extensions and improvements of quantitative measurement thanks to Bayesian estimation; perhaps the leading case is "ideal point estimation" in political science, wherein scholars attempt to use a sequence of decisions by members of a collective body (Congress, the Supreme Court) to estimate the "ideal policy" of the members of that body in some underlying "policy space" that structures and relates alternative choices to one another (e.g., Martin and Quinn [2002], Clinton et al. [2004]). Any actual treatment of Bayesian statistics is beyond the scope of these notes (see Berger [1985], Gelman et al. [2004], Gelman and Hill [2006], and Gill [2007] for in depth treatments), but this section introduces the approach in simple terms to give students a flavor for it.

The main point of Bayesian statistics is that DGP parameters are quantities we are uncertain about, and therefore we should be able to speak of them probabilistically. Indeed, this is the motivation for the Bayesian view of the meaning of probability as discussed in Chapter 4. Probability as a language of uncertainty ought to apply to quantities the values of which we are not certain.

So where a classical or frequentist confidence interval has a somewhat convoluted interpretation as "a formula that leads to intervals of random length and location that cover the true parameter in $(1 - \alpha)\%$ of samples," a Bayesian analogue (called a "credible set") can simply assert, "The parameter is in this interval with probability $(1 - \alpha)$." Moreover, Bayesian statistics is also strongly associated with decision theory and as such leads to much more nuanced tradeoffs of Type I and Type II error than classical statistics procedures typically allow, better tradeoffs of variance and bias of estimators than is typical in frequentist statistics.

The flavor of Bayesian estimation can be gained from a simple example. Whereas classical estimation arrives at a point estimator and its sampling distribution, the end result of Bayesian estimation is a posterior distribution for the DGP's parameter. The expected value of that posterior can then be computed if one desires a single "best guess" about its value, or one can use the mode of the posterior (i.e., the value of the parameter that maximizes it – that leads to the "highest posterior density [HPD]" in Bayesian parlance) to obtain the single most likely value of the parameter, for example. In the latter case, note again that the interpretive funambulism of maximum likelihood, and the technical difference between likelihood and probability, estimators are completely superfluous.

Consider a random variable X with range $\mathcal{X} = \{0, 1\}$ and following a Bernoulli distribution with parameter ξ. This parameter in turn can take one of two values: $\xi_1 = 0.25$ or $\xi_2 = 0.75$. Assume that $\Pr[\xi = \xi_1] = 0.5$. This is the prior distribution of ξ. Thus X follows a Bernoulli distribution, and the parameter ξ of this distribution of X itself is a draw from a Bernoulli distribution. The parameter of the prior distribution on ξ, 0.5, is a *hyperparameter*. A draw ξ from the prior determines the distribution of X, called the data distribution. Both the hyperparameter and the functional form of the prior are taken as given in this example; where they might come from in applications is discussed briefly later.

Thus, a parameter is drawn from a distribution and inserted into the distribution of X. Then a draw is taken from the distribution of X. The first draw (determining ξ) is not observed by the analyst but the second draw (determining x) is. We can see our data but not the parameter of the DGP that generated it. The object of Bayesian estimation is to update the prior distribution on the basis of the observed data $X = x$ and arrive at the posterior distribution $f(\xi|x)$ over ξ. Then a variety of analyses can be performed on the posterior, such as determining its mean and its most likely value, and so on.

Given data $X = x$, the posterior of ξ is simply determined by Bayes's theorem. As noted in Chapter 4, this theorem specifies $f(\xi|x) = \frac{\Pr(x|\xi)\Pr(\xi)}{\Pr(x)}$. Suppose for example that $X = 1$ is drawn from the data distribution. If $\xi = 0.25$, this has probability 0.25, and $\xi = 0.25$ has probability 0.5 as given in the prior. That is the numerator of $f(0.25|1)$. The denominator is $0.25 \times 0.5 + 0.25 \times 0.5 = 0.5$. Therefore, $f(\xi = 0.25|X = 1) = 0.25$. Similarly, $f(\xi = 0.75|X = 1) = 0.75 = 1 - 0.25$. This is the posterior distribution of ξ given that the sample is observed as $x = 1$.

Note that the posterior distribution is also a Bernoulli distribution: a Bernoulli prior combined with a Bernoulli data distribution led to a Bernoulli posterior. When a prior from family A combined with a data distribution from family B leads to a posterior also in family A, it is a happy situation. A and B are said to form a *conjugate pair*. In more realistic applied work, the normal distribution is a conjugate family with itself. Conjugate pairs make posterior computations simple, and when applied statistics was limited to puny computers and pen-and-paper methods, Bayesians were often hamstrung by the need to work with conjugate families. Expanding computer power has made this much less of an issue because a posterior can be simulated quickly with great accuracy for a huge variety of prior and data distributions, conjugate pair or not.

The posterior contains all information an analyst could want for making specific statements about the parameter's value or the probability that it is in a particular part of the parameter space. As noted, one point estimation approach is to use the parameter value that maximizes the posterior probability distribution or a highest posterior density (here, mass) estimator. The parameter value that maximizes the posterior in this example is $\xi = 0.75$, which makes sense. Large sample observations are more likely when the parameter is relatively large than when it is relatively small, and a large sample observation did actually occur. So the posterior probability of the larger parameter value has gone up, relative to its prior probability.

This parameter value leading to the highest posterior probability (or density, in case of a continuous parameter space) is one type of parameter estimator in Bayesian statistics. In general, a Bayesian estimator like this is called a *highest posterior density* or *HPD* estimator.

The expected value of the posterior is another possible estimator: for this posterior and given $x = 1$ is the sample, this expectation is $E(\xi | X = 1) = 0.25^2 + 0.75^2 = 0.625$. Note that the posterior mean is not a possible parameter value, which could lead to interpretive oddities when the parameter is discrete-valued, but that is unusual in applied settings. In any case, the oddity is no worse than any interpretation of a mean that is not a member of the range of possible values. Whether one prefers the posterior mean or the maximizer of the posterior mass function as the estimator is of course a judgment call and exactly the same as whether one prefers to summarize a distribution with its mean or its mode.

Obviously, the prior chosen for this problem exerts considerable influence on the posterior, and therefore over any conclusions an analyst might draw about the DGP. In principle the choice of prior – its functional form and hyperparameters – is a judgment call for an analyst. However, Bayesians do have approaches to avoid the suspicion that the analyst's unexamined personal beliefs, or worse, desires to obtain interesting results, have led him or her to "cherry pick" a favorable prior. Often Bayesians use a *diffuse prior*, that spreads the prior weight uniformly over the parameter space. Or an analyst may use a *maximum entropy prior*, which is a tactic to ensure formally that the prior distribution is as uninformative about the location of the parameter as it can possibly be (in a specific sense). That then leaves the data to do most of the talking and puts the prior in the background, yet still allows for the interpretive benefits of a Bayesian approach, as well as its modeling flexibility. In addition, Bayesian analysis often explores the sensitivity of the conclusions to the specification of the prior to help ensure that the prior is not unjustifiably driving the results. This ethos of Bayesian estimation is clearly explicated in practical settings by Gelman and Hill [2006] and Gill [2007].

Bayesians used to be and sometimes still are criticized for demanding significant changes in statistical methods for what are, once you get used to frequentist ideas, rather modest interpretive gains. A frequentist confidence interval is not *that* counterintuitive, and in any case, once we get used to it as a range of reasonable guesses, it is rather informative.

But as computer power has increased, Bayesian methods have grown into a flexible modeling tool that reflects a variety of important social processes. This is especially true in *hierarchical modeling*, wherein a behavior is determined by several levels of a social process. Consider turnout behavior in the United States – it is possible that some states have a richer political culture than others, which determines the political engagement within neighborhoods or even households. An individual turnout decision could be affected by parameters at both of these hierarchical levels: state-level culture affects neighborhood-level culture, which in turn affects idiosyncratic personal benefits of voting.

In general, there is no social science question or concept that can be modeled with Bayesian methods but not frequentist methods, or vice versa, but it can be more natural to model a process in one framework – and take account of numerous statistical complications – than another.

9.5 EXAMPLES

In this section, we return to the examples from recent literature initially discussed in Chapter 6 on attitudes toward high- and low-skilled immigration in the United States and protest events in the former Soviet Union.

9.5.1 Attitudes toward High- and Low-Skilled Immigration

Recall that Hainmueller and Hiscox [2010] analyzed the economic and sociocultural determinants of Americans' attitudes toward immigration by high- and low-skilled workers (see Chapter 6, Section 6.9.1). The dependent variable is an expressed opinion (ordered 1 to 5) on whether the United States should allow more immigration by people of a given skill level (high or low), with larger values reflecting a more positive attitude toward immigration.

The authors estimated an ordered probit model with the following linear regression specified for the latent variable Y^*:

$$E(Y^*|X_1, X_2, Z) \equiv \mu = \alpha + \beta_1 X_1 + \beta_2 X_2 + \beta_3 X_1 X_2 + \beta_4 Z. \qquad (9.14)$$

The covariates measure respondents' skill[16] (X_1), whether they were asked about high-skilled ($X_2 = 1$) or low-skilled ($X_2 = 0$) immigration, and a vector of respondent demographics (Z). The labor competition theory implies $\beta_3 < 0$, and additionally, $\beta_3 < -\frac{\beta_2}{4}$.

In Section 6.9.1, we looked only at the estimated values of the βs, with no consideration of the uncertainty about the DGP values of these parameters based on the estimates from the sample. There we saw that although the estimate of β_3 is indeed negative, the estimates of β_2 and β_3 did not satisfy $\beta_3 < -\frac{\beta_2}{4}$. Even ignoring uncertainty about the parameter estimates, the evidence labor competition theory was at best mixed.

---

[16] Specifically, highest degree of formal schooling completed.

But after the last few chapters, it is clear that these parameter estimates are not the same as the parameters themselves – if a different sample were drawn, with just as much connection to the DGP as this one, the estimates would change. Now we are in a position to consider the estimation of the βs as well, and the uncertainty in those estimates (i.e., standard errors).

Because the ordered probit model fully specifies the parametric form of the DGP (Equation 6.29 to determine discrete values of Y from the latent index Y^*, combined with normality of the latent variable Y^*) and the link of its regression to covariates (Equation 6.30, MLE is a compelling approach. If these modeling assumptions are correct or reasonably good approximations, then the resulting MLEs are consistent, asymptotically efficient, and asymptotically normal.

To form the ordered probit likelihood function, we must express the probability of each particular answer to the survey item (1 through 5) by each respondent. As noted in Equation 6.29, $Y = 5$, for example, if $Y^* = \mu + \varepsilon > u_4$, where u_4 is the cutoff which the latent "warmth" Y^* must exceed so that the survey answer Y changes from 4 to 5. Because ε is the only random variable in this expression (μ and u_l are DGP parameters), the probability of $Y = 5$ is $\Pr[\varepsilon > u_4 - \mu]$. Letting Φ denote the normal CDF, this is equivalent to $1 - \Phi(u_4 - \mu)$. The probability of each other possible response can similarly be expressed as Φ applied to u_ls and μ. Note also that because μ is in turn specified in terms of the βs of theoretical interest (Equation 9.14), the probability of each possible response by a given respondent is a function of the regression model of interest. This is crucial in MLE: the point is to maximize probability of observing the actual sample data, with respect to the parameters in the regression model we're interested in.

Assuming survey responses are independent across respondents (a credible assumption in this survey), the likelihood function is simply

$$L(\beta_1, \beta_2, \beta_3 | X) = \prod_{i=1}^{N} \Pr[Y_i = k], \qquad (9.15)$$

where k is a a survey response. Again, the important point is that $\Pr[Y_i = k]$ depends on the βs, so L can be maximized with respect to them. The business end of this maximization focuses on the log likelihood function,

$$\mathcal{L}(\beta_1, \beta_2, \beta_3 | X) = \sum_{i=1}^{N} \ln \Pr[Y_i = k]. \qquad (9.16)$$

Except for relatively avant-garde models, statistics software packages already have routines established for forming and maximizing the likelihood function with respect to the β parameters of interest. One needs to open a dataset in the software and express in the software's language that one wants to estimate an ordered probit model (or some other kind of GLM) with variables specified by

TABLE 9.4. *Attitudes toward*
Immigration: Parameter Estimates
and Standard Errors

Variable	$\widehat{\beta}$	$\widehat{SE}$
X_1	0.27	0.05
X_2	0.73	0.20
$X_1 X_2$	−0.07	0.07

the user. The computer software does the rest to obtain parameter estimates for all the GLMs we have encountered in this book, including ordered probit.[17]

Hainmueller and Hiscox obtained the parameter estimates and standard errors of those estimates shown in Table 9.4.

Although $\widehat{\beta}_3 < 0$ as implied by the labor competition theory, the estimate is not significantly different from 0. Because MLEs are approximately normally distributed, the z statistic $\frac{-0.07-0}{0.07} = -1$ is a draw from an approximately standard normal distribution. Because about 68% of draws from a standard normal distribution are between -1 and 1, the p-value in the (two-tailed) test of $H_0 : \beta_3 = 0$ is about 0.32. Informally, $\widehat{\beta}_3$ differs from 0 by about a typical amount (1 standard error), assuming H_0 is true. It is easy to explain the observation $\widehat{\beta}_3 = -0.07$ as a result of chance error, even if the labor competition theory has no explanatory power in the data. Thus if one starts out skeptical of the labor competition theory, this data does not force abandonment of that position; it is, in that sense, not a compelling demonstration of the theory's importance.

On the other hand, the parameter estimates for both respondent's education level (X_1) and whether the respondent was asked about highly skilled immigrants (X_2) are significantly different from 0. The z statistics are each much larger than 2 in absolute value. More educated respondents are significantly more favorable about immigration in general, and (holding education constant) a given respondent is more favorable about immigration of high-skill than low-skill workers. It is difficult to explain the observed responses on the assumption that these sociocultural factors have no effect on opinion.

9.5.2 Protest Movements in the Former Soviet Union

As we discussed in Chapter 6, Section 6.9.2, Beissinger [2002] analyzed the number of ethnonationalist protest events for each of 47 (non-Russian) ethnicities in the last few years of the USSR's existence, 1987–1991. Beissinger

---

[17] While it is good to have people in social science and related disciplines to question and probe the quality and stability of the optimization routines used in various software, exploring this is beyond the scope of this treatment.

TABLE 9.5. *Determinants of Number of Ethnonationalist Protests in Former USSR, by Nationality*

Variable	$\widehat{\beta}$	Z Statistic	$e^{\widehat{\beta}}$
Pop. size, 1000s (natural log)	0.658	4.42	1.931
Linguistic assimilation	−0.072	−4.12	0.930
Urbanization	0.066	2.95	1.068
No. protests, 1965–1986	0.057	0.96	1.059
Communist party membership per 1000	−0.003	−0.24	0.997
Dummy for Islamic culture	−0.328	−0.65	0.720
Constant	−3.001		
LRT against Poisson	$\chi^2 = 628.42$		
LRT against null model	$\chi^2 = 42.38$		
Model log likelihood	−167.59		
N	47		

observed that the dependent variable is a count and elected to invoke a DGP for Y that matches this structure. Although Chapter 6 discussed the relatively simpler Poisson model in some detail, Beissinger actually used a negative binomial distribution for Y, as is common in applications of count models. The reason is that it is usually hard to maintain the assumption that the mean and variance of the DGP are the same, conditional on covariates, as the Poisson assumes. But the basic approach is the same; the negative binomial supplies the DGP of Y, and the mean of this DGP is specified as a function of covariates that reflect substantive considerations.

Estimation of model parameters is typically executed by maximum likelihood. The basic steps to obtain estimates from computer software are to open a dataset, then give the software the command for negative binomial regression with the dependent variable and covariates specified by the user. This will direct the computer to assume that Y follows a negative binomial distribution, that the natural log of its mean is a linear function of the covariates (just like the Poisson model), and to maximize the likelihood function to obtain parameter estimates and standard errors. This is "plain vanilla" negative binomial; a wide array of optional specifications are possible, but they are beyond the scope of an introductory treatment.

Parameter estimates and Z scores from one of Beissinger's models, as well as a few other bits of model output, are in Table 9.5. All of these results except the third column are part of the standard output from negative binomial models, and the third column is easy enough to obtain, either in optional software commands or by hand.

Consider first the output at the bottom of the table, which we have not seen much of before. There are two likelihood ratio tests, which are typically performed automatically by computer software when estimating MLEs for negative binomial models. The first is a likelihood ratio test against a Poisson model. This is a test of whether the Poisson assumption of equal conditional mean and variance is a reasonable description of the DGP, based on the data. The null hypothesis is that a Poisson model is in fact appropriate. This is a hopeful case: the Poisson does not require estimation of a separate conditional variance for each collection of covariates. The Poisson model concentrates all of the information in the sample on estimates of α and β parameters from the model. Because it has fewer parameters to estimate, it gives more precise estimates of them than the negative binomial model, assuming the equal mean-variance assumption holds up. So by default, MLE routines for negative binomial models test this assumption. The alternative is that the DGP exhibits overdispersion, or conditional variance greater than the conditional mean. The likelihood is maximized assuming a Poisson distribution, then assuming a negative binomial distribution, and the likelihoods are compared in an LRT. Here, as is common, the null hypothesis of a Poisson model is easily rejected; the p-value for this χ^2 statistic is less than 0.0001.

The second likelihood ratio test result is about a "null" model, one in which $\beta = 0$ simultaneously for each covariate. This has a similar flavor to the overall F test in regression models (Chapter 8): the null is that the model the researcher has specified adds no explanatory power for Y beyond it is a negative binomial random variable with constant conditional mean as a function of the specified covariates. Here again, the p-value for this χ^2 statistic is less than 0.0001; specifying this model adds a significant increase in the likelihood of observing this sample data.

Beissinger's results also indicate the log likelihood from the model, -167.59. The likelihood is the probability of observing the specific sequence of 47 observations in this sample, assuming they are drawn from a negative binomial distribution and assuming the parameters of that distribution are the α and β estimates from the table. With all that information, it is simple arithmetic for a computer to calculate the probability of observing this sample. The log of this likelihood is negative because natural logs of numbers less than 1 are negative. Although it is common to report the log likelihood of the model, it is not a particularly informative or compelling measure of model fit.

The sample size, $N = 47$, often gives pause to researchers steeped in traditions such as survey research, where $N > 1,000$ is common (and even that may be considered "small"). The appealing properties of MLEs are asymptotic – asymptotic consistency, efficiency, and normality – meaning that they are convergence results as $N \to \infty$. Can we really invoke $N = 47$ as an "approximation" to ∞? No, but we can't invoke $N = 3,000$ or $30,000$ that way either. As far as ∞ is concerned, any of these Ns is triflingly small; 3,000 is not "closer" to ∞ than 47 in any meaningful sense. We study the asymptotic properties of MLEs because we are able to do so analytically, the hope (or faith) being that an estimator that performs well in one context where we can judge it rigorously will also perform well in other contexts where analytical evaluation of its performance is intractable.

In addition to these model diagnostics, Beissinger presented parameter estimates with associated z scores. Each of these z scores tests the null hypothesis that the parameter in question is actually 0. Some analysts report standard errors of parameter estimates; others report z scores; others report p-values. All of these approaches convey qualitatively similar information, and it is not worth getting bent out of shape about using one versus another. Many researchers also use stars, asterisks, or other notations on various statistics to indicate statistical significance (including Beissinger in his original table). This is useful for making quick scans of a table but is not a substitute for reporting actual estimates of uncertainty in the parameters or observed significance levels.

The z statistics on these parameter estimates actually show that sociodemographic attributes of ethnic groups have statistically significant effects on the number of protest events in this model, but institutional connection to the USSR (measured by number of Communist Party members in an ethnic group) and the historical protest behavior of that ethnic group do not. However, as is usually the case in detailed and comprehensive analyses of a complex phenomenon, Beissinger estimated a number of other models besides this one, including other covariates to measure institutional position of ethnic groups with respect to the wider USSR in particular. In those models, institutional factors also have a statistically significant effect on protest movements. The point is that in statistical modeling, we almost never specify the one single model that captures all facets of the problem and call it a day; there are almost always multiple specifications and operationalizations of variables to deploy. It is rash to make sweeping conclusions about broad categories of factors based on one operationalization in one model and more judicious to explore a variety of measures and models and distill conclusions that hold up across a number of them.

At the same time, as even-handed as that all sounds, it opens the door to specification searches, which leads to a problem of evaluating published evidence that is closely related to the "file-drawer" problem (see Chapter 8). If one's pet theory indicates that a certain variable or category of variables has a statistically significant effect on the mean of Y, it is tempting not to take "no" for an answer from the model. If one operationalization of that concept doesn't lead to significant results, try others; if one set of covariates doesn't work, try others; if one functional form for the model doesn't work, try others. Then, as soon as one's favored variable is significant, stop; we are more than happy to take "yes" for an answer and not probe further. Because all of these measures, functions, and specifications allow the possibility of false positives in hypothesis tests (or artificially small p-values due to random chance), the actual p-values associated with these models may be much higher than the claimed, published p-values (which are always impressively small).

9.6 CONCLUSION

Point estimation and hypothesis testing/interval estimation are complementary aspects of empirical modeling in social science. Point estimators give a sense of magnitude of a relationship or other parameter – how much does the mean of Y change for a unit change in X in a regression model, for example? That question is answered by a point estimator. Point estimators are designed to give the "best guess" about the parameter value, in some sense. Maximum likelihood estimation is arguably the leading theory (and computational method) of identifying point estimators in statistical modeling, but other approaches (including Bayesian estimation and the method of moments, not covered here) have been gaining ground in the last couple decades. For the applied researcher, it is probably not worth fastidious insistence that we have found the One True Theory of Inference. As far as modeling techniques go, it is better for us in the "user community" to be pragmatic and flexible about models that theoreticians have identified as sensible and robust in specific cases, and/or that have stood the test of time.

Interval estimators give a sense of the range of credible guesses about the value of a parameter. Because confidence intervals implicitly give an entire range of hypothesis test results in one estimator, they are in a sense more informative and more comprehensive than hypothesis tests of specific parameter values. The exact, specific parameter value specified by H_0 in a hypothesis test is rarely a credible guess (often by design, if H_0 embodies a skeptic's argument against one's own theory), so hypothesis tests focused on just that parameter can be somewhat artificial. In any case, both approaches are widely used in quantitative social science to convey the degree of credibility or sample support for possible values of the parameters.

By now, this book has considered the core of the theory of probability (Chapters 4, 5, and 6) and the theory of statistical inference (Chapters 7, 8, and 9). We have explored how statements about social theory can be expressed in terms of DGP. We have seen how the connections between DGPs and observable data can be used to make statements about DGPs supported by sample data, and thereby evaluate the importance of our theories in explaining observed events.

But theories in social science do not simply specify relationships; they identify reasons relationships should exist. In other words, they spell out cause-and-effect links. Yet all the modeling and inference theory we have developed thus far is about assessing correlation, not causation. Moreover, essentially every recommendation of a specific policy rests on a cause–effect argument: if a specific policy is adopted, it will cause a specific desired result to occur or to be more likely to occur. Therefore, it is important to know whether and when the evidence we can adduce about DGPs also supports a causal interpretation about the links between covariates and dependent variables. That is the subject of the next and final chapter of this book. That chapter develops a widely used framework for making and evaluating causal statements, called the *potential outcomes model* of causation. It then explores a variety of approaches to validating causal statements based on observable data.

PROBLEMS

1. Gallup routinely polls Americans about whether they think economic growth should have a higher priority in public policy making than protecting the environment. In March 2009, for the first time in 25 years, a majority of respondents answered yes. Of 625 American adults polled at that time, 51% stated that economic growth should have higher priority. Assume the poll comes from a simple random sample, that is, the 625 respondents are independently sampled from the population.[18]

   (a) Test the hypothesis that half of American adults believe that economic growth should have higher priority than protecting the environment. State the type of hypothesis test you perform. Compare the p-value to conventional significance benchmarks.

   (b) Did you have to bootstrap the standard error to execute this test?

   (c) What is the margin of error in this poll, that is, what is half the width of the 95% confidence interval?

2. In an opinion poll the party preference of 220 men and 243 women who self-identified as affiliated with a major political party was recorded. Ninety men identified as Democrats, and 145 women identified as Democrats.

   (a) Form the 95% confidence interval for the share of men and women that identify as Democrats.

   (b) Test the hypothesis that female party-affiliated voters are equally likely to identify as Republican and Democrat, and repeat for males.

   (c) Test the hypothesis that the male and female shares of Democratic identifiers are different.

3. Suppose two normally distributed random variables are estimated. It is sometimes said that if their respective 95% confidence intervals overlap, they are not significantly different. Is this true? That is, is it possible that a 95% confidence interval for their difference that does not include 0, even if their respective 95% confidence intervals overlap?

4. The confidence intervals we dealt with in this chapter are called "two-sided" because the range of reasonable parameter values falls on either side of an estimate. Suppose an estimator $\hat{\theta}$ follows a normal sampling distribution. What is the formula for a one-sided 95% confidence interval? Why is it wider than a two-sided interval?

---

[18] This data is real except the sample size was changed to make computations easy.

5. A researcher studying the distribution of resources by groups has data from a laboratory experiment on votes by group members to approve a particular distribution of resources. A formal theory of voting and bargaining she is interested in holds that voters should be more likely to vote in favor of a proposed distribution as their own share of that distribution ("own share") rises, and more likely to vote against as their own payoff in case the proposal fails to be approved ("disagreement value") rises. Furthermore, the theory predicts that the effect of own-share should be the same as the effect of the disagreement value, but with the sign reversed. The researcher estimates a logit model of vote choice by maximum likelihood with no constraints on the parameters, and the log likelihood is −720. She then estimates the logit model with the theoretical restriction imposed on the parameters and obtains a log likelihood of −759. With the theoretical restriction imposed, there are three parameters to estimate in the model.

   (a) Why are the log likelihoods negative? Is this alarming, given the definition of a likelihood function? ~~O+1~~ ~~Footnote 14~~

   (b) State the theoretical restriction as a null hypothesis and the failure of the restriction as an alternative hypothesis.

   (c) Without knowing anything else about the theory, statistical model, or coefficients, does the theoretical restriction seem sensible in light of these results? Be specific.

6. Let $X_1, \ldots, X_N$ be iid draws from a Normal$(\theta, 1)$ distribution. Suppose that it is substantively meaningless or impossible to have $\theta < 0$. What is the MLE of θ? Why can't the usual MLE of θ be used?

7. Suppose that a guess θ_0 is made about a parameter θ such that $|\theta_0 - \theta| = \Delta$ and that the likelihood $L(\theta|x)$ has a unique maximum for each x. Discuss the relationship between the Fisher information for θ, $\mathcal{I}(\theta) \equiv E[(\frac{\partial}{\partial \theta} \ln f(x|\theta))^2]$ and the ability of a likelihood ratio test to detect whether θ_0 is "far" from θ (i.e., whether Δ is "large").

8. (a) Show that a Bernoulli PMF can be written as $f(y|p) = p^y(1-p)^{(1-y)}$.

   (b) Write the likelihood function for a sample of N iid draws from a Bernoulli distribution. Make sure it is a function only of a sufficient statistic, not the entire sample.

   (c) Write down the log likelihood function.

   (d) Maximize the log likelihood function using analytic methods (i.e., not a computer simulation) and identify the MLE of p. Explain why your method for finding the maximum is valid in this problem and why you are sure there are no other maximizers other than the MLE.

9. Consider an experiment in which a coin is flipped four times. Its parameter p is either .5 or .75.

   (a) What is the likelihood of each parameter, as a function of the number of heads observed?

(b) For $L(p|2)$, what is the likelihood ratio for $p = .75$ versus the MLE? What is the likelihood ratio for $p = .51$ versus $p = .5$ (which we did not cover explicitly)?

(c) For $L(p|4)$, what is the likelihood ratio for $p = .75$ versus the MLE?

(d) Are the likelihood ratios for the $p = .75$ relative to the MLE different? Why or why not? (Think about the shape of the likelihood function in each case.) Explain what this means about the degree of support the data provides for the $H_0 : p = .75$ in each "data set."

10

Causal Inference: Inferring Causation from Correlation

We have ignored the elephant in the room long enough. Social science theory does not just imply relationships. It often implies *causal relationships* – that a change in an explanatory factor causes a change in the dependent variable for some specified reason. Yet all the methods and concepts we have covered are simply about assessing relationships, causal or not. We have tools to describe relationships in observed data, and tools to make inferences about whether the relationships observed in data hold in the underlying process that generated the data or whether they can be ascribed to idiosyncratic chance. We have tools to make a best guess about the relationships that hold in the data-generating process (DGP) and quantify our uncertainty about those guesses. But none of this deals in a sustained fashion with whether relationships are causal relationships.

When we spin theories, we often spin them in causal terms. And when we make policy recommendations, we often do so on the belief that the recommended intervention will cause a change in some important outcome. But causation is not just a theoretical concept. "Correlation does not imply causation" has reached the status of a truism. In light of this maxim, it might seem that the best approach to inferring causation from correlation is not to try it. But this causal nihilism is not reasonable. Claims of causation are more credible in some empirical research than others. We need to ask why this is so, and if possible, try to make empirical research with causal aspirations follow a template that makes causal claims credible.

Over the past couple decades, statisticians and social scientists have made significant headway in understanding these issues. In this chapter, we introduce a model of causation to help evaluate such issues more precisely. We review the types of arguments people construct when they want to claim that an observed relationship is *not* a causal relationship. And we briefly analyze methods that are useful for identifying causal relationships in the face of these critiques.

We only scratch the surface here; for more in-depth recent treatments, see Morgan and Winship [2007] and Angrist and Pischke [2008]. A marginally fuller treatment of the issues in this chapter – methods for establishing credible causal inference and further issues in the theory of causal inference – are covered in the online appendix to this chapter at the book's website.

10.1 TREATMENTS AND COUNTERFACTUALS: THE POTENTIAL OUTCOMES MODEL

In this section, we lay out a basic model of causation to assess what the term means and to assess what we need to know to identify it. The model elaborated here is a simple case of the *potential outcomes* of causation, which has emerged as a unifying model for many different approaches to causal inference.[1]

To keep the exposition simple, we are going to focus on a fairly basic situation, formally speaking. To keep things concrete, we will use a running example that should be of reasonably widespread interest: the causal link between the printing press and the Protestant Reformation in Europe. The link is at least plausible and has been noted by historians for as long as the Reformation has been studied (cf. Febvre and Martin [1958] for just one example). Most basically, the development of the printing press in Europe and the Reformation were contemporary events. Beyond this, the Protestant Reformation was predicated on the idea that individual Christians could, in contrast to standard Catholic practice of the time, engage the Bible themselves, without the aid of a priest. The printing press held out the promise of dramatically reducing the costs to individuals of doing this. Moreover, the printing press allowed for distribution of pro-Reformation or anti-Catholic propaganda on a broad scale.[2]

There are two ways to think about this relationship. One is to ask, What caused the Reformation? And more specifically, Was it the printing press? This approach asks about the *cause of an effect*. The outcome or effect is fixed – the Reformation occurred – and the object of inquiry is its cause. It scarcely requires noting that a social event of such scale as the Reformation depends on the interaction of numerous factors, none sufficient by itself, so that a one-variable theory of this event based on the printing press is a bit absurd.

The second approach asks, Was the printing press one of the many causes the Reformation, or did cause advancement in the Reformation? This approach asks about the *effect of a cause*. The potentially causal variable – the printing

---

[1] This model is also referred to as the *Rubin causal mode* or the *Neyman-Rubin model*, among others. Original development is credited to the statistician Jerzy Neyman in the early 20th century. The model was revived and elaborated by D. Rubin [1974] and Holland [1986]. For a recent review of numerous philosophical approaches to understanding causation, see Brady [2008].

[2] J. Rubin [2011] is a recent attempt to address the causal effect of the printing press on the Reformation.

press – is the object of inquiry; we ask if changes in the occurrence of this variable caused changes in another variable (the extent or occurrence of the Reformation).

Both of these are perfectly reasonable objects of inquiry. Statistical models are better suited to answering the latter issue, on effects of a cause. These models are naturally suited to the context in which we have variation in the explanatory factor (the "cause") and want to determine whether this variation causes variation in the dependent variable.

The cause whose effect on the dependent variable we wish to ascertain is also called a *treatment*. To keep things simple, we will consider the case of two possible treatments; the treatment is either administered to a unit of observation or it is not. The results here are easily generalizable to a treatment with any finite number of values, but it runs into some technical problems and requires more assumptions if its value lies in a continuum.

The treatment is denoted T. $T = 1$ if it is received by the unit and $T = 0$ if it is not received. This language is a little abstract. "Received by" obscures by whom the treatment might have been administered. That is important, but we need to leave it aside for now. The point is that the unit might or might not be treated.

The dependent variable that the treatment may or may not affect is Y. This is also sometimes the *response variable* or *outcome*. Y can either be thought of as a fixed number conditional on the treatment received or as a random variable conditional on the treatment received. Standard developments of the potential outcomes model start with the former (Rubin [1974], Holland [1986]), so the only sources of randomness in what is observable are sampling uncertainty (in the parlance of Chapter 3) and possibly randomness in the assignment of treatment to units. But it does not cause any conceptual problems to think of Y as a random variable itself, conditional on the treatment and apart from sampling uncertainty. It might be random due to "fundamental" or "theoretical" uncertainty (cf. Chapter 3).[3]

If we think of Y as a random variable, it is useful to avoid issues of sampling uncertainty and statistical inference for the time being. So pretend we can observe infinitely large samples or, equivalently, that we know the real DGP. Then we can deal with expected values of Y, not just sample means. Again, this expectation is with respect to the DGP governing Y as a random variable. We can allow for the possibility of this while remaining agnostic about exactly what that distribution is or exactly where it comes from.

Let $E(Y_0)$ denote the expected outcome that would occur if the unit were untreated, and $E(Y_1)$ the expected outcome that would occur if it were treated. These are the *potential outcomes*.

---

[3] This is a bit metaphysical for some people, and if it causes discomfort, this section can be read the same way by pretending all the $E(\cdot)$s in it are not there. But the formulation with the $E(\cdot)$s makes it easier to move from here to regression models for estimating causal effects.

For the effect of the printing press on the Reformation in Europe, we could take the whole area in various years as the unit of analysis. Or we could take individual cities as the unit of analysis. The printing press was available in different cities at different times, and some cities were more aligned with the Reformation than others. The availability of the printing press is the treatment, and the degree of "alignment with the Reformation" (suitably measured) is the outcome.

Let $E(Y)$ with no subscript denote the expected value of the outcome for a unit that is actually observed by a researcher (or at least estimable, in a finite sample). We can write this as an "accounting identity":

$$E(Y) \equiv (1 - T)E(Y_0) + TE(Y_1). \tag{10.1}$$

If $T = 1$ so treatment is received, the first term drops out and $E(Y) = E(Y_1)$ is observed. The opposite happens if $T = 0$. Equation 10.1 shows clearly that only one of the two potential outcomes can be observed for the unit of observation in question.

This is something of a problem, because the definition of a *causal effect of the treatment* is

$$\Delta \equiv E(Y_1) - E(Y_0). \tag{10.2}$$

This is also sometimes known as the *treatment effect*. It is the difference in the two potential outcomes for a given unit. They seem bland and unassuming, but a lot of information is wrapped up in that comparison. It means that the unit must be compared under circumstances that are completely identical in every way except for the treatment. That is the one and only difference between $E(Y_1)$ and $E(Y_0)$, so if the potential outcomes are different, it can only be because of the treatment. That is why the difference is called a treatment effect. It is a difference in the outcomes that is caused by the treatment. For the case of the printing press and the Reformation, we would like to know what would have happened to the degree of alignment with the Reformation in a given place given that it did have the printing press and compare it to a scenario in which it did not have the printing press but was in every other way the same.

Now, for a given treatment assignment to the unit, one of these outcomes occurred and the other one did not. The one that didn't occur is the *counter-factual outcome*. And once one of the treatments is received, in the strictest sense the counterfactual can never be observed again. We can't just change the treatment administered to the unit at a future point in time, even if it were up to us to do so. The unit could be different in some way because of having received the other treatment first, and it could have changed autonomously in the mean time. So we couldn't say that we're observing the unit under exactly the same conditions as before, with the only difference being due to the treatment.

So it is not convincing to compare what happened to alignment with the Reformation before and after it got the printing press. The penetration of both around Europe increased with the passage of time (over a particular interval of years when the Reformation was growing, anyway), and they may occur or not occur together for reasons that have nothing to do with each other. Such a relationship is sometimes called *spurious*. Or it is possible that the same willingness to challenge existing belief systems that allowed the Reformation to flourish in certain places also made people in those places especially interested in (or able to read) printed materials, and so more likely than average to have a printing press show up there.

The fact that a single unit cannot be observed both with and without the treatment under otherwise identical conditions is called the *fundamental problem of causal inference*. At the level of an individual unit, observing causal effects is impossible by this definition of causation. This is an exacting standard, but in fields in which we are often far too credulous about claims of causation, that is probably not a bad thing.

So at the individual level, hope for identifying causation is lost. But if we observe several units, we might be able to say something about the average causal effect of the treatment for the whole group of them. We could observe some units with the treatment (the *treated group* or *treatment group*), and some units without the treatment (the *untreated group*), and compare their average outcomes. Or we could estimate the OLS regression of Y on T to measure the mean difference – it would simply be the slope from the regression. If this works, it would tell us the average causal effect over the whole collection of units – still interesting.

Let $E(Y_i|T)$ denote unit *i*s expected outcome as a function of the actual treatment assignment. So $E(Y_i|T = 1)$ is the expected outcome if it receives the treatment, and $E(Y_i|T = 0)$ is *i*s expected outcome if it does not receive the treatment. As in Equation 10.1, this can be written for each unit as $E(Y_i|T) \equiv (1 - T_i)E(Y_{i0}|T = 0) + T_i E(Y_{i1}|T = 1)$. Unit *i* still has two potential outcomes; now they are just indexed by *i*. It might seem redundant to introduce the dependence of Y_i on T because it's already in the subscript, but this will prove useful. Remember that a T in the subscript refers to a potential outcome, and a T in the condition of the expectation (the part after the vertical bar) refers to an observable treatment assignment.

So the observed difference in expected outcomes for the treated and untreated groups is

$$\overline{E}(Y_i|T = 1) - \overline{E}(Y_i|T = 0) = \overline{E}(Y_{i1}|T = 1) - \overline{E}(Y_{i0}|T = 0)$$
$$= \left[\overline{E}(Y_{i1}|T = 1) - \overline{E}(Y_{i0}|T = 1)\right]$$
$$+ \left[\overline{E}(Y_{i0}|T = 1) - \overline{E}(Y_{i0}|T = 0)\right], \quad (10.3)$$

where $\overline{E}(\cdot)$ refers to the mean of the expected outcomes across units.

First, the arithmetic: the first = sign follows just by using the identity $E(Y_i|T) \equiv (1 - T_i)E(Y_{i0}|T = 0) + T_i E(Y_{i1}|T = 1)$ (which holds for the mean across units because it holds for each unit). The second follows by adding and subtracting $\overline{E}(Y_{i0}|T = 1)$ in the first line. Because this adds 0, it doesn't change anything.

Now, the idea: the left-hand side (in the first line) is an observable quantity. On the right-hand side, the quantity $E(Y_{i0}|T = 1)$ seems kind of strange. The indicator for T in the subscript is 0, but the indicator for T in the parentheses is 1. This quantity is the value of Y_i we would have expected to occur for units that received the treatment, if instead they had not received it. The T in the subscript indicates that this is the potential outcome of units under a treatment they might have received; the T in parentheses refers to the treatment these units did in fact receive.

So think of cities that had a printing press. Their actual treatment is $T = 1$. What would have happened to the Reformation in these particular cities, if their treatment had instead been 0? That is what $E(Y_{i0}|T = 1)$ captures. It is a counterfactual outcome. We are looking at a counterfactual whenever the T in the subscript conflicts with the T in the parentheses. That is why it's important to have both; we need to represent counterfactuals to analyze causation.

This also means that the part $[\overline{E}(Y_{i1}|T = 1) - \overline{E}(Y_{i0}|T = 1)]$ is an observed expected outcome for the treated units, less the counterfactual expected outcome for those same units. This is the causal effect of the treatment, on those units that actually received the treatment. It is the *average treatment effect on the treated* or *ATT*.[4] We observe the progress of the Reformation in cities that got the printing press, and to establish causation, we need to compare it to what would have happened in those same cities (i.e., identical in every way) if they had not gotten the printing press. That's the ATT.[5]

Because the latter is a counterfactual, we cannot observe it. The next best thing to the counterfactual outcome for $T = 1$ units, had they received $T = 0$, is to look at the actual outcome for units that really did receive $T = 0$. This is $\overline{E}(Y_{i0}|T = 0)$, the last part of Equation 10.3.

Now, $\overline{E}(Y_{i0}|T = 0)$ and $\overline{E}(Y_{i0}|T = 1)$ might be different. Cities that actually had a printing press might have been wealthier, more socially progressive in some sense, more distant from Rome and more weakly held in the Catholic orbit, for example, than cities that did not have a printing press. Those cities might have had a higher expected value of Y than the cities with $T = 0$, even if the printing press had never been invented. The difference between $\overline{E}(Y_{i0}|T = 0)$ and $\overline{E}(Y_{i0}|T = 1)$ captures all the outcome-relevant ways in which each group of units might be different, besides the treatment itself.

Back to Equation 10.3 as a whole: given the definition of ATT, it is purely a matter of arithmetic that if $\overline{E}(Y_{i0}|T = 1) - \overline{E}(Y_{i0}|T = 0) \neq 0$, the observable

---

[4] The first line of Equation 10.3 also contains the quantity $\overline{E}(Y_{i1}|T = 1) - \overline{E}(Y_{i0}|T = 0)$, the *average treatment effect* or ATE.

[5] It is perfectly possible and may be perfectly interesting to focus on the average treatment effect on the untreated, instead of ATT. This would fall out of Equation 10.3 if we had added and subtracted $\overline{E}(Y_{i1}|T = 0)$ as the counterfactual outcome.

difference $\overline{E}(Y_i|T = 1) - \overline{E}(Y_i|T = 0)$ will not capture the average treatment effect on the treated. In this case, the observable difference $\overline{E}(Y_i|T = 1) - \overline{E}(Y_i|T = 0)$ gives a biased view of ATT. The term $\overline{E}(Y_{i0}|T = 1) - \overline{E}(Y_{i0}|T = 0)$ tells us the sign and size of the bias. This term is the *causal bias* or *selection bias* in the observable mean difference.

Selection bias is a good description because the bias comes from how the units are selected for each treatment. When selection bias is not zero, some of the things associated with the selection of a treatment for a unit are also associated with its expected outcome. This is particularly natural when units *self-select* their treatments, so that this is also sometimes called *self-selection bias*. But the problem of treatment selection correlated with outcomes is not limited to cases where units select their own treatments, so the name and the problem are more general than just self-selection.

In summary: the quantity that we can hope to observe in data is $\overline{E}(Y_i|T = 1) - \overline{E}(Y_i|T = 0)$, the left-hand side of Equation 10.3. Essentially, this is a correlation between the treatment and the outcome. This can be decomposed into the ATT (which we want to know) plus causal bias (which we hope we don't and wish we didn't have). The entire question of whether observable differences reflect causal effects comes down to whether we can approximate the counterfactual $\overline{E}(Y_{i0}|T = 1)$ that we need with the data $\overline{E}(Y_{i0}|T = 0)$ that we have. If we can, the causal bias is approximately 0, and the observable difference in means reflects ATT.

So "correlation is not causation" is a true statement. The equation shows that correlation is causation (to wit, ATT) + selection bias. Put differently, within the potential outcomes framework, an empirical argument that the treatment has a causal effect on the outcome requires (*i*) observing a correlation between the two and (*ii*) arguing that selection bias is small enough not to outweigh the ATT of interest.

10.2 CAUSAL INFERENCE IN REGRESSION: THE PROBLEM

It is particularly interesting, in terms of possible attempts to deal with selection bias as well as the issue of bias in OLS regression, to put this explicitly in terms of a regression model. The dependent variable is Y, the outcome variable we're interested in. Assume that all units have the same DGP and the DGP regression is linear so we have as few complications regarding bias as possible. For now consider only one covariate, T, the treatment. Finally, assume that the treatment effect is identical for all units. This simple case of constant treatment effects can be generalized, but that is not necessary for the core ideas.

In this case, the regression we can try to estimate using observed data is $E(Y_i|T_i) = \alpha + \beta T_i$. That β is the same for each unit i reflects the causal homogeneity, or identical treatment effects, we are assuming in this simple case. If this equation captures the true link in the DGP, then we know that *for a given unit* where everything is fixed except T, β is the effect of changing T

on $E(Y)$. Slopes in DGPs capture causal effects as a matter of assumption. For instance, for a unit that happens to receive the treatment in observed data, if this function describes the DGP accurately, then $E(Y_{i1}|T = 1) - E(Y_{i0}|T = 0) = \beta$ is the first line, the average treatment effect (ATE), from Equation 10.3.[6]

The regression error is $\varepsilon_i \equiv Y_i - E(Y_i|T_i)$. This is the difference between the "actual" outcome for a unit and the expected outcome given the treatment T. For instance, for a unit that happens not to receive treatment in observed data, the error is $\varepsilon^0 = Y_{i0} - E(Y_{i0}|T_i = 0)$. If that same unit with the same outcome receive the treatment instead, the regression error is $\varepsilon^1 = Y_{i0} - E(Y_{i0}|T_i = 1)$. So $E(\varepsilon^1) - E(\varepsilon^0) = E(Y_{i0}|T_i = 1) - E(Y_{i0}|T_i = 0)$. If this is not 0, it means that the expected regression error is not flat as a function of T – in other words, that T and ε are correlated.

There are two important points about this. First, $E(\varepsilon^1) - E(\varepsilon^0)$ is exactly what each unit "contributes" to the causal bias in Equation 10.3. If this difference is 0, then the β that can be estimated in this regression is an unbiased estimate of ATT from Equation 10.3. Second, correlation between the error and the covariate in a regression is another name for *endogeneity of the regressor*, which we saw in Chapter 7. There, we saw that endogeneity leads to bias in ordinary least squares (OLS) regression coefficients. Here we see that in this simple model, bias due to endogeneity and selection bias are the same thing.

Substantively, ε captures the myriad factors that lead a variable to depart from its conditional expectation in particular cases. Availability of the printing press may give us an expectation of the progress of the Reformation in a city, but it is obviously not the only factor affecting that outcome. As noted, one might expect social progressivity or greater education among elites to have an effect on the progress of the Reformation. Because they are not captured in the bivariate model $E(Y_i|T_i) = \alpha + \beta T_i$, they show up in the error of the success of the Reformation in a city around its conditional mean given T.

If these factors are about the same for both values of T, they just show up as noise in ε. But if they tend to be larger for one value of T than the other, they lead to endogeneity. So if the elites are more educated or socially progressive in printing press cities than in nonprinting press cities, and these factors also push up the expected depth of the Reformation in a city, then the variable T will be endogenous.

When a regressor is endogenous, OLS regression in observed data gives a biased estimate of β for that regressor. We saw earlier that β in the DGP really does define a causal effect, so the upshot is that endogeneity means OLS does not produce good estimates of causal effects in the sense of bias. Statistical significance has nothing to do with this. The OLS slope may be many standard errors away from 0; whatever this slope is estimating, the causal effect of T

---

[6] This will still hold after averaging across units with $\overline{E}(\cdot)$ because β is the same for each unit, so the average across units is β as well.

on $E(Y|T)$ isn't it. More precision doesn't change this. If causal inference is the goal, precision just gives a better estimate of the wrong parameter.

We saw in Chapter 5 that if the DGP and the model of $E(Y|X)$ are correctly specified, then $Cov(T, Y - E(Y|T)) = 0$. What is happening here is not a violation of this result. It is that we have not specified a complete model of the regression.

The problem is not just with OLS or with regression models. Any approach that reads causal effects off of observed differences of treated and untreated units has the same problem. The problem is that inferring causation from observed data requires assuming that the units actually untreated are about the same as what would have happened to the treated units, if they too had been untreated. Logit, probit, Poisson, and assorted other parametric generalized linear models (as well as qualitative methods such as qualitative comparative analysis (QCA); see Ragin [1987, 2000], Seawright [2005]) will not fare any better than linear regression in this respect.

10.2.1 Endogeneity Critiques in Applied Research

Any researcher presenting findings from statistical modeling runs a gauntlet of critique. Are the concepts in the theory in question adequately operationalized? Is the functional form of the model suitable for the type of data analyzed? Is a linear model postulated where a nonlinear one might be preferable? Are the model results excessively sensitive to the model employed? Are the standard errors of model coefficients robust to likely failures of iid? Are the key hypotheses in the theory adequately represented in the hypothesis tests executed? Are the results substantively meaningful in addition to being merely statistically significant? And these are just based on the relatively basic issues covered in this book.

All that said, the sort of critique that is usually a showstopper is a credible argument of endogeneity bias. This critique means that even if all the preceding points are granted to the researcher advancing a new finding, the results still do not tell us what we want to know about the DGP. If the endogeneity bias is strong enough, the estimated slopes of the model may not even have the same sign as the slopes in the DGP. If this is the case, then what we "learn" from the data is the opposite of the "truth."

Endogeneity critiques can amount to the simple argument that a researcher has excluded a relevant variable (correlated with both Y and other covariates in the model) from the model, leading to omitted variable bias.

Any process that leads to a correlation between T and ε produces endogeneity bias. In offering a critique of claims of causal inference in regression, it is often most compelling to spin a simple theory that would induce this correlation. For example, it is not particularly far-fetched to suppose that the same elite education or social progressivity that would (positively) affect the success of the Reformation in a city would also affect its demand for a printing press.

It is important to become good at ferreting out endogeneity critiques of any possible association that might arise in observational data. It is often the best argument that can be leveled against empirical research. It may not be especially constructive for an individual paper to learn that it is hopelessly unable to meet its causal aspirations, but it is constructive for a literature as a whole because it is informative.

And for one's own research, skill in spotting endogeneity critiques will make one less susceptible to them. If they are anticipated well, an attempt at a solution is possible, along the lines identified in the rest of this chapter. If all else fails, the nature of the claims made in the research can be moderated so that, even if they are not splashy, they are at least defensible. Staid but credible is better than splashy but not credible.

10.3 CAUSAL INFERENCE AND CONTROLLED EXPERIMENTS

Causal inference in social science has come to focus more in the past 20 or so years on *design-based solutions* to the endogeneity problem. The nice thing about design-based solutions, in contrast to *model-based solutions* discussed later, is that the nature of the comparisons that lead to causal inferences is relatively transparent, and the assumptions under which these comparisons allow for causal inference are less delicate. Design-based solutions are ideal when they are available, but for reasons I lay out later, they often are not.

The gold standard of design-based solutions to endogeneity problems is experimentation. For our purposes, an *experiment* is a research design in which a researcher directly controls treatment assignment for units.[7] There are a variety of usages for "experiment" in common parlance, including the somewhat amorphous idea of an experiment as observation of outcomes in a "controlled" setting. For causal inference, "experiment" has a somewhat specialized usage in which "control" refers to treatment assignment.

Consider in particular an experiment in which a researcher collects a group of N units and assigns a random number from to each drawn from $\{1, \ldots, N\}$ without replacement. Then the researcher assigns treatment $T = 0$ to the units with numbers 1 to $\frac{N+1}{2}$ and assigns treatment $T = 0$ to the rest. This is a *randomized controlled experiment* because the treatment assignment is determined by random chance that is controlled by the researcher. In practice, randomized assignment may not be entirely so simple, but this is the idea.

The point of randomized controlled experiments is straightforward. Because treatment assignment is based on a random number drawn by the experimenter, it cannot be correlated with a unit's nontreatment characteristics. Therefore, randomized treatment assignment ensures independence of treatment and potential outcomes and eliminates selection bias. As a result, treatment

---

[7] Morton and Williams [2010] employed the more general and abstract, but similar in spirit, definition of an experiment as a design in which the researcher intervenes in the DGP.

effects estimated from randomized experiments can give an unbiased estimate of true treatment effects. Moreover, part of the beauty of random assignment is that it often eliminates the need to assume intricate and contestable parametric models for the DGP; simple difference in means comparisons are sufficient to estimate causal effects of a binary treatment.

Because of the robust promise of experiments for causal inference, they provide a useful way to structure one's thinking about problems even if an experiment is impossible in practice. When setting out to collect data and evaluate a treatment effect, ask yourself: What experiment would I perform – what treatment would I randomize over what units, and what outcomes would I observe – if I had unlimited resources and no ethical considerations in experimental design? This simple question helps one stay focused on the treatment effect of interest and the kinds of manipulations of treatments that make it possible to estimate this effect. In addition, keeping this question in mind helps one keep an eye on anything that is randomly assigned to some group in the real world. Spotting these "natural experiments" is often a good way to obtain a causal estimate of something.[8]

As transparent as this is, we actually must be clear on what we mean by "cannot be correlated." In fact, it is quite possible in any one experiment for the random assignment number to be correlated with nontreatment factors. Suppose we wish to analyze the effect of attending an "elite" university for undergraduate studies on annual income after graduation. Simply put, the question is, Does attending an elite university cause an increase in postgraduate income? Obviously, we cannot answer this by comparing students who do and do not attend an elite university. The treatment is selected in part on the basis of the student's intelligence, work ethic, and family history of "elite" education. And all of these factors could have an effect on postgraduate income as well. So the treatment of interest is horrendously endogenous.

Although no student would (I hope) ever consent to it, and even if students did, no university institutional review board or human subjects committee would ever approve it, we can at least imagine a randomized experiment to address this endogeneity. Randomly assign a group of N graduating high school students to either an "elite" or "nonelite" university.

Now, it is entirely possible that, purely by chance, the students assigned to the "elite" university happen to have more intelligence or "grit" or whatever nontreatment factors lead to greater postgraduate income than the students assigned to the "nonelite" university. Randomized assignment means we do not expect this, just as we do not expect the first 5 out of 10 flips of a fair coin to be heads. But it is possible. Unless the researcher observes all these nontreatment

---

[8] There is still a challenge to figuring out exactly what natural experiments allow a causal inference *of*. Sekhon and Titiunik [2012] reviewed a number of applications of the "natural experiment" approach, and argued that the actual randomization is not done in the way that researchers might want or need for the treatment effect of interest.

factors for each student that might affect the outcome, there is no way to determine whether it happened or not in any one case. (If the researcher *does* observe all the nontreatment factors, randomization isn't necessary anyway; the researcher can just solve the endogeneity problem by controlling for these other factors.) And if it does so happen that, purely by chance, the treated individuals are different from the untreated in terms of their nontreatment factors, the estimated treatment effect of attending an "elite" university may be different from the true effect in the DGP. In principle, it does not even have to have the same sign. The reason is that, within this particular set of observed data, there is a relationship – a correlation – between nontreatment factors and treatment.

What we mean by "cannot be correlated" is different from this. It means that if we repeated the experiment many times with the same units, who each have the same nontreatment factors, we would expect zero correlation between these factors and treatment assignment. In other words, ex ante, before treatment is assigned, we don't expect a relationship between treatment and nontreatment factors under random assignment. But ex post, there might be. What we mean by "cannot be correlated" is the former. This is what gives randomized experiments the potential to yield unbiased estimates of treatment effects. "Unbiased" means that we expect them to give the "right answer" in repeated sampling, and in fact, that is the same thing that unbiased has always meant in this book.

The idiosyncratic chance event in which treatment and nontreatment factors are correlated amounts to a failure of randomization to do its job. We don't expect that to happen, but it can. It can also be checked in the data: if various nontreatment factors are measured for each unit, we can simply use hypothesis tests to analyze whether they are significantly different between the treatment and no-treatment groups. This is a *randomization check* or *balance test*. Obviously, these tests cannot be based on unobserved attributes that might be correlated with Y, so these kinds of tests can never prove randomization was successful ex post on every relevant dimension. But they are helpful. In addition, the problem should not be overstated. If the researcher actually does control assignment randomly, even a modest number of units observed in the sample makes serious idiosyncratic differences between the treatment and no-treatment groups fairly unlikely.

Experimentation has been accepted in some social science disciplines for a long time. For instance, social psychology – in both its sociological and psychological manifestations – has welcomed experimental methods for decades. Educational research also has a long-standing tradition of random assignment of treatments. Other disciplines, particularly economics and political science, have seen a more recent explosion of interest in experimentation for causal inference (Druckman et al. [2006], Morton and Williams [2010]), though these disciplines also have established traditions of experimental research (e.g., Palfrey [1991], Palfrey and Kinder [1993]).

10.4 SOLUTIONS BY CONTROLLING FOR SELECTION BASED ON OBSERVABLE COVARIATES

The intuition behind the description of endogeneity bias also suggests a way around it. If the problem is that some variable X is correlated with both the outcome Y and the treatment T, why not simply gather observations of that variable too and control for them? The variable X is a *confounding variable* because it confounds our estimation of the causal effect of T on Y. So if we can observe the confounding variable and adjust or control for it, we might be able to recover an unbiased estimate of treatment effects (e.g., ATT).

In other words, if X is a factor that determines units' selection of treatment, and X is also correlated with Y, it will induce selection bias in our assessment of the causal effect of T on Y. The assumption that confounding factors of this nature can be observed and controlled to yield an unbiased estimate of causal effects is called *selection on observables*.

10.4.1 Confounding Variables and Conditional Independence in Regression

If X is included in the regression of $E(Y|T, X)$ and we continue to assume this is linear,[9] then we have $E(Y|T, X) = \alpha + \beta_T T + \beta_X X$. A condition that encapsulates the assumption that X controls the selection problem is *conditional independence of treatment and potential outcomes*. This is often shortened simply to *conditional independence*. Conditional independence is a sufficient condition for unbiased estimation of causal effects.[10] If conditional independence holds, the treatment is "as good as randomly assigned" to the units. That is another way to see the benefits of controlled randomization: when the treatments really are randomly assigned by the researcher, conditional independence holds.

The "independence" part means that Y_{i0} and Y_{i1} are independent of T_i for all i. This does not mean that T is assumed to have no effect on the outcome Y. It means that T is not assigned to units in a way that is correlated with their *potential* outcomes. This independence means that units don't come to the state $T = 1$ on the basis of their potential outcomes; they come to that state for reasons that have nothing to do with either of their potential outcomes. The point is not that Y_{i0} and Y_{i1} are the same but that $E(Y_{i0}|T = 1)$ is well approximated by $E(Y_{i0}|T = 0)$.

---

[9] Linearity is useful for developing this because it is an easy case for identifying unbiased estimates. The point is that even in this easy case, eliminating causal bias is difficult. It doesn't get easier if the regression is nonlinear.

[10] Conditional independence is actually sufficient only if another assumption, called the "stable unit treatment values assumption," also holds. This is discussed explicitly later in the chapter. Here it has been implicitly assumed away by defining potential outcomes for a unit only as a function of that unit's T_i. In addition, because conditional independence is sufficient, it can be weakened in some cases; see Heckman and Vytlacil [2007].

The "conditional" part means that this independence only has to hold when X is taken as given. Unconditionally, treatment and potential outcomes may be correlated because X determines both the selection into T and (part of) the outcome Y_{iT}. But conditional on X, T is not correlated with either of the potential outcomes.

The assumption that we have a complete list of confounding factors is a big one. We can't prove it in actual datasets (i.e., when we don't see the real DGP). Rather, this approach to causal inference rests on an untestable theory that all the relevant confounds have been controlled. So whenever this regression approach is used, that theory should be made as explicit as possible to the reader, even if it cannot be proven by the ensuing empirical analysis. This way, at least the assumptions behind the claim of causal inference are clearer to the reader (and writer).

There are other strong assumptions here that are necessary to make an OLS estimate unbiased, most conspicuously linearity in the DGP regression. We have not justified that at all, and in real applications, we should be suspicious of it. Conditional independence, and even controlled randomization, do not justify the other assumptions behind OLS (Freedman [2010b]). So the point here is not that OLS is sure to work fine for causal inference if we can just observe all the confounding factors. Rather, it is that controlling for confounding factors is an important part of the justification for OLS.

10.4.2 Matching

An interesting, some would say problematic, aspect of regression is that it "controls" for X, even though it never requires a direct comparison of Y for two units with different T_is but the same value of X. Regression uses linearity to "create" information about the expected Y_j in case unit j has unit i's X value instead of its own real one.

An arguably more transparent meaning of "control" for X, when estimating the effect of T, is to line up cases that have a given value of X but different values of T, and then determine the average change in Y as T changes. This could be done, in principle, for each possible value of X, and resulting effects of T on Y averaged over the range of Xs. This is the idea behind *matching estimators* (Rosenbaum and Rubin [1983], Rosenbaum [2002]).

In practice, this degree of transparency in how comparisons are made between treated and untreated is not attainable. For even a few covariates that can take just a few values each, there are often no exact matches on numerous combinations of covariates between the treated and untreated groups. Even if there were exact matches on each, very large samples are necessary to obtain reasonable precision on average outcomes for treated and untreated for each combination of covariates. And if one or more covariates are continuous variables, exact matches are impossible. Completely dispensing with a model to structure comparisons across covariate values requires inordinate amounts of information in a sample. This is exactly the sense in which models give the researcher some degrees of freedom "for free."

So in practice, matching estimators implement some way to find cases of treated and untreated units that are "similar" in terms of other covariates. Thus some degree of extrapolation across nonidentical covariates between treated and untreated groups is necessary. This makes actual matching estimators used in research somewhat closer in spirit to regression models than the fully model-free, exact matching benchmark described above.

There are numerous variants of matching estimators. Common to all is an attempt to achieve *covariate balance*. The idea in covariate balance is that nontreatment covariates tend to be similar, in some sense, across units. Sometimes balance is understood to require similar means; ideally matched covariates would have the same distribution across treated and untreated groups. Matching estimators differ in how they operationalize "similar."

Matching, like regression, requires selection on observables to deliver credible causal inferences. Unobserved covariates, by definition, cannot be matched on, and if they are correlated with both treatment and potential outcomes conditional on observed (and balanced) covariates, selection bias remains. The argument for matching as an alternative to regression is not that it delivers believable causal estimates in cases where regression does not. It is that matching lessens the dependence of whatever estimates one obtains on an underlying model (in particular, the specific function linking covariates and parameters) and is in this sense more transparent (Sekhon [2008]).

10.4.3 Regression Discontinuity

The power of randomized controlled experiments, in terms of causal inference, is based on controlled assignment of treatments. Even if that control is not available to a researcher, in some cases assignment is still formally controlled in some way on the basis of a known, transparent rule. It is always a good idea to keep an eye out for such oddities in real life because they can form the basis of credible estimates of treatment effects under an alternative design-based approach called *regression discontinuity* or RD. RD is a relatively recent innovation in causal inference (e.g., see discussion in Campbell and Stanley [1963]) but has caught on fast because it yields good estimates of treatment effects when it is available.

The key to RD is a treatment that is dichotomous around some continuous latent variable, and treatment jumps discontinuously at a particular value of X. The variable X is called the *forcing variable* in RD. Formally, $T = 1$ if $X \geq X_c$, and $T = 0$ if $X < X_c$. Here X_c is a cutoff value of the forcing variable that determines treatment assignment. In this setup, T is a deterministic function of X. This is called *sharp RD*.

The main idea in RD is to exploit this process of treatment assignment, which ensures that treated and untreated units are similar by design, at least in terms of the forcing variable X, right around the cutoff X_c. So RD takes the observations just above the cutoff as providing roughly counterfactual information for those just below – the ones above are just about like the ones below, in terms of the forcing variable but not in terms of the treatment. If the threat to causal inference is that the forcing variable carries all of the explanatory weight of Y and the treatment variable has no effect, this is just the right kind of counterfactual to examine.[11]

10.5 SOLUTIONS WITH SELECTION ON UNOBSERVABLES

The promise of randomized assignment for causal inference is clear. But there are countless cases in which we'd like to estimate causal effects and no reasonable experiment is possible. How could we use controlled, randomized treatment assignment to analyze, for example, the effects of political institutions on long-term economic outcomes? One could certainly implement a laboratory experiment in which individuals participate in an "economy" that is affected by "policies" selected through "institutions" that are randomly assigned by an experimenter. Because most of the participants presumably have to be home for dinner at some point, "long term" is somewhat limited here. More generally, one would forgive most social scientists for doubting that such an experiment has a lot to say about the actual economic history and distribution of economic performance according to political institutions around the world. For many types of issues we study, many social scientists have a strong preference for identifying causal effects with "real data."

Yet it is also true that solutions by controlling for selection are always vulnerable to further critique. Maybe the control variables do not really solve the selection problem, and the relevant basis of selection, although observable, is still uncontrolled. Maybe the functional form of the model that does so much of the work of controlling is not credible.

Maybe treatment selection is not based on variables that are observable to a researcher at all. This is a problem of *selection on unobservables*. If treatment selection is based on a concept that cannot be credibly operationalized or is inherently the private information of a unit which they have no incentive to reveal, approaches for dealing with selection on unobservables are all we have for observational data.

10.5.1 Difference-in-Differences and Fixed Effects Regression Models

When endogeneity problems persist despite attempts to control omitted variables, confounders, and the like, we usually cannot hope to solve them just by

---

[11] Of course, other explanatory factors for Y besides X can be included in the model, but there is no reason to believe that there is any particular value of another covariate at which treated and untreated units are essentially the same other than the treatment.

observing the units, their treatments, and their outcomes at more points in time. The problem behind selection bias is not that we lack sufficient data but that all the data in the world doesn't make the untreated units a good stand-in for what would have happened to the treated units without treatment. Whatever social process, treatment selection, and omitted variables lead to endogeneity problems when units are observed at a time period t will also lead to the same problems at time $t + 1$.

There is one exception to this. If the unobserved differences between any pair of units is more or less stable over time, for example, because it arises from some fixed trait or attribute of the units, then observing the N units at multiple points in time actually can help substantiate causal inference. Recall from Chapter 2 that the N observations at a single point in time for each unit constitute a cross section, and observing the N units at T different points in time (adding a time series dimension) turns this into panel (or longitudinal or time series–cross-sectional, depending on one's usage) data.

Panel data is the key ingredient in an approach called *fixed effects regression* and a special case of it, *difference-in-differences* or D-in-D estimation. Besides the assumption of relatively fixed unobservable differences among units, this approach also requires some variation in treatment assignment over time for at least some units. Without both of these assumptions, fixed effects models are not helpful for causal inference.

Fixed effects regression essentially elaborates the D-in-D approach to allow for more units, more time periods, and more explanatory factors for Y besides treatment.[12] But fixed effects tries to solve the same problem as D-in-D. It is able to do so only if the same conditions hold: fixed differences across units that are correlated with treatment, and some variation over time in treatment assignment for some units.

A simple example of a classic fixed effects regression model is

$$E(Y_{it}|X, T, t) = \alpha + \gamma_i + \theta_t + \beta_X X_{it} + \beta_T T_{it}. \tag{10.4}$$

So there is an overall intercept α, and a unit-specific intercept shift γ_i. This is the fixed effect for each unit. It just means that there is one regression for each unit, $E(Y_t|X, T, t) = \tilde{\alpha} + \theta_t + \beta_X X_t + \beta_T T_t$, where $\tilde{\alpha} \equiv \alpha + \gamma_i$. This clarifies that all that is happening in fixed effects is that the unit-intercept is the overall intercept plus each unit's fixed attribute.

The unobserved factor γ_i must be correlated with treatment assignment across units for fixed effects to make sense for causal inference. (The fixed effect cannot be correlated with treatment for a given unit over time because

---

[12] Actually difference in differences can account for more covariates too, but it is easier to get the idea if they are left out.

it is constant for a single unit.) It is this correlation of γ_i and T_{it} across units i that causes selection bias. Because the bias arises from the variation of fixed effects across units, it is sometimes specifically called *heterogeneity bias* in this context.

The fixed effects estimator of β_T can be obtained by OLS for this model.[13] The idea is first to compute the mean value of each variable for each unit, giving a unit-specific mean for each. Then for each unit at each time period, compute the difference between each variable at that time and the unit-specific mean. This data is said to be *de-meaned*. Note that γ_i drops out of this de-meaned data: it is constant for each unit, so the observation of it in each time period is the same as the mean. Also, any units for which treatment does not vary over time are also dropped out of the de-meaned data, because the treatment in each period is equal to its average. These units do not help to identify the treatment effect β_T in fixed effects models.

OLS on the de-meaned data gives the fixed effects estimator of β_T.[14] The idea behind de-meaned data is that the regression only tries to explain variation of each unit's behavior in time t around its average over all time periods. It does not try to explain variation in means across units. In other words, de-meaned data forces OLS to use only *within-unit variation* in estimating parameters, and it throws away *between-unit variation*. Because the between-unit variation in T is correlated with between-unit variation in γ, that variation is what causes the heterogeneity bias. Fixed effects solves the problem by ignoring the information that is the source of the bias. OLS on the original (non-de-meaned) data utilizes both the within-unit and between-unit variation.

By the same token, because fixed effects by design does not use all the information in the data, it is not as efficient as OLS when heterogeneity bias is not present. For this reason, and because the assumption of an exactly fixed term γ is often sketchy, some statisticians believe that insisting on using only de-meaned data is too high a price to pay for the benefits obtained. Including some portion of the between-unit variation to estimate parameters is the subject of a huge literature on *hierarchical models*, of which fixed effects is but one example (see Gelman and Hill [2006]). Some people are efficiency people, others are bias people. The bias people don't see the point of a more efficient estimator of what they are sure is the wrong quantity.

---

[13] Fixed effects estimators have been developed for nonlinear or generalized linear regression models as well (e.g., fixed effects or conditional logit; see Cameron and Trivedi [2005]). The underlying idea, of the problem to be solved and the conditions under which fixed effects will do it, is the same.

[14] Fixed effects models are not estimated by including a dummy variable for each unit as a covariate in a regression. If sample size increases by increasing both N and T, adding another parameter to be estimated for each unit (the slope on a unit-specific dummy) keeps on using up new information in the sample as quickly as it is added. So the resulting estimator is not consistent. Consistency depends on lots (and lots) of observations per parameter estimated.

10.5.2 Instrumental Variables Regression

Although fixed effects models are clever and powerful within the domain where their assumptions are credible, there are many applications where they are not. *Instrumental variables regression* is another, more powerful approach to addressing endogeneity with selection on unobservables in observational data.[15] On the plus side, it is more flexible than fixed effects in the types of endogeneity problems it can handle (they do not just have to arise from correlation of a fixed effect with treatment). On the down side, it only works under certain assumptions, and it is difficult to examine whether they are satisfied in many applications.

The idea is that a treatment T might affect an outcome Y, but OLS regression is biased because of endogeneity or some omitted variable that cannot be controlled. But suppose we can find another variable Z that is correlated with T but, except through that correlation, does not affect Y. That variable Z is an *instrumental variable*.

In the case of political institutions and economic performance, we certainly cannot credibly identify a causal effect by regressing, say, a country's gross domestic product on various facets of its institutional regime. The same social, political, and economic factors that allow a country to develop and stabilize, say, relatively open and competitive political systems may also partly explain its economic fortunes.

To formalize this, consider a DGP such that $E(Y|T, X) = \alpha + \beta_T T + \beta_X X$. Because this is an assumed relation in the DGP, β_T is the causal effect of T on Y. If we had observations of both T and X, we'd be in good shape to recover β_T with standard regression methods. This is just a solution of the causal estimation problem by control.

The issue with solutions by control is that the relevant controls may not be available or observable, even in principle. Excluding X from a regression of Y on T poses an obvious threat of selection bias, if T and X are correlated. So if Y and T are observable, but X is not, we have a problem.

Now enter an instrument Z – an observable variable that is correlated with T but not otherwise correlated with Y. This means, in particular, that Z is not correlated with X. So we have

$$E(T|Z) = \gamma + \delta Z. \tag{10.5}$$

This expectation for T is necessarily uncorrelated with X. Some other factors besides Z might help to explain T, but we don't have to pay much attention to them for this simple presentation. The important point is that X, which is the source of the endogeneity of T, is left out of this.

---

[15] See Angrist and Pischke [2008] for a treatment of causal inference in empirical research that is very sanguine to instrumental variables Cameron and Trivedi [2005] and Wooldridge [2009] contain in-depth textbook treatments.

So how about instead of the actual T, which is correlated with X, we use $E(T \mid Z)$, which is not, in the regression for Y? Then we get

$$E(Y \mid Z) = \alpha + \beta_T \, E(T \mid Z)$$

$$= \alpha + \beta_T \, (\gamma + \delta Z)$$

$$= \tilde{\alpha} + \tilde{\beta} Z, \qquad (10.6)$$

where $\tilde{\alpha} \equiv \alpha + \beta_T \gamma$, and $\tilde{\beta} \equiv \beta_T \delta$. Because we're in the land of the DGP and given the assumed structure of $E(Y \mid T, X)$, β_T is the right coefficient to include on the first line. A one-unit increase in T causes an β_T-unit increase in Y all else (in particular, X) constant. When $E(T \mid Z)$ increases by one unit, it is an increase in T that we have already assumed allows X to be held constant. This is important because nothing good comes from instrumental variables unless the actual treatment effect of interest can be written in here.

The magic of instrumental variables regression is

$$\beta_T = \frac{\tilde{\beta}}{\delta}. \qquad (10.7)$$

So to obtain the treatment effect we're interested in, we just divide the coefficient from the regression of Y on Z by the coefficient from the regression of T on Z.[16] Both coefficients can be estimated adequately by OLS, so the treatment effect can be estimated too. This arrangement is instrumental variables regression.

Now some instrumental variables terminology. Equation 10.5 is called the *first-stage regression*. We excluded X from this because we assumed $Cov(Z, X) = 0$, which is called the *exclusion restriction*. Equation 10.6 is called the *second-stage* or *reduced form regression*. The treatment effect of interest is the ratio of the second- and first-stage coefficients. People often refer to estimation of β_T in this two-equation (10.5 and 10.6) setup as *two-stage least squares* estimation, although computer software does not actually implement the estimator by estimating two OLS equations.

Besides the usual, and very serious, assumptions about linearity of these links in the DGP, the big assumptions in IV regression are (*i*) that Z has a reasonably sizable affect on T in the first stage and (*ii*) that the exclusion restriction $Cov(Z, X) = 0$ holds. With all these assumptions, the IV estimator of β_T is consistent, but not unbiased. In small samples, the bias can be serious.

The second assumption, the exclusion restriction, is the source of most of the heat and light in IV regression. This is what social scientists are getting at when they refer to a variable as *plausibly exogenous*. This technical-sounding language is another way to say "we are assuming the exclusion restriction holds because it's hard to see why it wouldn't." Although the strength of the instruments can be formally tested, the exclusion restriction usually comes down to a

---

[16] When T is binary, as it is here, the instrumental variables estimator of β_T is called a *Wald estimator*.

theoretical argument. So most papers using IV regression have a section before the data analysis explaining what the instrument is, and arguing theoretically that it is "plausibly exogenous." The exclusion restriction is impossible to test directly because X is not observed, which is the reason we are doing this in the first place rather than just controlling for X. That is the price of causal inference with "real" data in IV: it rests on the untestable assumption behind the exclusion restriction.

10.6 CONCLUSION

Interest in causal inference has grown rapidly in many social science disciplines. The potential outcomes model is a unifying structure behind attempts to deal with causation in empirical data, where, strictly speaking, only correlation can be observed. The potential outcomes model is useful because it tells us what causation means, what is knowable and not knowable about it even in principle and what we must believe about treatment assignment in empirical research to make pretensions of causal inference credible.

Although correlation does not imply causation in general, we cannot conclude that all observed correlations are equally informative or equally suspect in terms of causal inference. Research design, in the sense of how individuals or units are assigned to treatment – whether this is manipulated directly or at least observable and controllable in a statistical sense – is of paramount importance. When the basis of selection cannot be observed and controlled (selection on unobservables), the nature of the endogeneity problem in any situation is the key issue. This can be theorized about but not directly observed, and these theories have a lot to do with whether any (and in particular, which) approach to analyzing observational data can deliver a credible claim about causation.

PROBLEMS

1. A researcher is interested in the causal effect of union membership (X) on turnout behavior in elections (Y). The unit of analysis is an individual person.
   (a) Explain why estimating the model $E(Y|X) = \alpha + \beta X$ would probably not give an unbiased estimate of the causal effect of union membership on turnout.
   (b) The researcher obtains data on union membership of the parents of each individual in the dataset and proposes to use it as an instrument for the individual's union membership. What do the first- and second-stage regressions look like, assuming that X is the only covariate of interest and parents' union membership is the only instrument? What is the causal effect as estimated from these regressions, in terms of their parameters? Would you trust causal effects of X estimated in this way? Explain why or why not.

(c) The researcher obtains data on Y for union members before and after they join a union. Would you trust causal effects of X estimated with before-and-after comparisons of Y? Explain why or why not.

(d) The researcher also obtains data on Y for individuals who never join a union from the same elections for which the before-and-after data of union members was obtained. What must the researcher assume for a difference-in-differences estimator to give a credible estimate of the causal effect of X? Give a reason why this assumption might not hold.

2. Suppose you have data on adult earnings Y, intelligence X, and years of schooling Z for a large number of employed American adults.

(a) What do you suppose is the nature of the relationship between X and Z?

(b) Pretend you are sure that no other covariates correlated with X or Z have any effect on Y. If you estimate the regression $E(Y|X) = \alpha + \beta_X X + \beta_Z Z$, would you trust β_X as an estimate of the causal effect of intelligence on earnings?

(c) Would you trust β_Z as an estimate of the causal effect of years of schooling, on the same assumption that no other covariates that matter for Y are correlated with the regressors?

(d) Would dropping either regressor alleviate any problems you identified in the first two parts?

3. The "permanent income hypothesis" holds that a person's consumption and behavior patterns are driven by their "permanent" income rather than the "transitory" income that they earn in any particular time period. An analyst develops a theoretical model of permanent income as a function of several explanatory factors (human capital and the like), and transitory income is specified as permanent income plus a random shock. It is well known in the participation literature that transitory income has a significant positive effect on turnout. The analyst is interested in the treatment effect of permanent income on the decision to vote. She has cross-sectional survey data including (binary) participation decisions, transitory income, and all the postulated determinants of permanent income. She is willing to assume that all of these determinants of permanent income are exogenous to both transitory income and participation.[17]

(a) Suppose the analyst estimates a linear probability model for participation decisions, and she includes both transitory income in her model and all determinants of permanent income. She finds that transitory income has a significant positive effect, but most of the determinants of permanent income are insignificant. Is it safe to conclude that the permanent income hypothesis is false? Why might these results be obtained even if it is correct?

[17] Note: This problem will probably be harder if you try to think through it all in words; it is easier when translated into symbols and models relating them.

(b) In the model in the previous part, the analyst finds the estimated effect of transitory income is consistent with numerous other studies that examine the effect of transitory, but not permanent, income on participation. Why is this so?

(c) Should she include transitory income in the model if she wants to assess the permanent income hypothesis? Why or why not?

Afterword: Statistical Methods and Empirical Research

Statistical inference and modeling are different topics. One involves expressing the properties of DGPs in terms of parameters and parameters as functions of other variables. The other involves making inferences from observable data back to DGPs, whether those inferences are structured by a model or not.

Statistical inference is necessary to learn about a social process broader than the mere data in front of a researcher any time the process that generates that data or makes it observable has a stochastic element. Statistical modeling is not a necessary implication of any particular metaphysical view about DGPs. But it is helpful to social scientists attempting to learn about stochastic ones. First, statistical models allow for crisp expressions of the link between the positive theory that is often of ultimate interest in social science and data-generating processes (DGPs). Second, statistical models narrow the range of possible DGPs that might have generated the data considerably. This does a great deal of work in structuring the estimation and inference problems that researchers face. In a sense, a model represents a sort of "prior belief" about the workings of the social process under analysis. The analysis precedes from and is informed by that prior belief. And in another sense, models represent "free" information: generating equally certain, equally strong conclusions without a model as are possible with the aid of a model requires a massive increase in available data. As computing power has gotten cheap and space to store data plentiful, the availability of massive datasets has of course increased apace. But in many fields, for example, the study of wars throughout the world, there are simply substantive limits to how big datasets can be for any question. That "free information" explains both why models are promising and why they should be regarded with circumspection and skepticism.

The main idea in this book is that social scientists, who work in disciplines where models are often the coin of the empirical realm, need to learn statistical modeling and that they can learn something about statistical inference simultaneously. On modeling, we have covered theoretical foundations of regression in DGPs, some bases for assuming linearity in regression models, a number of well-known families of generalized linear models when DGPs and their parametric links to covariates do not work well with linear specifications, and some issues on model specification and interpretation. Finally, we have looked at conditions under which the results of effects of covariates in models can reasonably be given a causal interpretation.

On inference, we have covered the core theoretical topics of sampling distributions, which forms the key link between theoretical DGPs and observable data; hypothesis testing in terms of general principles and a number of specific tests; and interval and point estimation through the basic theory of maximum likelihood estimation of parameters in models. This discussion has focused on the theoretical justifications and foundations for commonly used approaches in estimation and inference and to some extent on what can be done when those justifications fall apart. It has also focused on the link between inference and social science theory and the issues social scientists should consider when reporting results.

There are two important things that introductory students should be willing to try next. The first is more advanced coursework that treats any of the topics in this book in greater depth – regression analysis in earnest (focusing less on recapitulating the basic theory of sampling distributions and inference for the ordinary least squares estimator, or plain-vanilla failures of homoskedasticity, and more on panel data, time series, estimation frameworks for more intricate estimators, etc.), Bayesian statistics (which we hardly dealt with at all), causal inference, semiparametric modeling, or whatever comes next in one's program. The second thing students should be willing to try is original empirical analysis, aiming at statistical inference and structured by statistical models. The basic issues are laid out in this book, and if they are reasonably well understood, the marginal gains in understanding from spending time with model specification and interpretation with real data of interest for one's own research are vastly greater than the marginal gains from additional time with textbooks. More formal training would certainly be necessary to develop theoretical mastery of these topics, but one should never wait for total theoretical mastery before beginning applied research with statistical models. Otherwise the research will never get started, let alone finished.

Bibliography

Daron Acemoglu and James A. Robinson. *Economic Origins of Dictatorship and Democracy*. Cambridge University Press, New York, 2005.

Christopher Achen. Toward a new political methodology: Microfoundations and art. *Annual Review of Political Science*, 5:423–450, 2002.

Philippe Aghion and Jeffrey G. Williamson. *Growth, Inequality, and Globalization: Theory, History, and Policy*. Cambridge University Press, New York, 1999.

R. Michael Alvarez and John Brehm. *Hard Choices, Easy Answers: Values, Information, and American Public Opinion*. Princeton University Press, Princeton, NJ, 2002.

Joshua D. Angrist and Jörn-Steffen Pischke. *Mostly Harmless Econometrics: An Empiricist's Companion*. Princeton University Press, Princeton, NJ, 2008.

Scott Ashworth, Joshua D. Clinton, Adam Meirowitz, and Kristopher W. Ramsay. Design, inference, and the strategic logic of suicide terrorism. *American Political Science Review*, 102:269–273, 2008.

Larry Bartels. *Unequal Democracy: The Political Economy of the New Gilded Age*. Princeton University Press, Princeton, NJ, 2008.

Nathaniel Beck and Jonathan N. Katz. What to do (and not do) with time-series cross-section data. *American Political Science Review*, 89:634–647, 1995.

Mark R. Beissinger. *Nationalist Mobilization and the Collapse of the Soviet State*. Cambridge University Press, New York, 2002.

James O. Berger. *Statistical Decision Theory and Bayesian Analysis* (2nd ed.). Springer, 1985.

Frederick J. Boehmke. The influence of unobserved factors on position timing and content in the nafta vote. *Political Analysis*, 14:421–438, 2006.

Carles Boix. *Democracy and Redistribution*. Cambridge University Press, New York, 2003.

Janet Box-Steffensmeier and Bradford S. Jones. *Event History Modeling: A Guide for Social Scientists*. Cambridge University Press, New York, 2004.

Henry Brady. Causation and Explanation in Social Science. In Janet M. Box-Steensmeier, Henry E. Brady, and David Collier, editors, *The Oxford Handbook of Political Methodology*, pp. 217–270. Oxford University Press, New York, 2008.

Henry Brady and David Collier. *Rethinking Social Inquiry: Diverse Tools, Shared Standards*. Cambridge University Press, New York, 2010.

Thomas Brambor, William Roberts Clark, and Matt Golder. Understanding interaction models: Improving empirical analyses. *Political Analysis*, 14:63–82, 2006.

Bruce Bueno de Mesquita, Alastair Smith, Randolph Siverson, and James Morrow. *The Logit of Political Survival*. MIT Press, Cambridge, MA, 2003.

A. Colin Cameron and Pravin K. Trivedi. *Microeconometrics*. Cambridge University Press, New York, 2005.

Donald Thomas Campbell and Julian C. Stanley. *Experimental and Quasi-Experimental Designs for Research*. Rand McNally, Chicago, 1963.

George Casella and Roger L. Berger. *Statistica Inference*. Duxbury Press, Pacific Grove, CA, 2002.

Michael Chernick. *Bootstrap Methods, A practitioner's guide* (2nd ed.). John Wiley and Sons, Hoboken, NJ, 2007.

Wendy Tam Cho. Contagion effects and ethnic contribution networks. *Political Analysis*, 47:368–387, 2003.

Wendy Tam Cho and Brian Gaines. The limits of ecological inference: The case of split-ticket voting. *American Journal of Political Science*, 48:152–171, 2004.

Nicholas A. Christakis and James H. Fowler. Explaining variance; or, stuck in a moment we can't get out of. *Political Analysis*, 14:268–290, 2006.

Nicholas A. Christakis and James H. Fowler. Understanding interaction models: Improving empirical analyses. *New England Journal of Medicine*, 357:370–379, 2007.

Jack Citrin and John Sides. Immigration and the imagined community in Europe and the United States. *Political Studies*, 56:33–56, 2008.

Joshua Clinton and John Lapinski. Measuring legislative accomplishment, 1877–1994. *American Journal of Political Science*, 50:232–249, 2006.

Joshua Clinton, Simon Jackman, and Doug Rivers. The statistical analysis of roll call voting: A unified approach. *American Political Science Review*, 98:355–370, 2004.

Gary W. Cox and Mathew D. McCubbins. *Setting the Agenda: Responsible Party Government in the U.S. House of Representatives*. University of California Press, Berkeley, CA, 2005.

Dato de Gruijter and Leo van der Kamp. *Statistical Test Theory for the Behavioral Sciences*. Chapman and Hall, New York, 2007.

James N. Druckman, Donald P. Green, James H. Kuklinski, and Arthur Lupia. The growth and development of experimental political science – experimental research in the american political science review. *American Political Science Review*, 100: 627–636, 2006.

Bradley Efron. Bootstrap methods: Another look at the jackknife. *The Annals of Statistics*, 7:1–26, 1979.

Lucien Febvre and Henri-Jean Martin. *The Coming of the Book: The Impact of Printing, 1450–1800*. Vereso, London, 1958.

Jessica Fortin. Measuring presidential powers: Some pitfalls of aggregate measurement. *International Political Science Review*, 34:91–112, 2013.

Robert Franzese and Jude C. Hays. Spatial-econometric models of cross-sectional interdependence in political-science panel and tscs data. *Political Analysis*, 15:140–164, 2007.

David A. Freedman. On "Solutions" to the Ecological Inference Problem. In David Collier, Jasjeet Sekhon, and Philip B. Stark, editors, *Statistical Models and Causal Inference: A Dialogue with the Social Sciences*, pp. 83–96. Cambridge University Press, New York, 2010a.

David A. Freedman. On Regression Adjustments in Experiments with Several Treatments. In David Collier, Jasjeet Sekhon, and Philip B. Stark, editors, *Statistical Models and Causal Inference: A Dialogue with the Social Sciences*, pp. 195–218. Cambridge University Press, New York, 2010b.

David A. Freedman. On the So-Called "Huber Sandwich Estimator" and "Robust Standard Errors." In David Collier, Jasjeet Sekhon, and Philip B. Stark, editors, *Statistical Models and Causal Inference: A Dialogue with the Social Sciences*, pp. 295–304. Cambridge University Press, New York, 2010c.

David A. Freedman, Robert Pisani, and Roger Purves. *Statistics* (4th ed.). W. W. Norton, New York, 2007.

Timothy Frye, J. Hellman, and Joshua Tucker. Database on political institutions in the post-communist world. Unpublished dataset, Ohio State University, 2000.

Sean Gailmard and Jeffery A. Jenkins. Negative agenda control in the Senate and House: Fingerprints of majority party power. *The Journal of Politics*, 69:689–700, 2007.

Andrew Gelman and Jennifer Hill. *Data Analysis Using Regression and Multilevel/Hierarchical Models*. Cambridge University Press, New York, 2006.

Andrew Gelman, John B. Carlin, Hal S. Stern, and Donald B. Rubin. *Bayesian Data Analysis* (2nd ed.). Chapman and Hall, New York, 2004.

Alan S. Gerber, Donald P. Green, and David Nickerson. Testing for publication bias in political science. *Political Analysis*, 9:385–392, 2001.

Jeff Gill. *Bayesian Methods: A Social and Behavioral Sciences Approach* (2nd ed.). Chapman and Hall, New York, 2007.

Gary Goertz and Harvey Starr. *Necessary Conditions: Theory, Methodology, and Applications*. Rowman and Littlefield, Lanham, MD, 2003.

William H. Greene. *Econometric Analysis* (7th ed.). Prentice Hall, Englewood Cliffs, NJ, 2011.

Jens Hainmueller and Michael J. Hiscox. Attitudes toward highly skilled and low-skilled immigration: Evidence from a survey experiment. *American Political Science Review*, 104:61–84, 2010.

Harry Horace Harman. *Modern Factor Analysis*. University of Chicago Press, Chicago, 1976.

James J. Heckman and Edward J. Vytlacil. Econometric Evaluation of Social Programs, Part II. In James J. Heckman and Edward Leamer, editors, *Handbook of Econometrics, Volume 6B*, pp. 4178–5134. North-Holland, New York, 2007.

Thomas Herndon, Michael Ash, and Robert Pollin. *Does High Public Debt Consistently Stifle Economic Growth? A Critique of Reinhart and Rogoff*. Working paper, Political Economy Research Institute, University of Massachusetts Amherst, 2013.

Michael Herron and Kenneth Shotts. Logical inconsistency of ei-based second stage regressions. *American Journal of Political Science*, 48:172–183, 2004.

Douglas Hibbs. Political parties and macroeconomic policy. *American Political Science Review*, 71:1467–1487, 1977.

Paul W. Holland. Statistics and causal inference. *The American Statistician*, 81:945–960, 1986.

Peter J. Huber. The behavior of maximum likelihood estimates under nonstandard conditions. *Proceedings of the Fifth Berkeley Symposium on Mathematical Statistics and Probability*, pp. 221–233, 1967.

Gary Jacobson. The effects of campaign spending in congressional elections. *American Political Science Review*, 72:469–491, 1978.

Luke J. Keele. *Semiparametric Regression for the Social Sciences*. John Wiley and Sons, New York, 2008.

Gary King. *A Solution to the Ecological Inference Problem*. Princeton University Press, Princeton, NJ, 1997.

Gary King. *Unifying Political Methodology: The Likelihood Theory of Statistical Inference*. Cambridge University Press, New York, 1998.

Gary King, Robert Keohane, and Sidney Verba. *Designing Social Inquiry: Scientific Inference in Qualitative Research*. Princeton University Press, Princeton, NJ, 1994.

Gary King, James Honaker, Anne Joseph, and Kenneth Scheve. Analyzing incomplete political science data: An alternative algorithm for multiple imputation. *American Political Science Review*, 95:49–69, 1995.

Gary King, Michael Tomz, and Jason Wittenberg. Making the most of statistical analyses: Improving interpretation and presentation. *American Journal of Political Science*, 44:347–361, 2000.

Gary King, Ori Rosen, and Martin A. Tanner. *Ecological Inference: New Methodological Strategies*. Cambridge University Press, New York, 2004.

Keith Krehbiel. *Information and Legislative Organization*. University of Michigan Press, Ann Arbor, MI, 1991.

Seymour Martin Lipset. Some social requisites of democracy. *American Political Science Review*, 53:69–105, 1959.

James Mahoney and Dietrich Rueschemeyer. *Comparative Historical Analysis in the Social Sciences*. Cambridge University Press, New York, 2003.

Andrew D. Martin and Kevin M. Quinn. Dynamic ideal point estimation via markov chain monte carlo for the u.s. supreme court, 1953–1999. *Political Analysis*, 10: 134–153, 2002.

Peter McCoullagh. What is a statistical model? *Annals of Statistics*, 30:1225–1310, 2002.

Allan Meltzer and Scott Richard. A rational theory of the size of government. *Journal of Political Economy*, 89:914–927, 1981.

Stephen L. Morgan and Christopher Winship. *Counterfactuals and Causal Inference: Methods and Principles for Social Research*. Cambridge University Press, New York, 2007.

Rebecca C. Morton and Kenneth Williams. *Experimental Political Science and the Study of Causality: From Nature to the Lab*. Cambridge University Press, New York, 2010.

Jum Nunnally and Ira Bernstein. *Psychometric Theory*. McGraw-Hill, New York, 2007.

Emily Oster. Hepatitis B and the case of the missing women. *Journal of Political Economy*, 113:1163–1216, 2003.

Adrian Pagan and Aman Ullah. *Nonparametric Econometrics*. Cambridge University Press, New York, 1999.

Thomas R. Palfrey (ed.). *Laboratory Research in Political Economy*. University of Michigan Press, Ann Arbor, MI, 1991.

Thomas R. Palfrey and Donald R. Kinder (eds.). *Experimental Foundations of Political Science*. University of Michigan Press, Ann Arbor, MI, 1993.

Keith T. Poole and Howard Rosenthal. *Ideology and Congress*. Transaction Publishers, Piscataway, NJ, 2007.

Robert D. Putnam. *Bowling Alone: The Collapse and Revival of American Community*. Simon & Schuster, New York, 2000.

Charles C. Ragin. *The Comparative Method*. University of California Press, Berkeley, 1987.

Charles C. Ragin. *Fuzzy-Set Social Science*. University of Chicago Press, Chicago, 2000.

Carmen M. Reinhart and Kenneth S. Rogoff. Growth in a time of debt. *American Economic Review (papers and proceedings)*, 100:573–578, 2010.

Paul R. Rosenbaum. *Observational Studies* (2nd ed.). Springer, New York, 2002.

Paul R. Rosenbaum and Donald B. Rubin. The central role of the propensity score in observational studies for causal effects. *Biometrika*, 70:41–55, 1983.

Donald B. Rubin. Estimating causal effects of treatments in randomized and nonrandomized studies. *Journal of Educational Psychology*, 66:688–701, 1974.

Donald B. Rubin. Inference and missing data. *Biometrika*, 63:581–592, 1976.

Jared Rubin. *Printing and Protestants: Reforming the Economics of the Reformation*. Unpublished working paper, Chapman University, 2011.

Jason Seawright. Qualitative comparative analysis vis-à-vis regression. *Studies in Comparative International Development*, 40:3–26, 2005.

Jasjeet Sekhon. Quantity meets quality: Case studies, conditional probability, and counterfactuals. *Perspectives on Politics*, 2:281–293, 2004.

Jasjeet Sekhon. The Neyman-Rubin Model of Causal Inference and Estimation via Matching Methods. In Janet M. Box-Steffensmeier, Henry E. Brady, and David Collier, editors, *The Oxford Handbook of Political Methodology*, pp. 271–300. Oxford University Press, New York, 2008.

Jasjeet Sekhon and Rocio Titiunik. When natural experiments are neither natural nor experiments. *American Political Science Review*, 106:35–57, 2012.

Matthew Soberg Shugart and John M. Carey. *Presidents and Assemblies: Constitutional Design and Electoral Dynamics*. Cambridge University Press, New York, 1992.

Sidney Siegel and John N. Castellan, Jr. *Nonparametric Statistics for the Behavioral Sciences*. McGraw-Hill, New York, 1988.

Beth A. Simmons and Daniel J. Hopkins. The constraining power of international treaties: Theory and methods. *American Political Science Review*, 99:623–631, 2005.

Theda Skocpol. *States and Social Revolutions: A Comparative Analysis of France, Russia, and China*. Cambridge University Press, New York, 1979.

Stephen Stigler. *The History of Statistics: The Measurement of Uncertainty before 1900*. Belknap Press, Cambridge, MA, 1986.

Laura Stoker and M. Kent Jennings. Life cycle transitions and political participation: The case of marriage. *American Political Science Review*, 89:421–433, 1995.

Edward R. Tufte. *The Visual Display of Quantitative Information*. Graphics Press, Cheshire, CT, 2001.

Jana Von Stein. Do treaties constrain or screen? Selection bias and treaty compliance. *American Political Science Review*, 99:611–622, 2005.

Halbert White. A heteroskedasticity-consistent covariance matrix estimator and a direct test for heteroskedasticity. *Econometrica*, 48:817–838, 1980.

Newey K. Whitney and Kenneth D. West. A simple, positive semi-definite, heteroskedas-
    ticity and autocorrelation consistent covariance matrix. *Econometrica*, 55:703–708,
    1987.

Jeffrey M. Wooldridge. *Introductory Econometrics: A Modern Approach* (4th ed.).
    Thomson-Southwestern, Mason, OH, 2009.

Index

OLS regression coefficient
and maximum likelihood estimation, 314
OLS regression coefficients
and hypothesis testing, 267
as best linear unbiased estimator (BLUE),
303
Comparing across models, 271
Comparing in hypothesis tests, 270
Confidence intervals, 294
Testing joint hypotheses about, 273
Variance–covariance matrix, 270
OLS regression coefficients
and omitted variable bias, 215
Approximate normality and central limit
theorem, 219
as linear estimator, 219
as random variables, 208
Bias, 211
Bias and endogeneity, 213
Bias under selection on dependent variable,
217
BLUE, 219
Bootstrapped standard error, 224
Heteroscedasticity-consistent standard
errors, 230
Newey-West standard errors, 231
Panel corrected standard errors, 231
Sampling distribution, 208
Standard error under iid sampling, 217
Standard errors under heteroscedasticity,
229
Unbiasedness under heteroscedasticity, 212
Unbiasedness under serial correlation, 212
OLS regression slopes
Reporting results in research, 269
Omitted variable bias, 215
One-tailed test, 241, 254
Operationalization of concepts, 16
Order statistic, 26
Ordinal measure, 15
Ordinal probit, 177
Outcome variable, 44
Outlier, 29
Overdispersion, 182, 329

p-value, 239
Panel data, 13
Parameter space, 240
Parameters, 114, 140, 188
Parametric family of DGPs, 140
Parent DGP of a sample, 188
Permutation, 94

Point estimation, 288, 290
Poisson distribution, 151
Poisson model, 153
Polychotomous variable, 16
Population, 74
Population distribution, 188
Positive relationship, 34
Positive theory, 4, 137, 236
Posterior probability, 96, 112
Potential outcomes, 337
Potential outcomes model, 332, 336
Prior probability, 96, 112
Probability, 87
Bayesian interpretation, 88
Frequentist interpretation, 87
Monty Hall problem, 96
probability density function, 104
Probability distribution, 82, 100
Conditional, 111
Joint distribution, 107
Marginal distribution, 109
Moments, 121
Probability limit, 305
Probability mass function, 103
Probability measure, 87
Properties, 89
Probability sample, 74
Probability zero, 105
Probit model, 149
Product series notation, 113
Publication bias, 250

Qualitative comparative analysis, 343
Quartiles, 26

Random sample, 188
Random variable, 98
Continuous, 99
Discrete, 99
Independent, 113
Joint, 106
Randomization check, 346
Randomized experiment, 344
Range matching, 141, 145
Regressand, 44
Regression
R^2, 50
Adjusted R^2, 56
and causation, 61
and mean squared error, 134
and prediction, 52
as MSE minimizer, 62